As a Reincarnated ARISTOCRAT, I'll Use My Appraisal Skill to Rise in the World

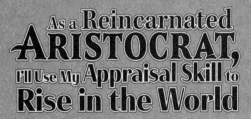

2

[Story] **Miraijin A**
[Art] **Natsumi Inoue**
[Character Design] **jimmy**

CONTENTS

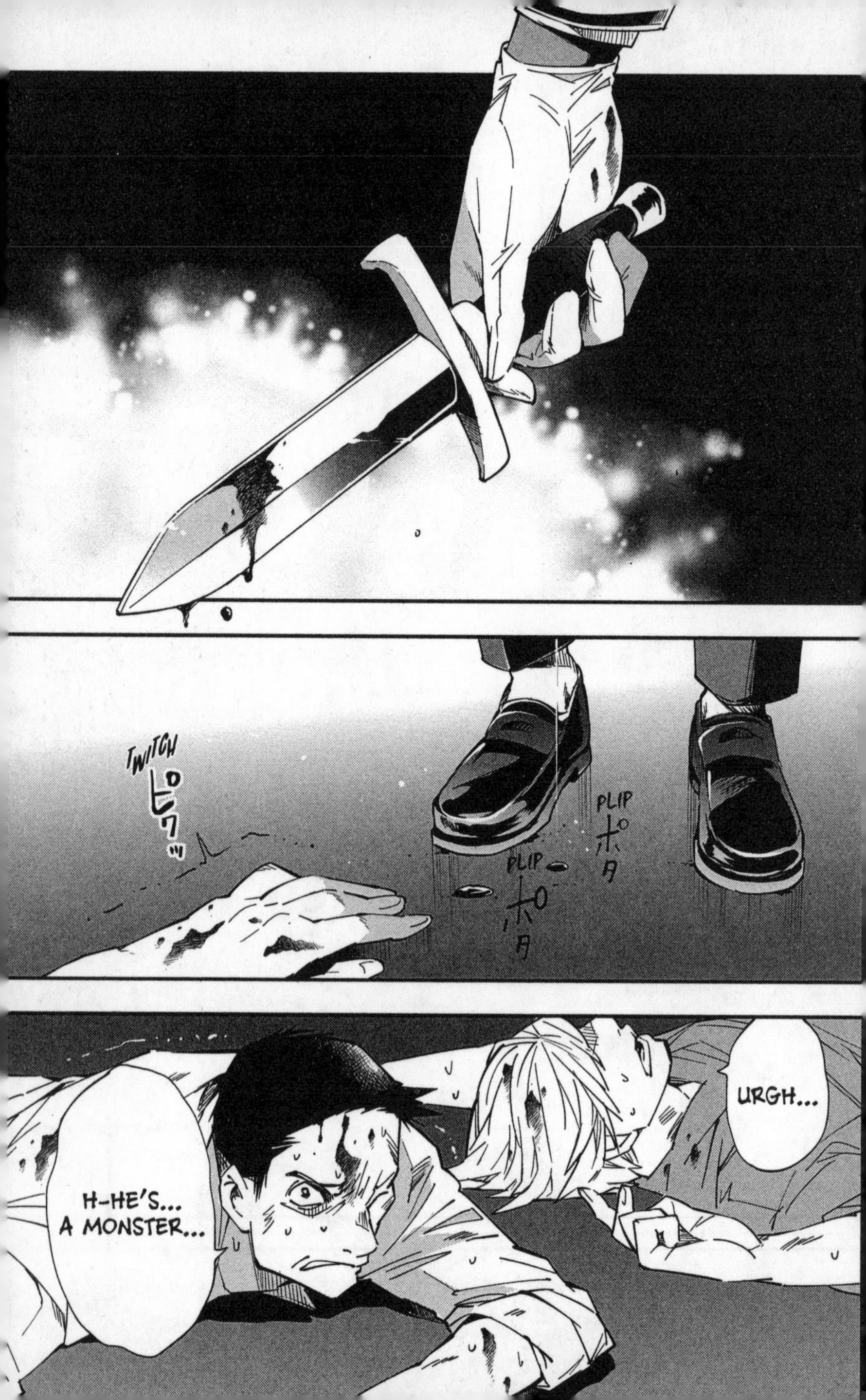
PLIP
ポタ
PLIP
ポタ
TWITCH
ピクッ
URGH...
H-HE'S... A MONSTER...

Chapter 9: The Clash

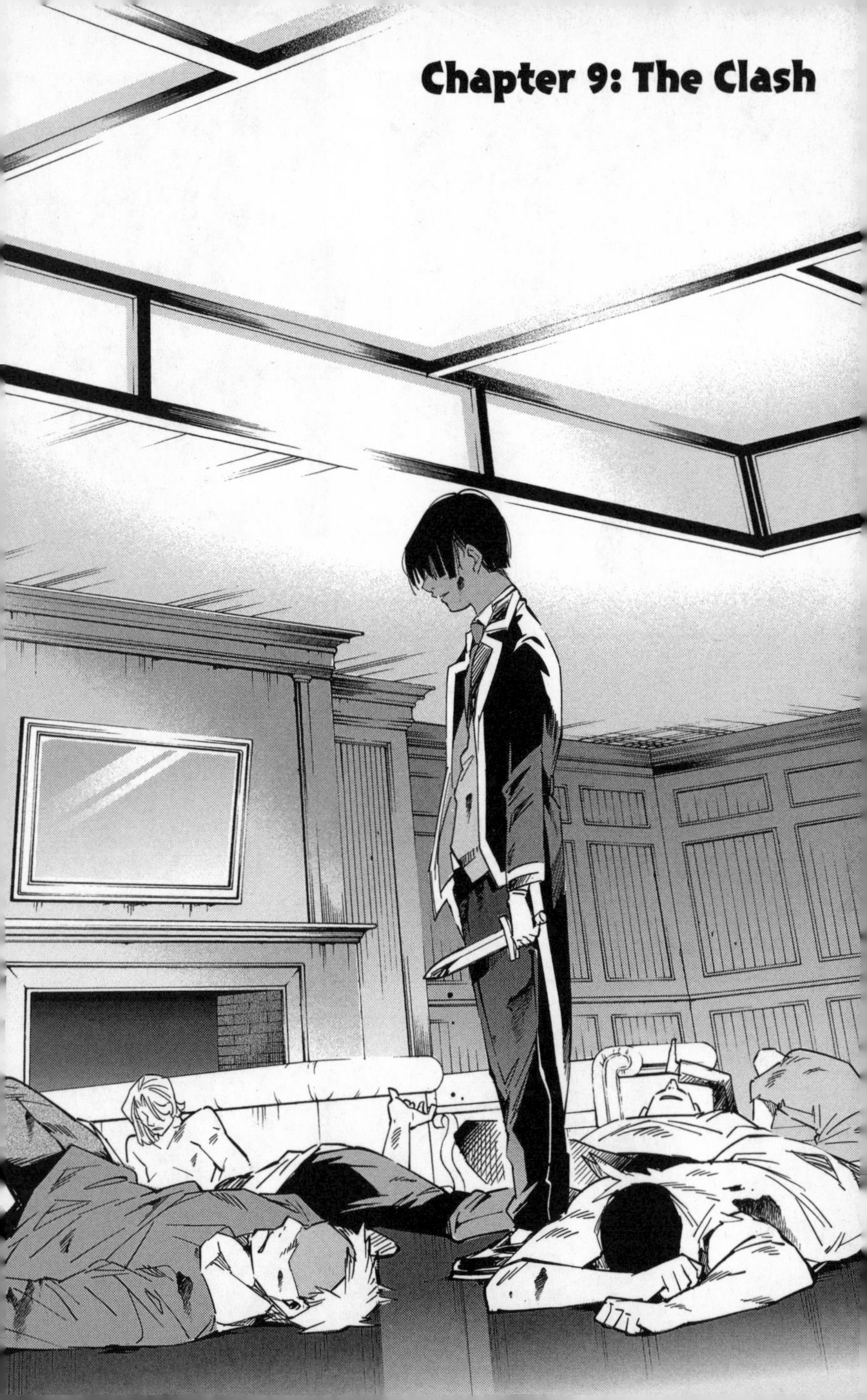

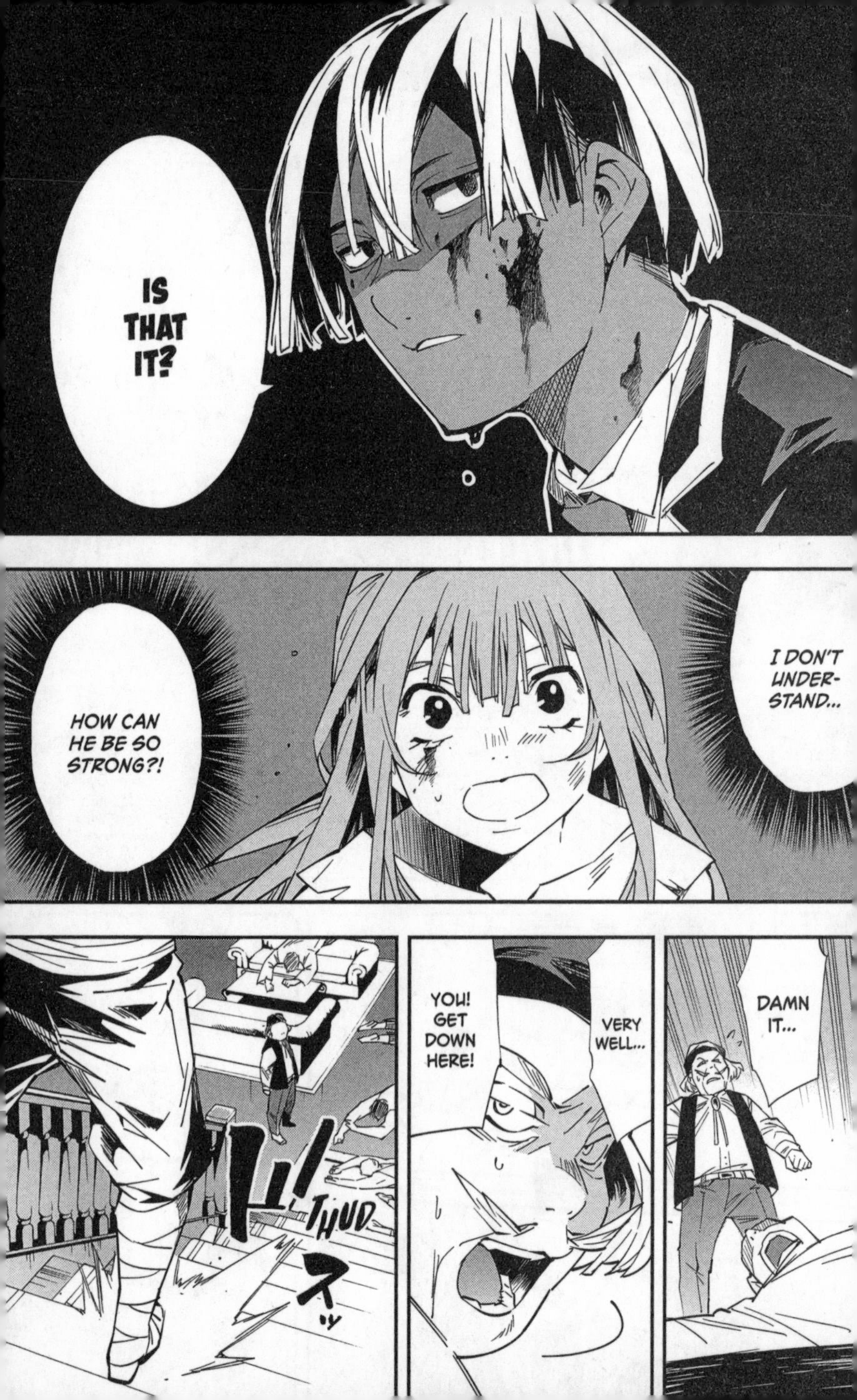
IS THAT IT?
I DON'T UNDERSTAND...
HOW CAN HE BE SO STRONG?!
DAMN IT...
VERY WELL...
YOU! GET DOWN HERE!
THUD

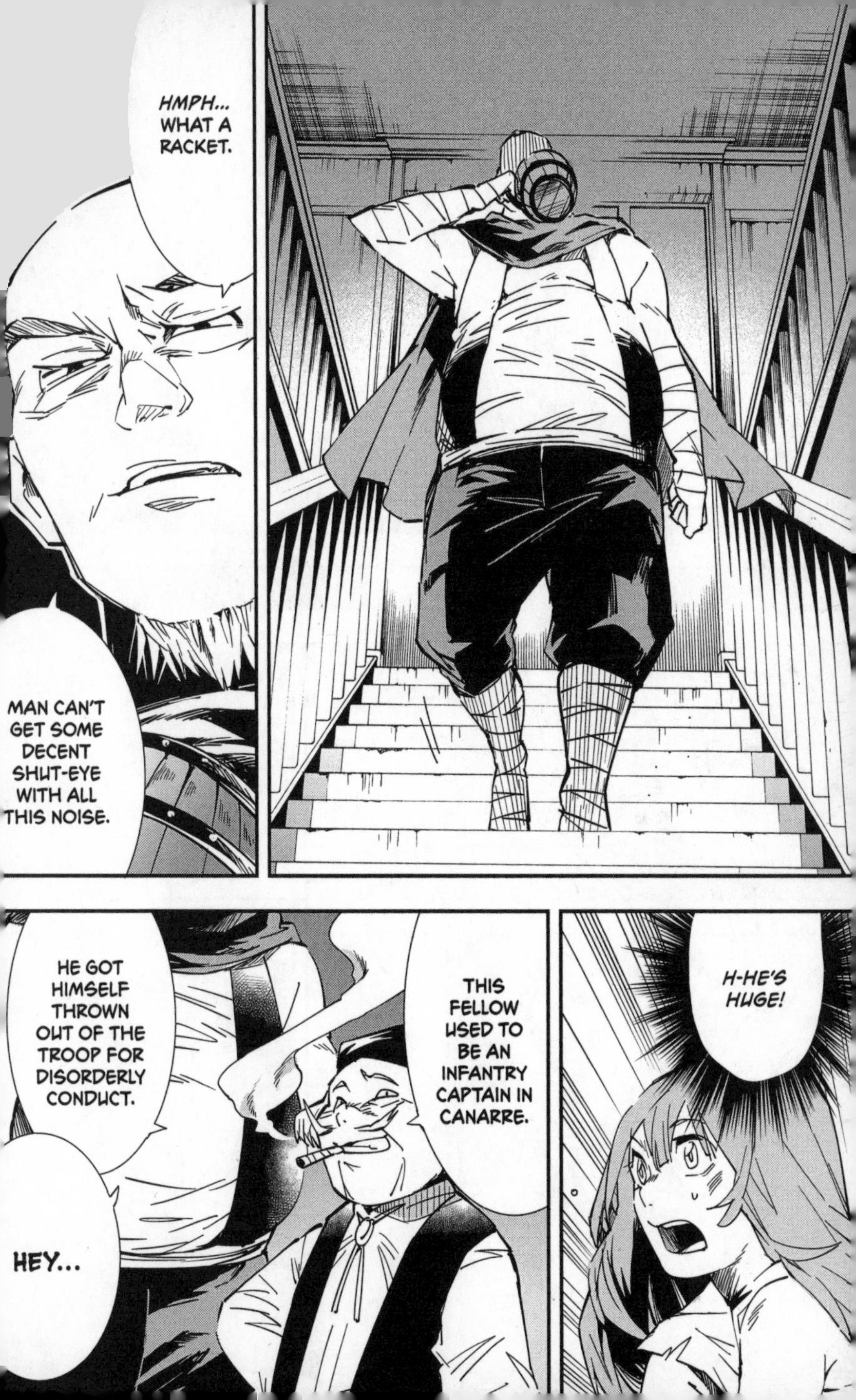
HMPH... WHAT A RACKET.
MAN CAN'T GET SOME DECENT SHUT-EYE WITH ALL THIS NOISE.
H-HE'S HUGE!
THIS FELLOW USED TO BE AN INFANTRY CAPTAIN IN CANARRE.
HE GOT HIMSELF THROWN OUT OF THE TROOP FOR DISORDERLY CONDUCT.
HEY...

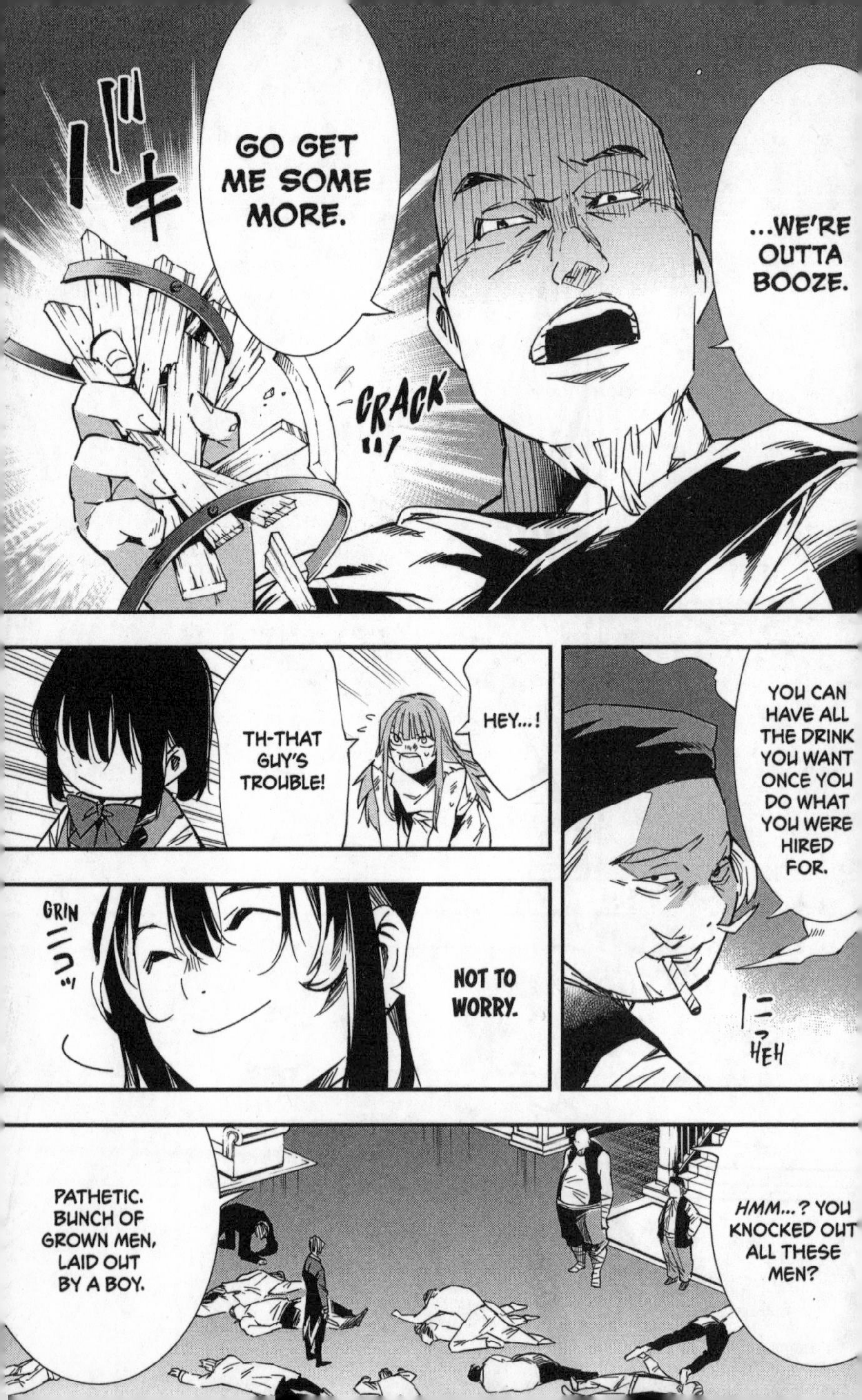
...WE'RE OUTTA BOOZE.
GO GET ME SOME MORE.
CRACK
YOU CAN HAVE ALL THE DRINK YOU WANT ONCE YOU DO WHAT YOU WERE HIRED FOR.
HEH
HEY...!
TH-THAT GUY'S TROUBLE!
NOT TO WORRY.
GRIN
HMM...? YOU KNOCKED OUT ALL THESE MEN?
PATHETIC. BUNCH OF GROWN MEN, LAID OUT BY A BOY.

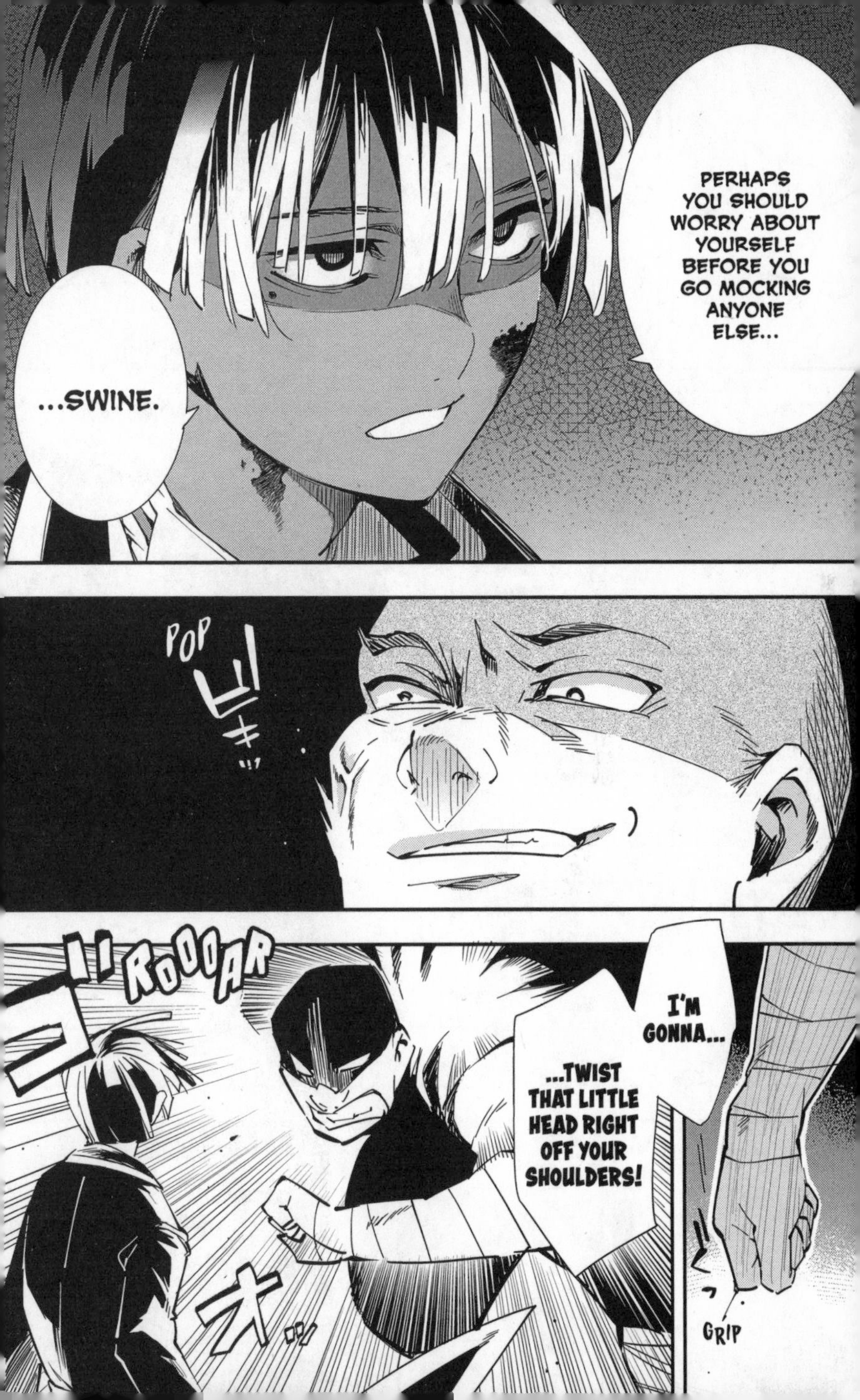
PERHAPS YOU SHOULD WORRY ABOUT YOURSELF BEFORE YOU GO MOCKING ANYONE ELSE...
...SWINE.
POP
I'M GONNA...
...TWIST THAT LITTLE HEAD RIGHT OFF YOUR SHOULDERS!
ROOOAR
GRIP

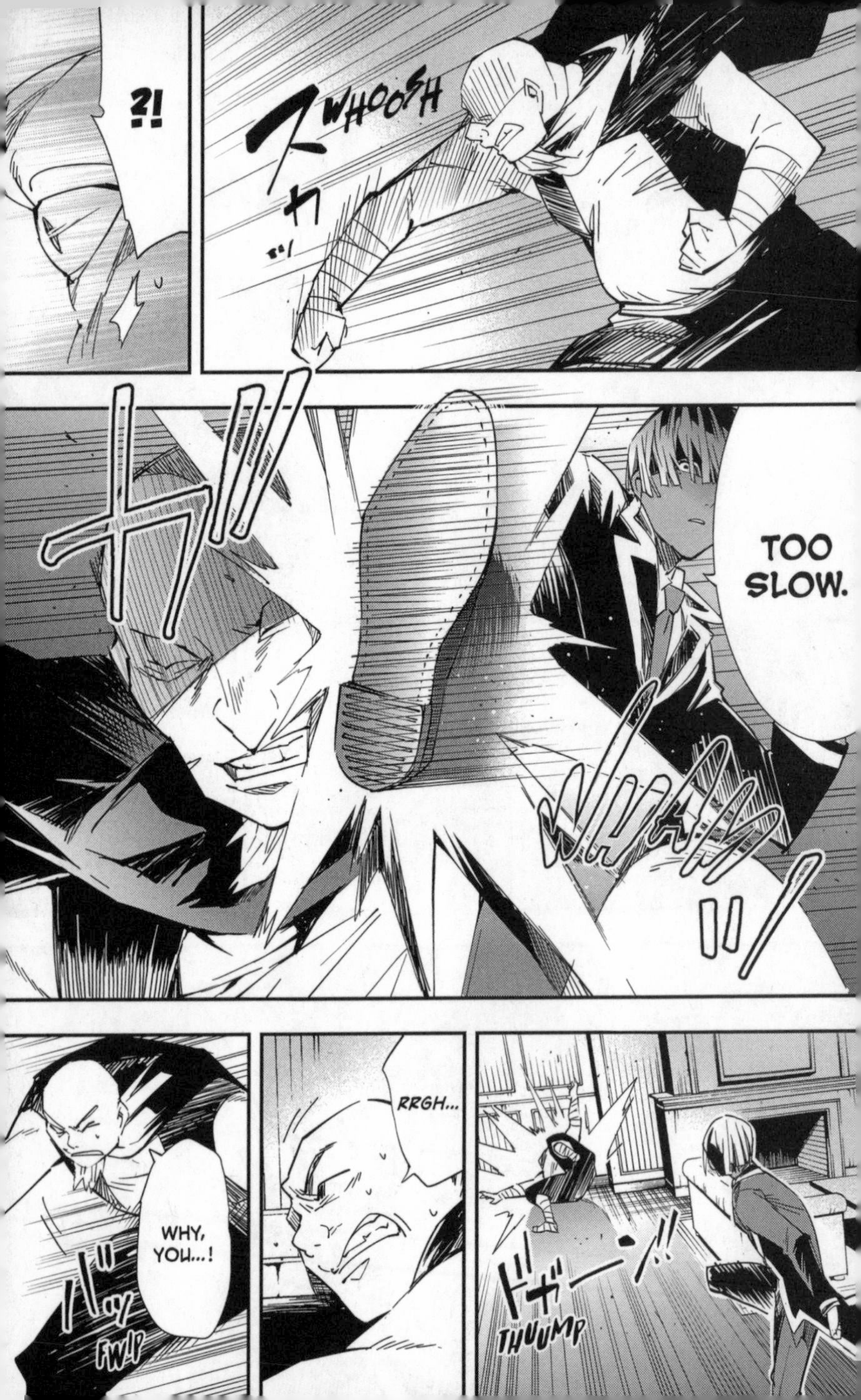
WHOOSH
?!
TOO SLOW.
WHAM
ドガーン!!
THUUMP
RRGH...
WHY, YOU...!
FWIP

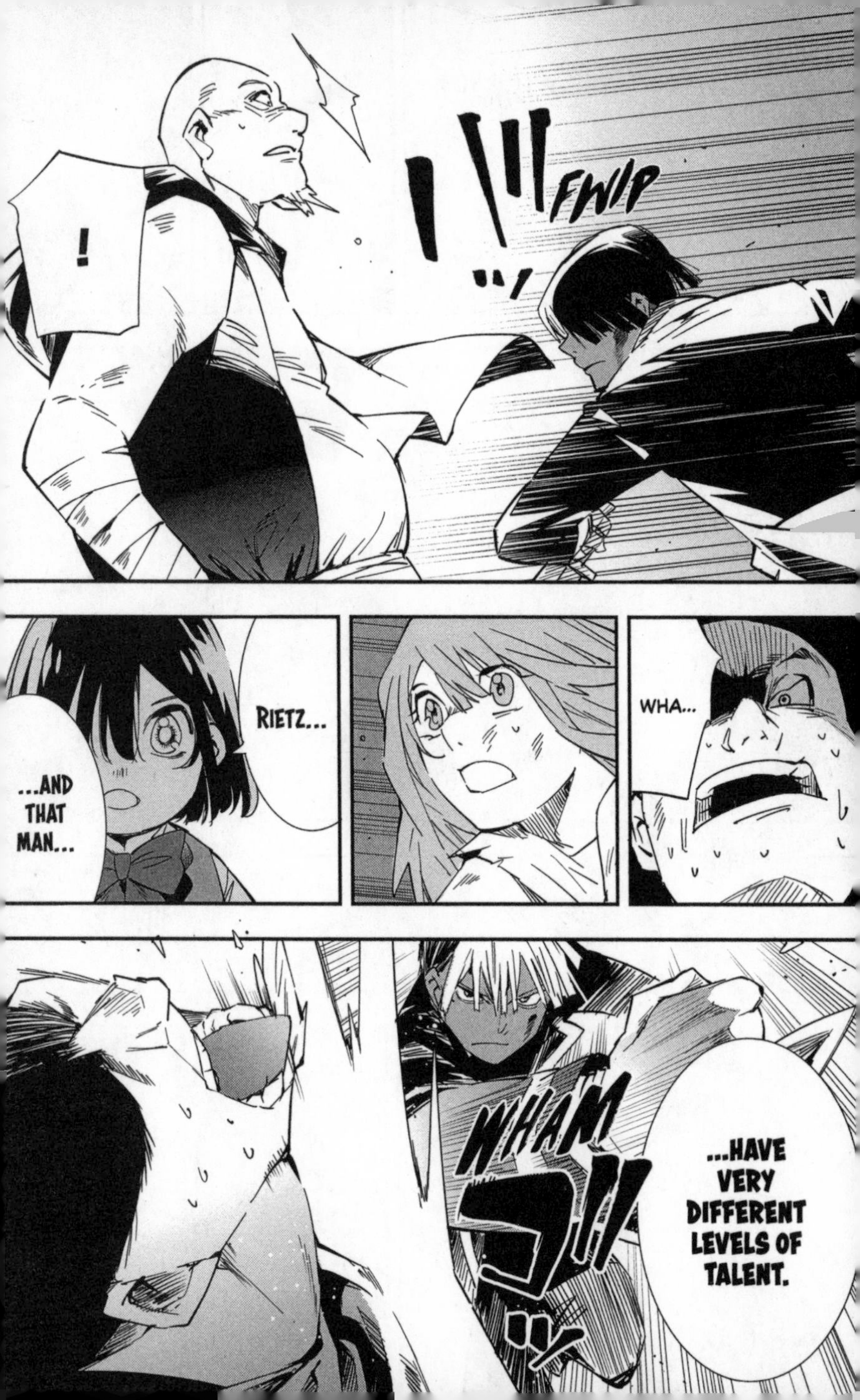
FWIP
!
WHA...
RIETZ...
...AND THAT MAN...
WHAM
...HAVE VERY DIFFERENT LEVELS OF TALENT.

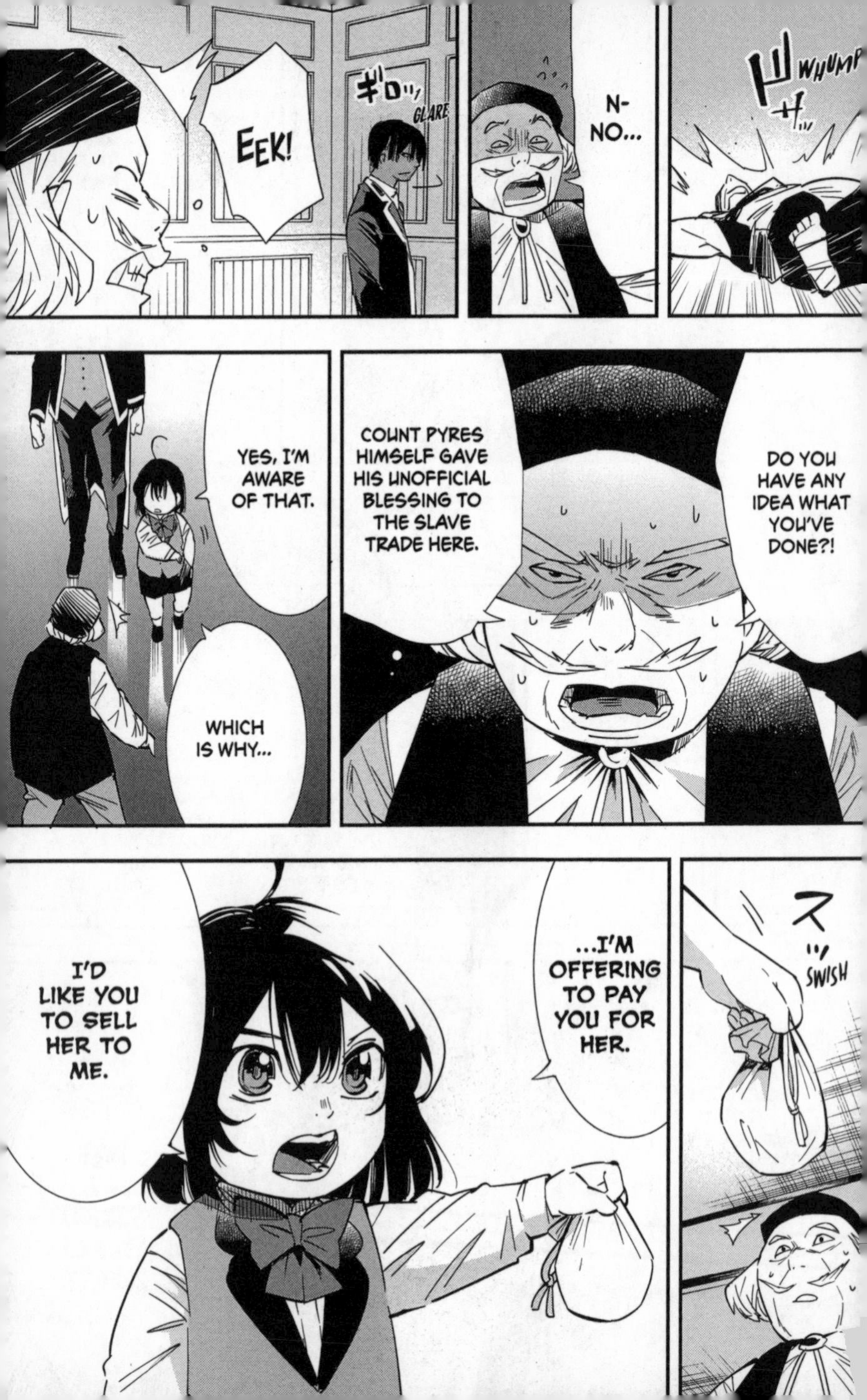
WHUMP
N- NO...
ギロッ
GLARE
EEK!
DO YOU HAVE ANY IDEA WHAT YOU'VE DONE?!
COUNT PYRES HIMSELF GAVE HIS UNOFFICIAL BLESSING TO THE SLAVE TRADE HERE.
YES, I'M AWARE OF THAT.
WHICH IS WHY...
SWISH
...I'M OFFERING TO PAY YOU FOR HER.
I'D LIKE YOU TO SELL HER TO ME.

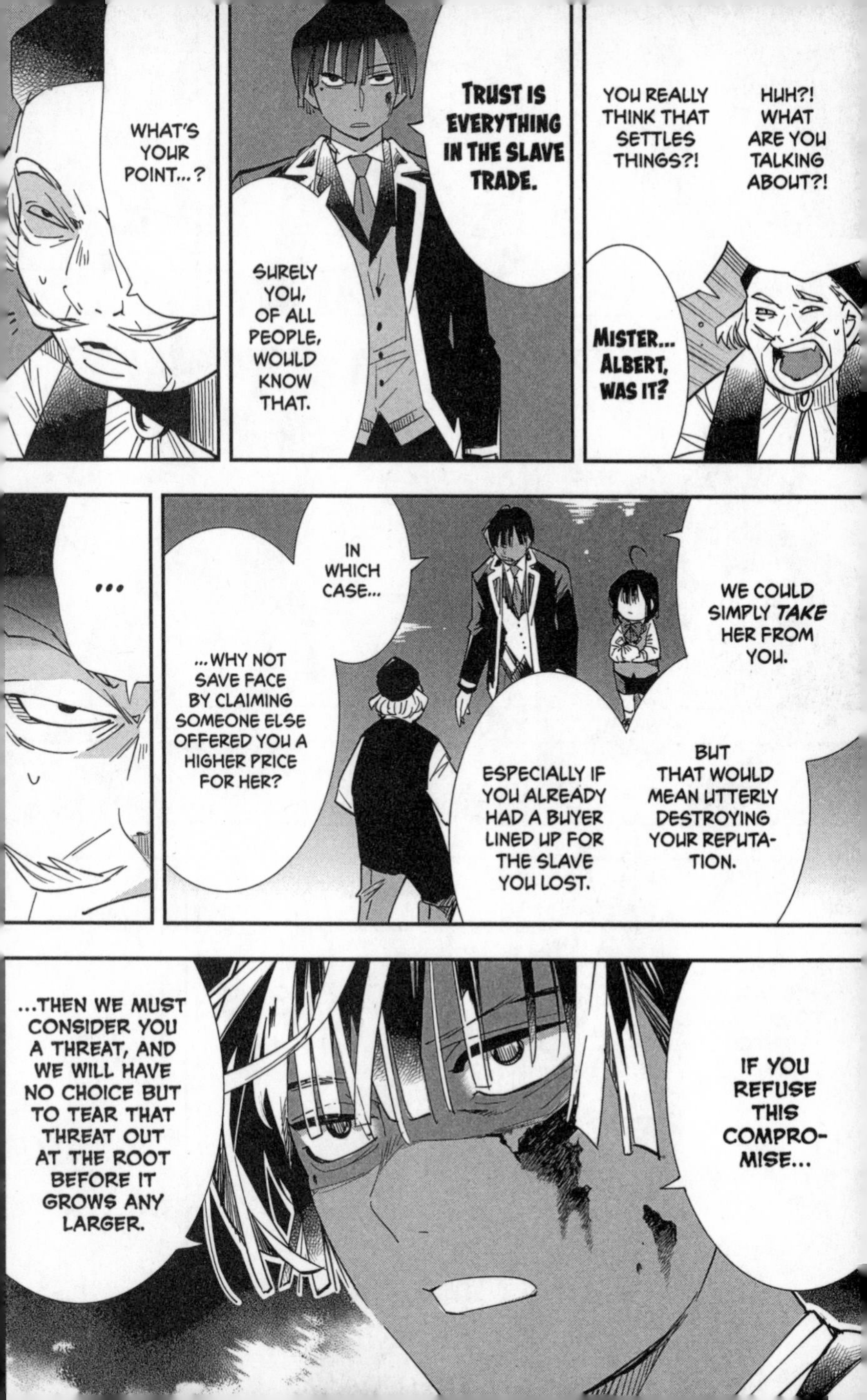
HUH?! WHAT ARE YOU TALKING ABOUT?!
YOU REALLY THINK THAT SETTLES THINGS?!
MISTER... ALBERT, WAS IT?
TRUST IS EVERYTHING IN THE SLAVE TRADE.
SURELY YOU, OF ALL PEOPLE, WOULD KNOW THAT.
WHAT'S YOUR POINT...?
WE COULD SIMPLY *TAKE* HER FROM YOU.
BUT THAT WOULD MEAN UTTERLY DESTROYING YOUR REPUTATION.
ESPECIALLY IF YOU ALREADY HAD A BUYER LINED UP FOR THE SLAVE YOU LOST.
IN WHICH CASE...
...WHY NOT SAVE FACE BY CLAIMING SOMEONE ELSE OFFERED YOU A HIGHER PRICE FOR HER?
...
IF YOU REFUSE THIS COMPROMISE...
...THEN WE MUST CONSIDER YOU A THREAT, AND WE WILL HAVE NO CHOICE BUT TO TEAR THAT THREAT OUT AT THE ROOT BEFORE IT GROWS ANY LARGER.

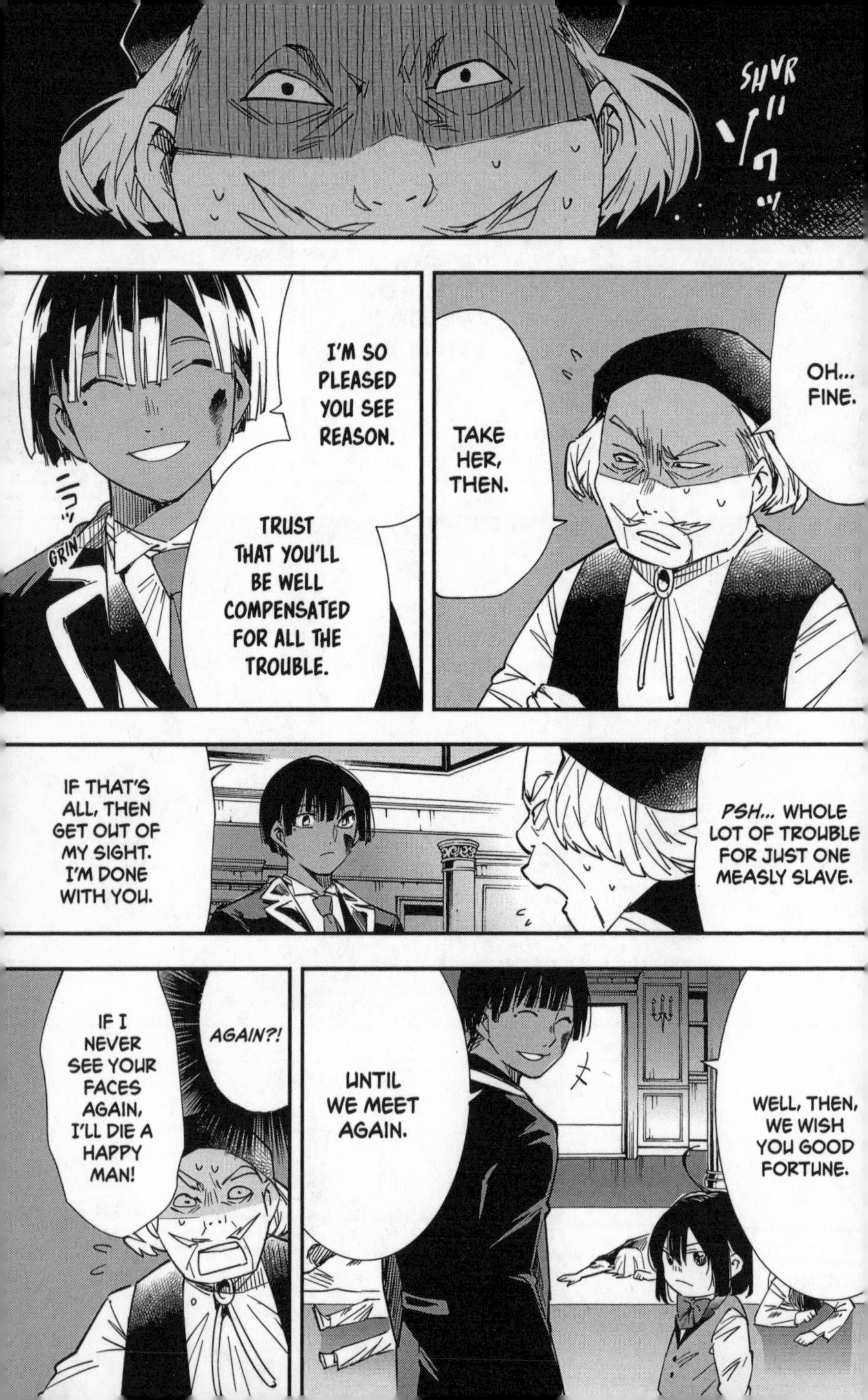
SHVR
ゾワッ
OH... FINE.
TAKE HER, THEN.
I'M SO PLEASED YOU SEE REASON.
TRUST THAT YOU'LL BE WELL COMPENSATED FOR ALL THE TROUBLE.
GRIN
PSH... WHOLE LOT OF TROUBLE FOR JUST ONE MEASLY SLAVE.
IF THAT'S ALL, THEN GET OUT OF MY SIGHT. I'M DONE WITH YOU.
WELL, THEN, WE WISH YOU GOOD FORTUNE.
UNTIL WE MEET AGAIN.
AGAIN?!
IF I NEVER SEE YOUR FACES AGAIN, I'LL DIE A HAPPY MAN!

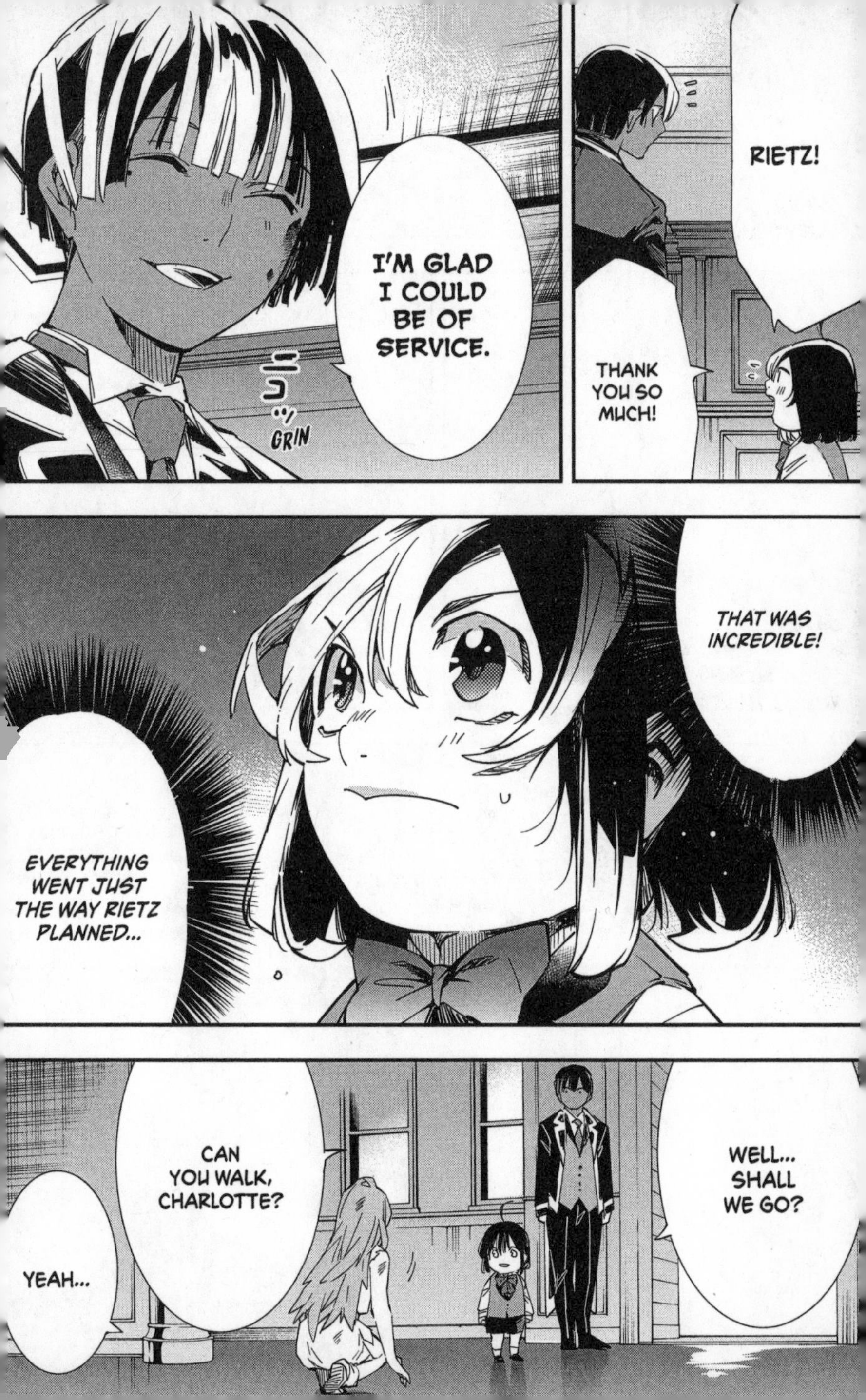
RIETZ!
THANK YOU SO MUCH!
I'M GLAD I COULD BE OF SERVICE.
ニコッ
GRIN
THAT WAS INCREDIBLE!
EVERYTHING WENT JUST THE WAY RIETZ PLANNED...
WELL... SHALL WE GO?
CAN YOU WALK, CHARLOTTE?
YEAH...

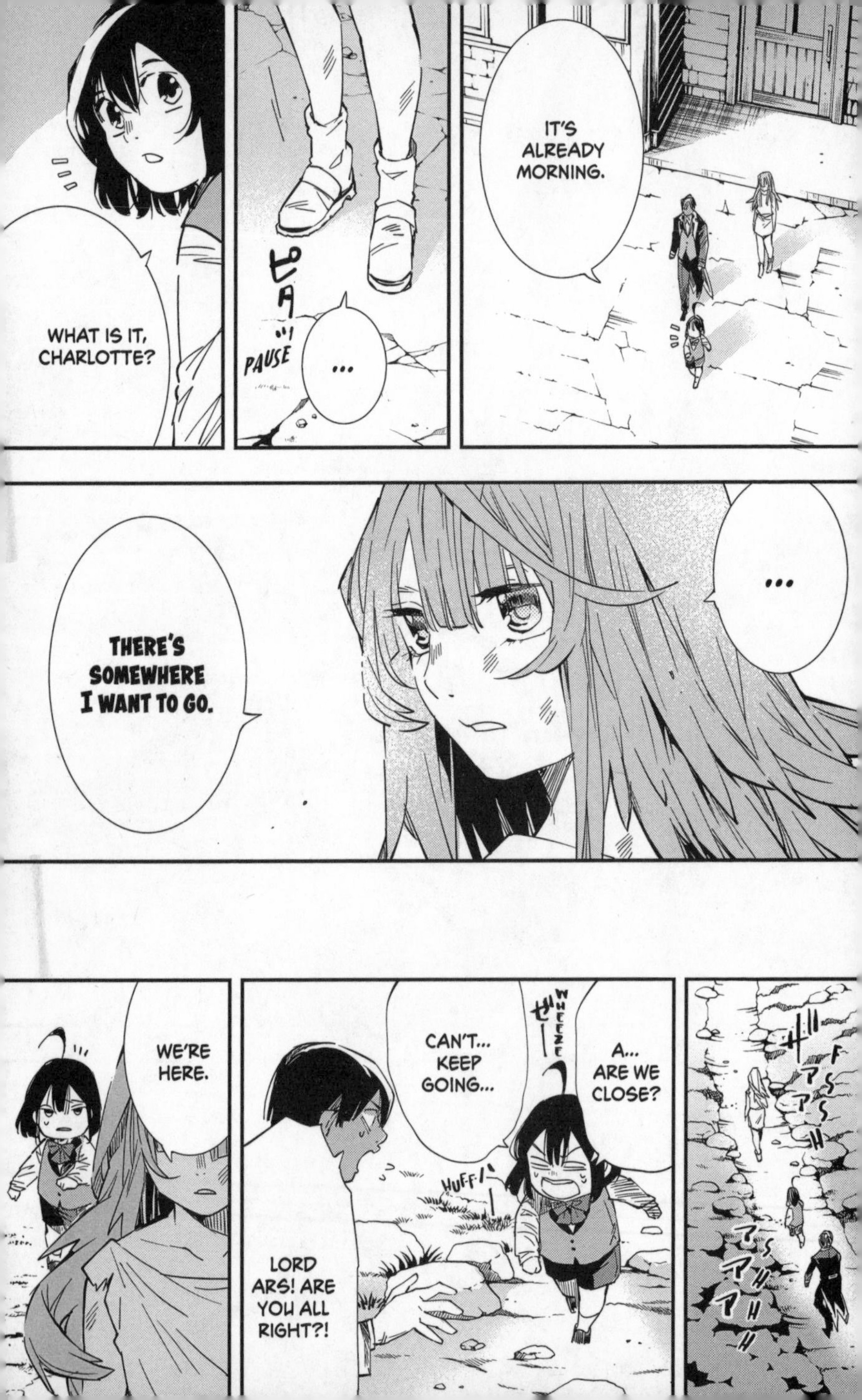
IT'S ALREADY MORNING.
ピタッ
PAUSE
...
WHAT IS IT, CHARLOTTE?
...
THERE'S SOMEWHERE I WANT TO GO.
FSSHH
SHHHH
A... ARE WE CLOSE?
ゼー
WHEEZE
CAN'T... KEEP GOING...
HUFF
LORD ARS! ARE YOU ALL RIGHT?!
WE'RE HERE.

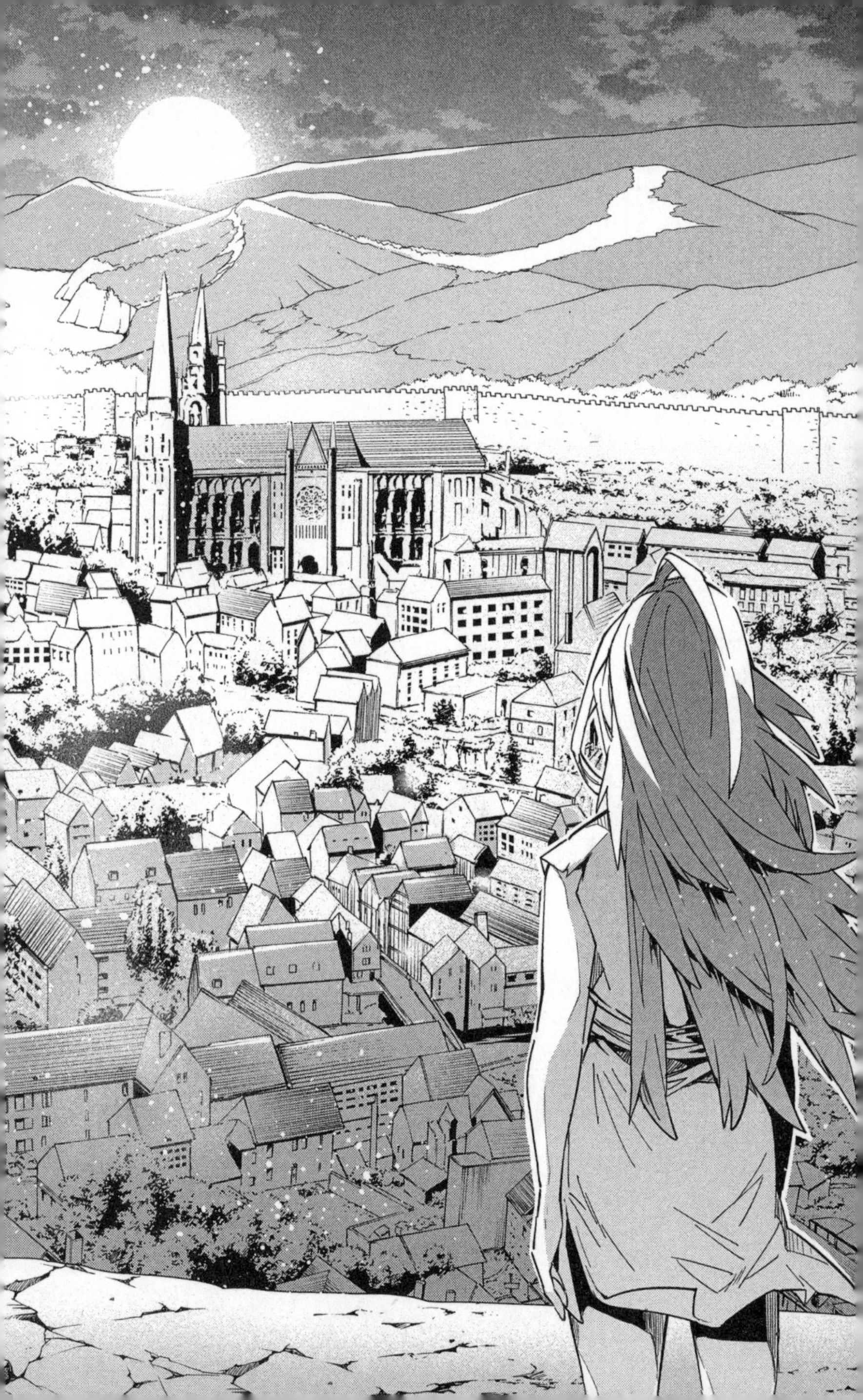

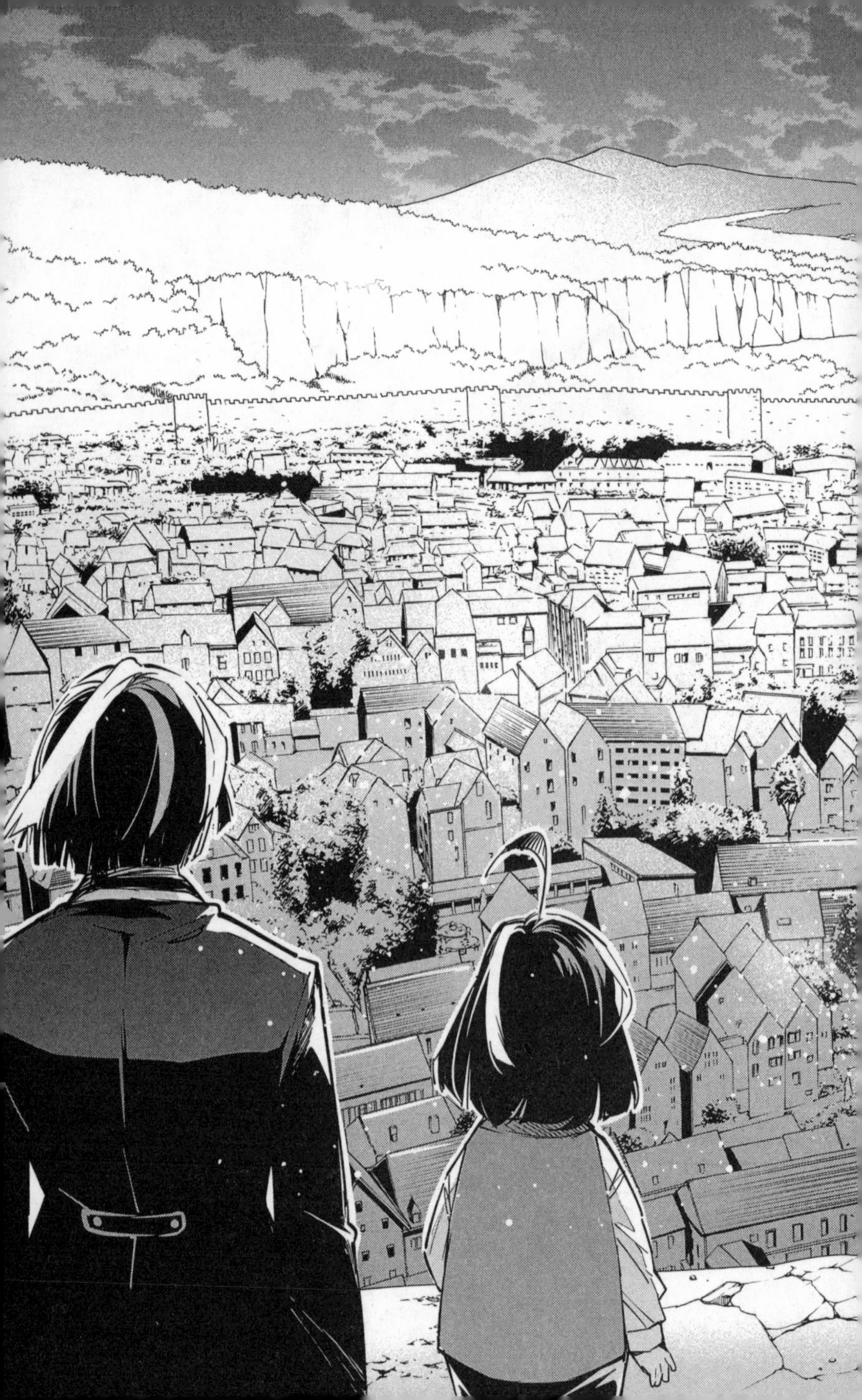

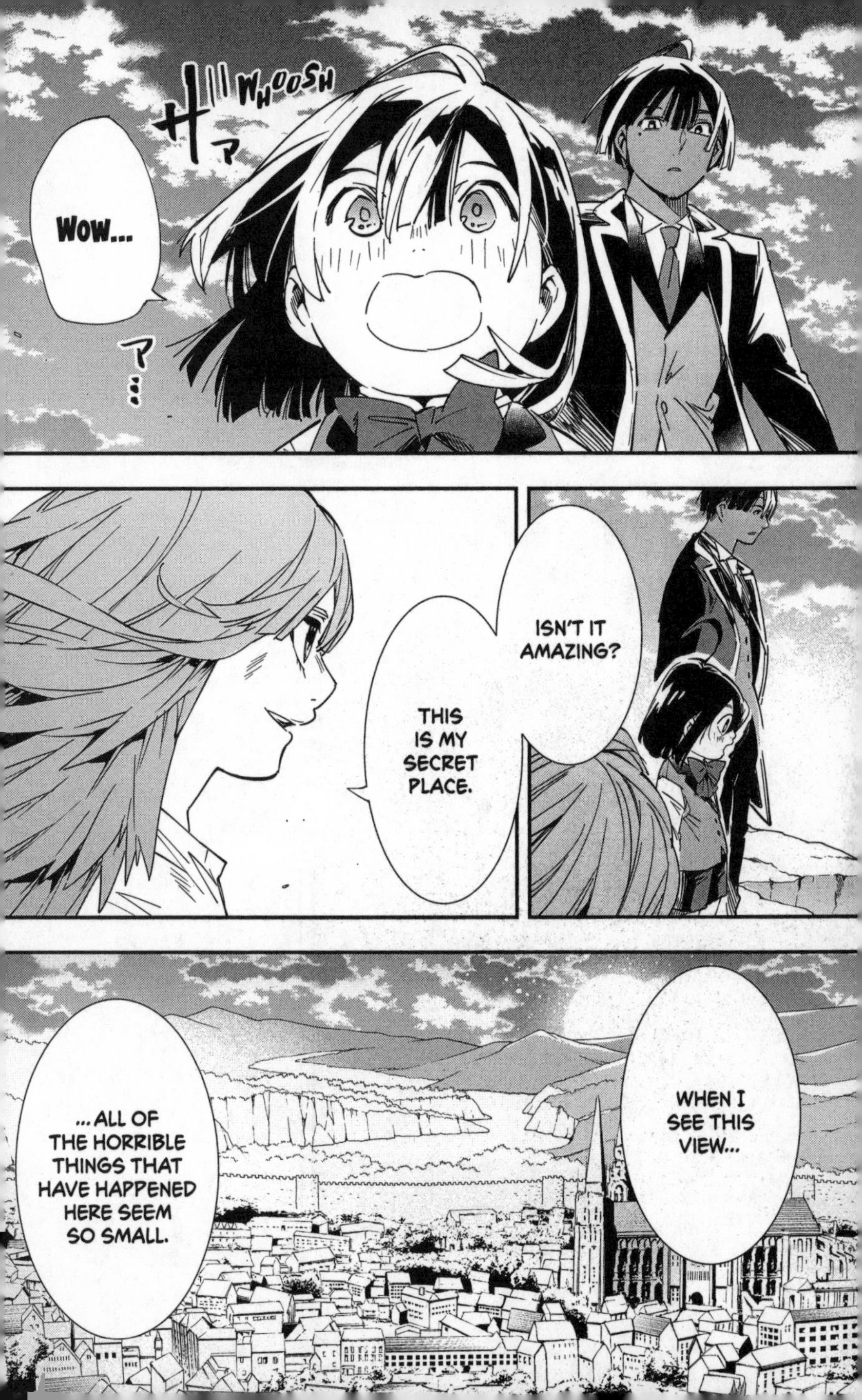
ザァ
WHOOSH
WOW...
ア…
ISN'T IT AMAZING?
THIS IS MY SECRET PLACE.
WHEN I SEE THIS VIEW...
...ALL OF THE HORRIBLE THINGS THAT HAVE HAPPENED HERE SEEM SO SMALL.

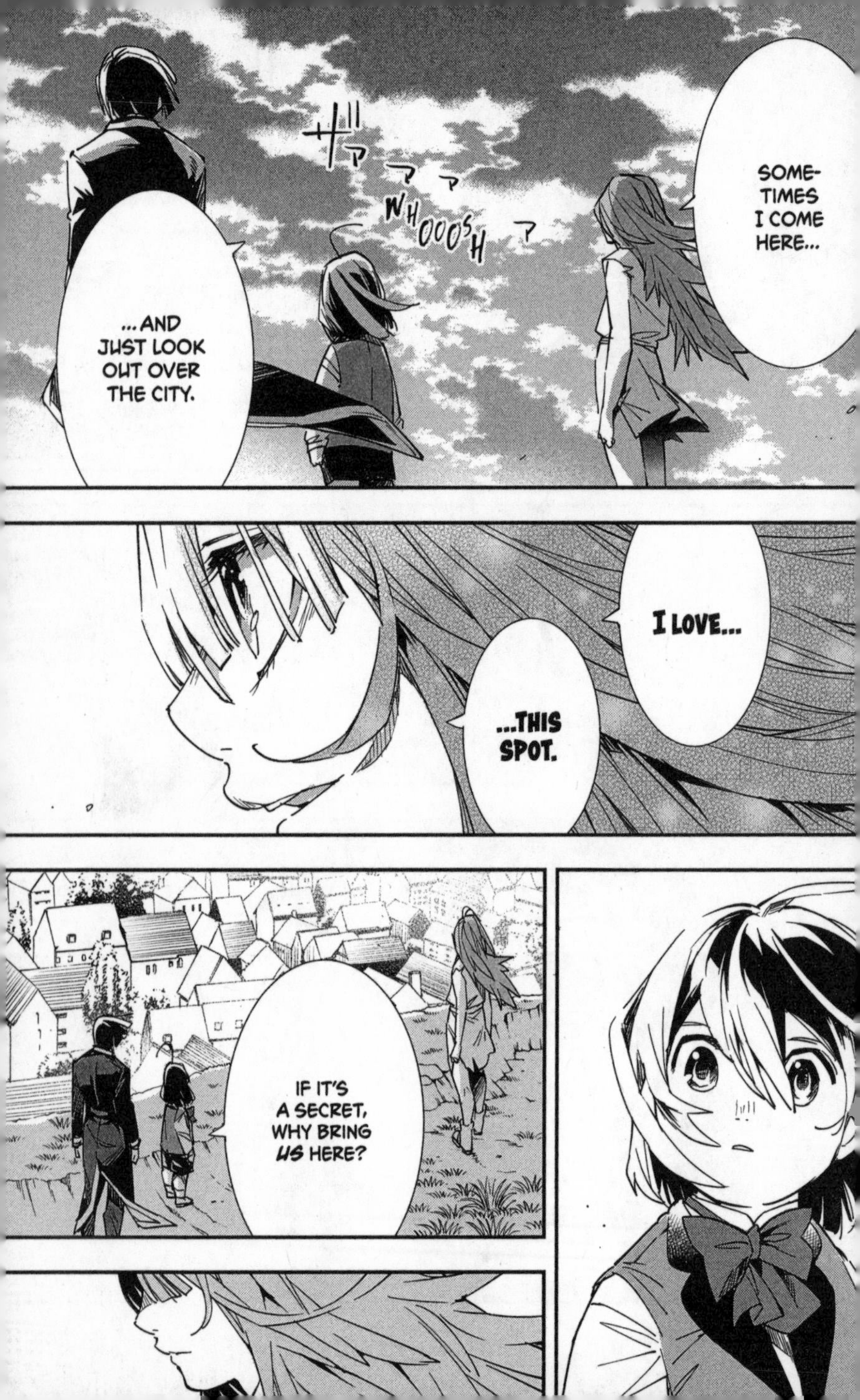
SOME-TIMES I COME HERE...
ザァァァ
WHOOOSH
...AND JUST LOOK OUT OVER THE CITY.
I LOVE...
...THIS SPOT.
IF IT'S A SECRET, WHY BRING *US* HERE?

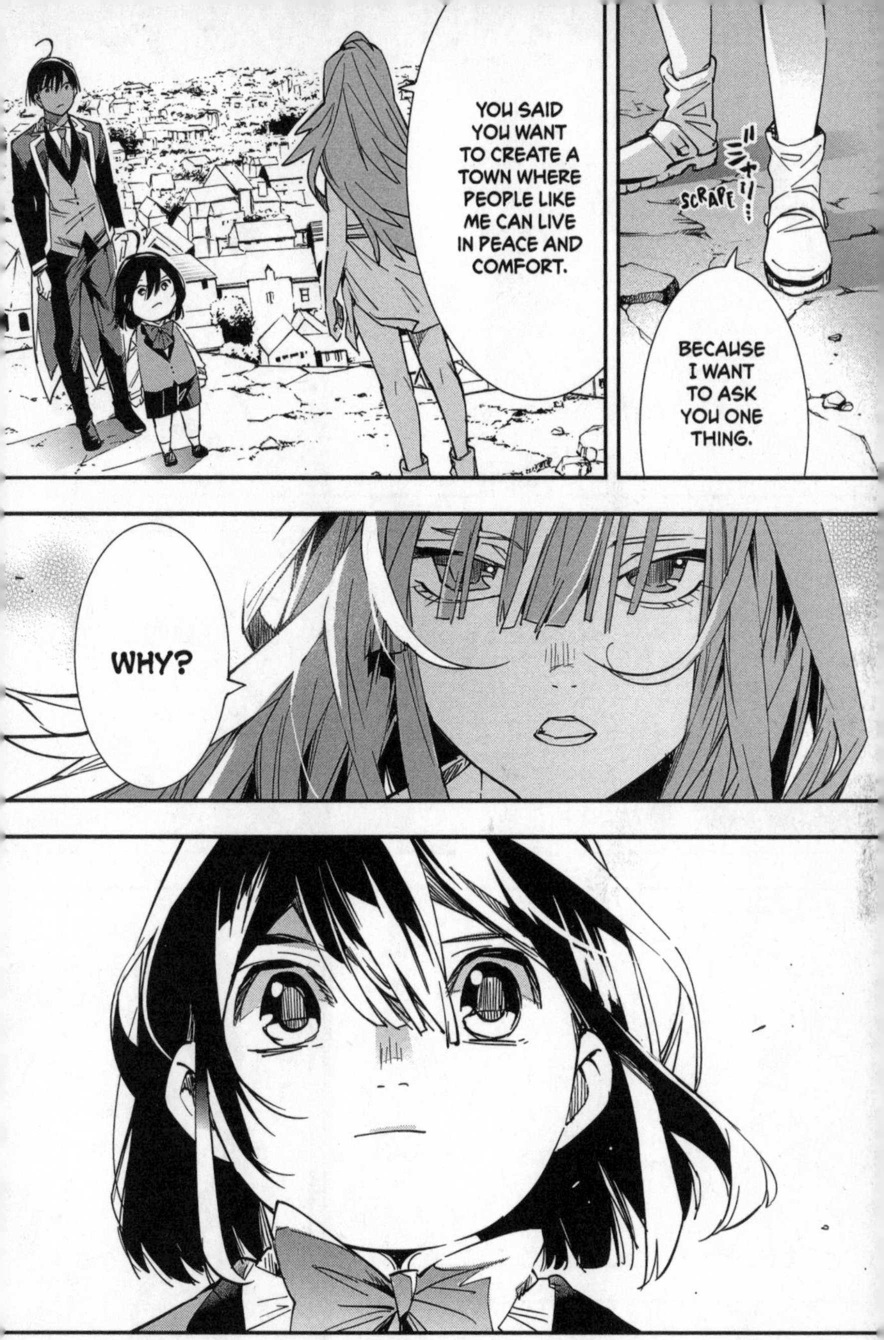
SCRAPE
BECAUSE I WANT TO ASK YOU ONE THING.
YOU SAID YOU WANT TO CREATE A TOWN WHERE PEOPLE LIKE ME CAN LIVE IN PEACE AND COMFORT.
WHY?

As a Reincarnated
ARISTOCRAT,
I'll Use My Appraisal Skill to
Rise in the World

As a Reincarnated
ARISTOCRAT,
I'll Use My Appraisal Skill to
Rise in the World

Chapter 10: The Answer

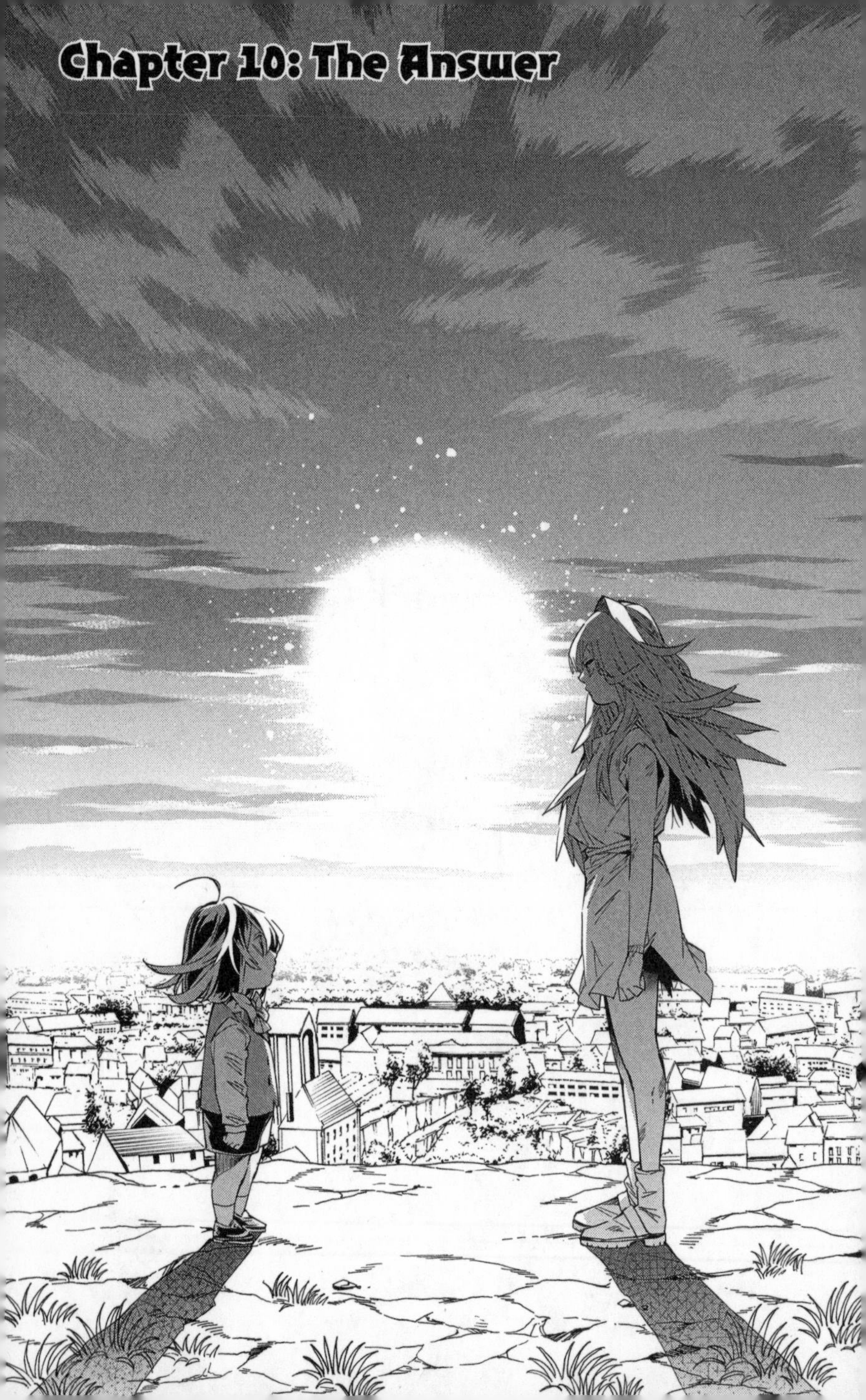

YOU SAID YOU WANT TO CREATE A TOWN WHERE PEOPLE LIKE ME CAN LIVE IN PEACE AND COMFORT.

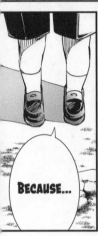

BECAUSE...

WHY?

...I LOVE CHILDREN.

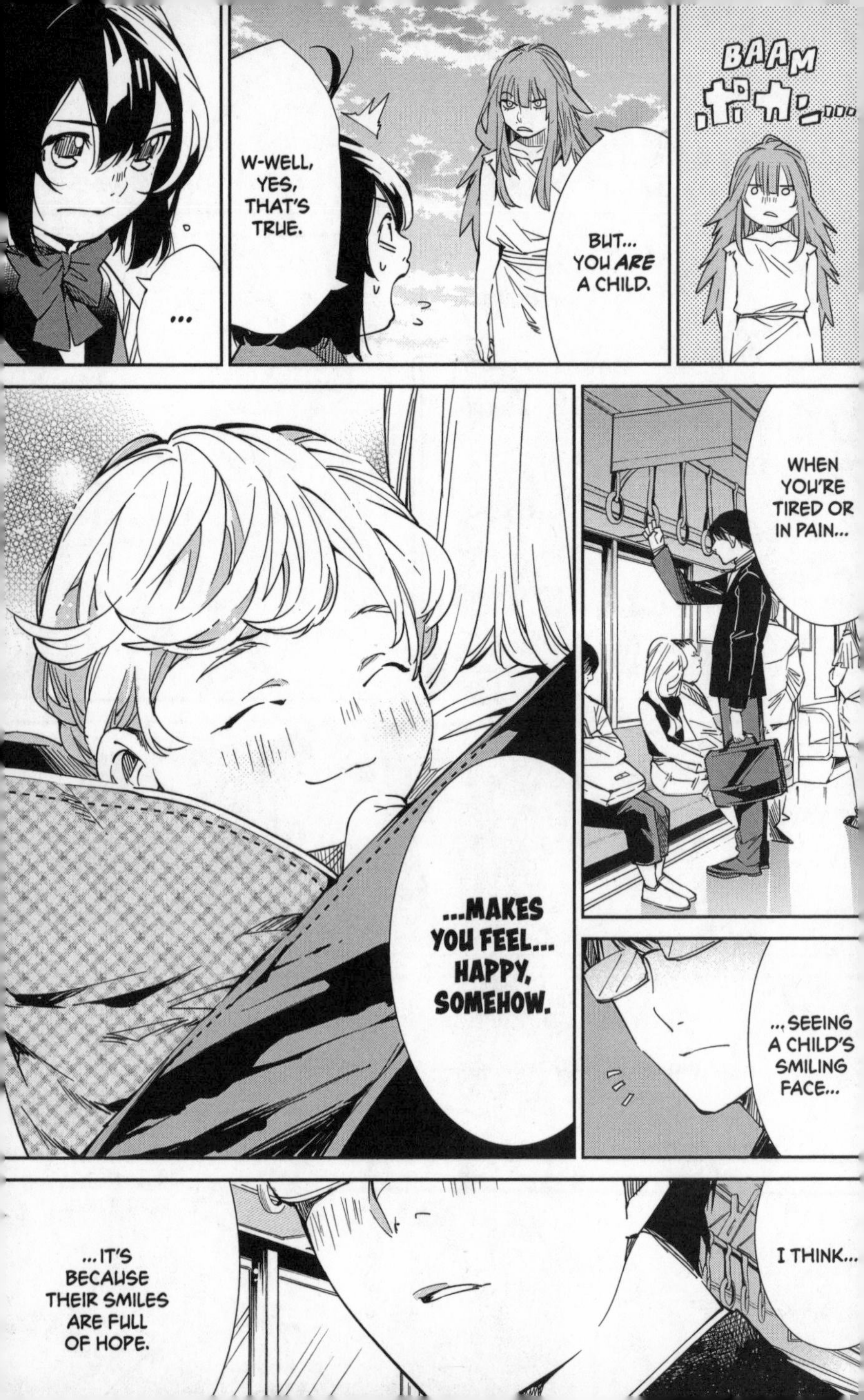

BAAM
ポカン…
BUT... YOU *ARE* A CHILD.
W-WELL, YES, THAT'S TRUE.
...
WHEN YOU'RE TIRED OR IN PAIN...
..., SEEING A CHILD'S SMILING FACE...
...MAKES YOU FEEL... HAPPY, SOMEHOW.
I THINK...
...IT'S BECAUSE THEIR SMILES ARE FULL OF HOPE.

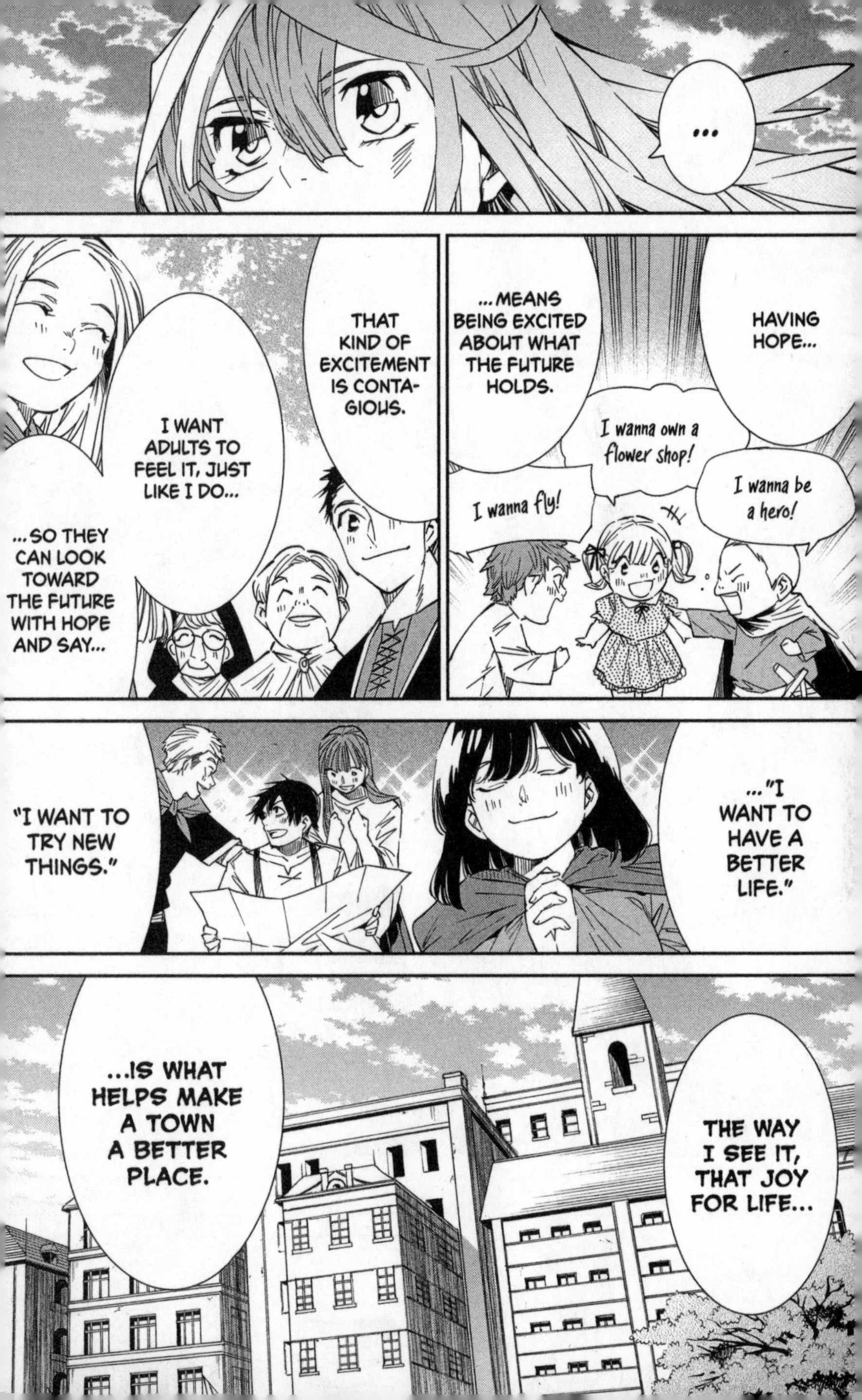
...
HAVING HOPE...
...MEANS BEING EXCITED ABOUT WHAT THE FUTURE HOLDS.
I wanna own a flower shop!
I wanna be a hero!
I wanna fly!
THAT KIND OF EXCITEMENT IS CONTA-GIOUS.
I WANT ADULTS TO FEEL IT, JUST LIKE I DO...
...SO THEY CAN LOOK TOWARD THE FUTURE WITH HOPE AND SAY...
..."I WANT TO HAVE A BETTER LIFE."
"I WANT TO TRY NEW THINGS."
THE WAY I SEE IT, THAT JOY FOR LIFE...
...IS WHAT HELPS MAKE A TOWN A BETTER PLACE.

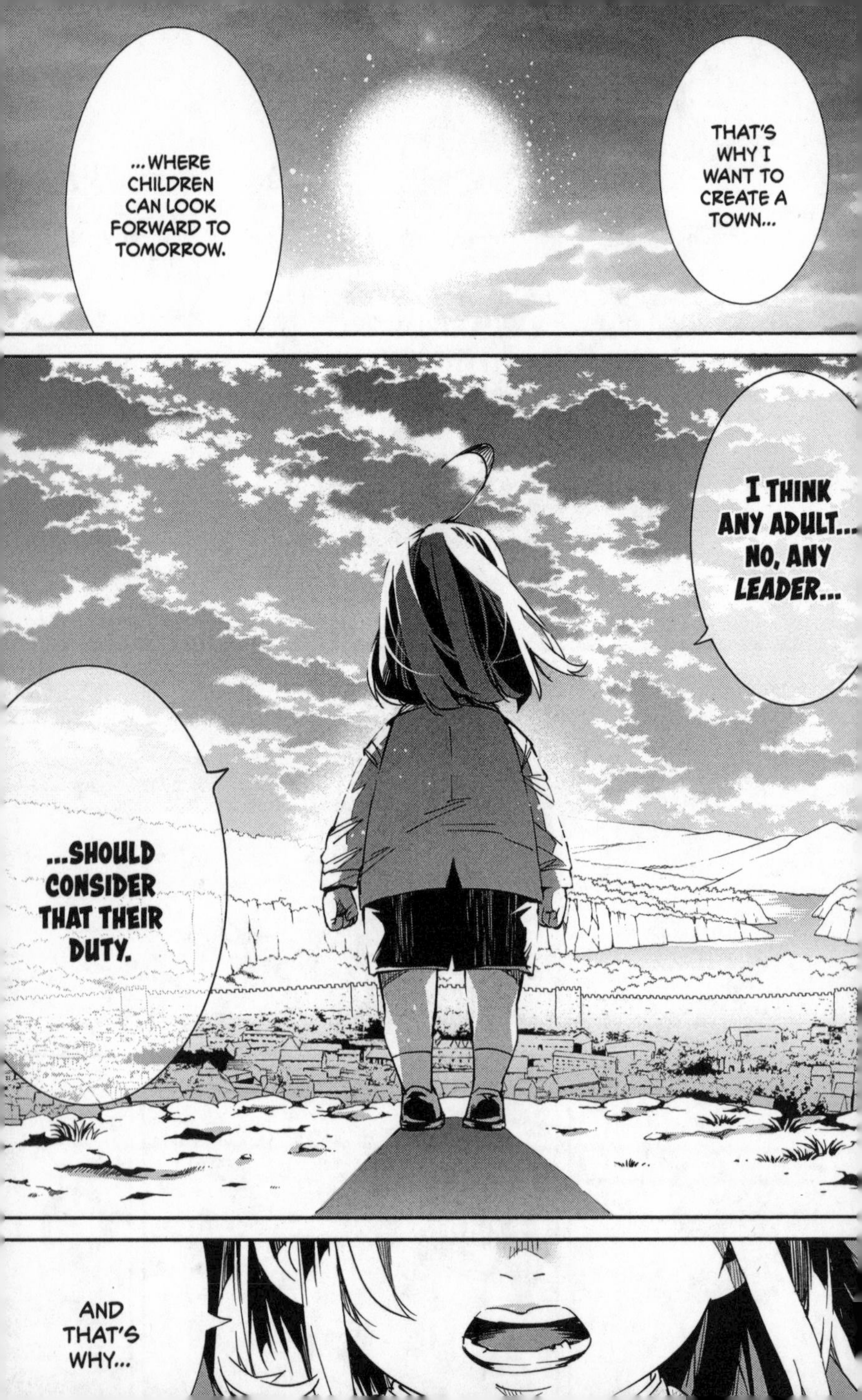
THAT'S WHY I WANT TO CREATE A TOWN...
...WHERE CHILDREN CAN LOOK FORWARD TO TOMORROW.
I THINK ANY ADULT... NO, ANY LEADER...
...SHOULD CONSIDER THAT THEIR DUTY.
AND THAT'S WHY...

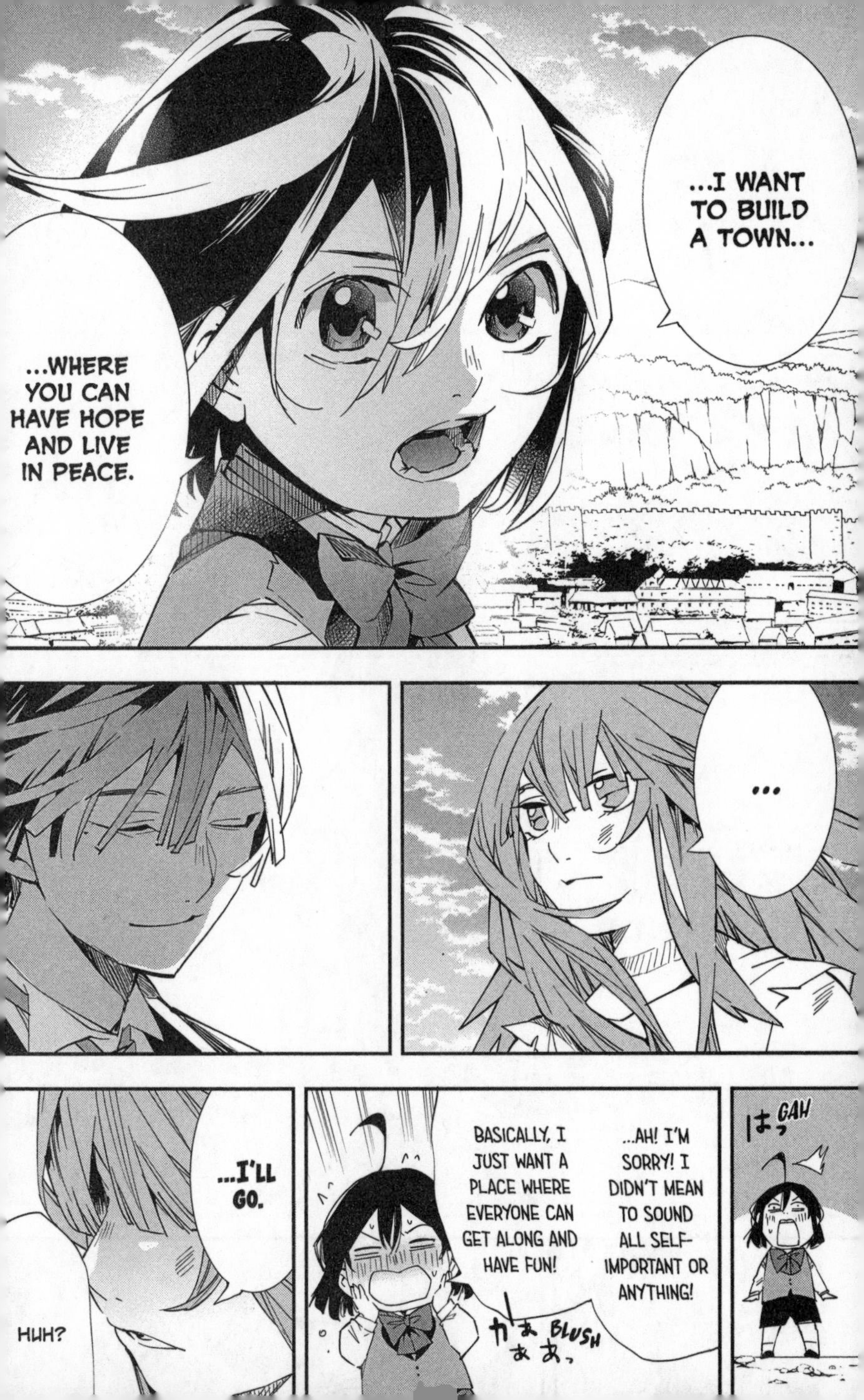
...I WANT TO BUILD A TOWN...
...WHERE YOU CAN HAVE HOPE AND LIVE IN PEACE.
...
はっ GAH
...AH! I'M SORRY! I DIDN'T MEAN TO SOUND ALL SELF-IMPORTANT OR ANYTHING!
BASICALLY, I JUST WANT A PLACE WHERE EVERYONE CAN GET ALONG AND HAVE FUN!
かあああっ BLUSH
...I'LL GO.
HUH?

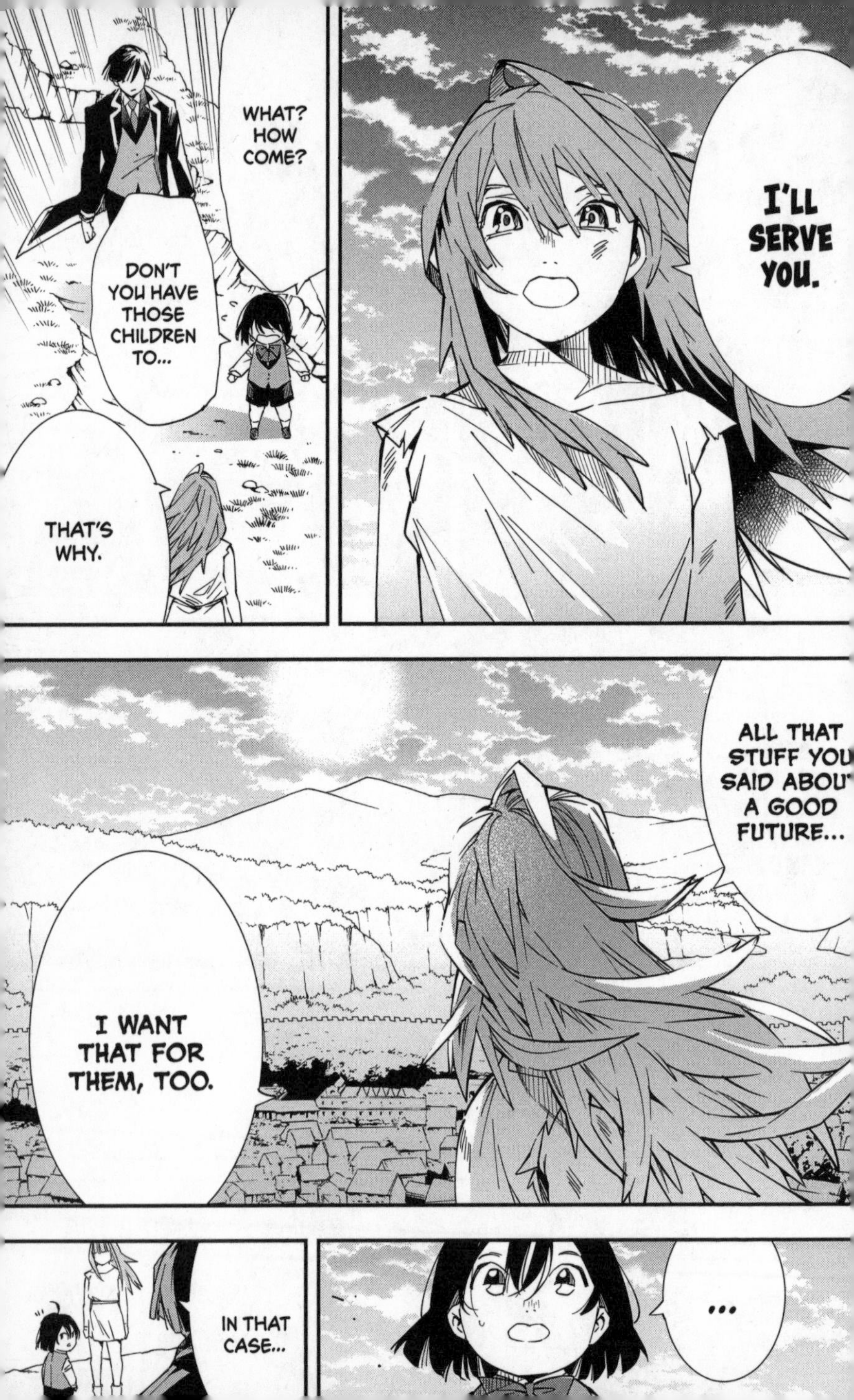
I'LL SERVE YOU.
WHAT? HOW COME?
DON'T YOU HAVE THOSE CHILDREN TO...
THAT'S WHY.
ALL THAT STUFF YOU SAID ABOUT A GOOD FUTURE...
I WANT THAT FOR THEM, TOO.
...
IN THAT CASE...

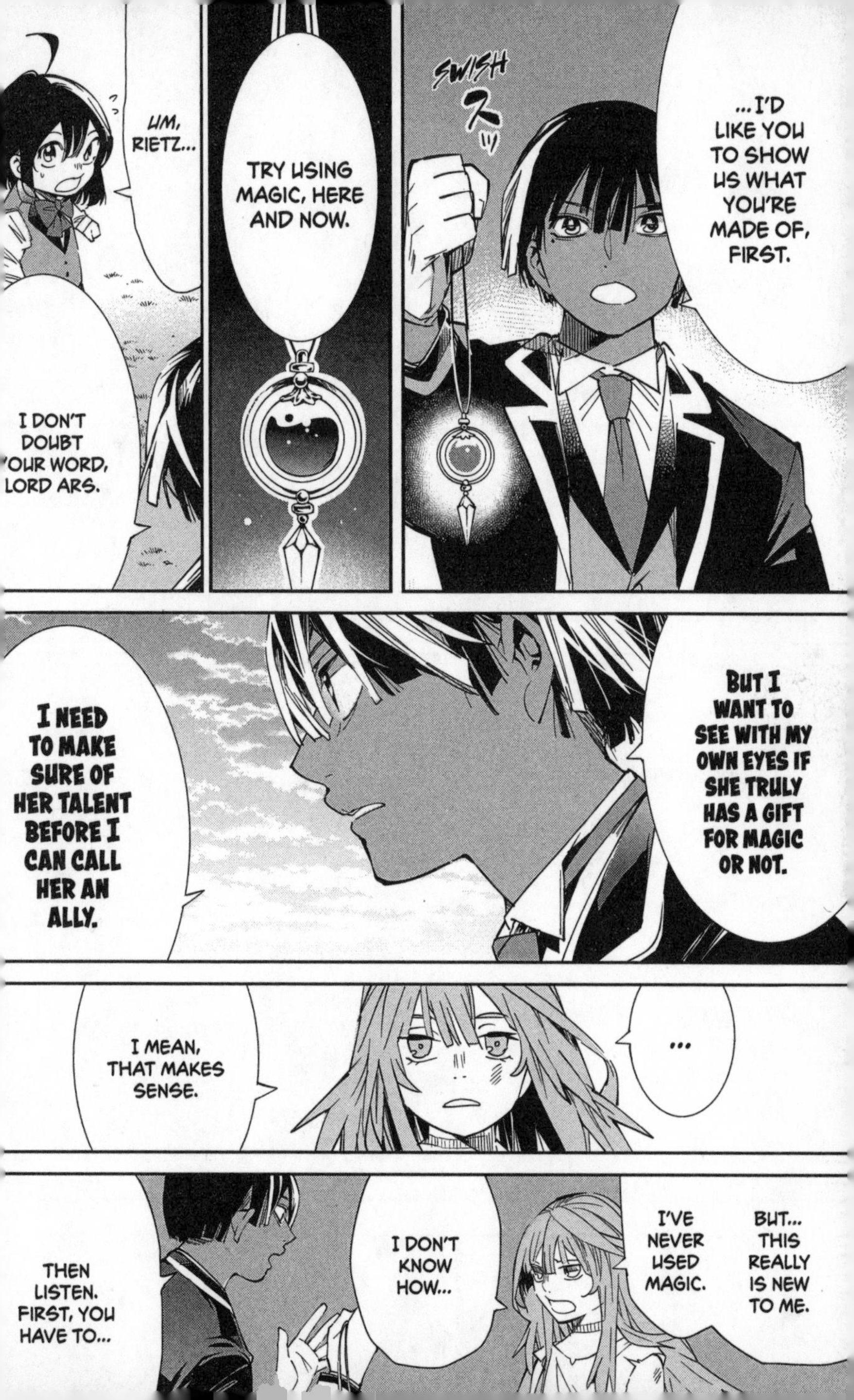
SWISH
スッ
...I'D LIKE YOU TO SHOW US WHAT YOU'RE MADE OF, FIRST.
TRY USING MAGIC, HERE AND NOW.
UM, RIETZ...
I DON'T DOUBT 'OUR WORD, LORD ARS.
BUT I WANT TO SEE WITH MY OWN EYES IF SHE TRULY HAS A GIFT FOR MAGIC OR NOT.
I NEED TO MAKE SURE OF HER TALENT BEFORE I CAN CALL HER AN ALLY.
...
I MEAN, THAT MAKES SENSE.
BUT... THIS REALLY IS NEW TO ME.
I'VE NEVER USED MAGIC.
I DON'T KNOW HOW...
THEN LISTEN. FIRST, YOU HAVE TO...

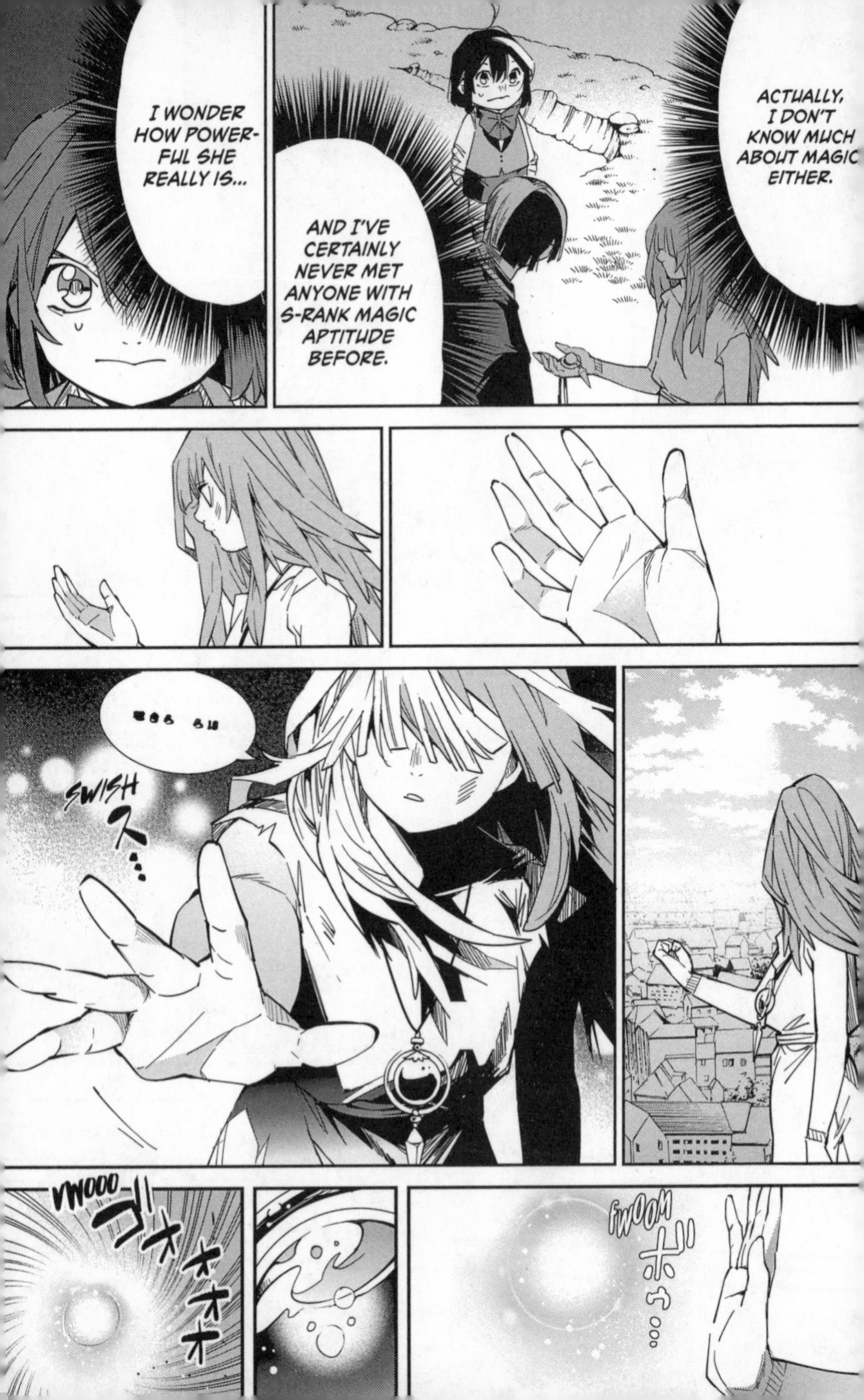
ACTUALLY, I DON'T KNOW MUCH ABOUT MAGIC EITHER.
AND I'VE CERTAINLY NEVER MET ANYONE WITH S-RANK MAGIC APTITUDE BEFORE.
I WONDER HOW POWER-FUL SHE REALLY IS...
SWISH
FWOOM
VWOOO--!!

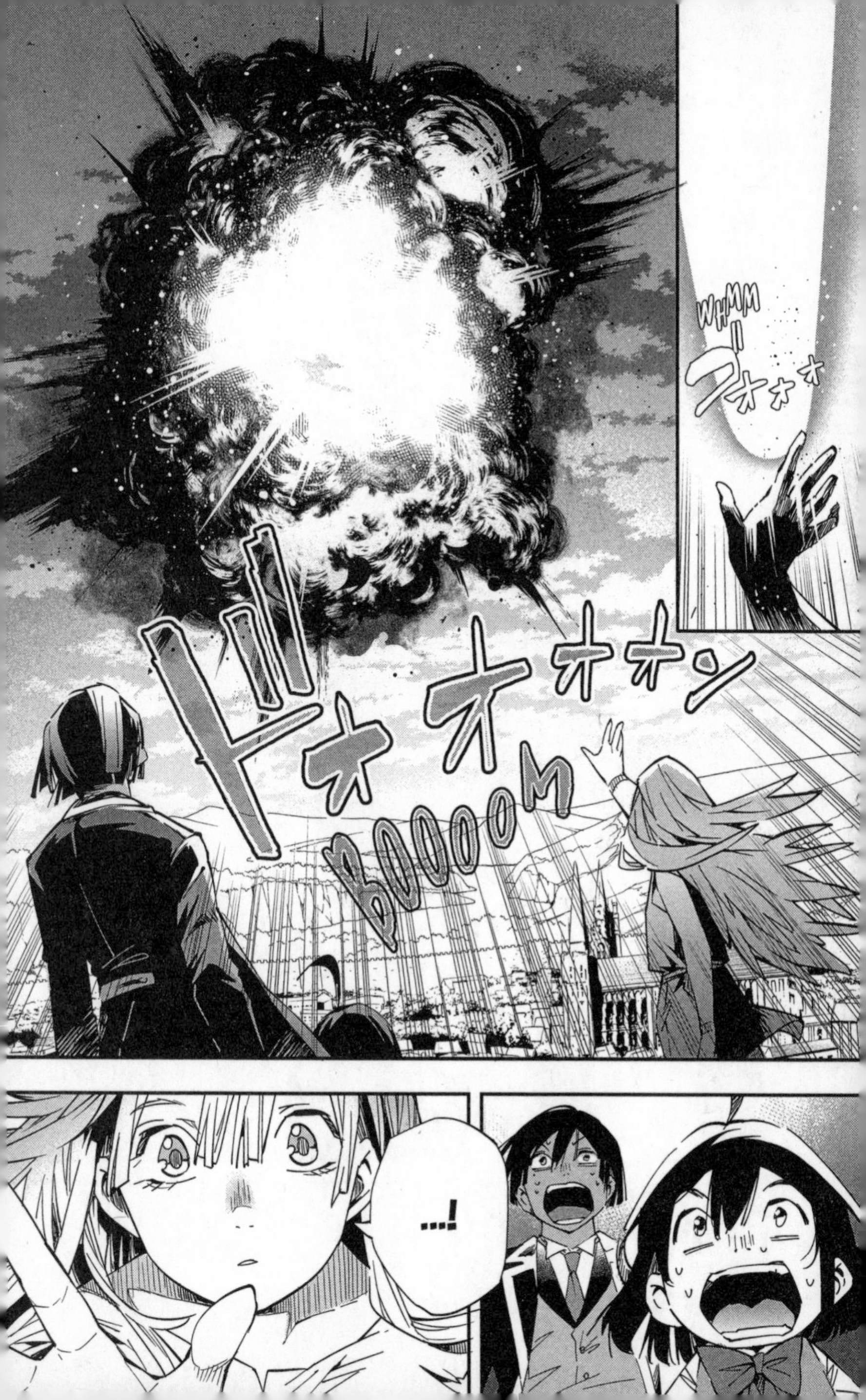
WHMM
ゴォォォ
ドォオオオオン
BOOOOM
...!

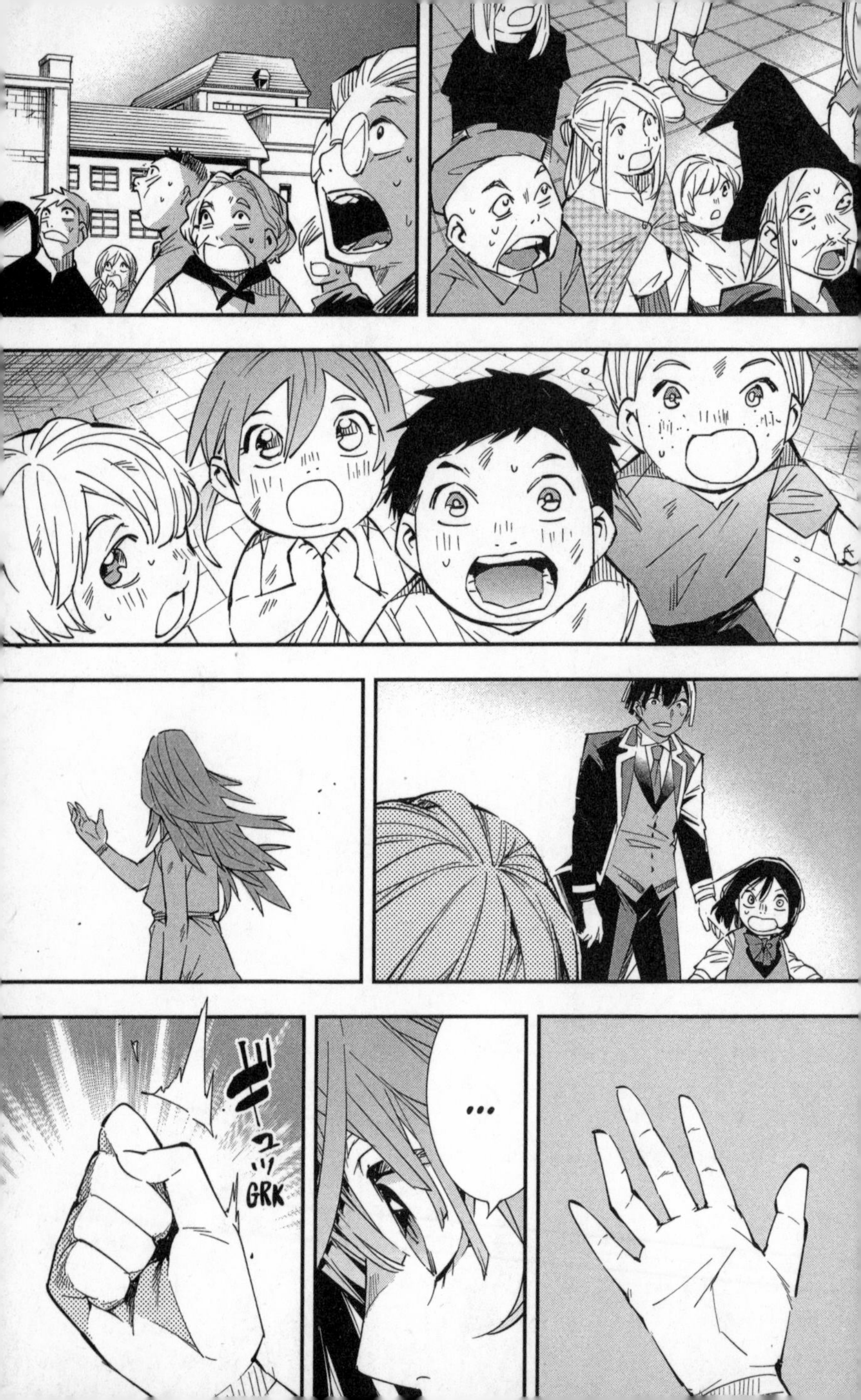

GRK
...

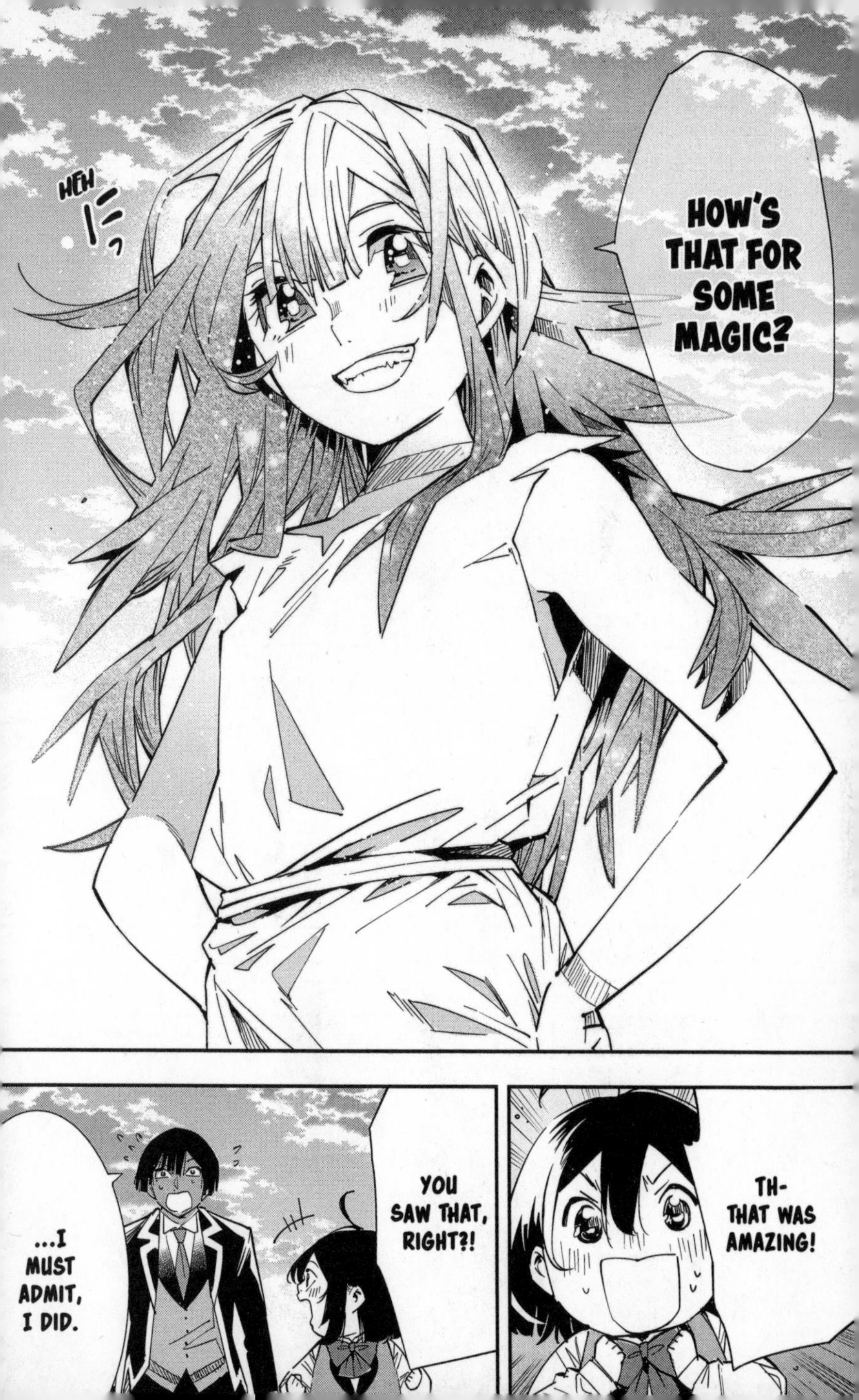
HOW'S THAT FOR SOME MAGIC?
HEH
TH- THAT WAS AMAZING!
YOU SAW THAT, RIGHT?!
...I MUST ADMIT, I DID.

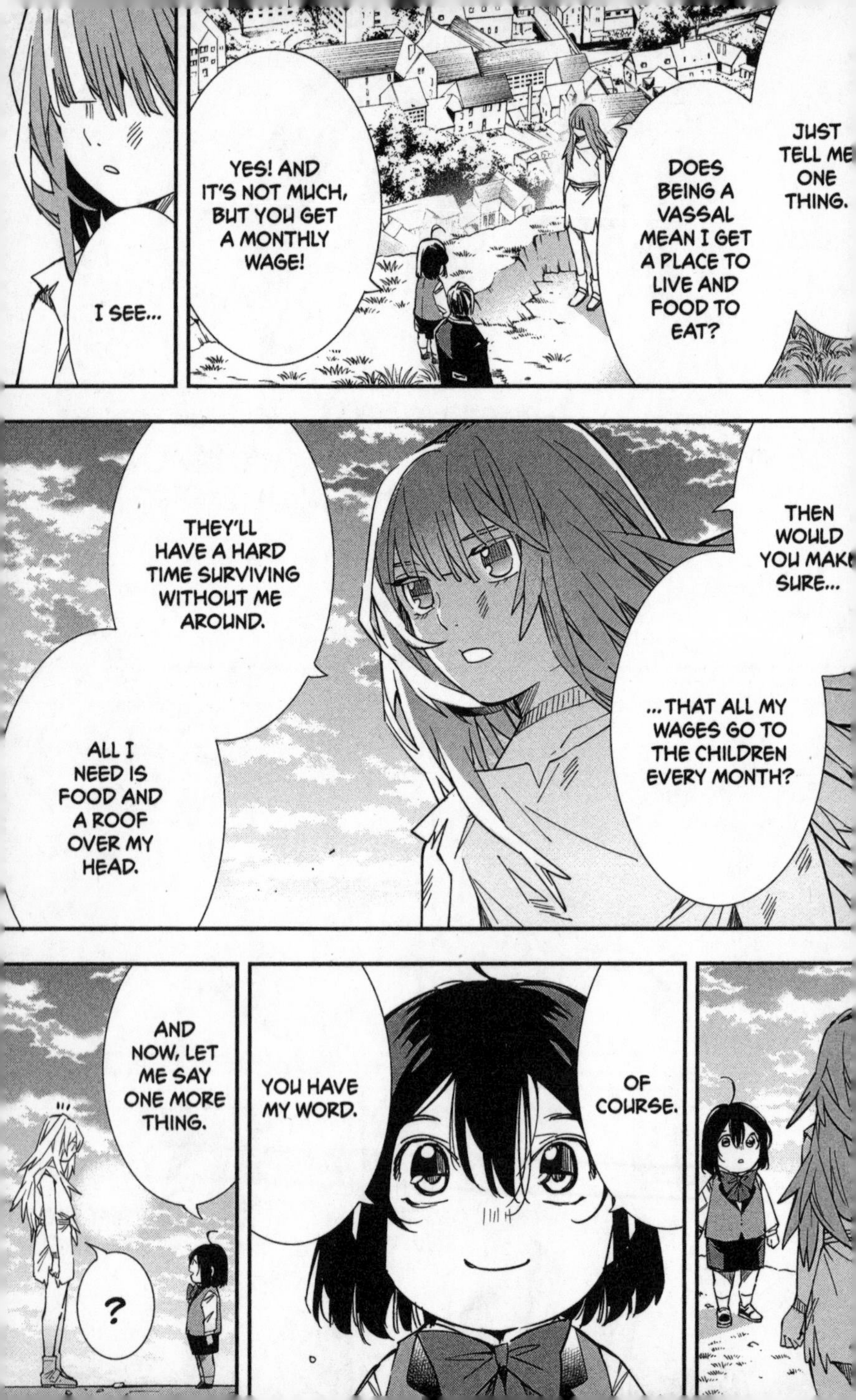
JUST TELL ME ONE THING.
DOES BEING A VASSAL MEAN I GET A PLACE TO LIVE AND FOOD TO EAT?
YES! AND IT'S NOT MUCH, BUT YOU GET A MONTHLY WAGE!
I SEE...
THEN WOULD YOU MAK SURE...
...THAT ALL MY WAGES GO TO THE CHILDREN EVERY MONTH?
THEY'LL HAVE A HARD TIME SURVIVING WITHOUT ME AROUND.
ALL I NEED IS FOOD AND A ROOF OVER MY HEAD.
OF COURSE.
YOU HAVE MY WORD.
AND NOW, LET ME SAY ONE MORE THING.
?

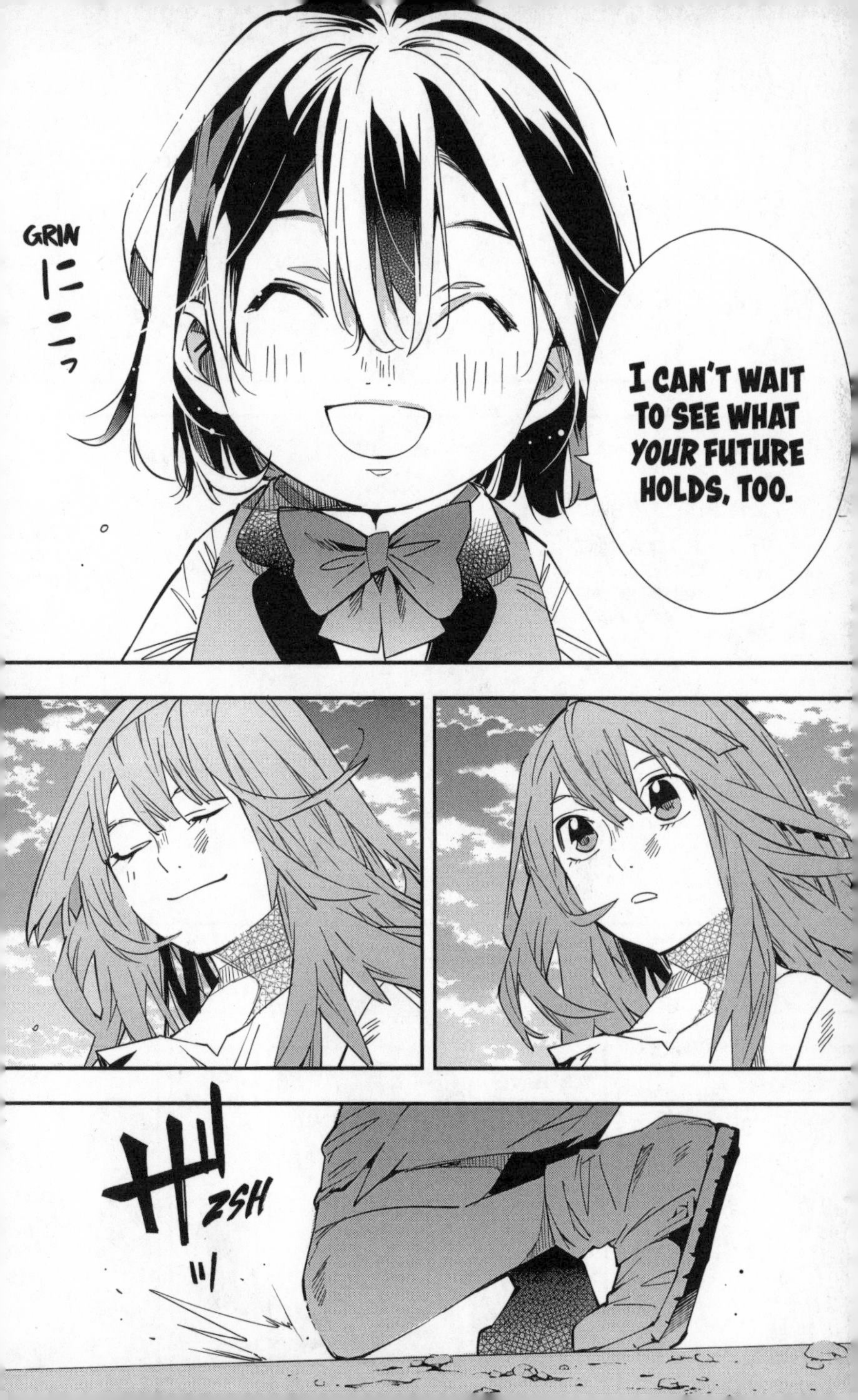
GRIN
I CAN'T WAIT TO SEE WHAT *YOUR* FUTURE HOLDS, TOO.
ZSH

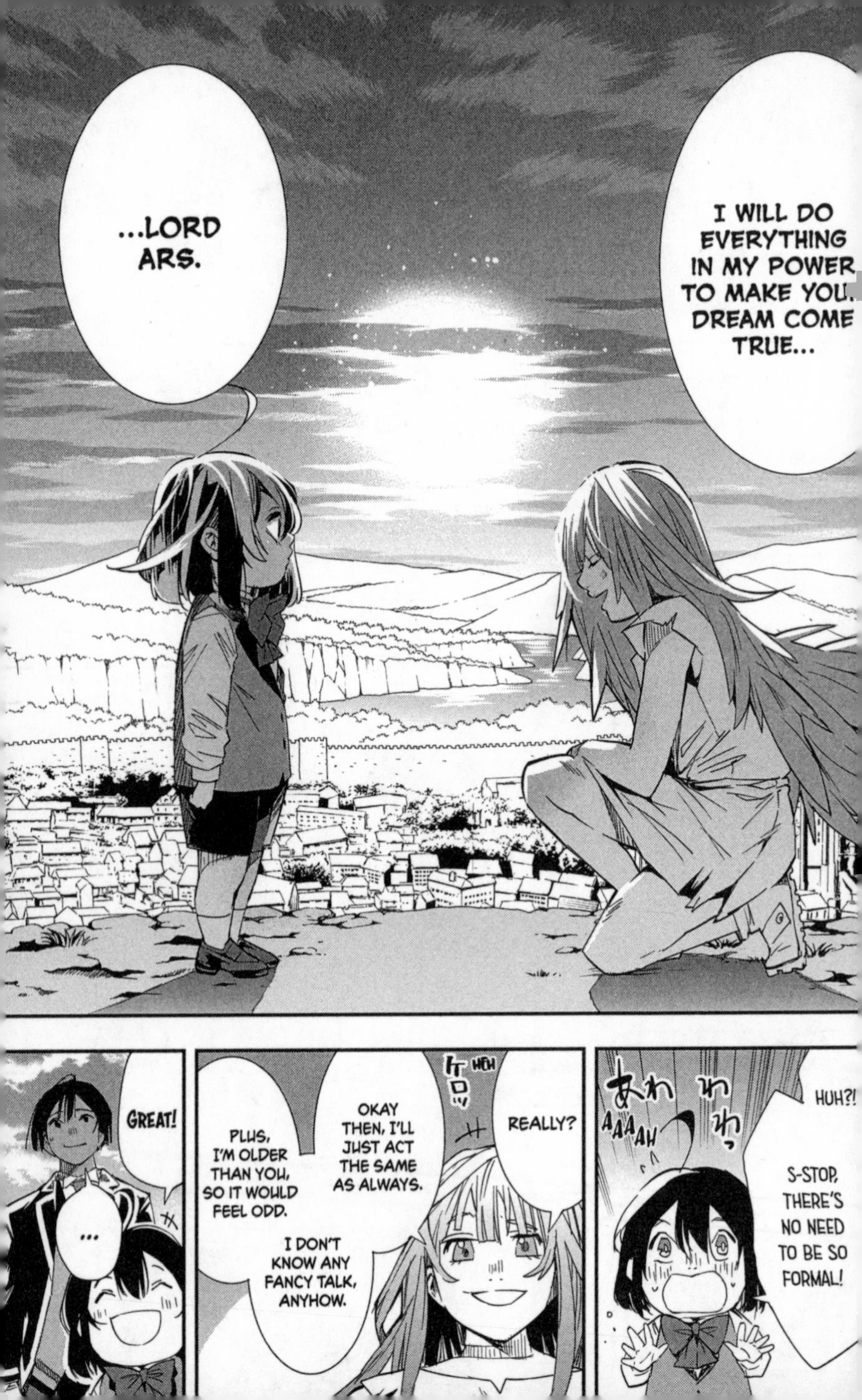
I WILL DO EVERYTHING IN MY POWER TO MAKE YOU DREAM COME TRUE...
...LORD ARS.
あわわわっ
AAAAH
HUH?!
S-STOP, THERE'S NO NEED TO BE SO FORMAL!
ケロッ
HEH
REALLY?
OKAY THEN, I'LL JUST ACT THE SAME AS ALWAYS.
PLUS, I'M OLDER THAN YOU, SO IT WOULD FEEL ODD.
I DON'T KNOW ANY FANCY TALK, ANYHOW.
GREAT!
...

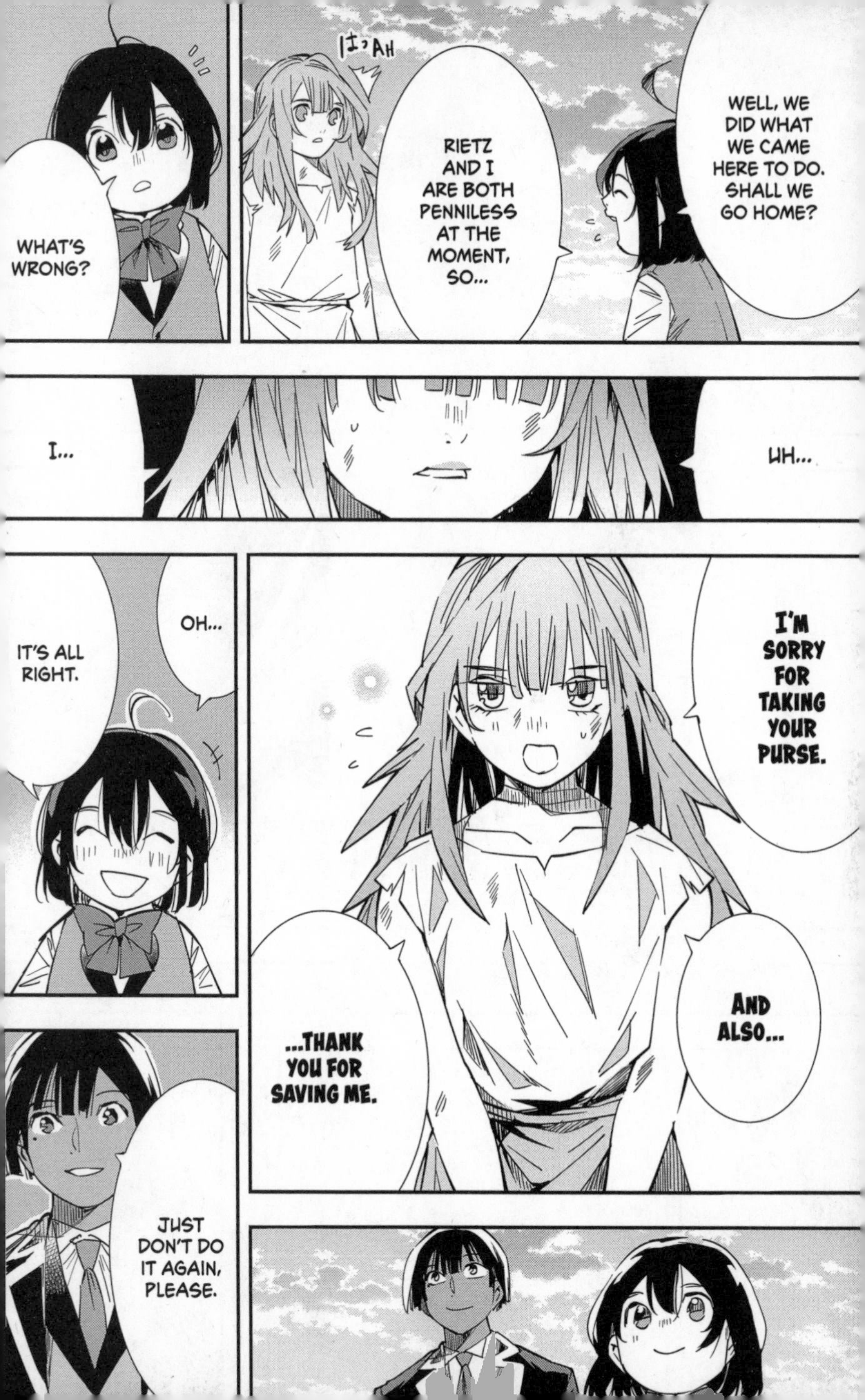
WELL, WE DID WHAT WE CAME HERE TO DO. SHALL WE GO HOME?
はっ AH
RIETZ AND I ARE BOTH PENNILESS AT THE MOMENT, SO...
WHAT'S WRONG?
UH...
I...
I'M SORRY FOR TAKING YOUR PURSE.
AND ALSO...
...THANK YOU FOR SAVING ME.
OH...
IT'S ALL RIGHT.
JUST DON'T DO IT AGAIN, PLEASE.

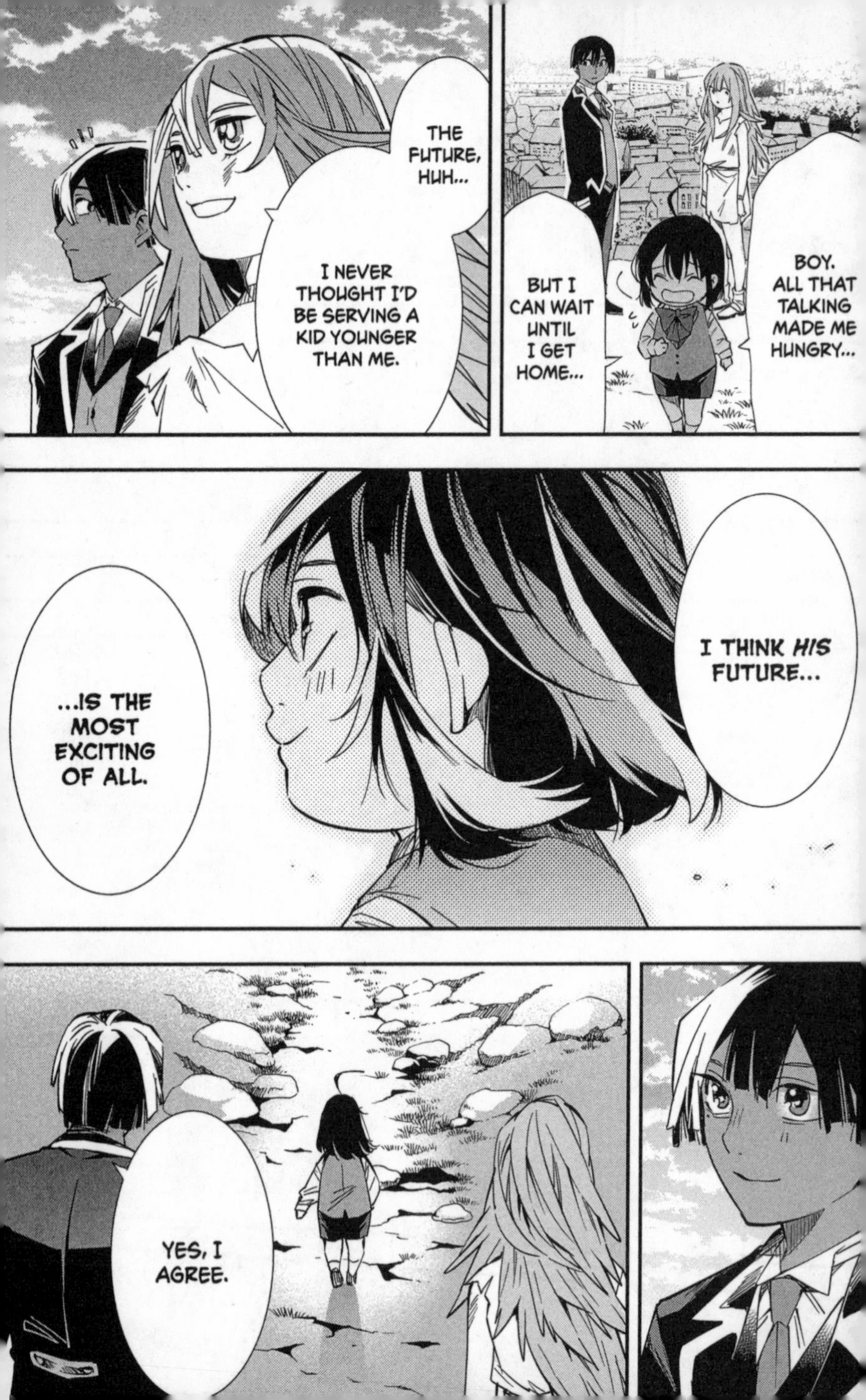

BOY. ALL THAT TALKING MADE ME HUNGRY...
BUT I CAN WAIT UNTIL I GET HOME...
THE FUTURE, HUH...
I NEVER THOUGHT I'D BE SERVING A KID YOUNGER THAN ME.
I THINK *HIS* FUTURE...
...IS THE MOST EXCITING OF ALL.
YES, I AGREE.

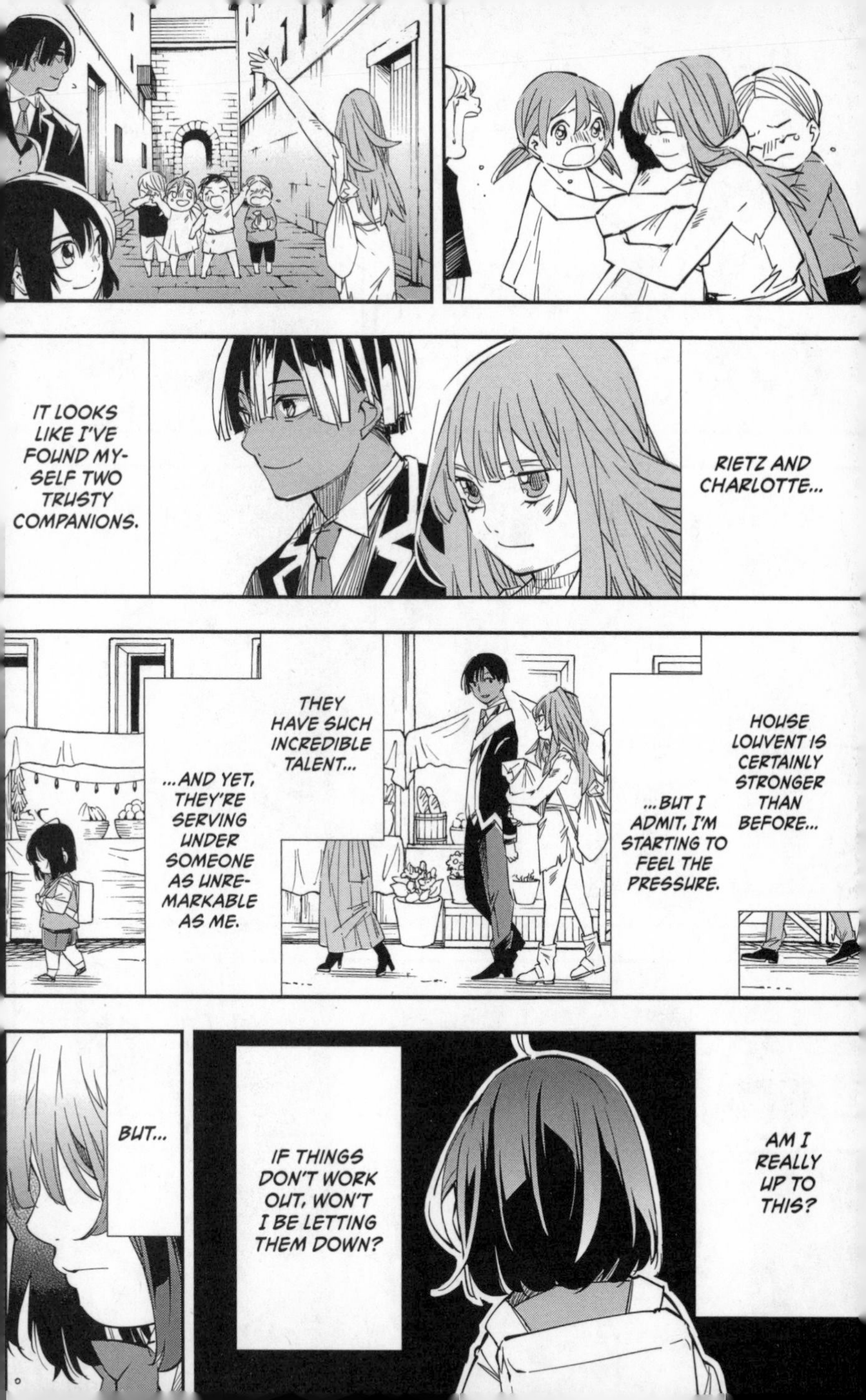
RIETZ AND CHARLOTTE...
IT LOOKS LIKE I'VE FOUND MYSELF TWO TRUSTY COMPANIONS.
HOUSE LOUVENT IS CERTAINLY STRONGER THAN BEFORE...
...BUT I ADMIT, I'M STARTING TO FEEL THE PRESSURE.
THEY HAVE SUCH INCREDIBLE TALENT...
...AND YET, THEY'RE SERVING UNDER SOMEONE AS UNREMARKABLE AS ME.
AM I REALLY UP TO THIS?
IF THINGS DON'T WORK OUT, WON'T I BE LETTING THEM DOWN?
BUT...

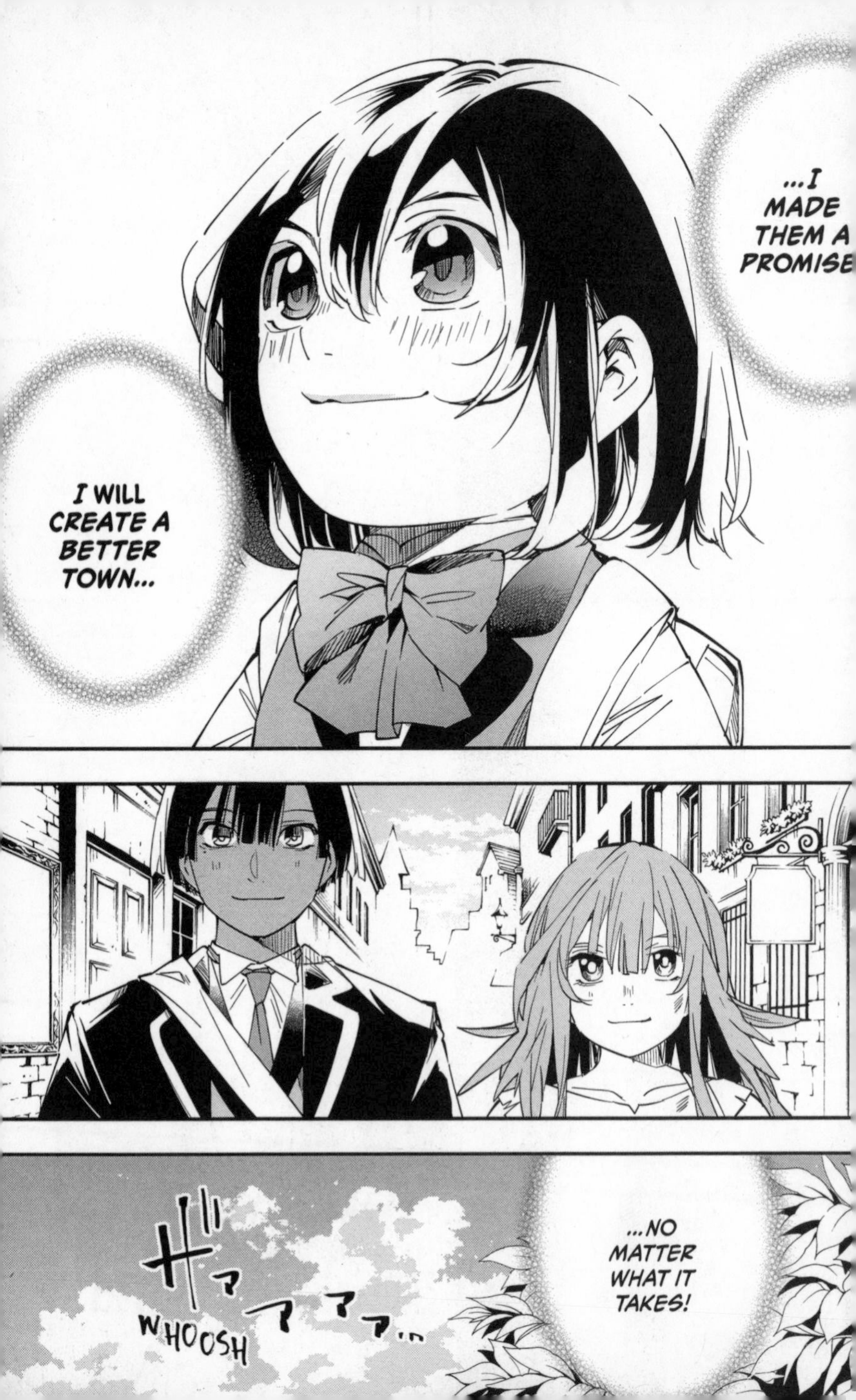
...I MADE THEM A PROMISE
I WILL CREATE A BETTER TOWN...
...NO MATTER WHAT IT TAKES!
ザァァァ...
WHOOSH

As a Reincarnated
ARISTOCRAT,
I'll Use My Appraisal Skill to
Rise in the World

Chapter 11: The Present State of House Louvent

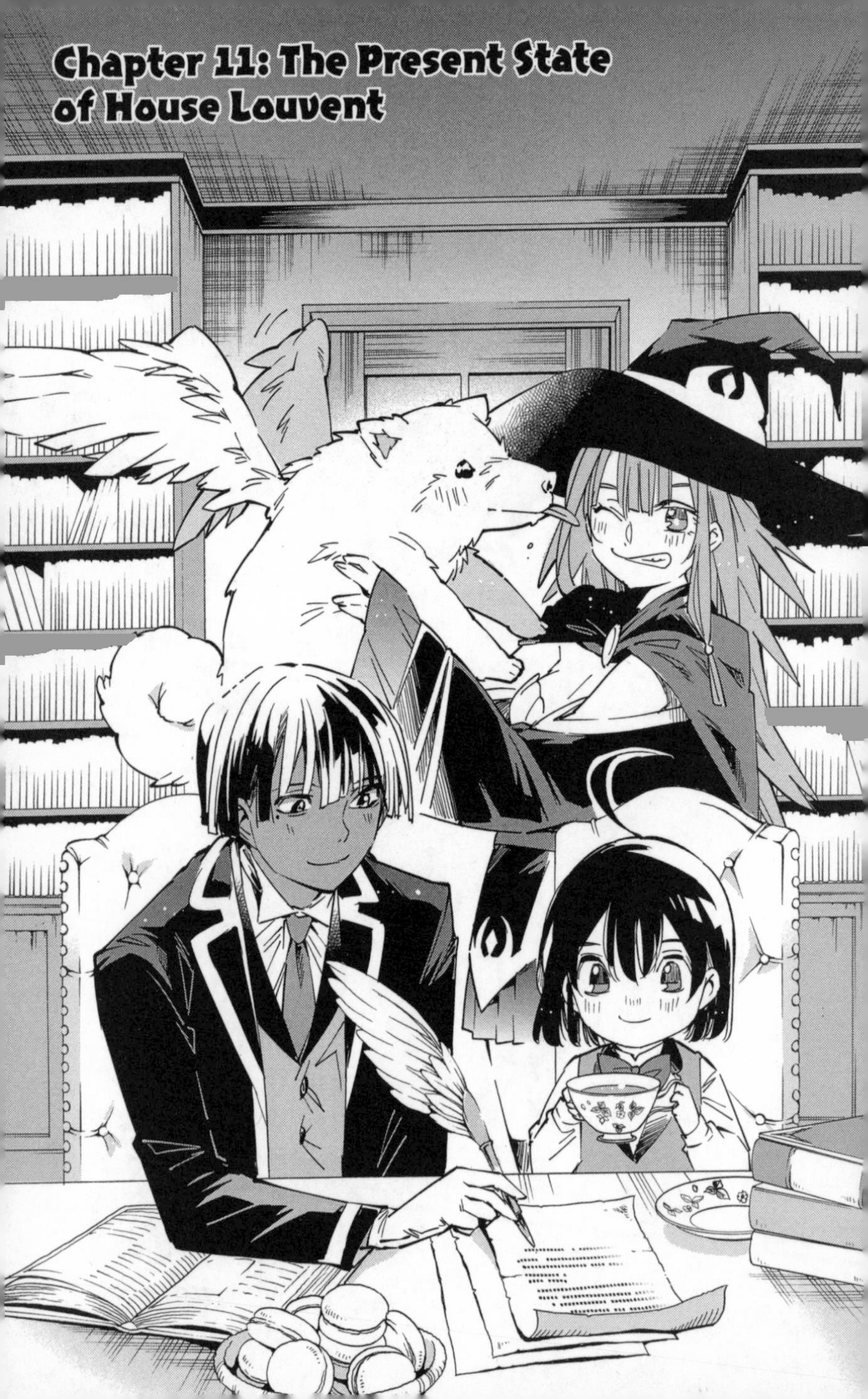

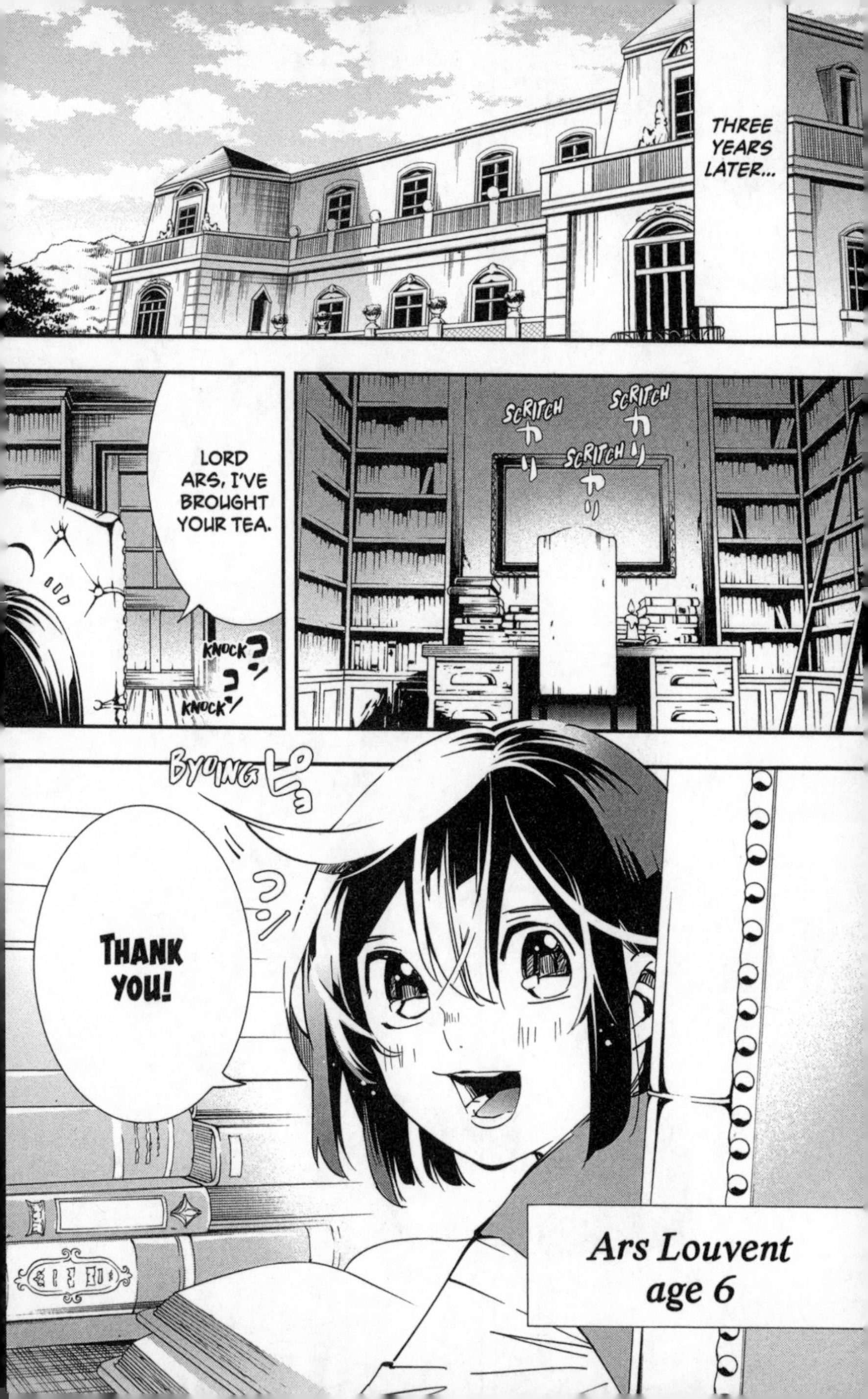
THREE YEARS LATER...
SCRITCH
SCRITCH
SCRITCH
LORD ARS, I'VE BROUGHT YOUR TEA.
KNOCK
KNOCK
BYOING
THANK YOU!
Ars Louvent
age 6

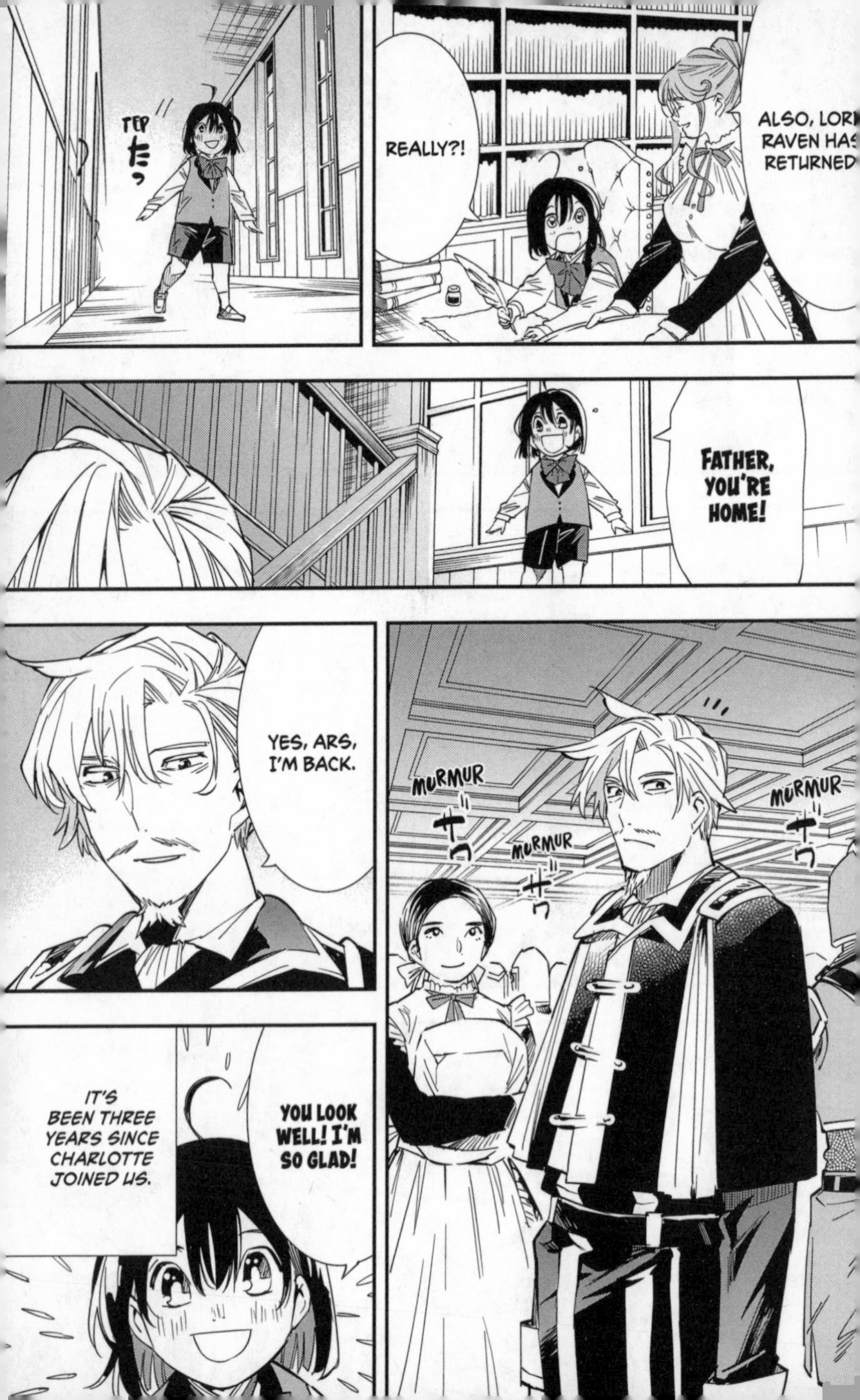
ALSO, LORD RAVEN HAS RETURNED
REALLY?!
TEP
たっ
FATHER, YOU'RE HOME!
MURMUR
ザワ
MURMUR
ザワ
MURMUR
ザワ
YES, ARS, I'M BACK.
YOU LOOK WELL! I'M SO GLAD!
IT'S BEEN THREE YEARS SINCE CHARLOTTE JOINED US.

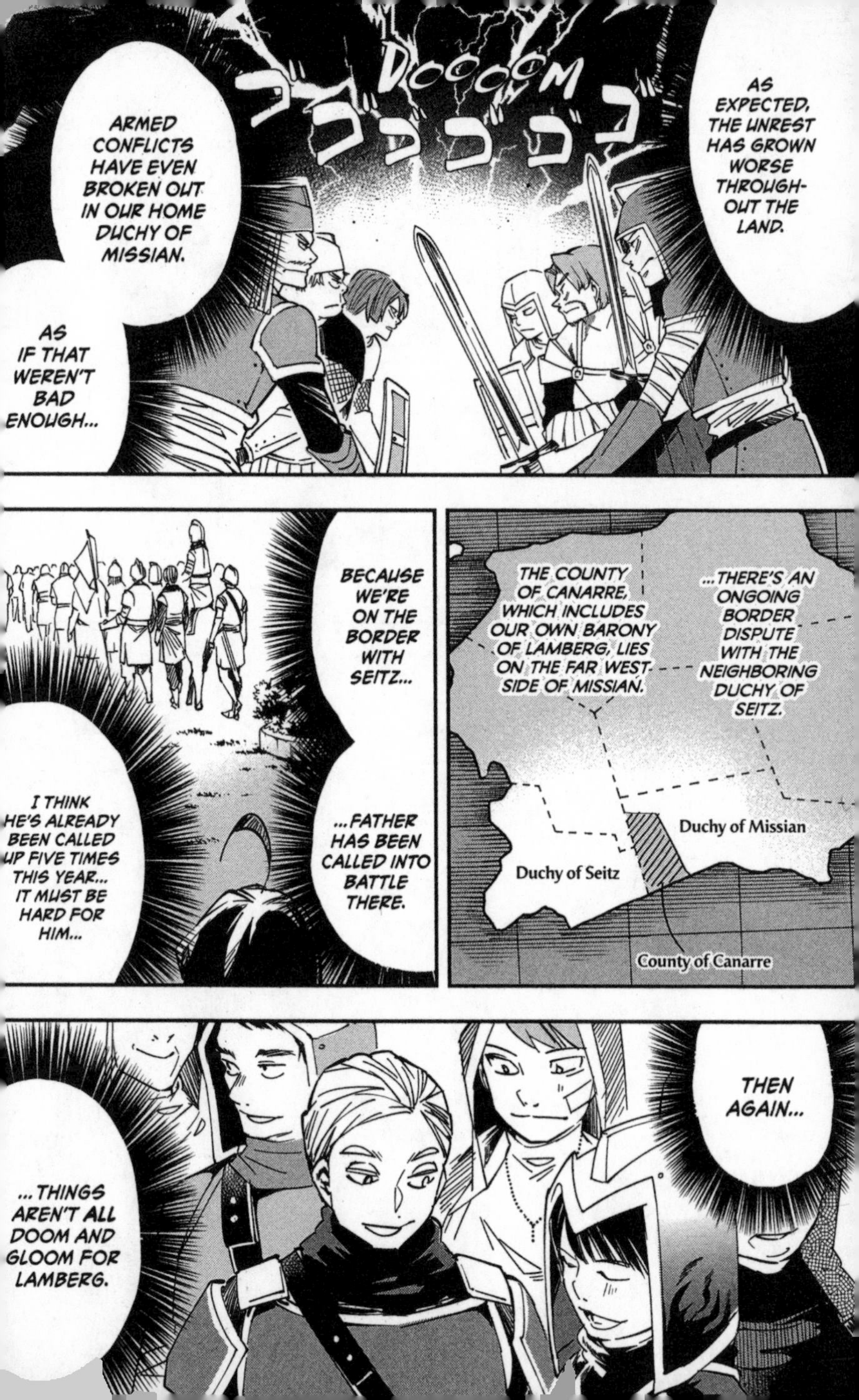
AS EXPECTED, THE UNREST HAS GROWN WORSE THROUGHOUT THE LAND.
DOOOOM
ゴゴゴゴゴゴ
ARMED CONFLICTS HAVE EVEN BROKEN OUT IN OUR HOME DUCHY OF MISSIAN.
AS IF THAT WEREN'T BAD ENOUGH...
THE COUNTY OF CANARRE, WHICH INCLUDES OUR OWN BARONY OF LAMBERG, LIES ON THE FAR WEST SIDE OF MISSIAN.
...THERE'S AN ONGOING BORDER DISPUTE WITH THE NEIGHBORING DUCHY OF SEITZ.
Duchy of Missian
Duchy of Seitz
County of Canarre
BECAUSE WE'RE ON THE BORDER WITH SEITZ...
...FATHER HAS BEEN CALLED INTO BATTLE THERE.
I THINK HE'S ALREADY BEEN CALLED UP FIVE TIMES THIS YEAR... IT MUST BE HARD FOR HIM...
THEN AGAIN...
...THINGS AREN'T ALL DOOM AND GLOOM FOR LAMBERG.

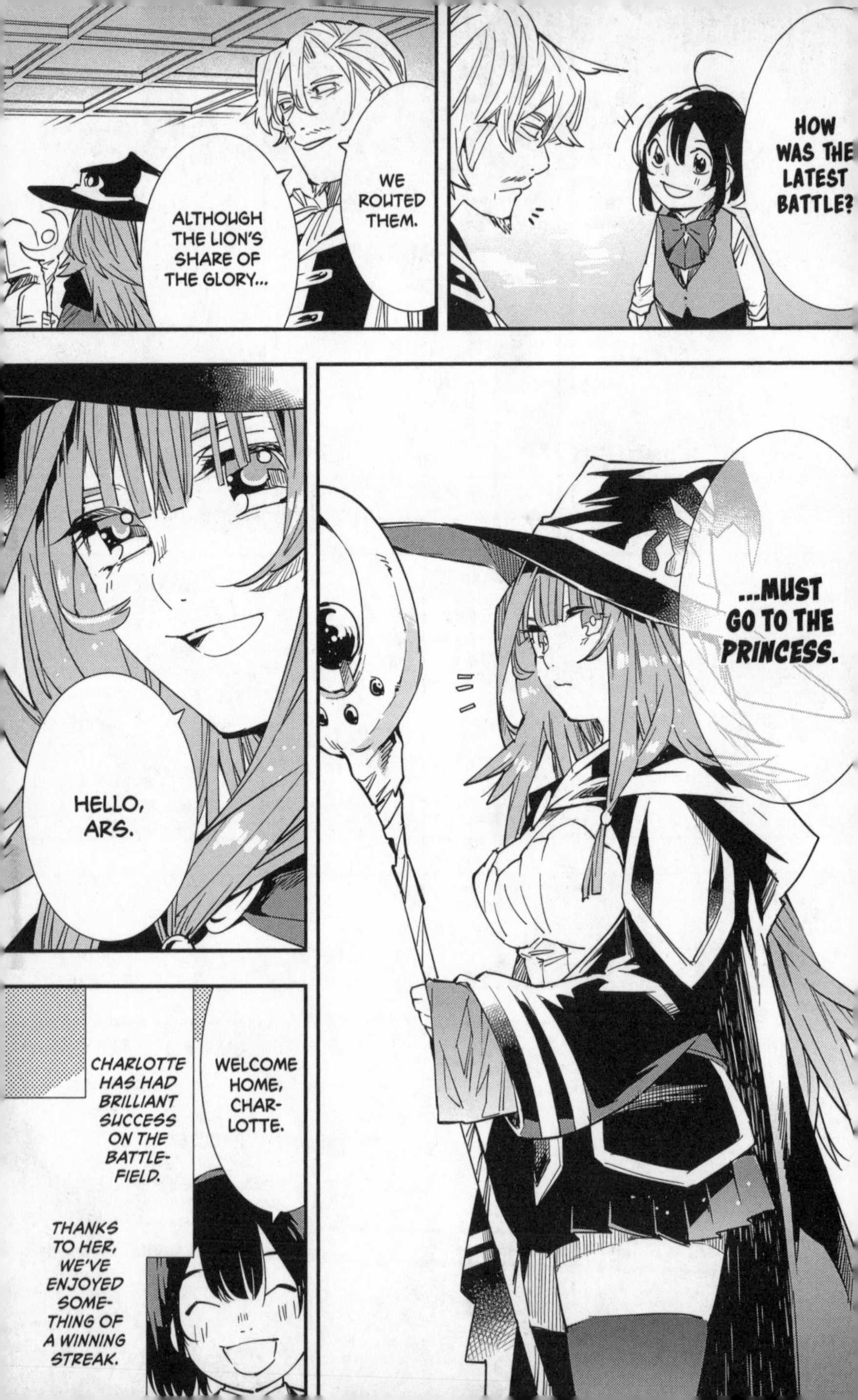
HOW WAS THE LATEST BATTLE?
WE ROUTED THEM.
ALTHOUGH THE LION'S SHARE OF THE GLORY...
...MUST GO TO THE PRINCESS.
HELLO, ARS.
WELCOME HOME, CHAR-LOTTE.
CHARLOTTE HAS HAD BRILLIANT SUCCESS ON THE BATTLE-FIELD.
THANKS TO HER, WE'VE ENJOYED SOME-THING OF A WINNING STREAK.

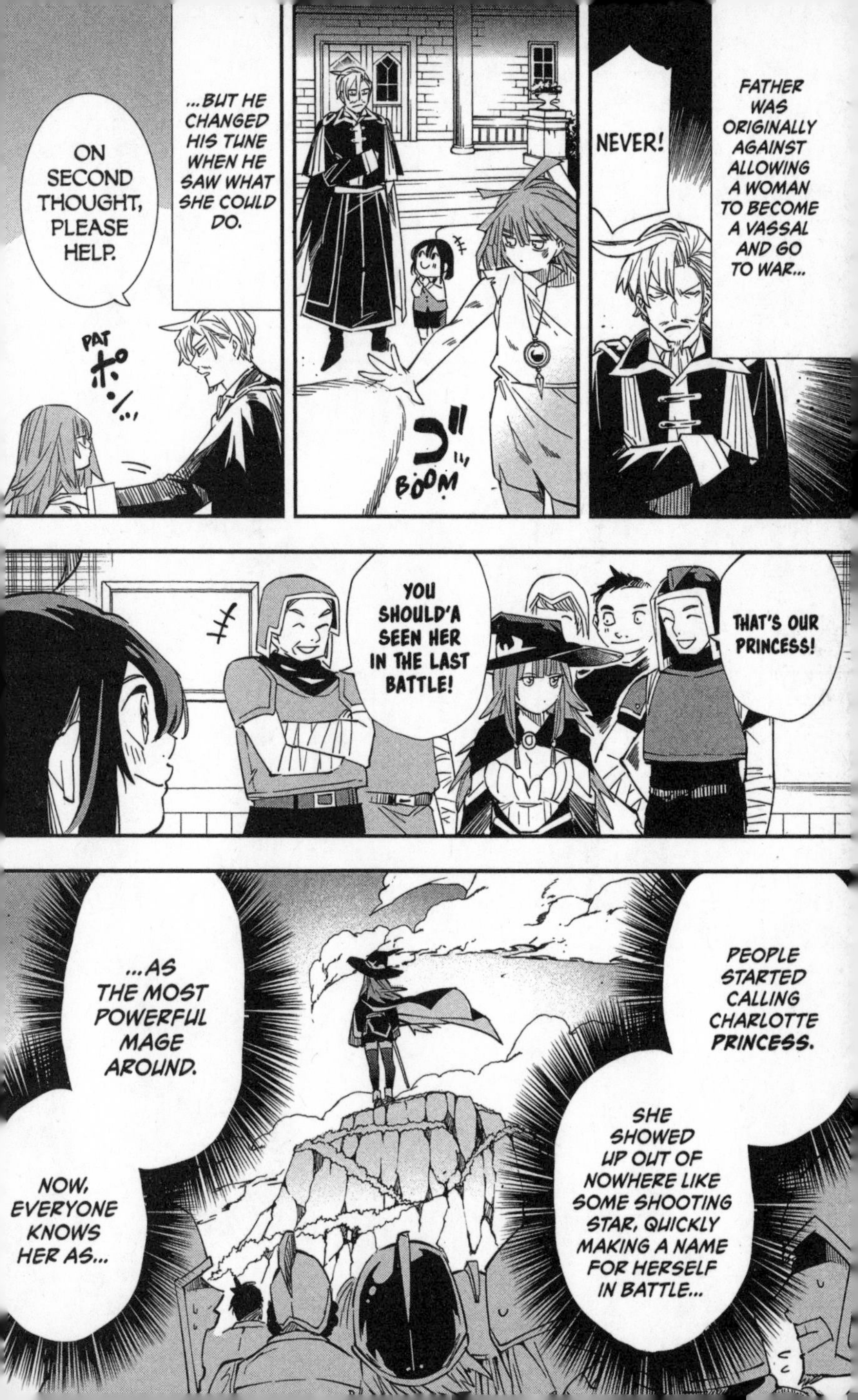
FATHER WAS ORIGINALLY AGAINST ALLOWING A WOMAN TO BECOME A VASSAL AND GO TO WAR...
NEVER!
BOOM
...BUT HE CHANGED HIS TUNE WHEN HE SAW WHAT SHE COULD DO.
ON SECOND THOUGHT, PLEASE HELP.
PAT
THAT'S OUR PRINCESS!
YOU SHOULD'A SEEN HER IN THE LAST BATTLE!
PEOPLE STARTED CALLING CHARLOTTE PRINCESS.
SHE SHOWED UP OUT OF NOWHERE LIKE SOME SHOOTING STAR, QUICKLY MAKING A NAME FOR HERSELF IN BATTLE...
NOW, EVERYONE KNOWS HER AS...
...AS THE MOST POWERFUL MAGE AROUND.

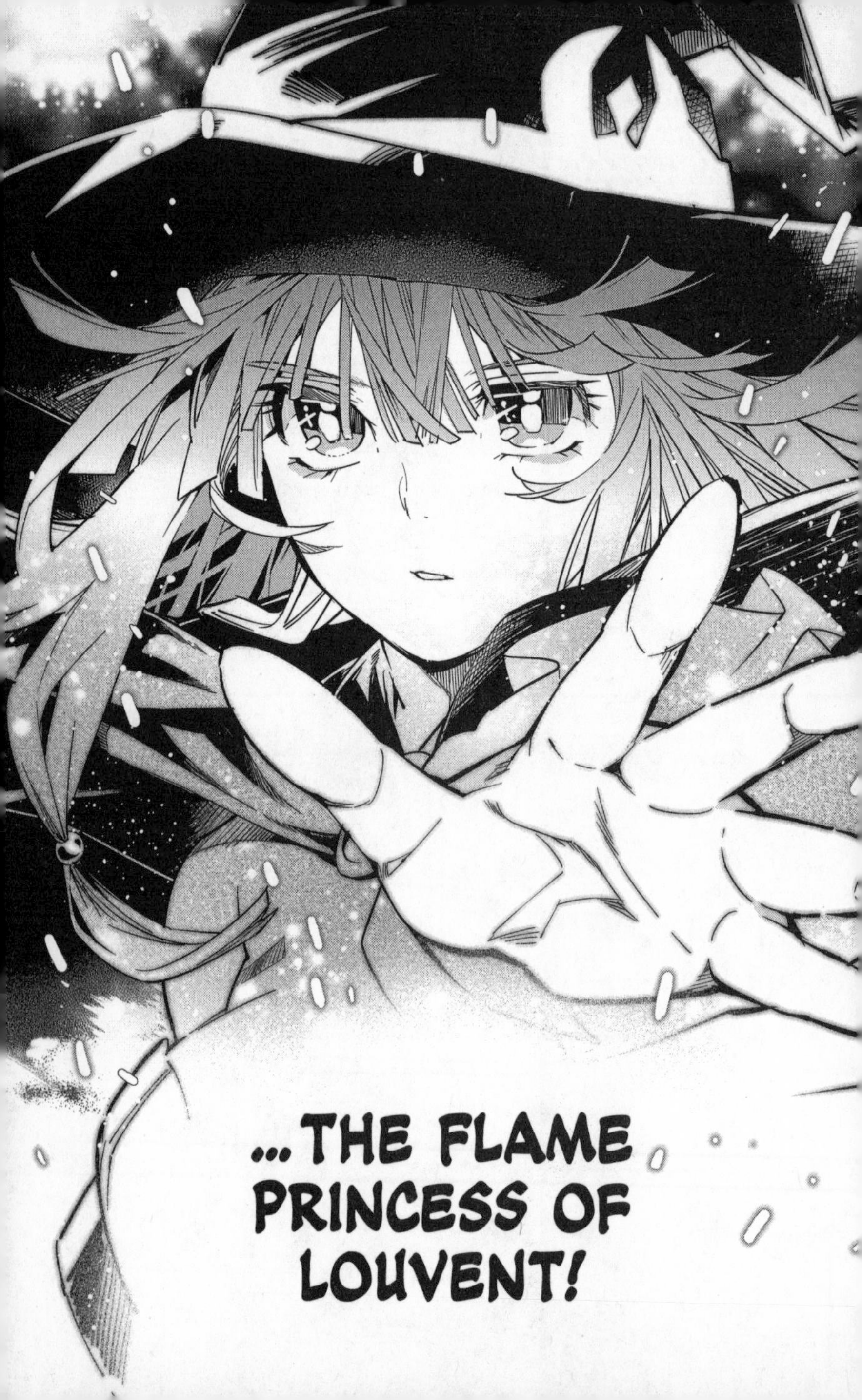
...THE FLAME PRINCESS OF LOUVENT!

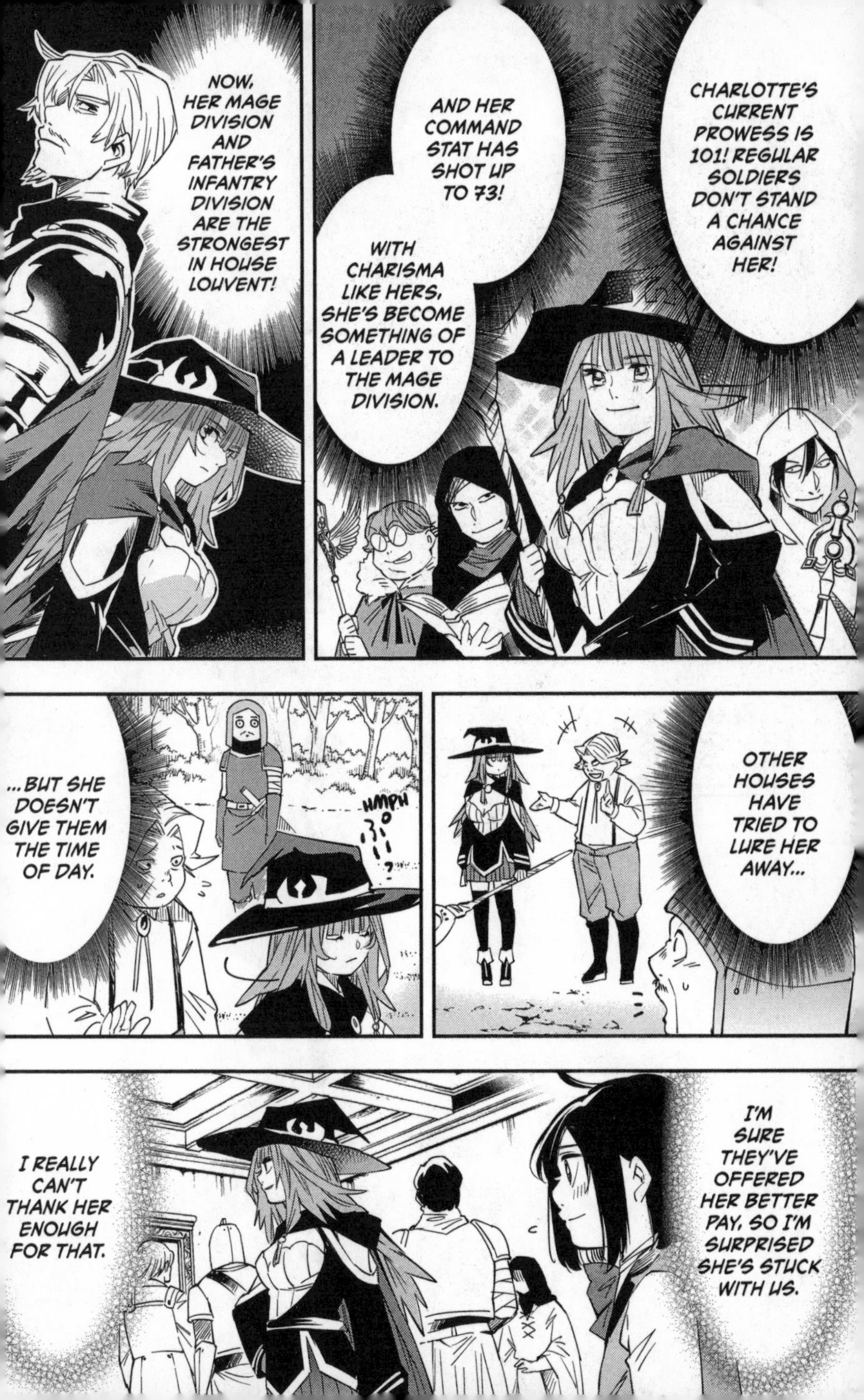
CHARLOTTE'S CURRENT PROWESS IS 101! REGULAR SOLDIERS DON'T STAND A CHANCE AGAINST HER!
AND HER COMMAND STAT HAS SHOT UP TO 73!
WITH CHARISMA LIKE HERS, SHE'S BECOME SOMETHING OF A LEADER TO THE MAGE DIVISION.
NOW, HER MAGE DIVISION AND FATHER'S INFANTRY DIVISION ARE THE STRONGEST IN HOUSE LOUVENT!
OTHER HOUSES HAVE TRIED TO LURE HER AWAY...
...BUT SHE DOESN'T GIVE THEM THE TIME OF DAY.
HMPH
I'M SURE THEY'VE OFFERED HER BETTER PAY, SO I'M SURPRISED SHE'S STUCK WITH US.
I REALLY CAN'T THANK HER ENOUGH FOR THAT.

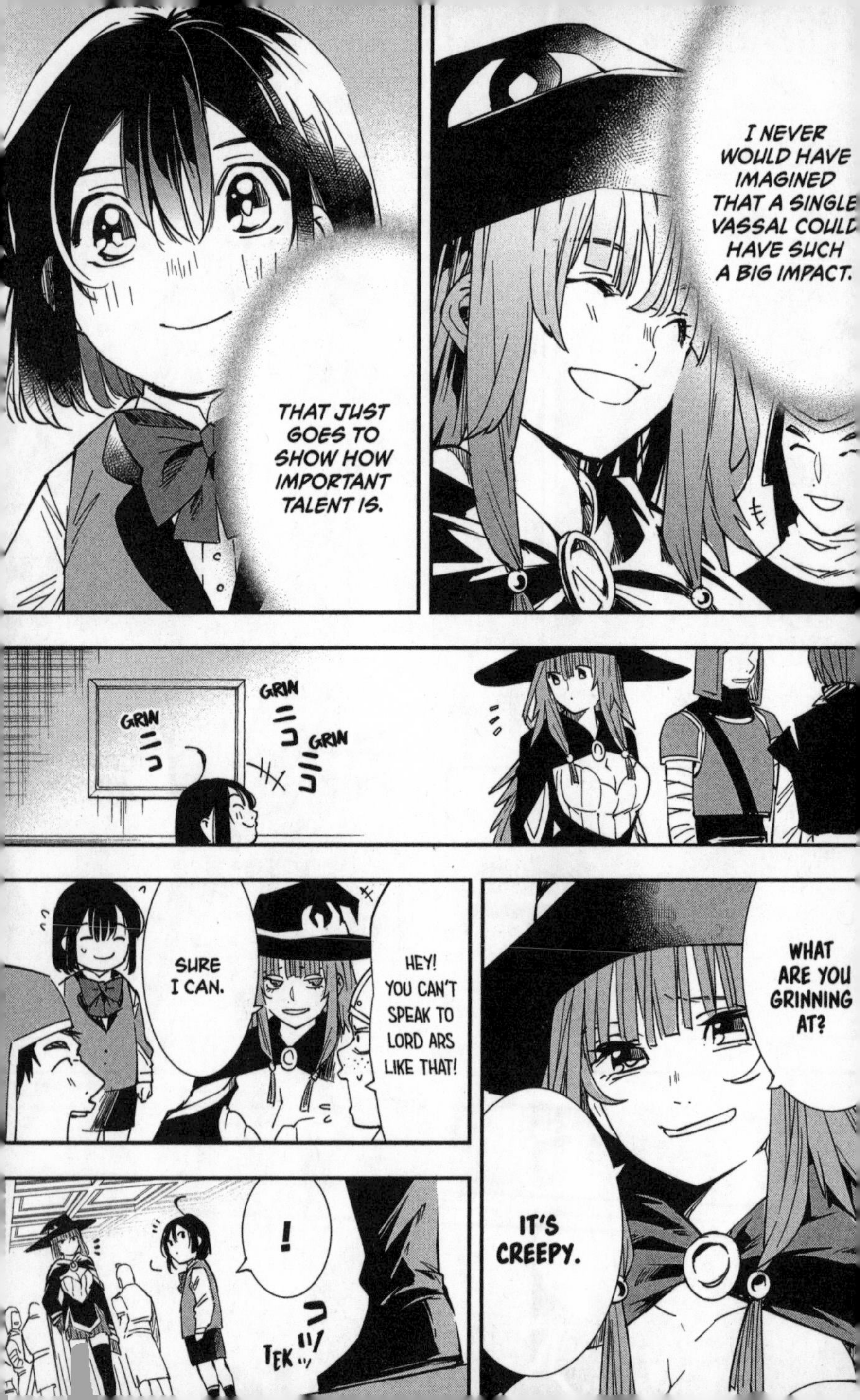
I NEVER WOULD HAVE IMAGINED THAT A SINGLE VASSAL COULD HAVE SUCH A BIG IMPACT.
THAT JUST GOES TO SHOW HOW IMPORTANT TALENT IS.
GRIN
GRIN
GRIN
WHAT ARE YOU GRINNING AT?
IT'S CREEPY.
HEY! YOU CAN'T SPEAK TO LORD ARS LIKE THAT!
SURE I CAN.
!
TEK

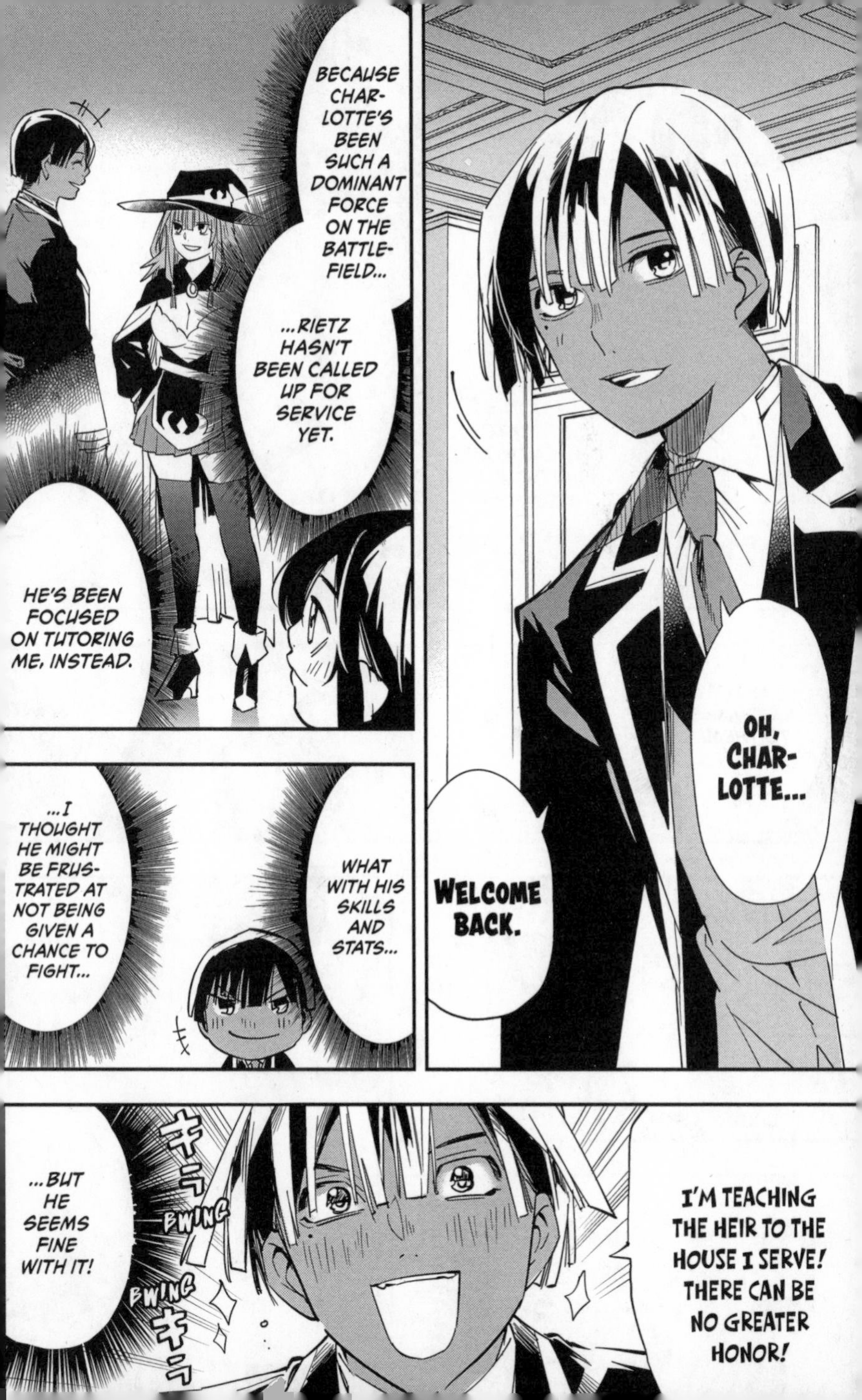
OH, CHAR-LOTTE...
WELCOME BACK.
BECAUSE CHAR-LOTTE'S BEEN SUCH A DOMINANT FORCE ON THE BATTLE-FIELD...
...RIETZ HASN'T BEEN CALLED UP FOR SERVICE YET.
HE'S BEEN FOCUSED ON TUTORING ME, INSTEAD.
WHAT WITH HIS SKILLS AND STATS...
...I THOUGHT HE MIGHT BE FRUS-TRATED AT NOT BEING GIVEN A CHANCE TO FIGHT...
I'M TEACHING THE HEIR TO THE HOUSE I SERVE! THERE CAN BE NO GREATER HONOR!
キラ
BWING
BWING
キラ
...BUT HE SEEMS FINE WITH IT!

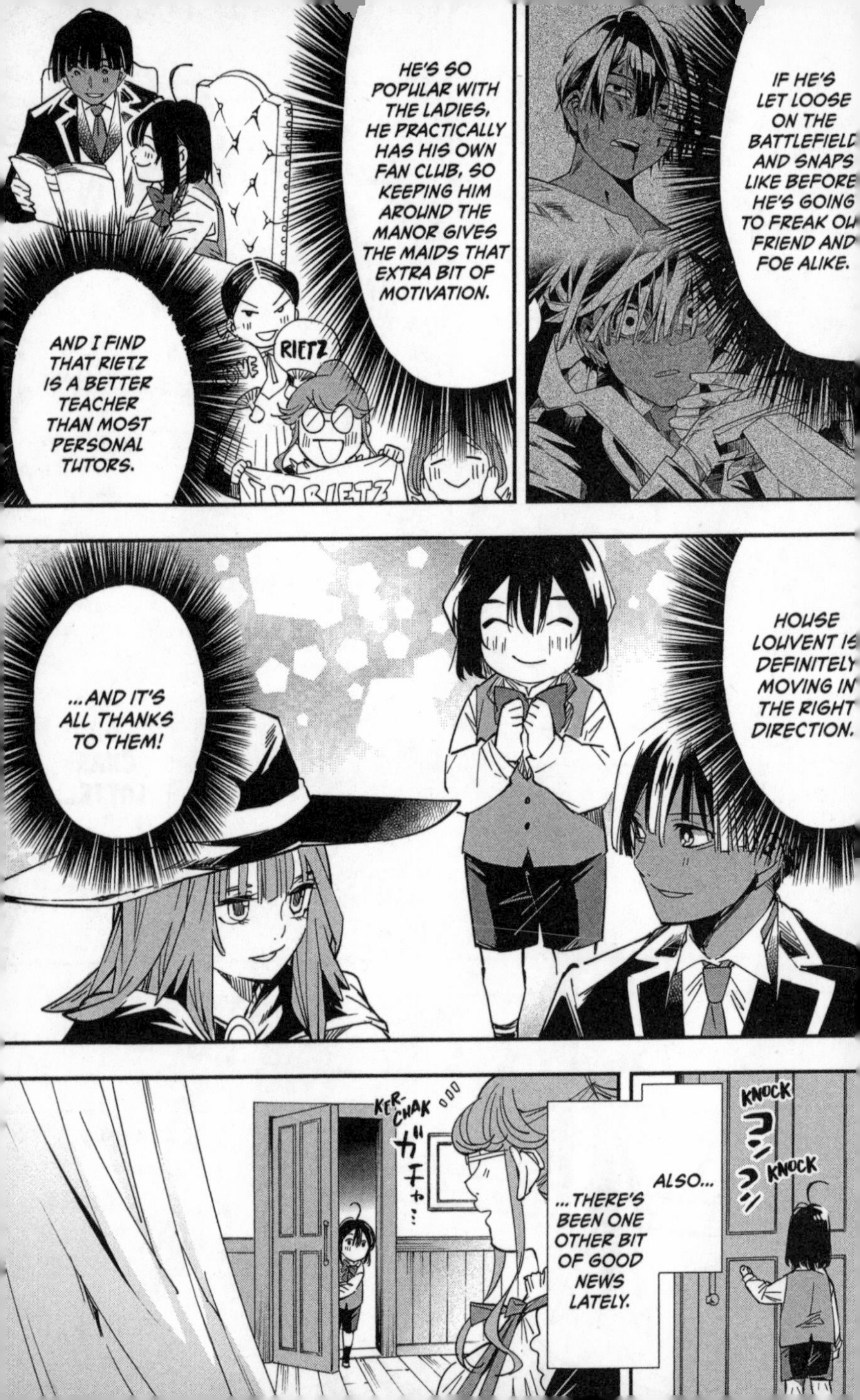
IF HE'S LET LOOSE ON THE BATTLEFIELD AND SNAPS LIKE BEFORE HE'S GOING TO FREAK OU FRIEND AND FOE ALIKE.
HE'S SO POPULAR WITH THE LADIES, HE PRACTICALLY HAS HIS OWN FAN CLUB, SO KEEPING HIM AROUND THE MANOR GIVES THE MAIDS THAT EXTRA BIT OF MOTIVATION.
RIETZ
LOVE
AND I FIND THAT RIETZ IS A BETTER TEACHER THAN MOST PERSONAL TUTORS.
HOUSE LOUVENT IS DEFINITELY MOVING IN THE RIGHT DIRECTION.
...AND IT'S ALL THANKS TO THEM!
KNOCK
コンコン
KNOCK
ALSO...
...THERE'S BEEN ONE OTHER BIT OF GOOD NEWS LATELY.
KER-CHAK
ガチャ

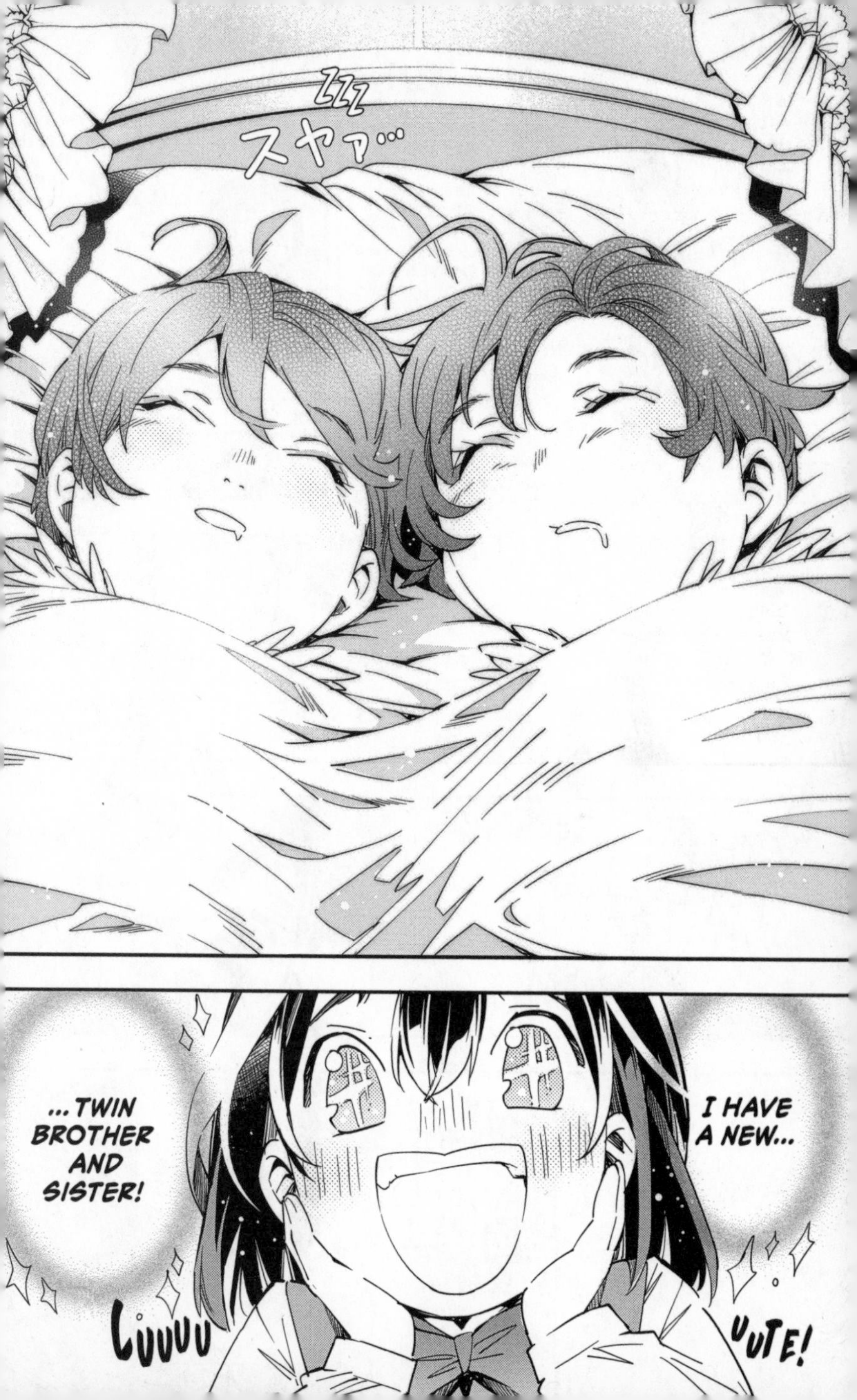
ZZZ
スヤァ゛
I HAVE A NEW...
...TWIN BROTHER AND SISTER!
CUUUU
UUTE!

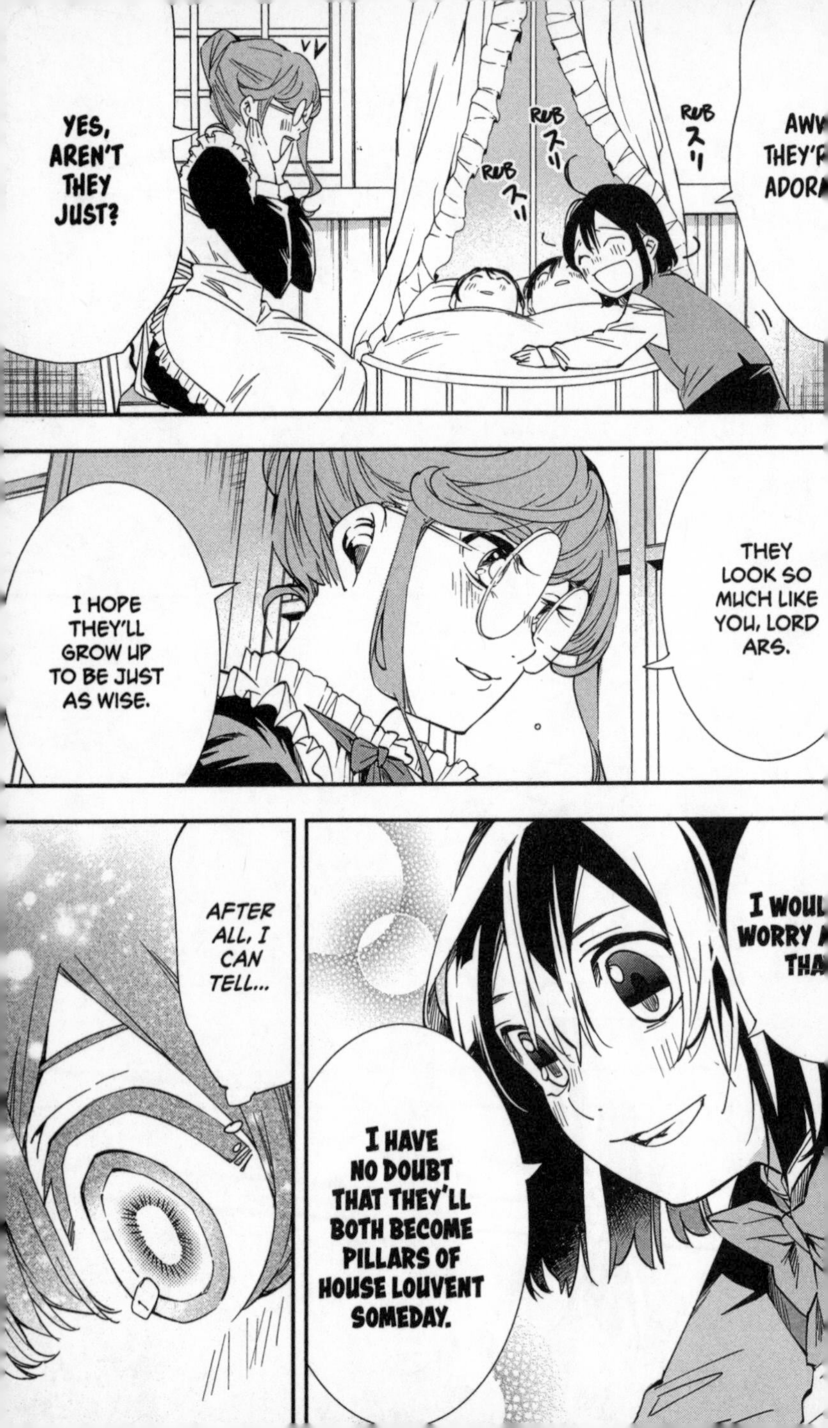
AWV THEY'R ADOR
RUB スリ
RUB スリ
RUB スリ
YES, AREN'T THEY JUST?
THEY LOOK SO MUCH LIKE YOU, LORD ARS.
I HOPE THEY'LL GROW UP TO BE JUST AS WISE.
I WOUL WORRY A THA
I HAVE NO DOUBT THAT THEY'LL BOTH BECOME PILLARS OF HOUSE LOUVENT SOMEDAY.
AFTER ALL, I CAN TELL...

Kreiz Louvent - Age 0 ♂

Stats

	CURRENT	MAX
Command	1	82
Prowess	1	89
Intellect	1	33
Diplomacy	1	21
Ambition	77	

Aptitude

Fighter S	Cavalier B	Archer A
Mage C	Engineer D	Armorer D
Mariner D	Pilot D	Tactician D

THEIR STATS ARE INCREDIBLE!

KREIZ, THE OLDER BROTHER, HAS GREAT COMMAND AND PROWESS, LIKE OUR FATHER.

HE HAS S-RANK FIGHTER APTITUDE, SO HE'LL BE GOOD WITH THE SWORD AND SPEAR!

HIS AMBITION'S THE MOST SURPRISING! HE'S MORE LIKELY TO BETRAY, BUT IT'S GOOD TO HAVE BIG DREAMS!

Ren Louvent - Age 0 ♀

Stats

	CURRENT	MAX
Command	1	22
Prowess	1	21
Intellect	1	91
Diplomacy	1	85
Ambition	33	

Aptitude

Fighter D	Cavalier D	Archer D
Mage D	Engineer C	Armorer B
Mariner C	Pilot B	Tactician A

THE YOUNGER SISTER, REN, HAS GREAT INTELLECT AND DIPLOMACY STATS!

SHE HAS A-RANK TACTICIAN APTITUDE, SO SHE COULD ALSO BECOME A MILITARY STRATEGIST.

THEY'RE STILL JUST BABIES, BUT THEY'RE BURSTING WITH POTENTIAL.

I WONDER WHAT THEY'LL BE LIKE WHEN THEY'RE OLDER...

...BUT I GREW UP AN ONLY CHILD, SO I'M REALLY HAPPY TO HAVE SIBLINGS.

I'M A BIT TOO OLD TO BE THEIR PLAYMATE...

AND I'M THEIR BIG BROTHER...

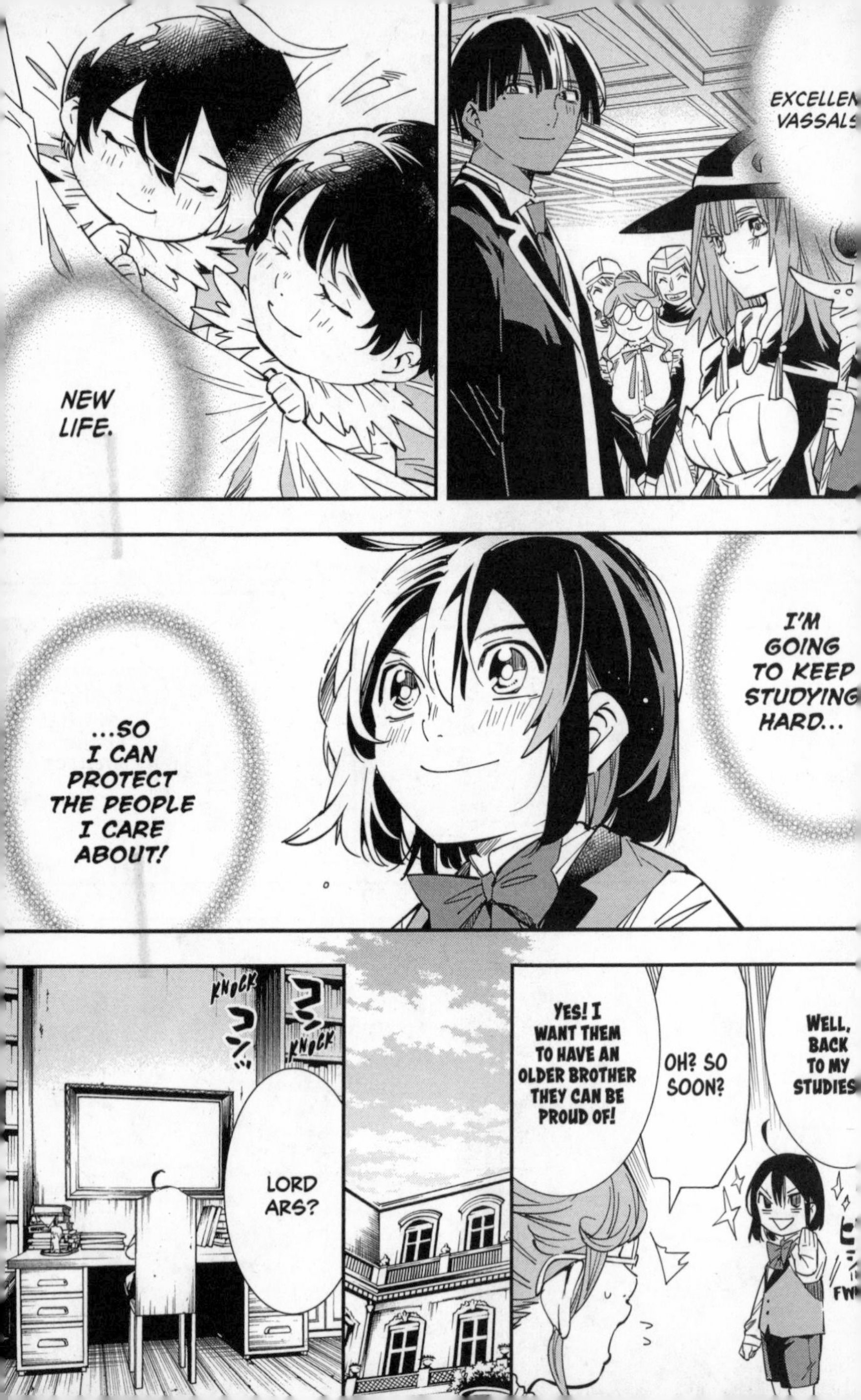
EXCELLEN VASSALS
NEW LIFE.
I'M GOING TO KEEP STUDYING HARD...
...SO I CAN PROTECT THE PEOPLE I CARE ABOUT!
WELL, BACK TO MY STUDIES
OH? SO SOON?
YES! I WANT THEM TO HAVE AN OLDER BROTHER THEY CAN BE PROUD OF!
KNOCK
KNOCK
LORD ARS?

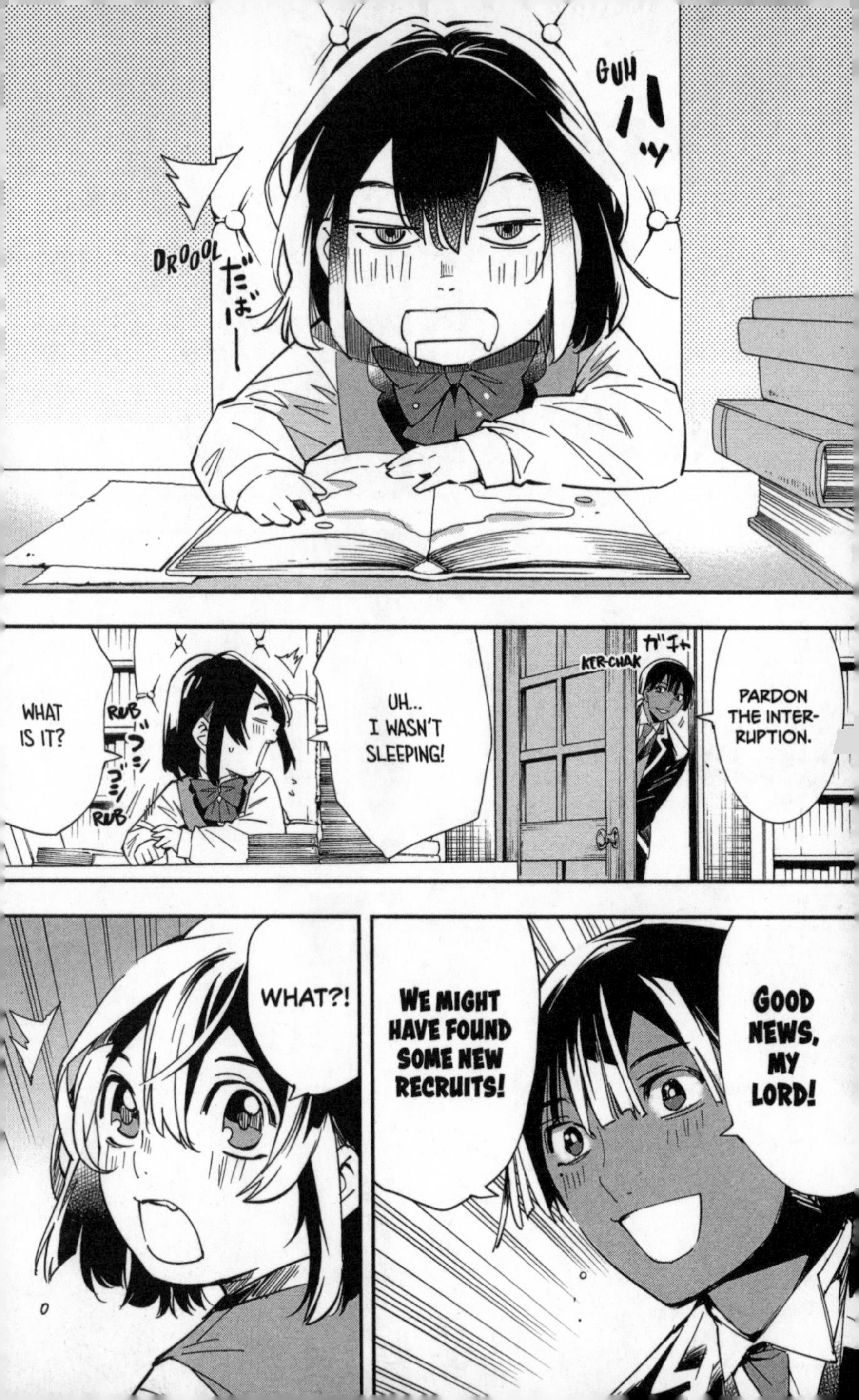
GUH
ハッ
DROOOL
だばー
KER-CHAK
ガチャ
PARDON THE INTER-RUPTION.
UH... I WASN'T SLEEPING!
RUB
RUB
WHAT IS IT?
GOOD NEWS, MY LORD!
WE MIGHT HAVE FOUND SOME NEW RECRUITS!
WHAT?!

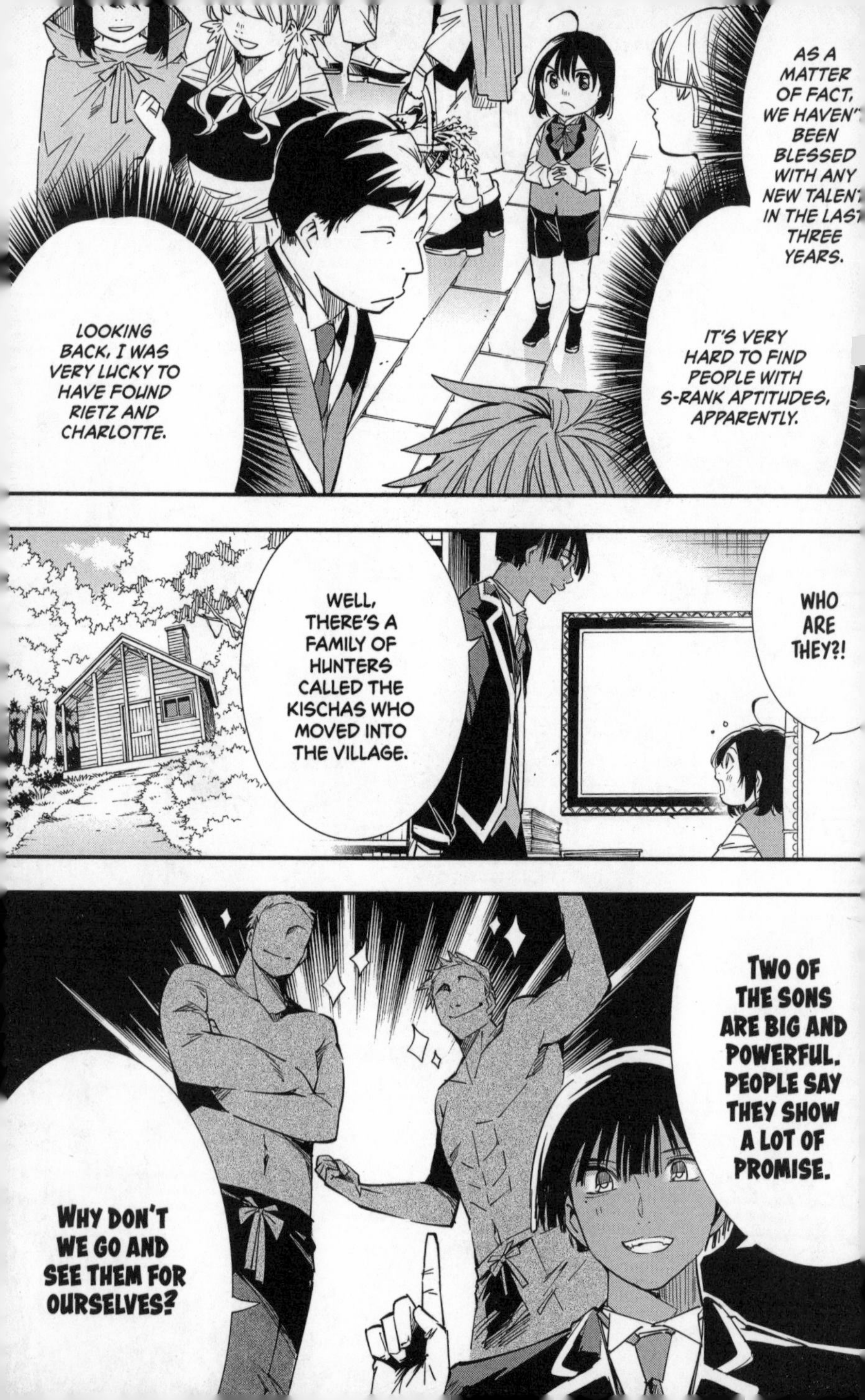

AS A MATTER OF FACT, WE HAVEN'T BEEN BLESSED WITH ANY NEW TALENT IN THE LAST THREE YEARS.
IT'S VERY HARD TO FIND PEOPLE WITH S-RANK APTITUDES, APPARENTLY.
LOOKING BACK, I WAS VERY LUCKY TO HAVE FOUND RIETZ AND CHARLOTTE.
WHO ARE THEY?!
WELL, THERE'S A FAMILY OF HUNTERS CALLED THE KISCHAS WHO MOVED INTO THE VILLAGE.
TWO OF THE SONS ARE BIG AND POWERFUL. PEOPLE SAY THEY SHOW A LOT OF PROMISE.
WHY DON'T WE GO AND SEE THEM FOR OURSELVES?

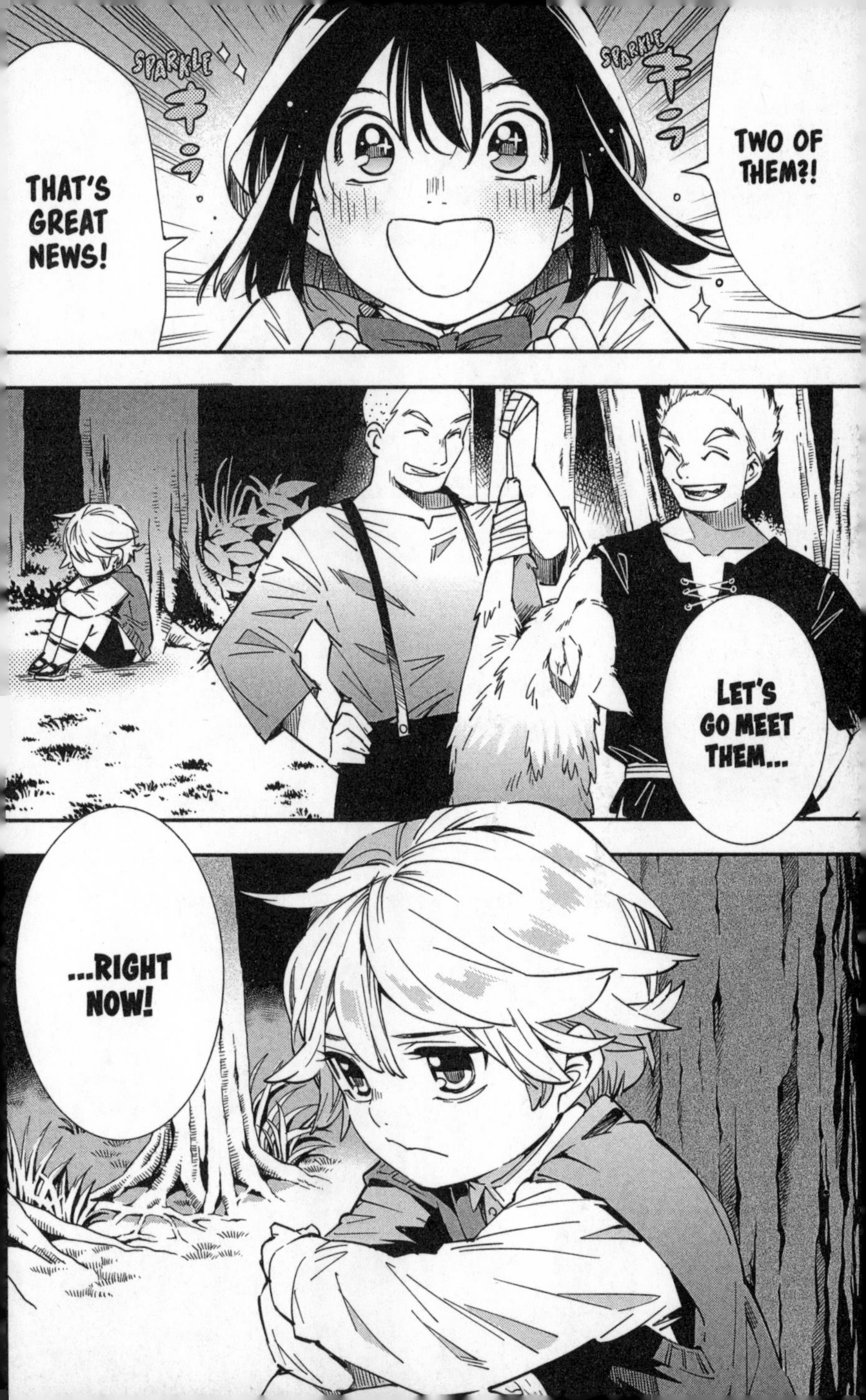
SPARKLE
キラ
TWO OF THEM?!
SPARKLE
キラ
THAT'S GREAT NEWS!
LET'S GO MEET THEM...
...RIGHT NOW!

As a Reincarnated
ARISTOCRAT,
I'll Use My Appraisal Skill to
Rise in the World

As a Reincarnated
ARISTOCRAT,
I'll Use My Appraisal Skill to
Rise in the World

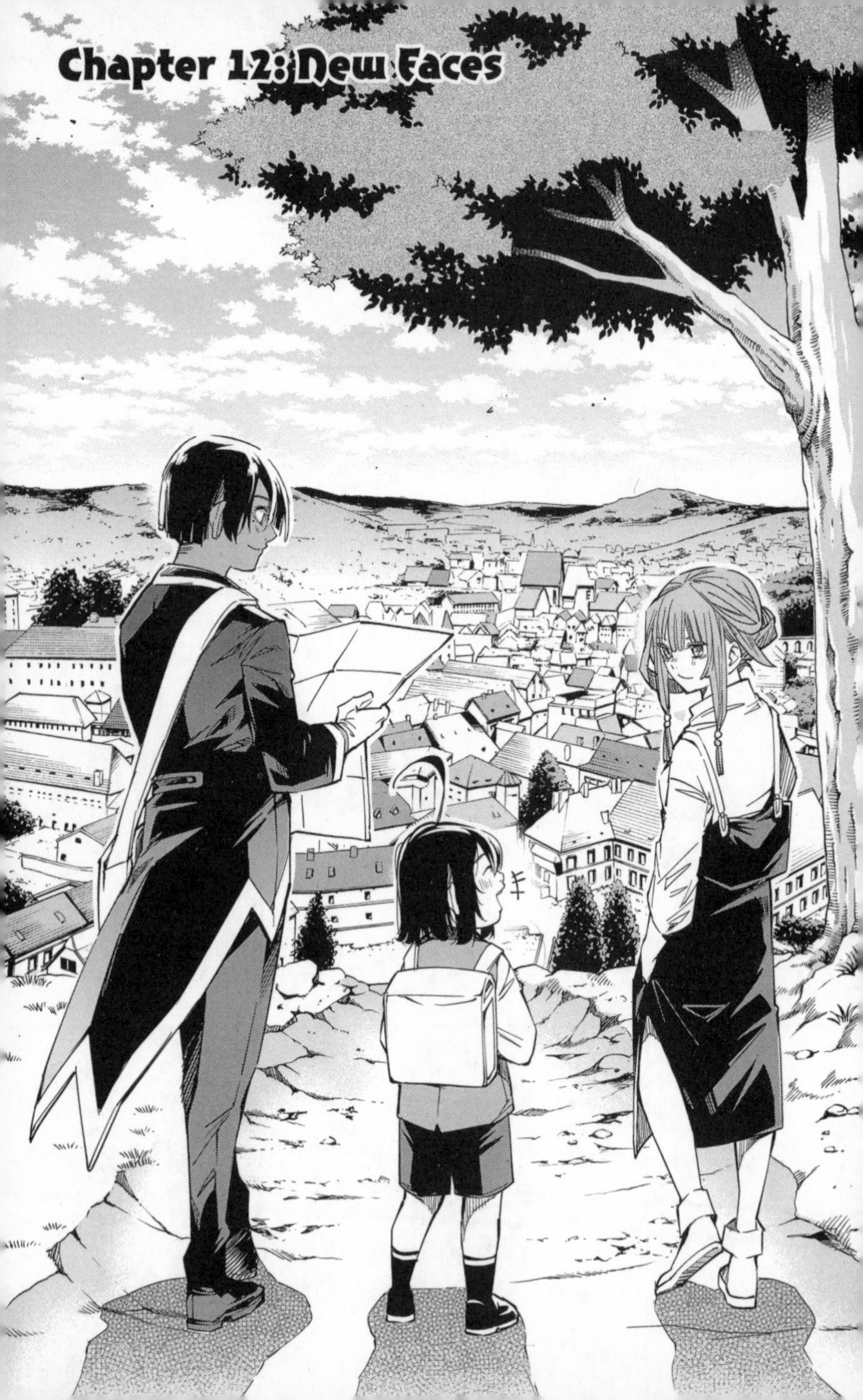
Chapter 12: New Faces

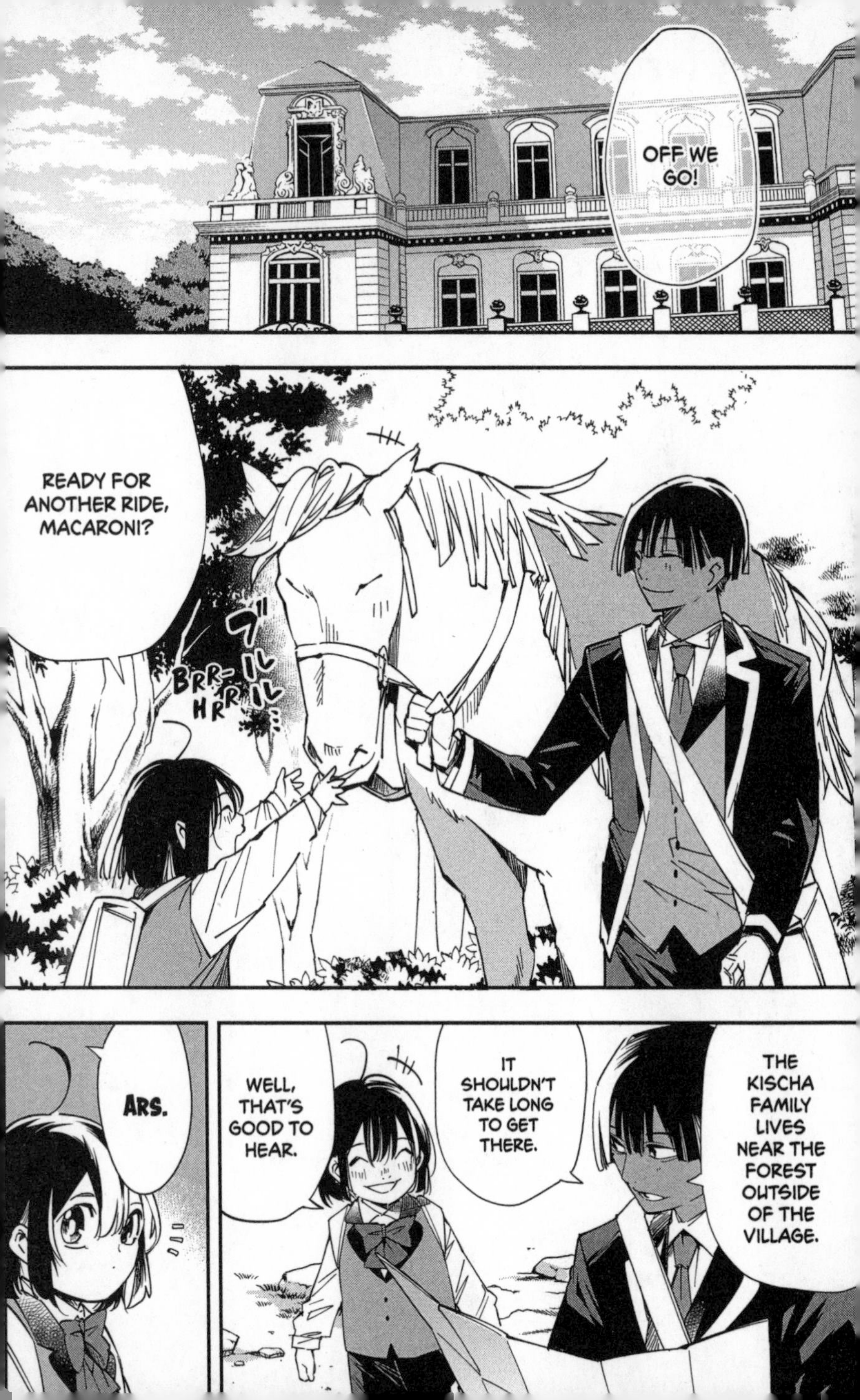
OFF WE GO!
READY FOR ANOTHER RIDE, MACARONI?
BRRR-HRRR
THE KISCHA FAMILY LIVES NEAR THE FOREST OUTSIDE OF THE VILLAGE.
IT SHOULDN'T TAKE LONG TO GET THERE.
WELL, THAT'S GOOD TO HEAR.
ARS.

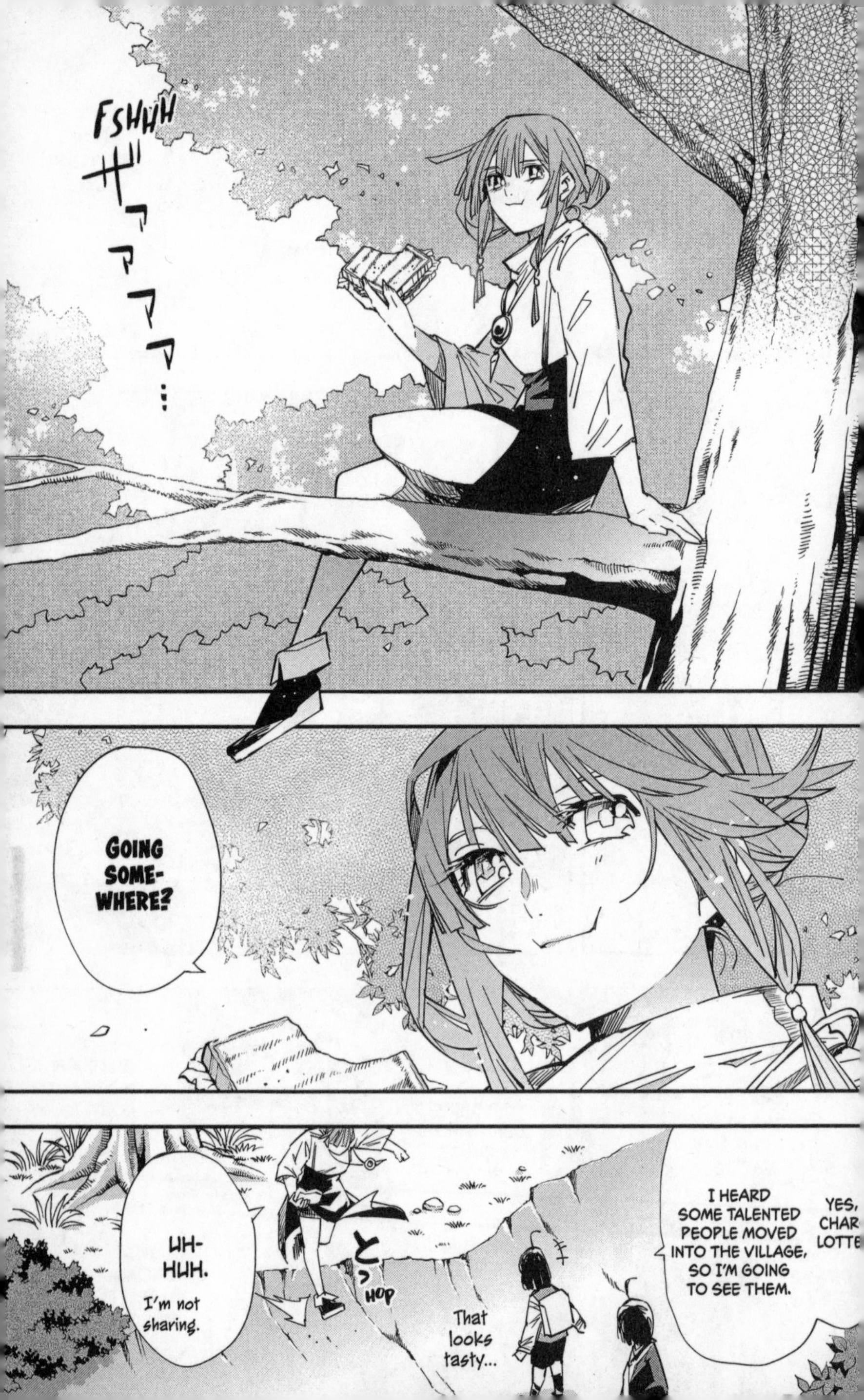
FSHHH
ザァァァ…
GOING SOME-WHERE?
YES, CHAR LOTTE
I HEARD SOME TALENTED PEOPLE MOVED INTO THE VILLAGE, SO I'M GOING TO SEE THEM.
That looks tasty...
とっ HOP
UH-HUH.
I'm not sharing.

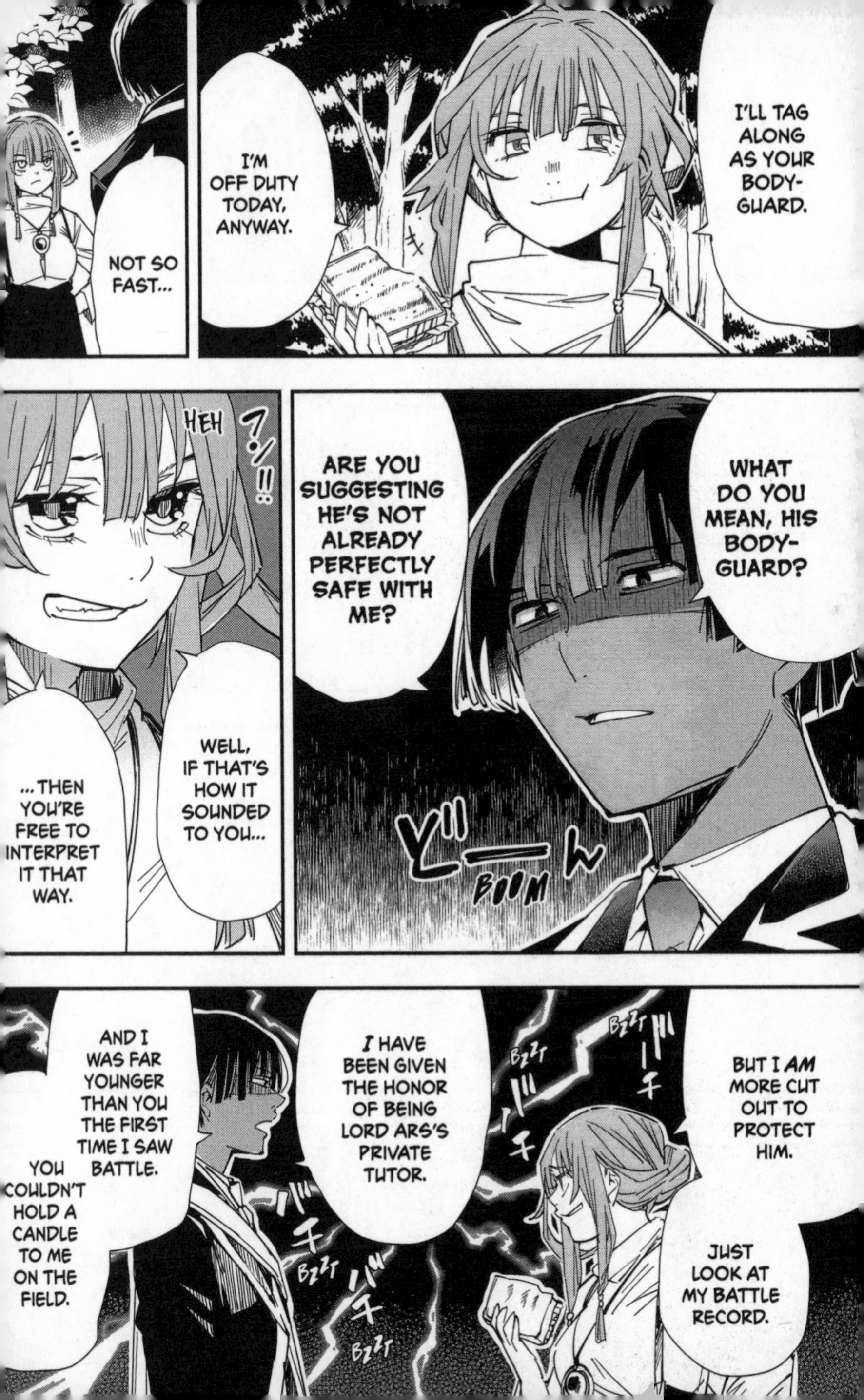
I'LL TAG ALONG AS YOUR BODY-GUARD.
I'M OFF DUTY TODAY, ANYWAY.
NOT SO FAST...
WHAT DO YOU MEAN, HIS BODY-GUARD?
ARE YOU SUGGESTING HE'S NOT ALREADY PERFECTLY SAFE WITH ME?
BOOM
HEH
WELL, IF THAT'S HOW IT SOUNDED TO YOU...
...THEN YOU'RE FREE TO INTERPRET IT THAT WAY.
BUT I *AM* MORE CUT OUT TO PROTECT HIM.
JUST LOOK AT MY BATTLE RECORD.
BZZT
I HAVE BEEN GIVEN THE HONOR OF BEING LORD ARS'S PRIVATE TUTOR.
BZZT
AND I WAS FAR YOUNGER THAN YOU THE FIRST TIME I SAW BATTLE.
YOU COULDN'T HOLD A CANDLE TO ME ON THE FIELD.
BZZT
BZZT

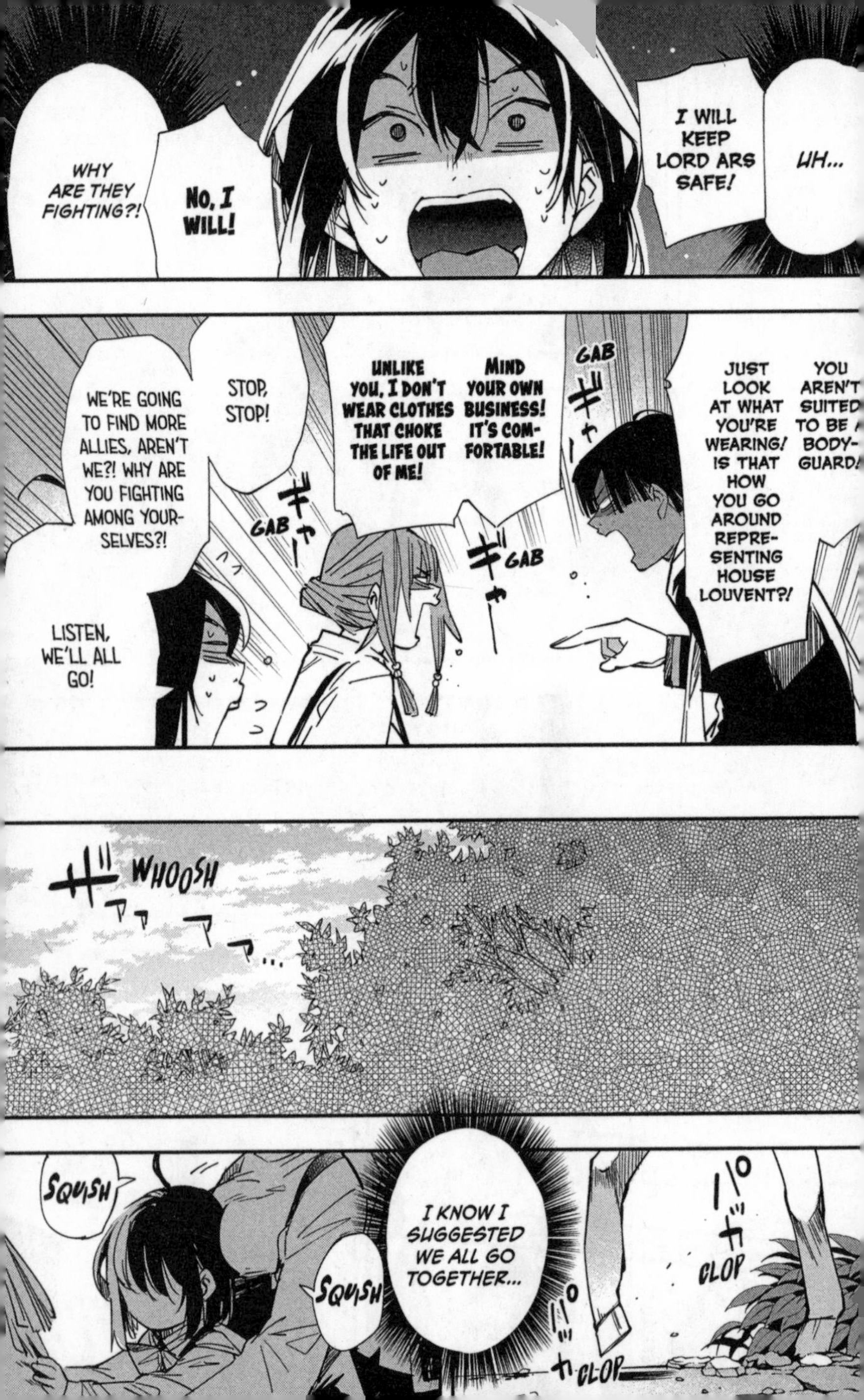
UH...
I WILL KEEP LORD ARS SAFE!
No, I WILL!
WHY ARE THEY FIGHTING?!
YOU AREN'T SUITED TO BE A BODY-GUARD!
JUST LOOK AT WHAT YOU'RE WEARING! IS THAT HOW YOU GO AROUND REPRE-SENTING HOUSE LOUVENT?!
GAB
MIND YOUR OWN BUSINESS! IT'S COM-FORTABLE!
UNLIKE YOU, I DON'T WEAR CLOTHES THAT CHOKE THE LIFE OUT OF ME!
GAB
GAB
STOP, STOP!
WE'RE GOING TO FIND MORE ALLIES, AREN'T WE?! WHY ARE YOU FIGHTING AMONG YOUR-SELVES?!
LISTEN, WE'LL ALL GO!
WHOOSH
CLOP
I KNOW I SUGGESTED WE ALL GO TOGETHER...
CLOP
SQUISH
SQUISH

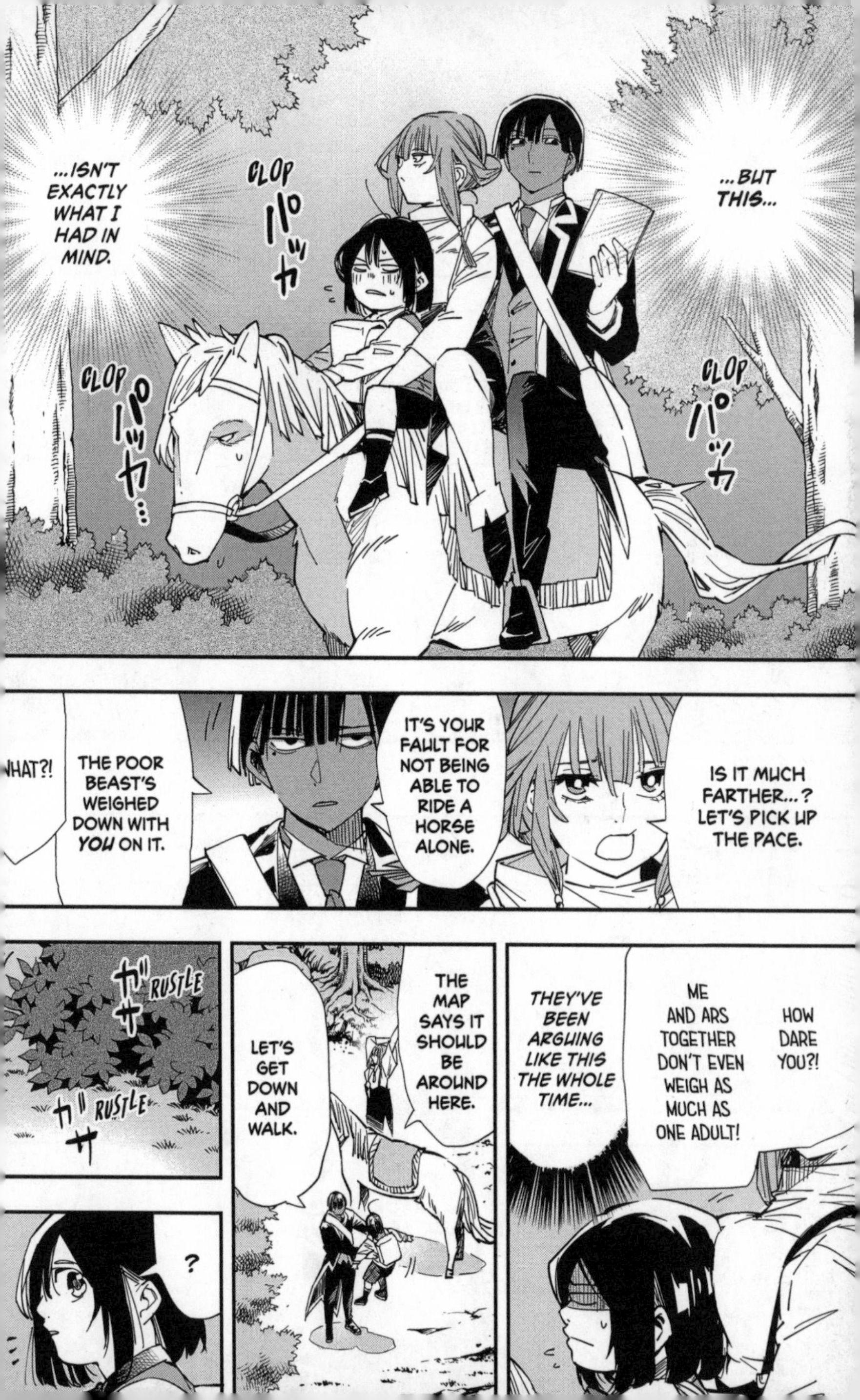
...BUT THIS...
CLOP パッカ
CLOP パッカ
...ISN'T EXACTLY WHAT I HAD IN MIND.
CLOP パッカ...
IS IT MUCH FARTHER...? LET'S PICK UP THE PACE.
IT'S YOUR FAULT FOR NOT BEING ABLE TO RIDE A HORSE ALONE.
THE POOR BEAST'S WEIGHED DOWN WITH YOU ON IT.
WHAT?!
HOW DARE YOU?!
ME AND ARS TOGETHER DON'T EVEN WEIGH AS MUCH AS ONE ADULT!
THEY'VE BEEN ARGUING LIKE THIS THE WHOLE TIME...
THE MAP SAYS IT SHOULD BE AROUND HERE.
LET'S GET DOWN AND WALK.
ガサ RUSTLE
ガサ RUSTLE
?

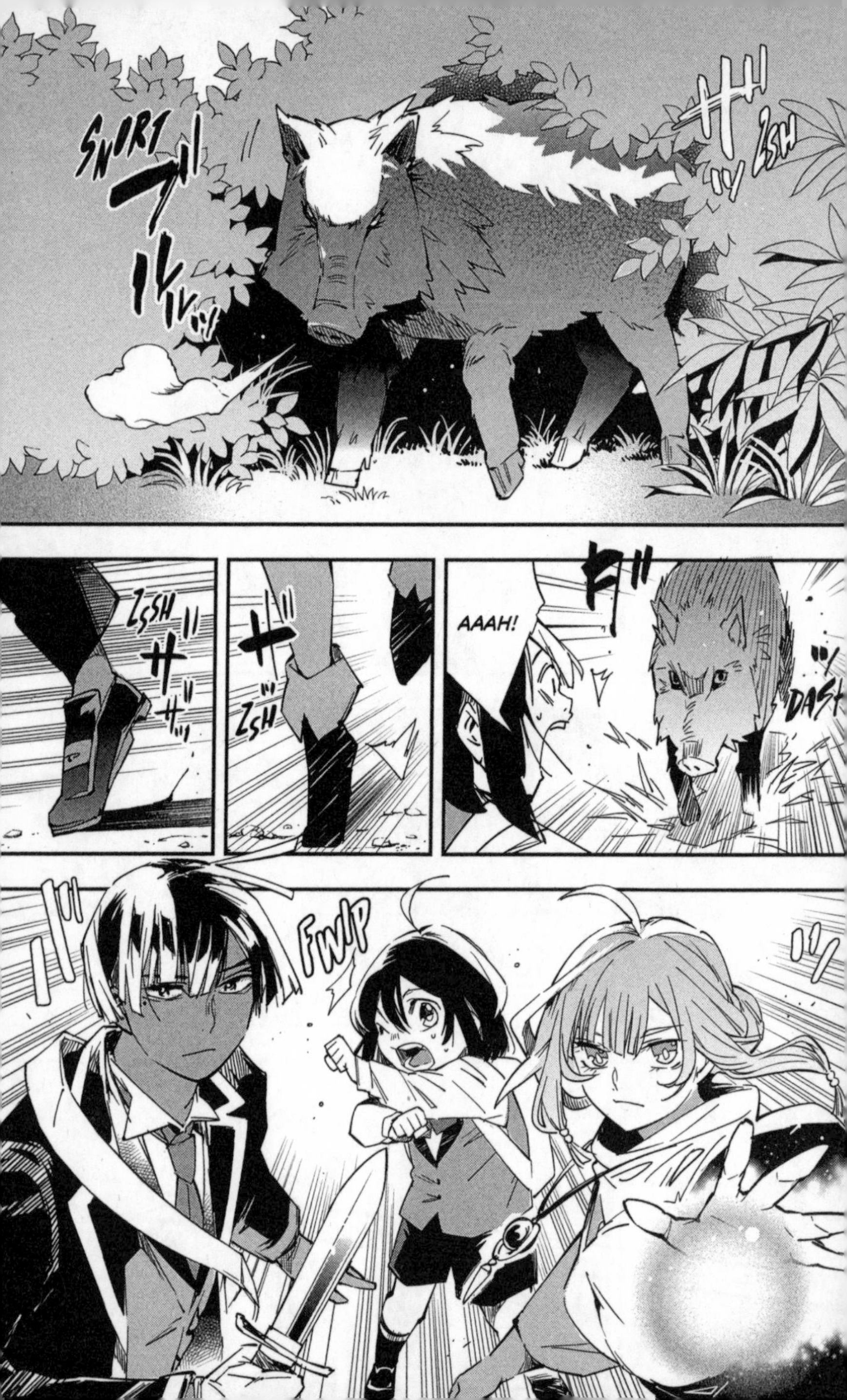
ZSH
SNORT
DASH
AAAH!
ZSH
ZSH
FWIP

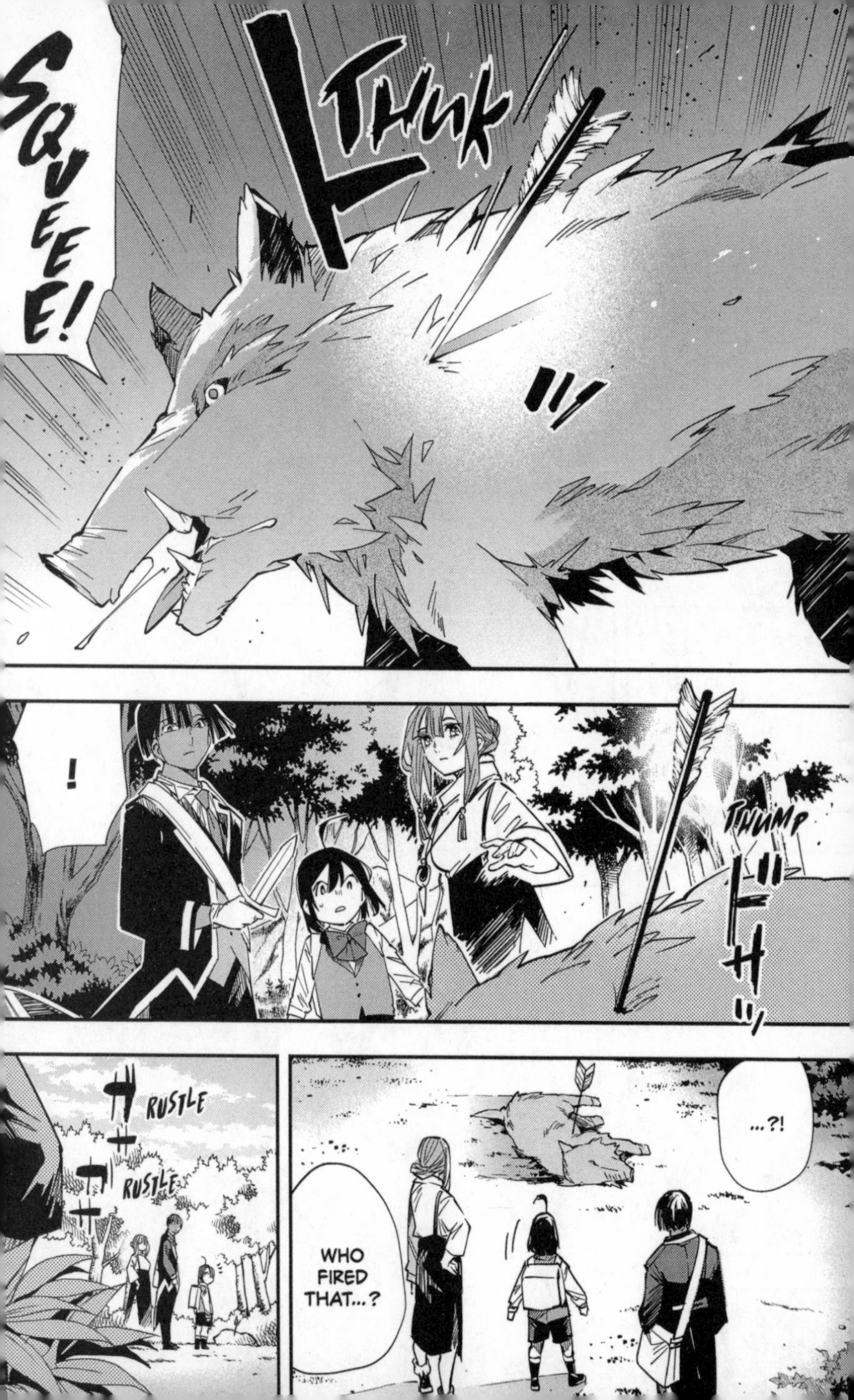
THUK
SQUEEEE!
THUMP
!
...?!
WHO FIRED THAT...?
RUSTLE
RUSTLE

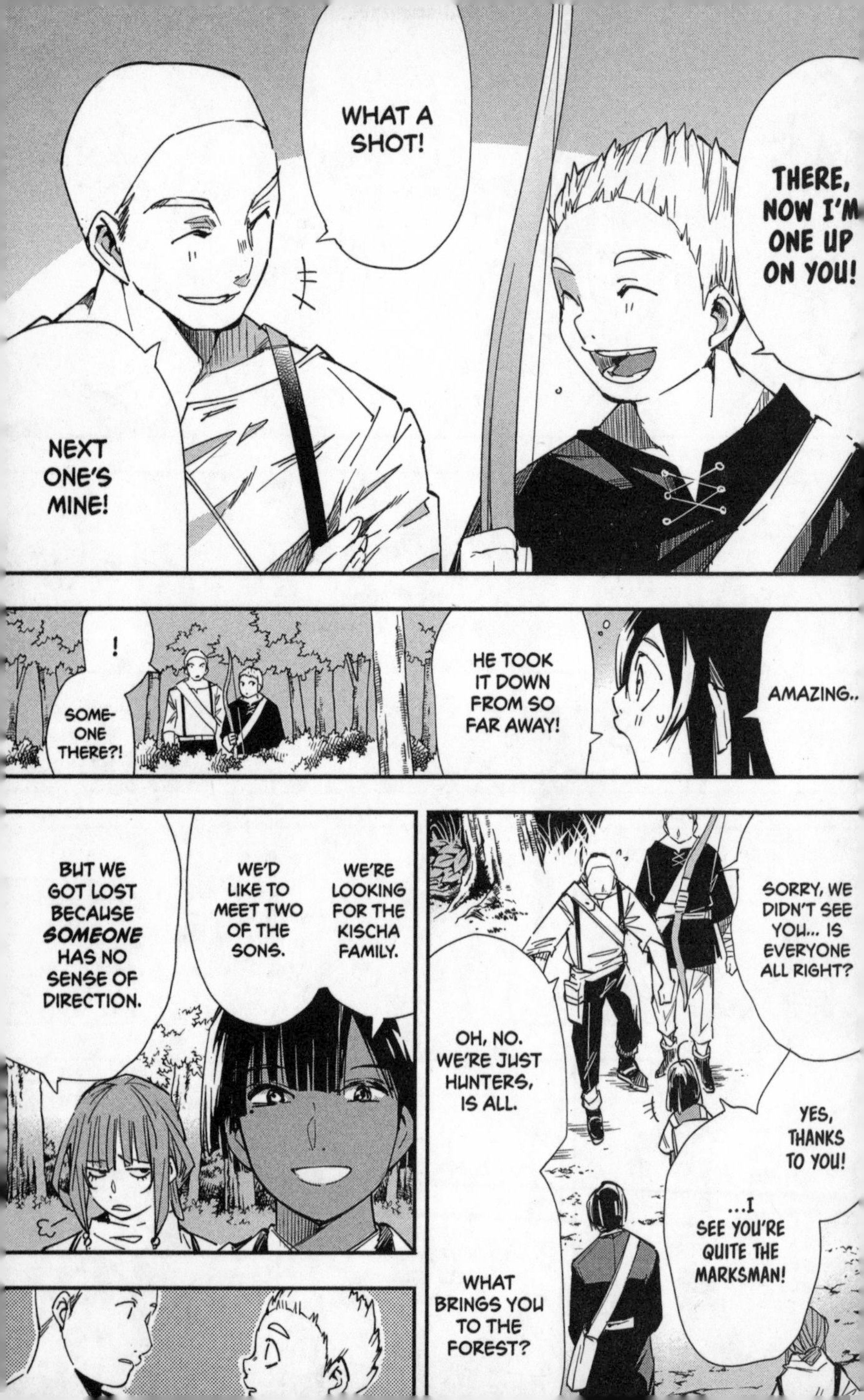

THERE, NOW I'M ONE UP ON YOU!
WHAT A SHOT!
NEXT ONE'S MINE!
AMAZING..
HE TOOK IT DOWN FROM SO FAR AWAY!
!
SOME-ONE THERE?!
SORRY, WE DIDN'T SEE YOU... IS EVERYONE ALL RIGHT?
YES, THANKS TO YOU!
...I SEE YOU'RE QUITE THE MARKSMAN!
OH, NO. WE'RE JUST HUNTERS, IS ALL.
WHAT BRINGS YOU TO THE FOREST?
WE'RE LOOKING FOR THE KISCHA FAMILY.
WE'D LIKE TO MEET TWO OF THE SONS.
BUT WE GOT LOST BECAUSE *SOMEONE* HAS NO SENSE OF DIRECTION.

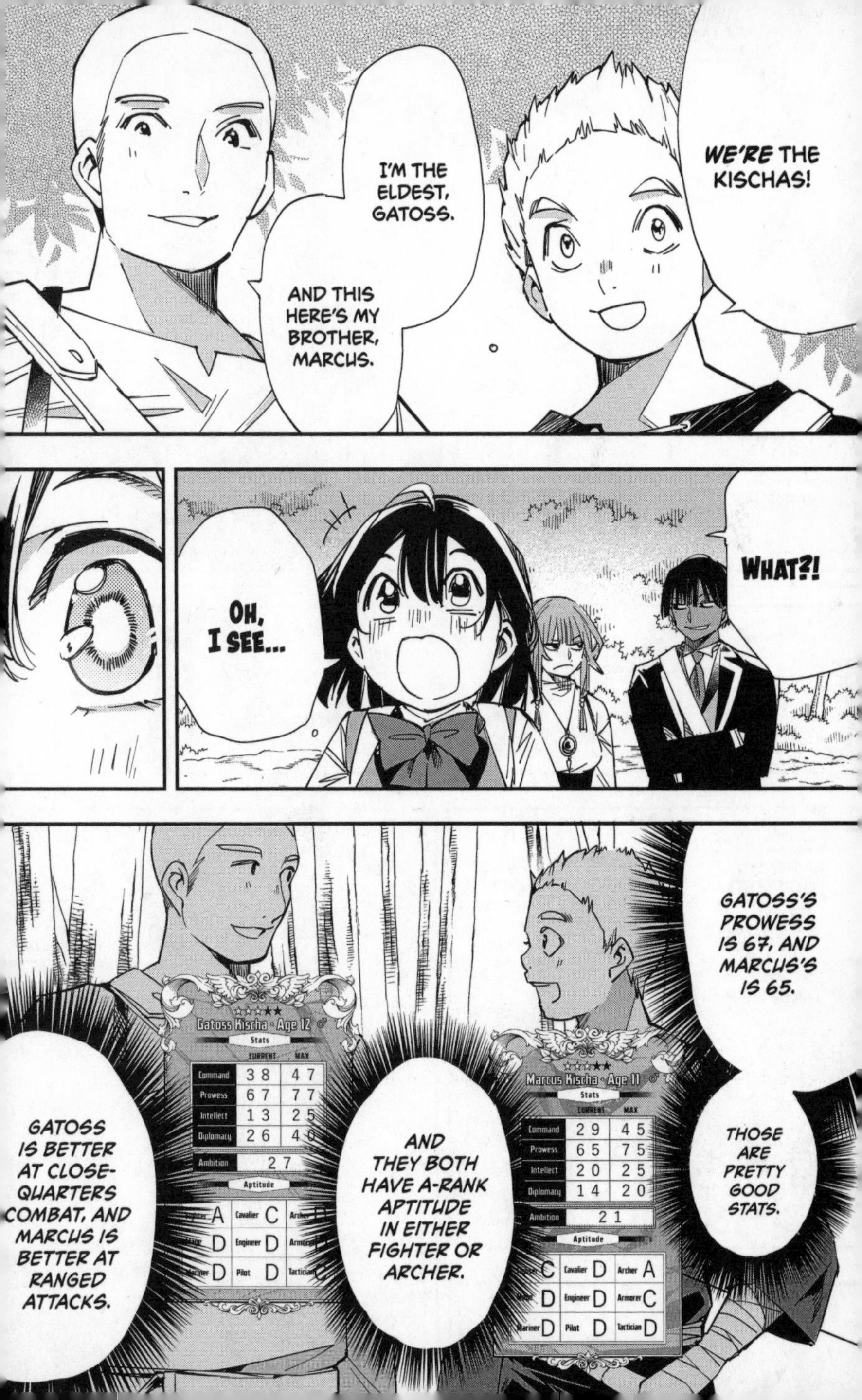
WE'RE THE KISCHAS!
I'M THE ELDEST, GATOSS.
AND THIS HERE'S MY BROTHER, MARCUS.
WHAT?!
OH, I SEE...
GATOSS'S PROWESS IS 67, AND MARCUS'S IS 65.
THOSE ARE PRETTY GOOD STATS.
Marcus Kischa · Age 11
Stats
CURRENT MAX
Command 29 45
Prowess 65 75
Intellect 20 25
Diplomacy 14 20
Ambition 21
Aptitude
C Cavalier D Archer A
D Engineer D Armorer C
Mariner D Pilot D Tactician D
AND THEY BOTH HAVE A-RANK APTITUDE IN EITHER FIGHTER OR ARCHER.
Gatoss Kischa · Age 12
Stats
CURRENT MAX
Command 38 47
Prowess 67 77
Intellect 13 25
Diplomacy 26 40
Ambition 27
Aptitude
A Cavalier C
D Engineer D
D Pilot D
GATOSS IS BETTER AT CLOSE-QUARTERS COMBAT, AND MARCUS IS BETTER AT RANGED ATTACKS.

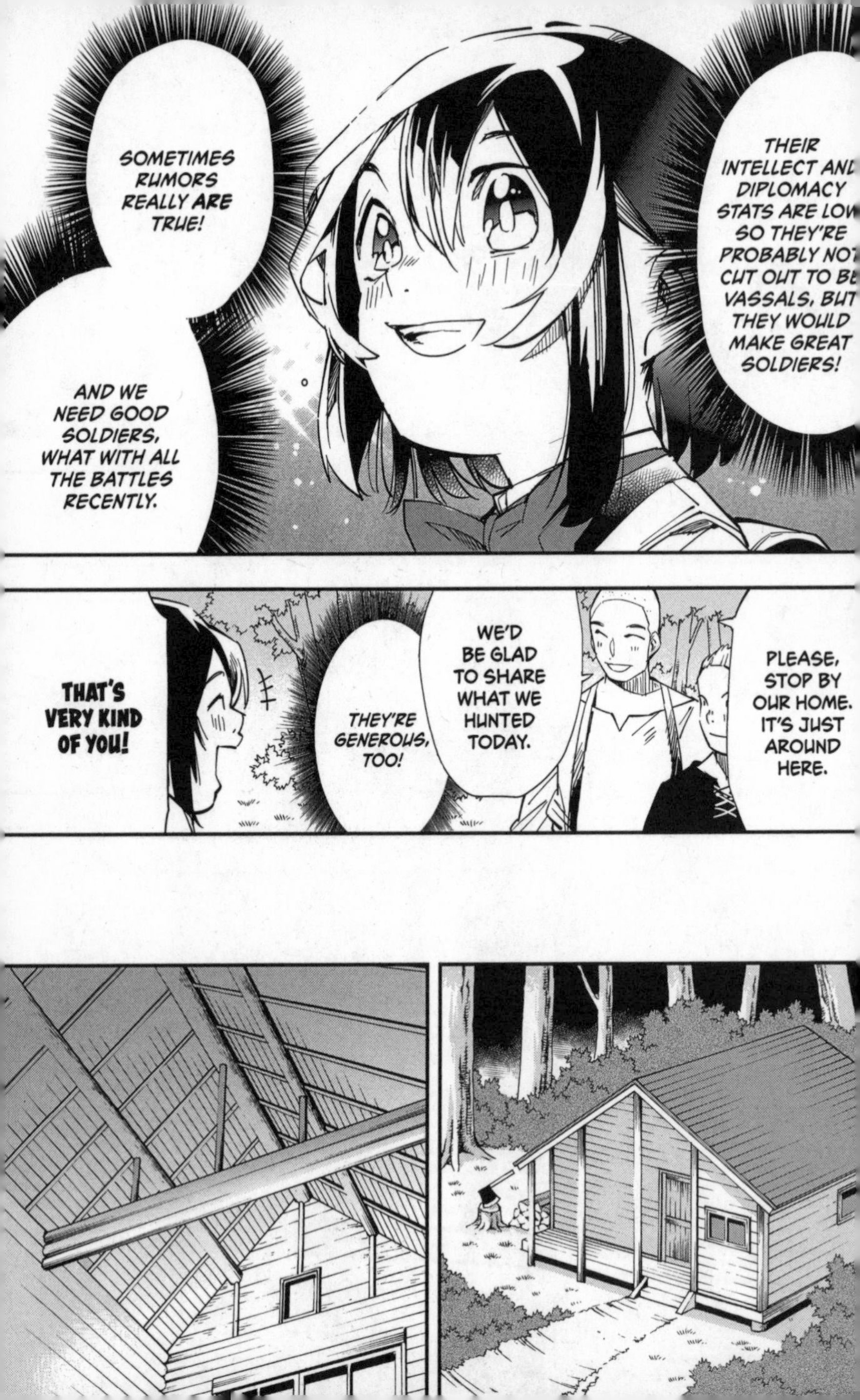

THEIR INTELLECT AND DIPLOMACY STATS ARE LOW SO THEY'RE PROBABLY NOT CUT OUT TO BE VASSALS, BUT THEY WOULD MAKE GREAT SOLDIERS!
SOMETIMES RUMORS REALLY ARE TRUE!
AND WE NEED GOOD SOLDIERS, WHAT WITH ALL THE BATTLES RECENTLY.
PLEASE, STOP BY OUR HOME. IT'S JUST AROUND HERE.
WE'D BE GLAD TO SHARE WHAT WE HUNTED TODAY.
THEY'RE GENEROUS, TOO!
THAT'S VERY KIND OF YOU!

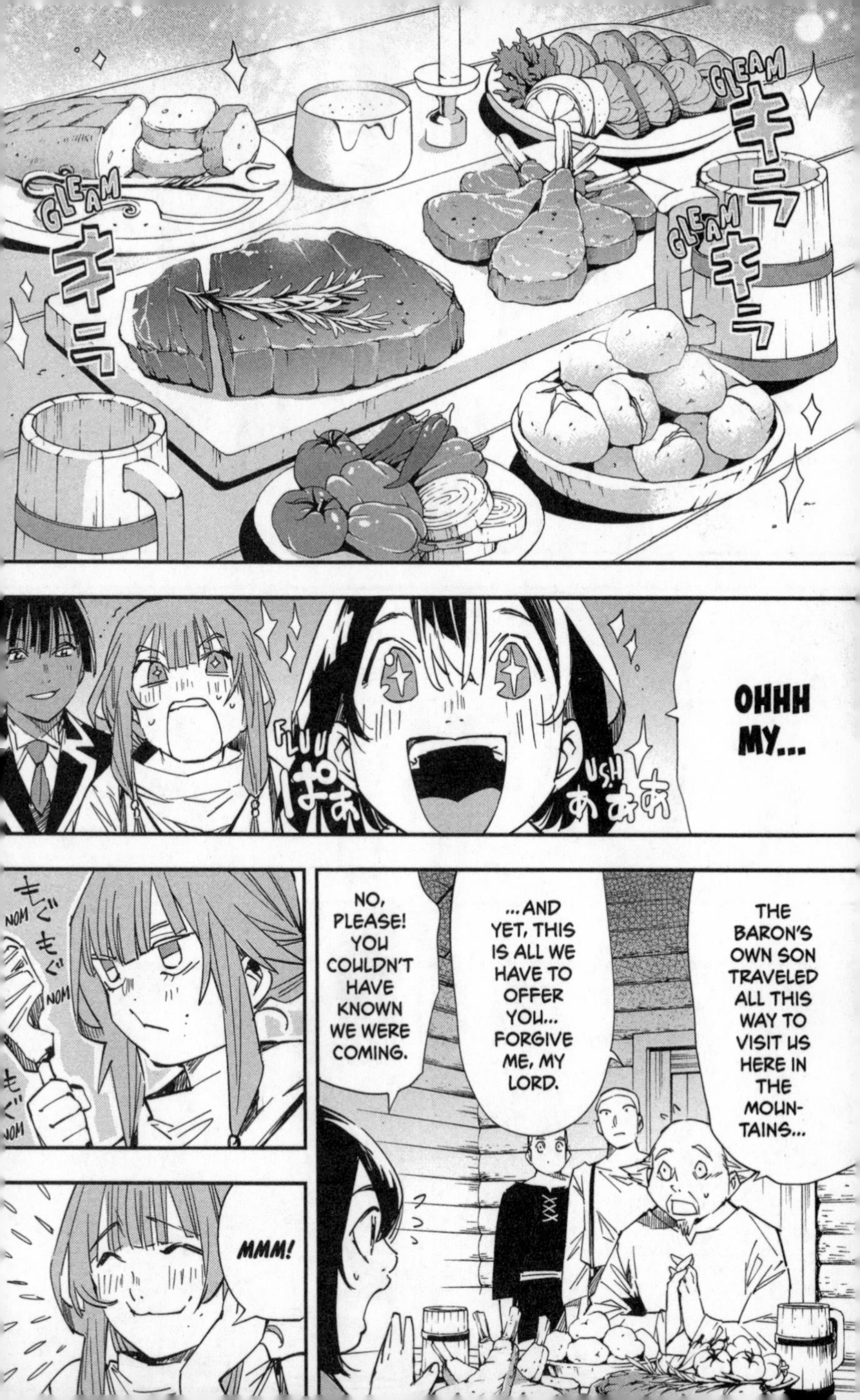
GLEAM
キラ
GLEAM
キラ
GLEAM
キラ
OHHH MY...
USH
あああ
FLUU
ぱあ
THE BARON'S OWN SON TRAVELED ALL THIS WAY TO VISIT US HERE IN THE MOUN-TAINS...
...AND YET, THIS IS ALL WE HAVE TO OFFER YOU... FORGIVE ME, MY LORD.
NO, PLEASE! YOU COULDN'T HAVE KNOWN WE WERE COMING.
もぐもぐ
NOM
NOM
もぐ
NOM
MMM!

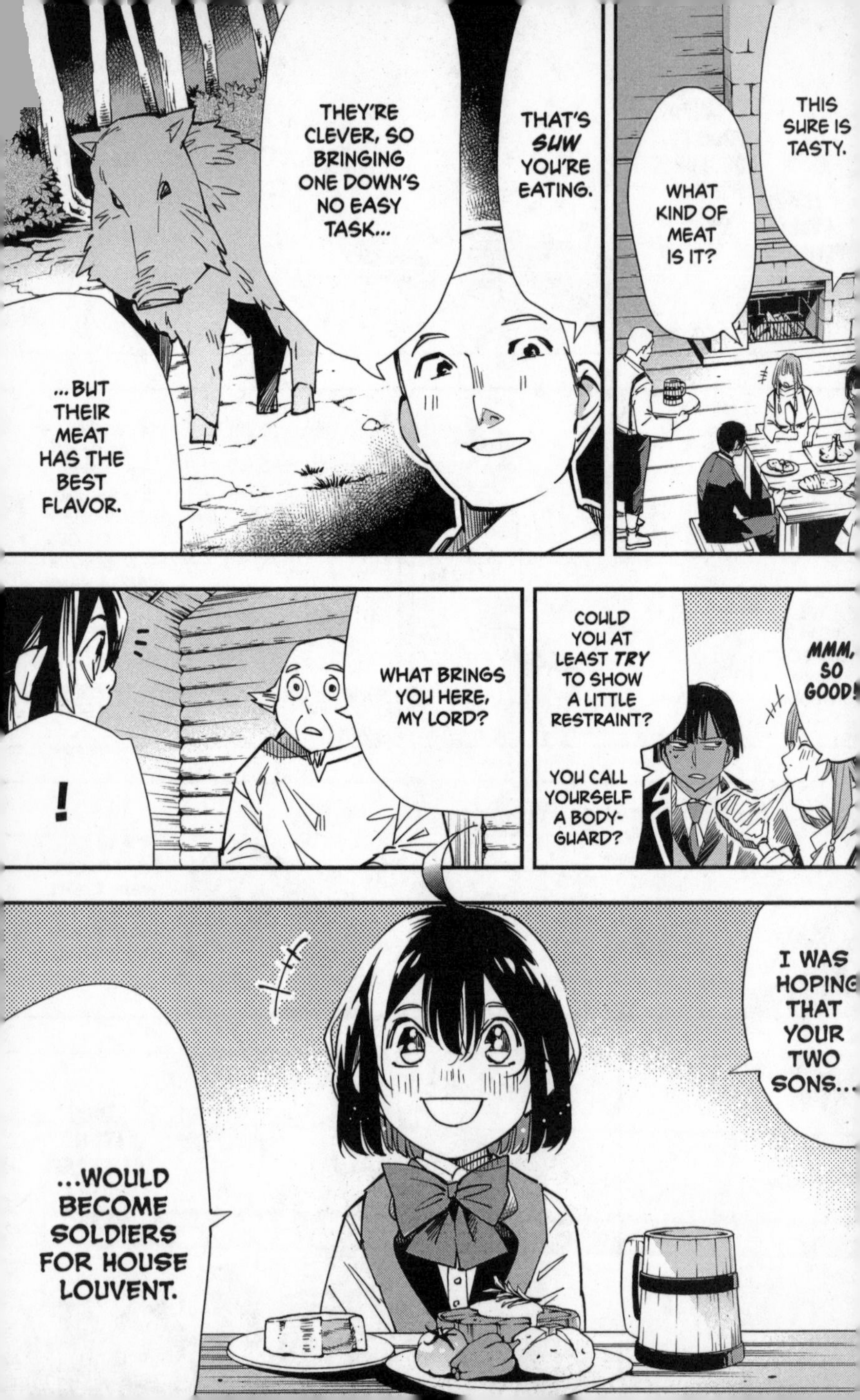
THIS SURE IS TASTY.
WHAT KIND OF MEAT IS IT?
THAT'S *SUW* YOU'RE EATING.
THEY'RE CLEVER, SO BRINGING ONE DOWN'S NO EASY TASK...
...BUT THEIR MEAT HAS THE BEST FLAVOR.
MMM, SO GOOD!
COULD YOU AT LEAST *TRY* TO SHOW A LITTLE RESTRAINT?
YOU CALL YOURSELF A BODY-GUARD?
WHAT BRINGS YOU HERE, MY LORD?
!
I WAS HOPING THAT YOUR TWO SONS...
...WOULD BECOME SOLDIERS FOR HOUSE LOUVENT.

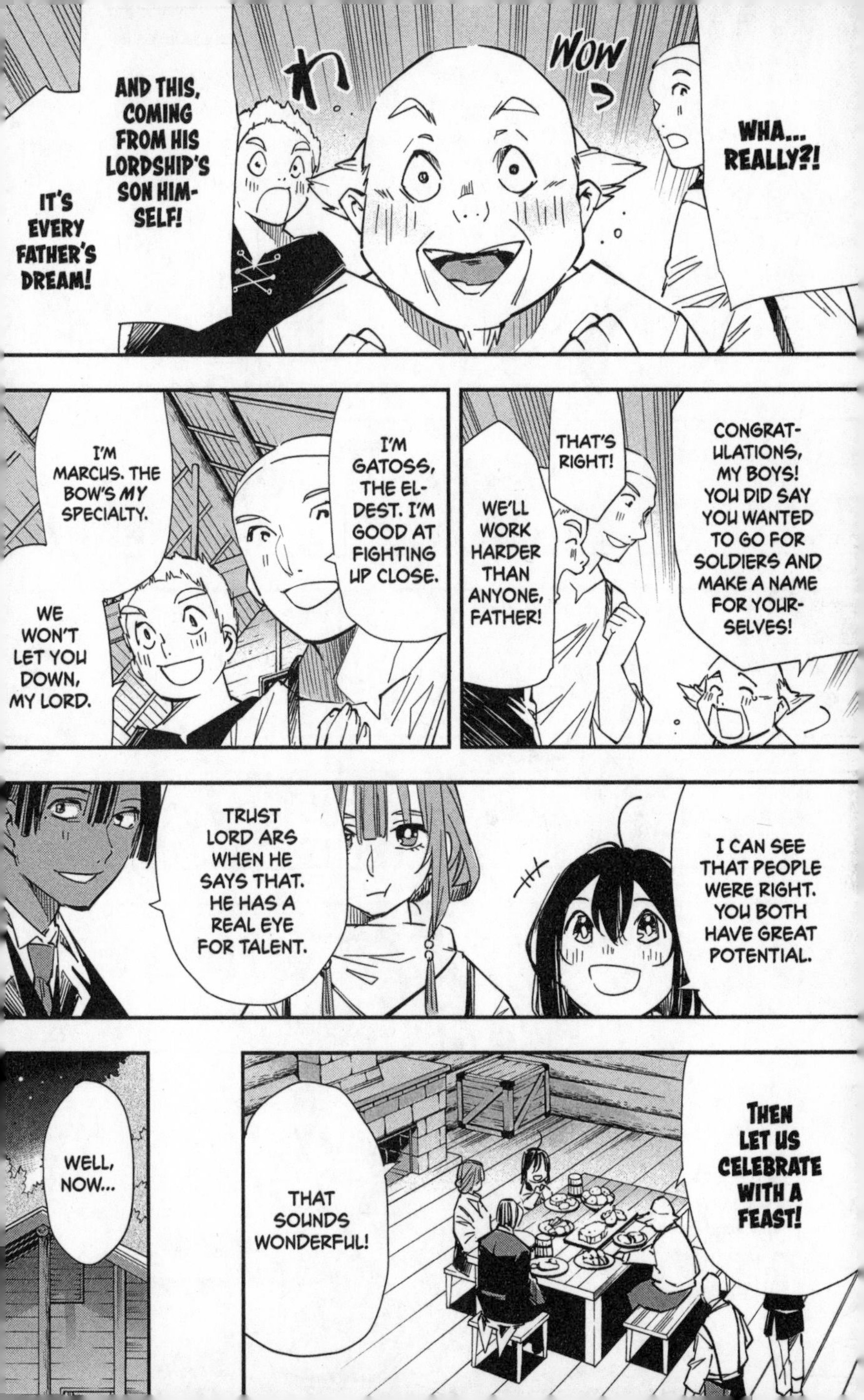
WHA... REALLY?!
WOW
わ
AND THIS, COMING FROM HIS LORDSHIP'S SON HIMSELF!
IT'S EVERY FATHER'S DREAM!
CONGRATULATIONS, MY BOYS! YOU DID SAY YOU WANTED TO GO FOR SOLDIERS AND MAKE A NAME FOR YOURSELVES!
THAT'S RIGHT!
WE'LL WORK HARDER THAN ANYONE, FATHER!
I'M GATOSS, THE ELDEST. I'M GOOD AT FIGHTING UP CLOSE.
I'M MARCUS. THE BOW'S *MY* SPECIALTY.
WE WON'T LET YOU DOWN, MY LORD.
I CAN SEE THAT PEOPLE WERE RIGHT. YOU BOTH HAVE GREAT POTENTIAL.
TRUST LORD ARS WHEN HE SAYS THAT. HE HAS A REAL EYE FOR TALENT.
THEN LET US CELEBRATE WITH A FEAST!
THAT SOUNDS WONDERFUL!
WELL, NOW...

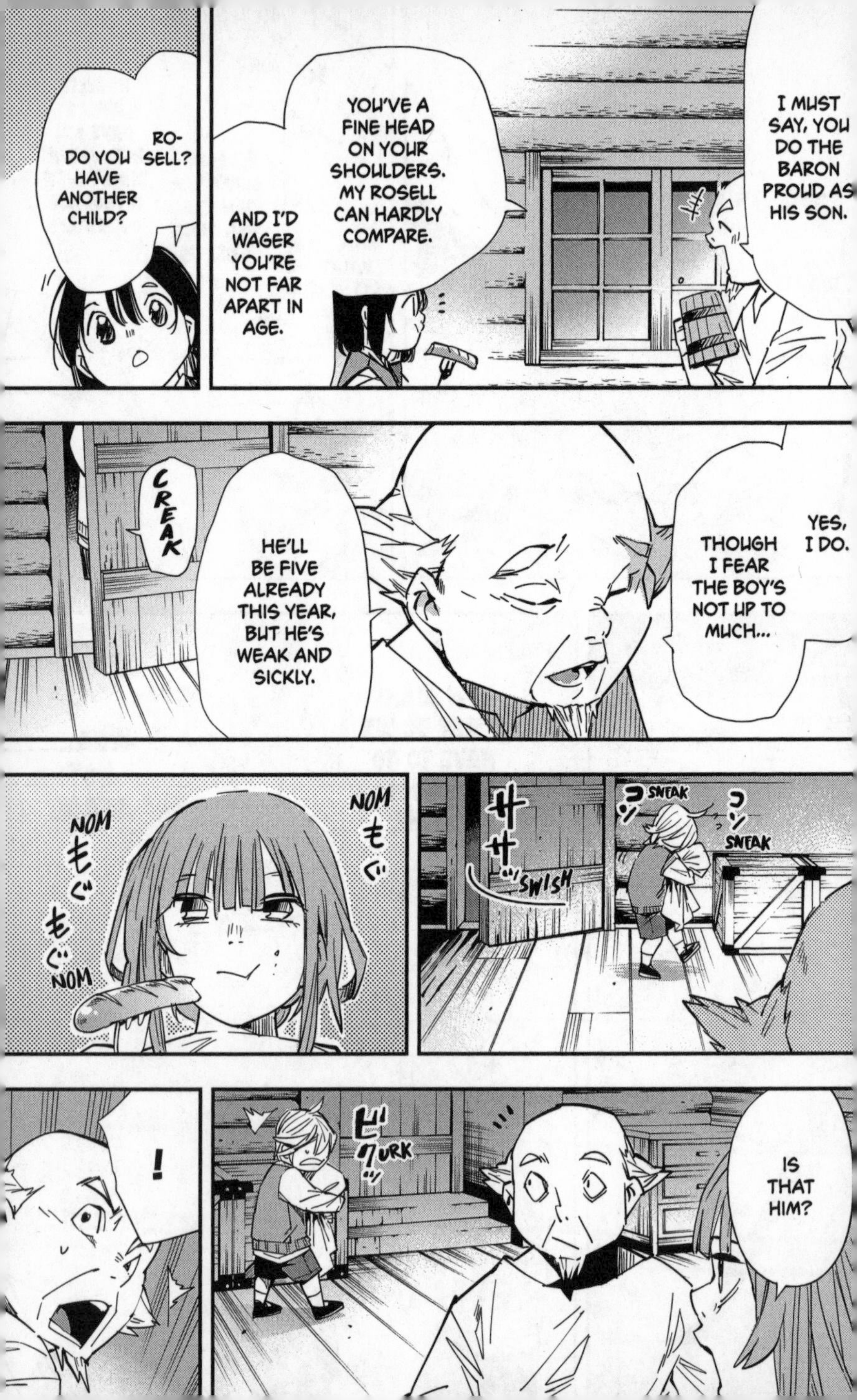
I MUST SAY, YOU DO THE BARON PROUD AS HIS SON.
YOU'VE A FINE HEAD ON YOUR SHOULDERS. MY ROSELL CAN HARDLY COMPARE.
AND I'D WAGER YOU'RE NOT FAR APART IN AGE.
RO-SELL?
DO YOU HAVE ANOTHER CHILD?
YES, I DO.
THOUGH I FEAR THE BOY'S NOT UP TO MUCH...
HE'LL BE FIVE ALREADY THIS YEAR, BUT HE'S WEAK AND SICKLY.
CREAK
SNEAK
SNEAK
SWISH
NOM
NOM
NOM
IS THAT HIM?
URK
!

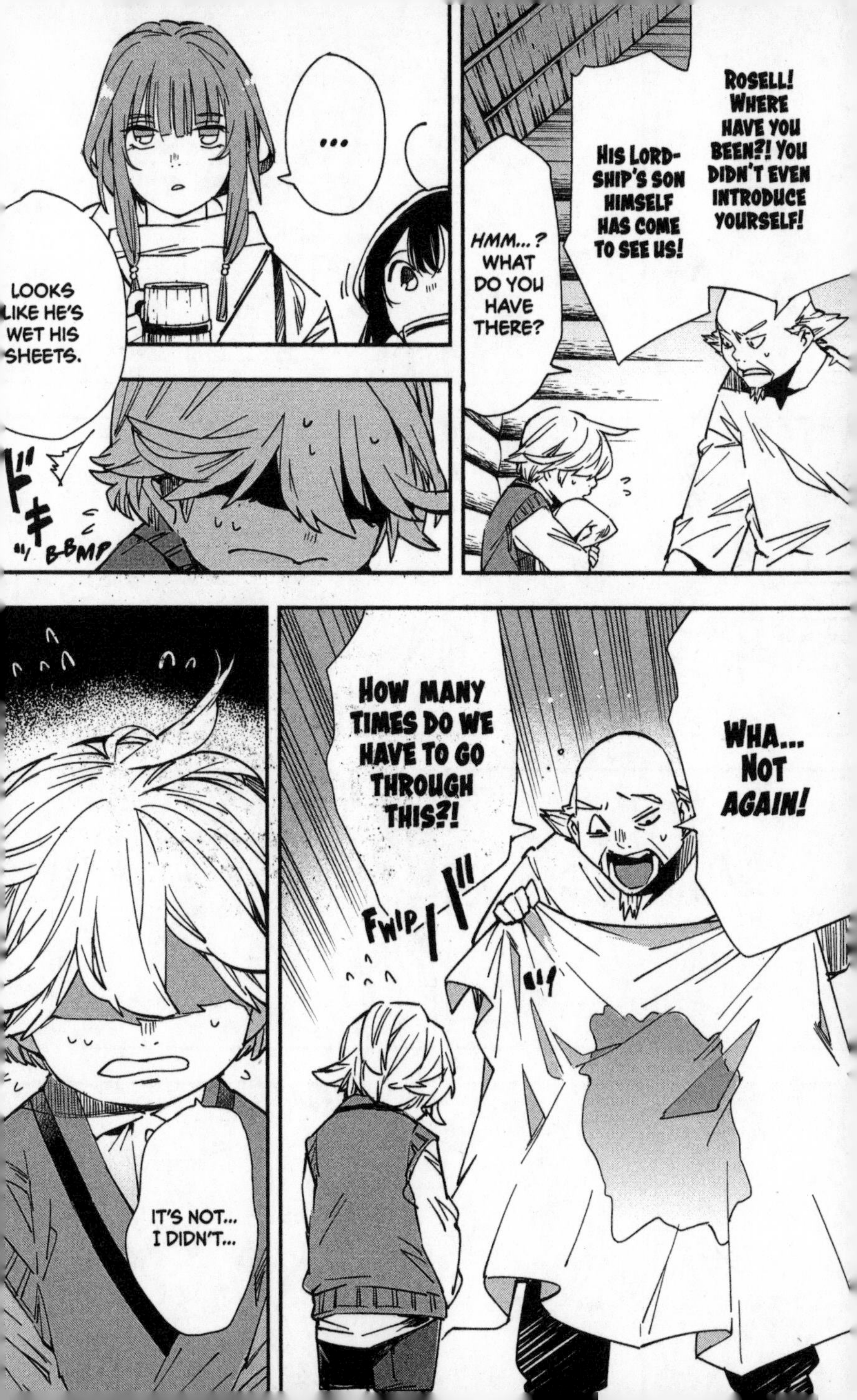

ROSELL! WHERE HAVE YOU BEEN?! YOU DIDN'T EVEN INTRODUCE YOURSELF!
HIS LORDSHIP'S SON HIMSELF HAS COME TO SEE US!
HMM...? WHAT DO YOU HAVE THERE?
...
LOOKS LIKE HE'S WET HIS SHEETS.
ドキ
B-BMP
WHA... NOT AGAIN!
HOW MANY TIMES DO WE HAVE TO GO THROUGH THIS?!
FWIP
IT'S NOT... I DIDN'T...

HAVING TO LIVE UP TO BROTHERS LIKE *THEM* MUST MAKE IT EVEN WORSE.

POOR KID.

HE CERTAINLY DOESN'T LOOK LIKE HE'S CUT FROM THE SAME CLOTH AS HIS BROTHERS.

REMINDS ME OF WHEN I HAD TO WASH THE LITTLE ONES' UNDER-CLOTHES...

HEH HEH WETTING THE BED...

☆☆☆☆☆
Rosell Kischa - Age 5 ♂

Stats

	CURRENT	MAX
Command	3 5	8 8
Prowess	1 1	3 2
Intellect	4 5	1 0 9
Diplomacy	3 2	9 5

Ambition	2 1

Aptitude

Fighter D	Cavalier D	Archer C
Mage C	Engineer A	Armorer A
Mariner C	Pilot A	Tactician S

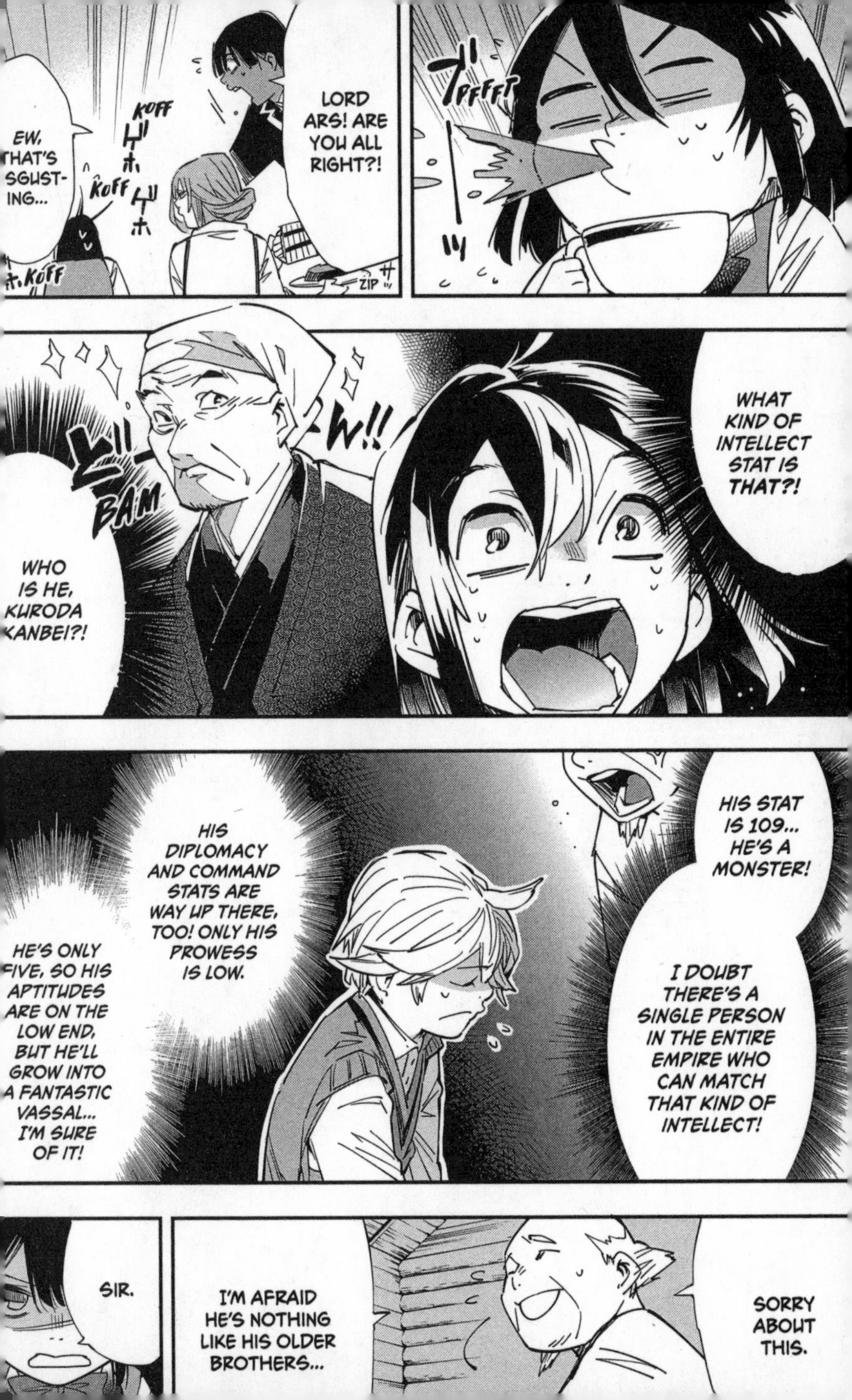
PFFFT
ZIP
LORD ARS! ARE YOU ALL RIGHT?!
KOFF
KOFF
EW, THAT'S SGUSTING...
KOFF
WHAT KIND OF INTELLECT STAT IS THAT?!
W!!
BAM
WHO IS HE, KURODA KANBEI?!
HIS STAT IS 109... HE'S A MONSTER!
I DOUBT THERE'S A SINGLE PERSON IN THE ENTIRE EMPIRE WHO CAN MATCH THAT KIND OF INTELLECT!
HIS DIPLOMACY AND COMMAND STATS ARE WAY UP THERE, TOO! ONLY HIS PROWESS IS LOW.
HE'S ONLY FIVE, SO HIS APTITUDES ARE ON THE LOW END, BUT HE'LL GROW INTO A FANTASTIC VASSAL... I'M SURE OF IT!
SORRY ABOUT THIS.
I'M AFRAID HE'S NOTHING LIKE HIS OLDER BROTHERS...
SIR.

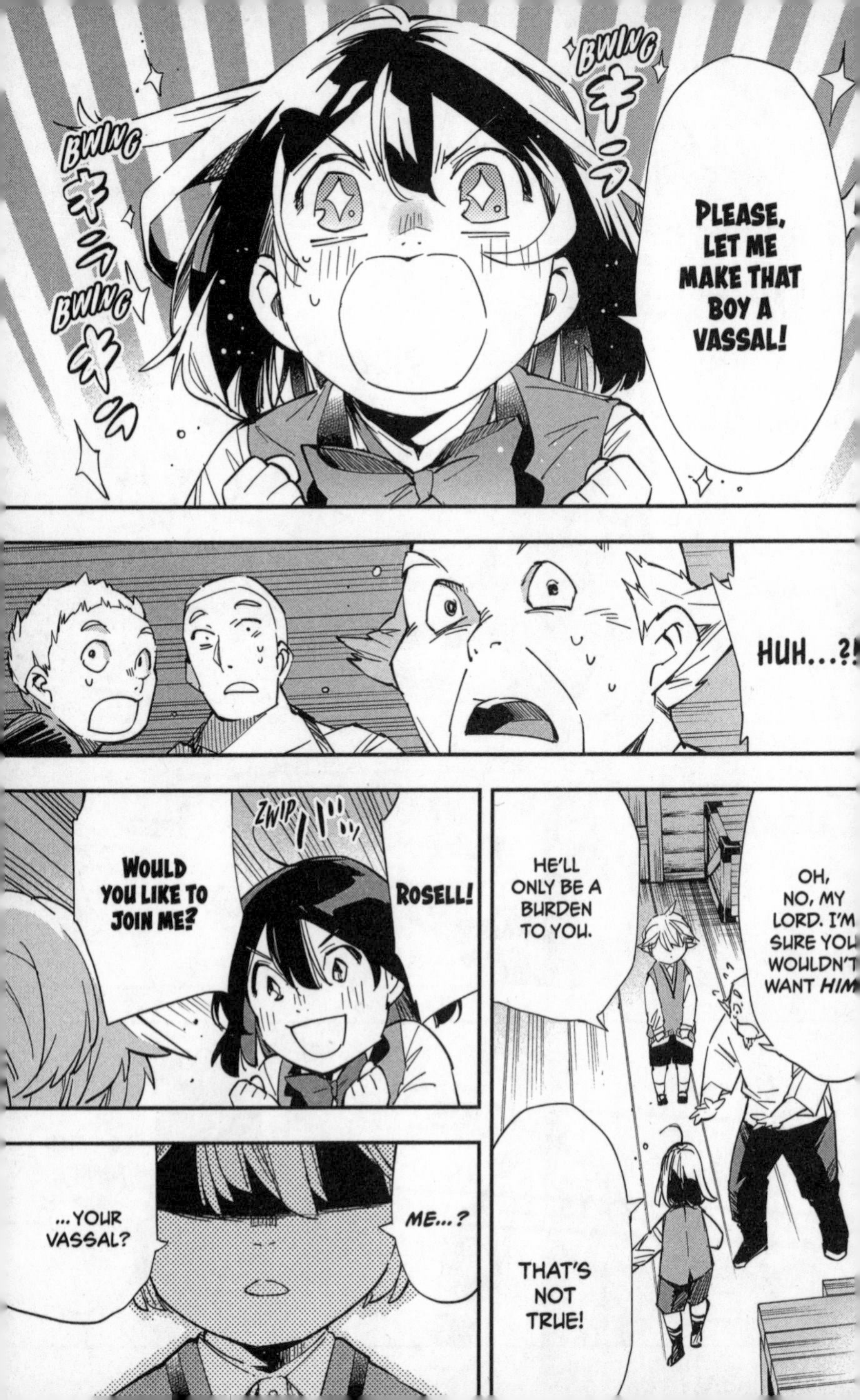
BWING
PLEASE, LET ME MAKE THAT BOY A VASSAL!
BWING
BWING
HUH...?!
OH, NO, MY LORD. I'M SURE YOU WOULDN'T WANT HIM
HE'LL ONLY BE A BURDEN TO YOU.
THAT'S NOT TRUE!
ZWIP
ROSELL!
WOULD YOU LIKE TO JOIN ME?
ME...?
...YOUR VASSAL?

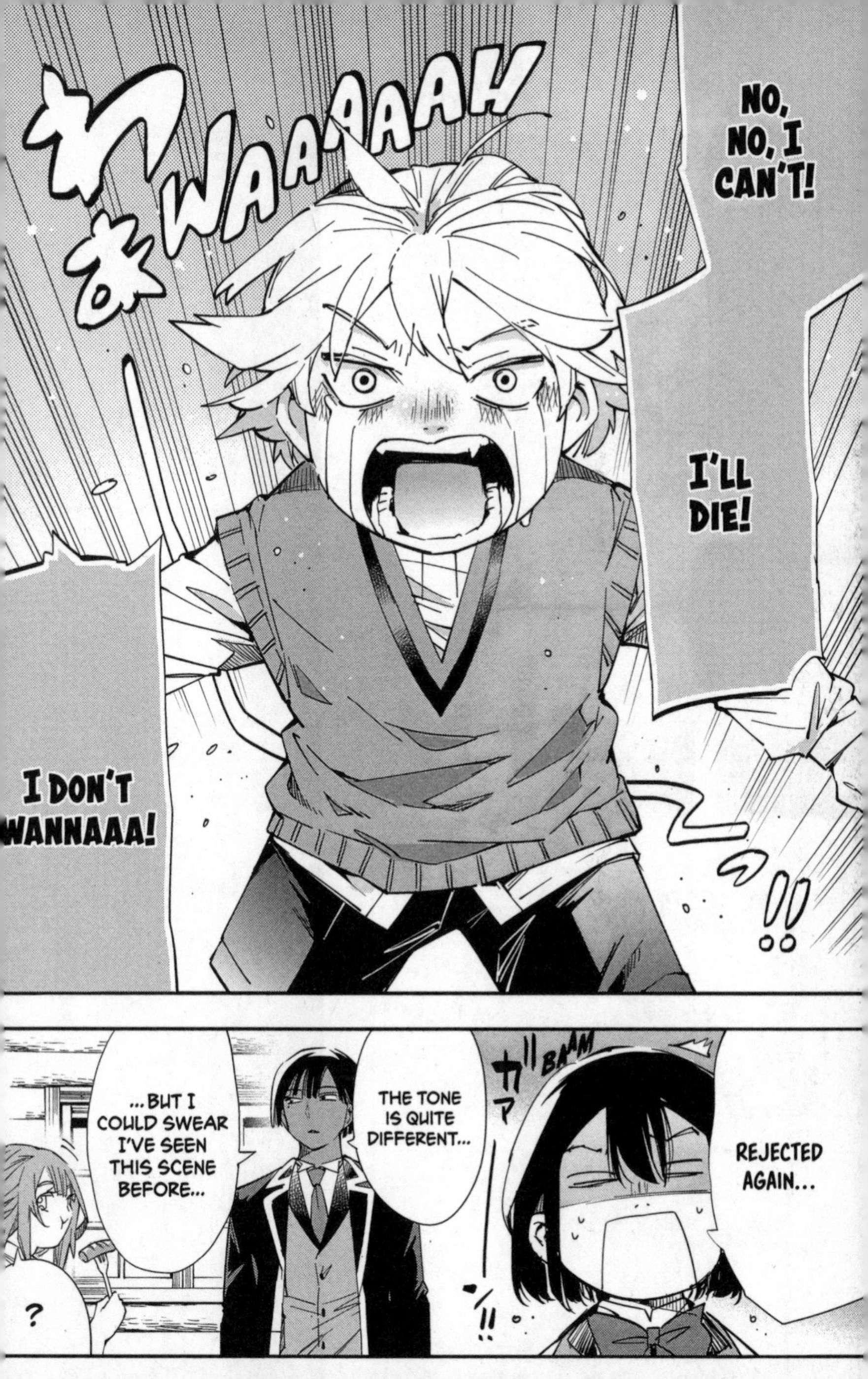
NO, NO, I CAN'T!
I'LL DIE!
WAAAAAAH
I DON'T WANNAAA!
BAAM
REJECTED AGAIN...
THE TONE IS QUITE DIFFERENT...
...BUT I COULD SWEAR I'VE SEEN THIS SCENE BEFORE...
?

As a Reincarnated
ARISTOCRAT,
I'll Use My Appraisal Skill to
Rise in the World

As a Reincarnated
ARISTOCRAT,
I'll Use My Appraisal Skill to
Rise in the World

Chapter 13: Rosell Kischa

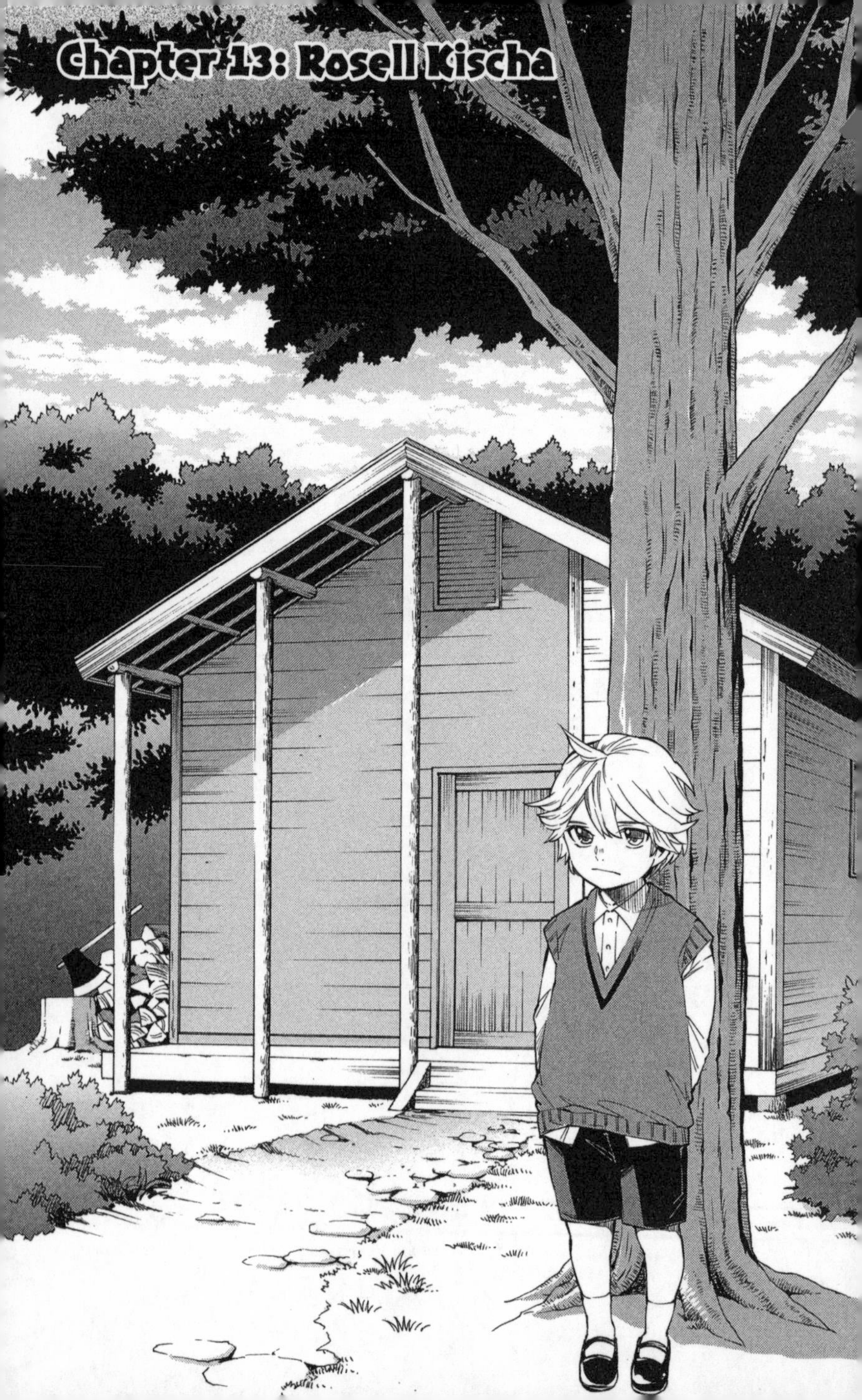

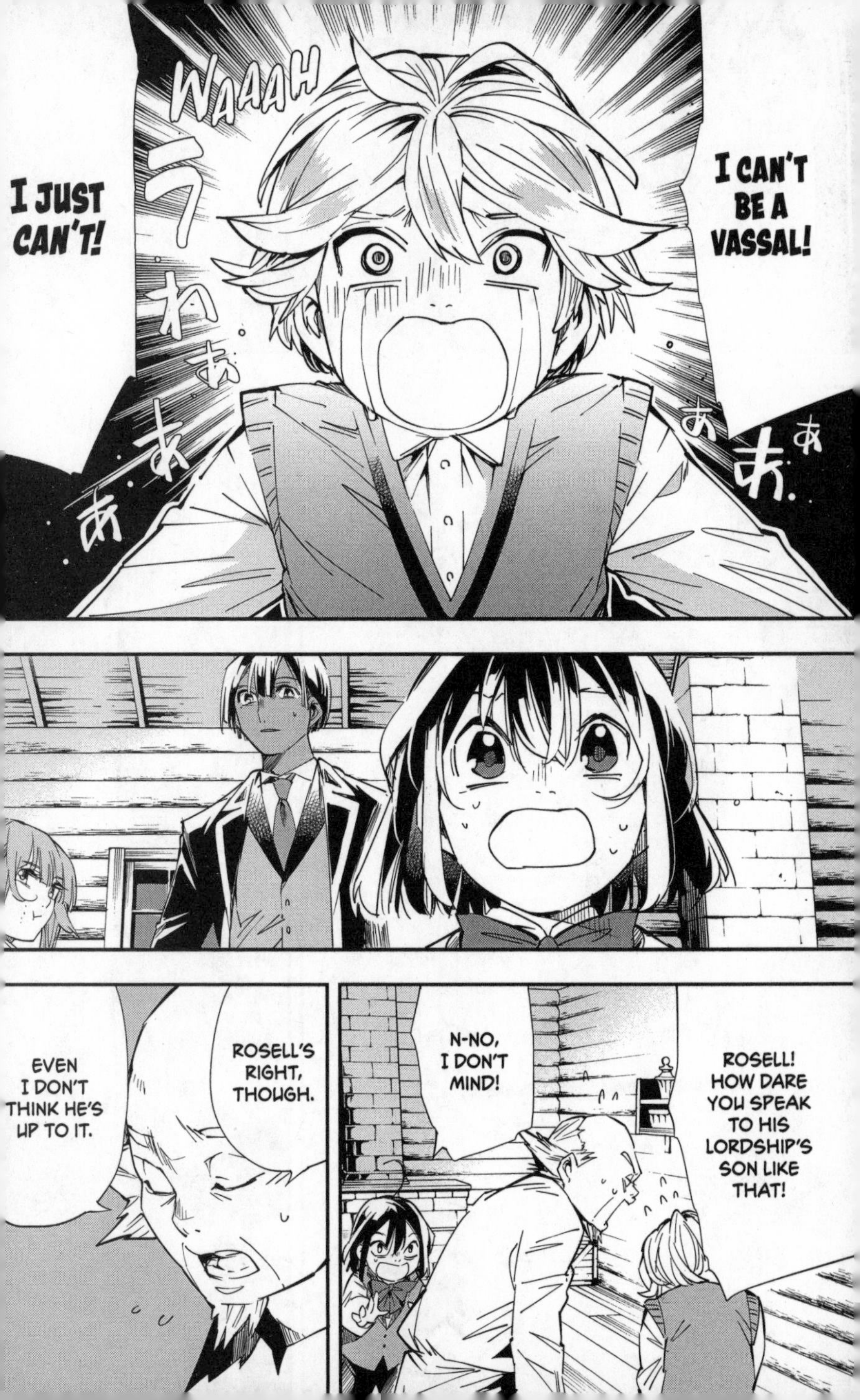
WAAAH
I CAN'T BE A VASSAL!
I JUST CAN'T!
うわぁああ
あああ
ROSELL! HOW DARE YOU SPEAK TO HIS LORDSHIP'S SON LIKE THAT!
N-NO, I DON'T MIND!
ROSELL'S RIGHT, THOUGH.
EVEN I DON'T THINK HE'S UP TO IT.

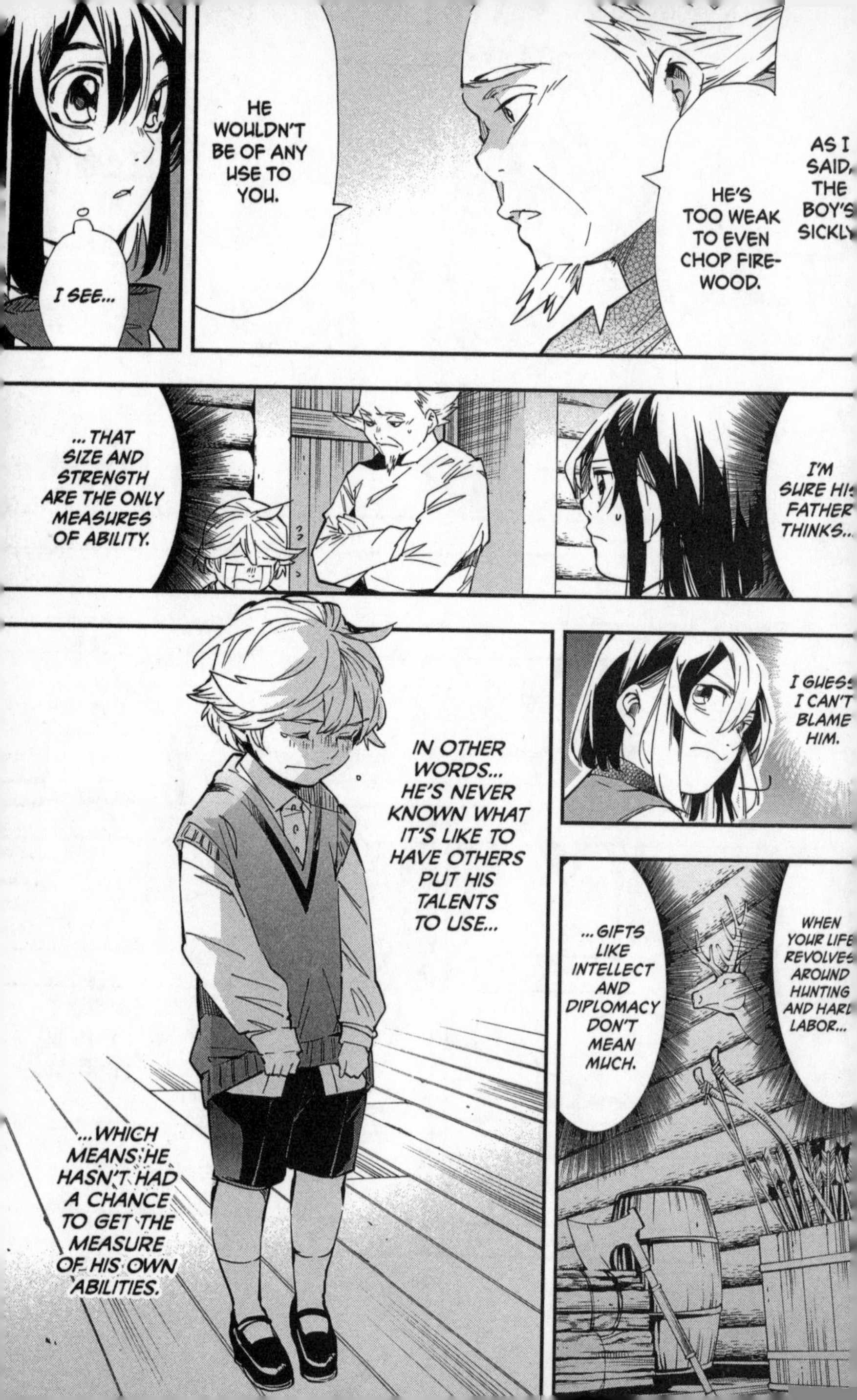
AS I SAID, THE BOY'S SICKLY.
HE'S TOO WEAK TO EVEN CHOP FIRE-WOOD.
HE WOULDN'T BE OF ANY USE TO YOU.
I SEE...
I'M SURE HIS FATHER THINKS...
...THAT SIZE AND STRENGTH ARE THE ONLY MEASURES OF ABILITY.
I GUESS I CAN'T BLAME HIM.
WHEN YOUR LIFE REVOLVES AROUND HUNTING AND HARD LABOR...
...GIFTS LIKE INTELLECT AND DIPLOMACY DON'T MEAN MUCH.
IN OTHER WORDS... HE'S NEVER KNOWN WHAT IT'S LIKE TO HAVE OTHERS PUT HIS TALENTS TO USE...
...WHICH MEANS HE HASN'T HAD A CHANCE TO GET THE MEASURE OF HIS OWN ABILITIES.

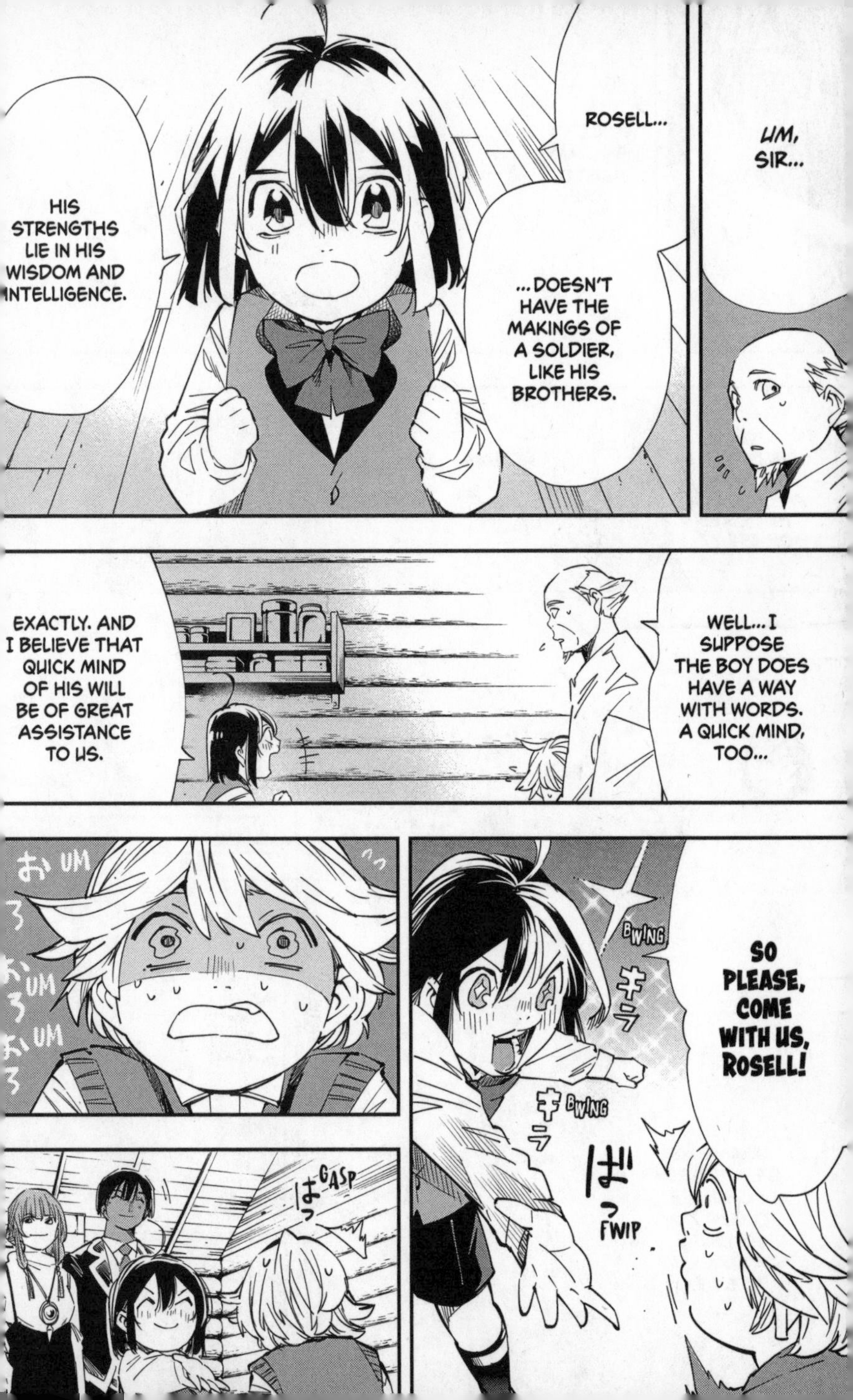
UM, SIR...
ROSELL...
...DOESN'T HAVE THE MAKINGS OF A SOLDIER, LIKE HIS BROTHERS.
HIS STRENGTHS LIE IN HIS WISDOM AND INTELLIGENCE.
WELL...I SUPPOSE THE BOY DOES HAVE A WAY WITH WORDS. A QUICK MIND, TOO...
EXACTLY. AND I BELIEVE THAT QUICK MIND OF HIS WILL BE OF GREAT ASSISTANCE TO US.
SO PLEASE, COME WITH US, ROSELL!
BWING
BWING
FWIP
UM
UM
UM
GASP

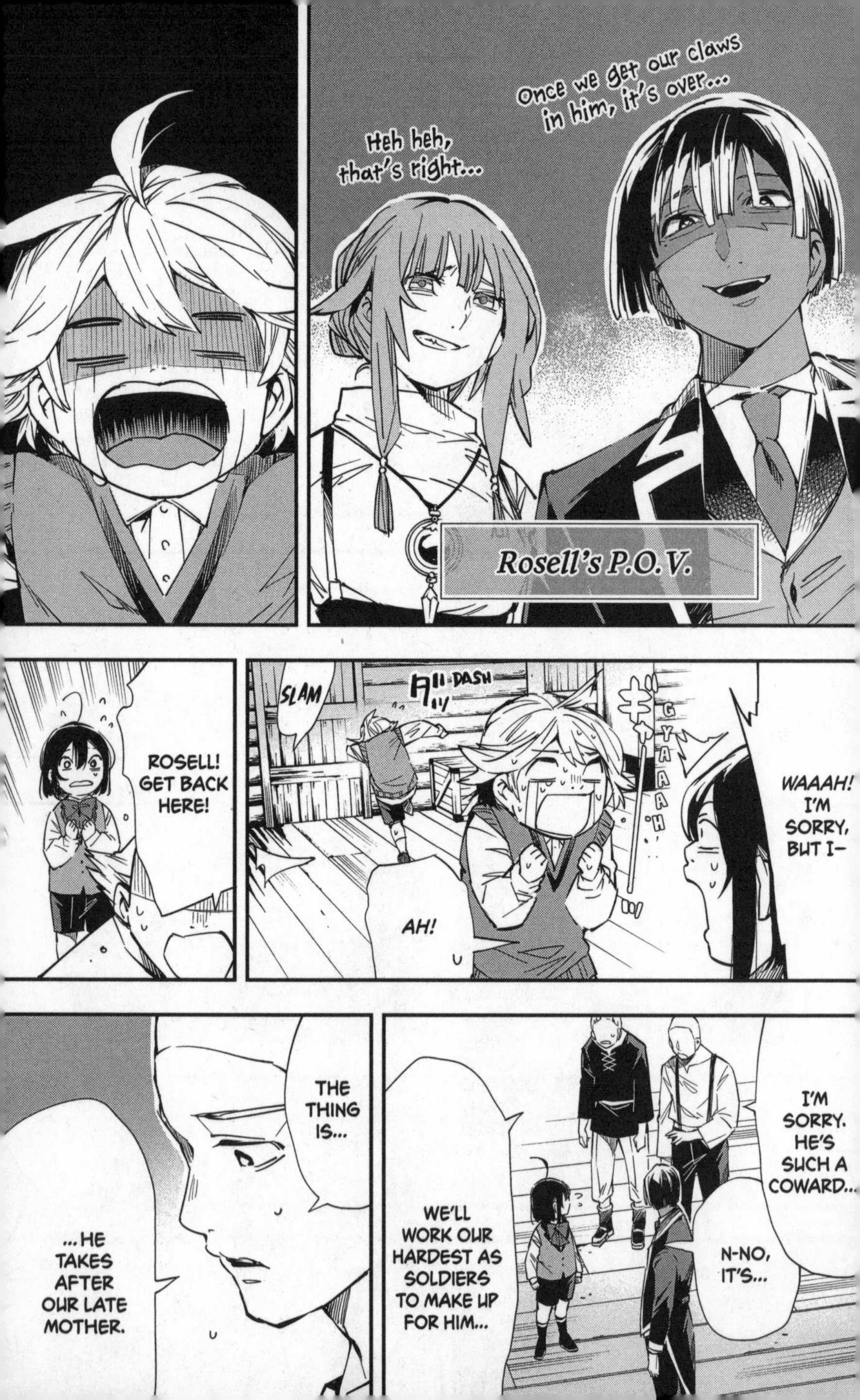

Once we get our claws in him, it's over...
Heh heh, that's right...
Rosell's P.O.V.
WAAAH! I'M SORRY, BUT I—
GYAAAAH
DASH
SLAM
AH!
ROSELL! GET BACK HERE!
I'M SORRY. HE'S SUCH A COWARD...
N-NO, IT'S...
WE'LL WORK OUR HARDEST AS SOLDIERS TO MAKE UP FOR HIM...
THE THING IS...
...HE TAKES AFTER OUR LATE MOTHER.

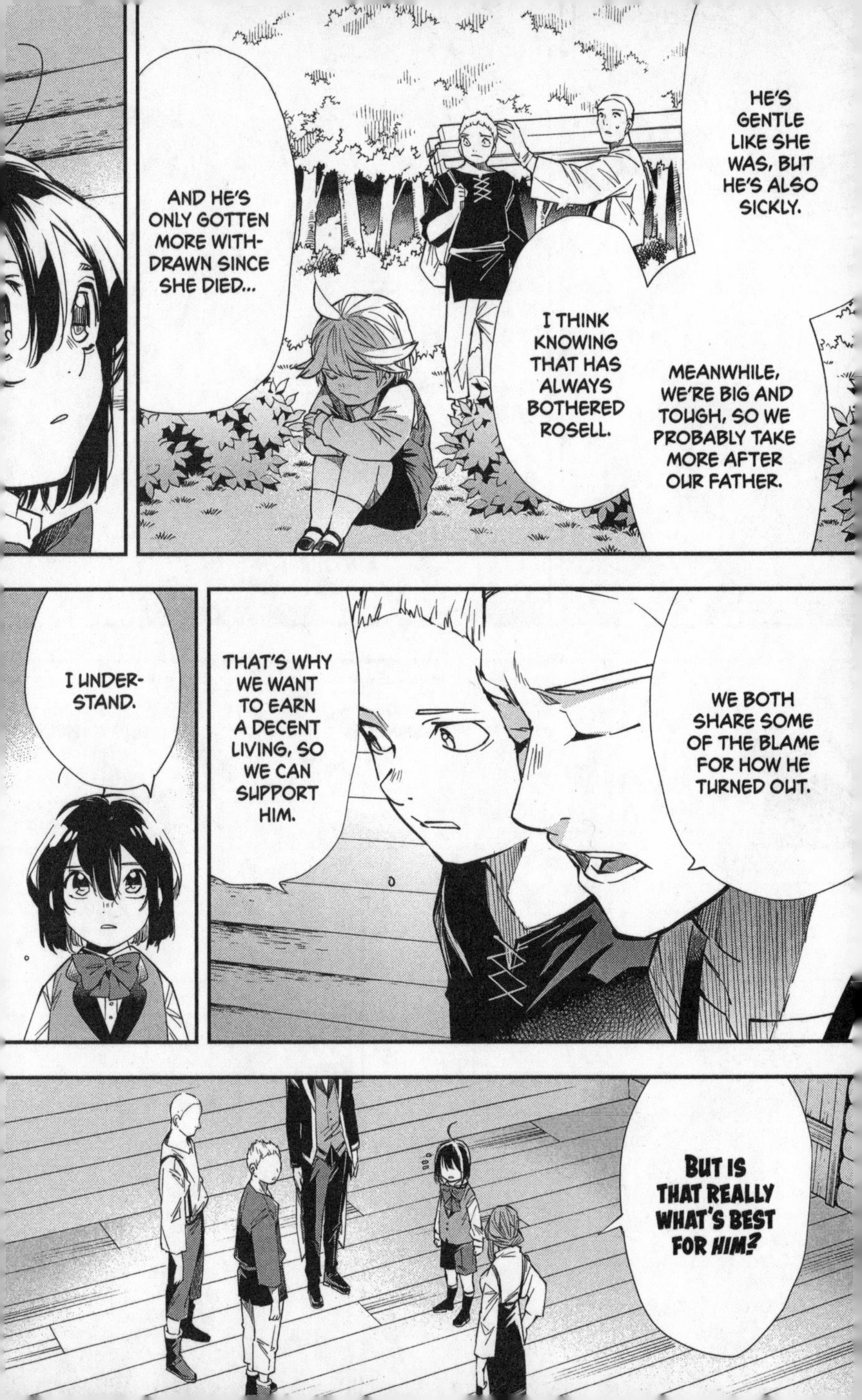
HE'S GENTLE LIKE SHE WAS, BUT HE'S ALSO SICKLY.
MEANWHILE, WE'RE BIG AND TOUGH, SO WE PROBABLY TAKE MORE AFTER OUR FATHER.
I THINK KNOWING THAT HAS ALWAYS BOTHERED ROSELL.
AND HE'S ONLY GOTTEN MORE WITH-DRAWN SINCE SHE DIED...
WE BOTH SHARE SOME OF THE BLAME FOR HOW HE TURNED OUT.
THAT'S WHY WE WANT TO EARN A DECENT LIVING, SO WE CAN SUPPORT HIM.
I UNDER-STAND.
BUT IS THAT REALLY WHAT'S BEST FOR *HIM*?

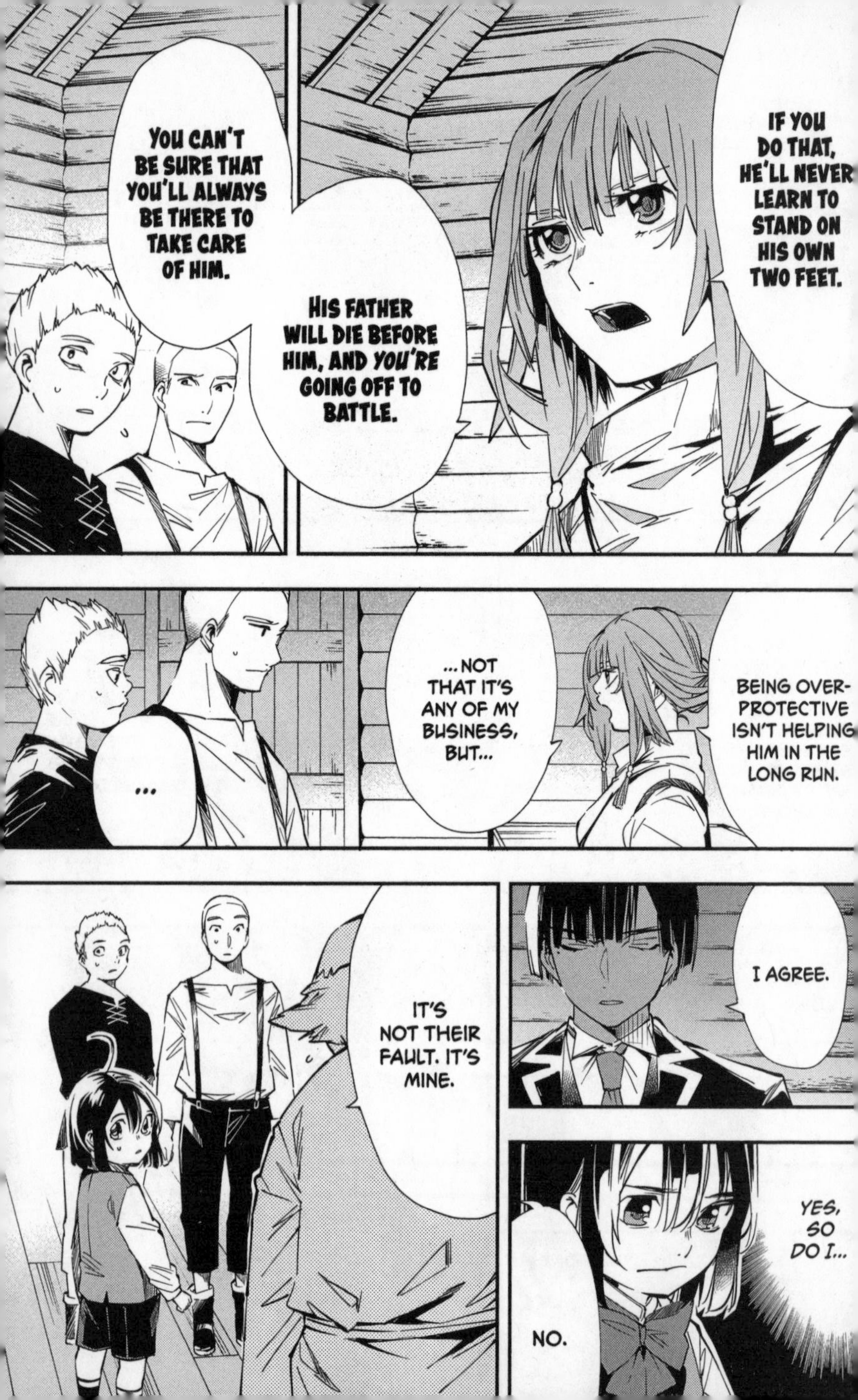
IF YOU DO THAT, HE'LL NEVER LEARN TO STAND ON HIS OWN TWO FEET.
YOU CAN'T BE SURE THAT YOU'LL ALWAYS BE THERE TO TAKE CARE OF HIM.
HIS FATHER WILL DIE BEFORE HIM, AND *YOU'RE* GOING OFF TO BATTLE.
BEING OVER-PROTECTIVE ISN'T HELPING HIM IN THE LONG RUN.
...NOT THAT IT'S ANY OF MY BUSINESS, BUT...
...
I AGREE.
YES, SO DO I...
NO.
IT'S NOT THEIR FAULT. IT'S MINE.

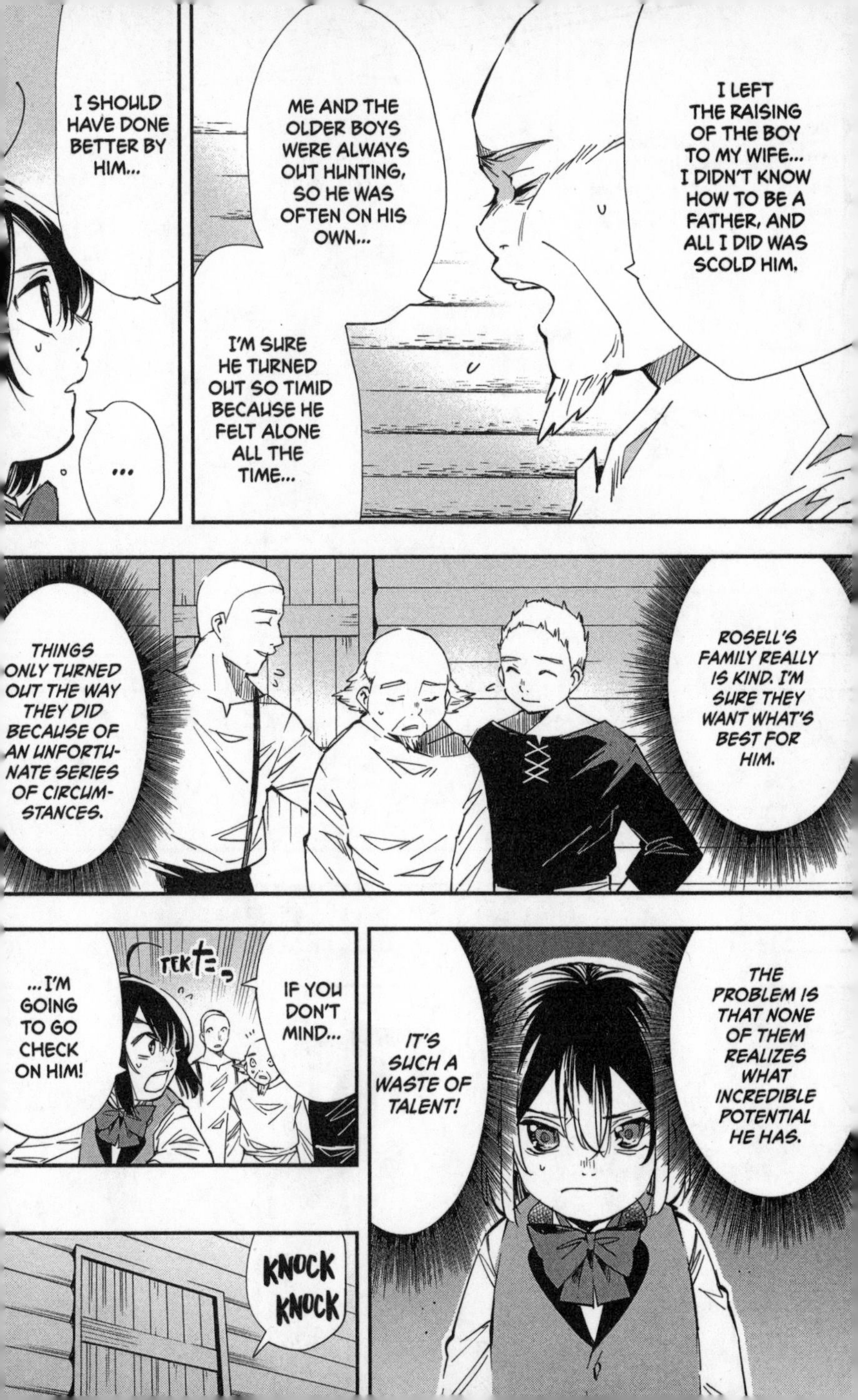
I LEFT THE RAISING OF THE BOY TO MY WIFE... I DIDN'T KNOW HOW TO BE A FATHER, AND ALL I DID WAS SCOLD HIM.
ME AND THE OLDER BOYS WERE ALWAYS OUT HUNTING, SO HE WAS OFTEN ON HIS OWN...
I'M SURE HE TURNED OUT SO TIMID BECAUSE HE FELT ALONE ALL THE TIME...
I SHOULD HAVE DONE BETTER BY HIM...
...
ROSELL'S FAMILY REALLY IS KIND. I'M SURE THEY WANT WHAT'S BEST FOR HIM.
THINGS ONLY TURNED OUT THE WAY THEY DID BECAUSE OF AN UNFORTUNATE SERIES OF CIRCUMSTANCES.
THE PROBLEM IS THAT NONE OF THEM REALIZES WHAT INCREDIBLE POTENTIAL HE HAS.
IT'S SUCH A WASTE OF TALENT!
IF YOU DON'T MIND...
TEK
...I'M GOING TO GO CHECK ON HIM!
KNOCK KNOCK

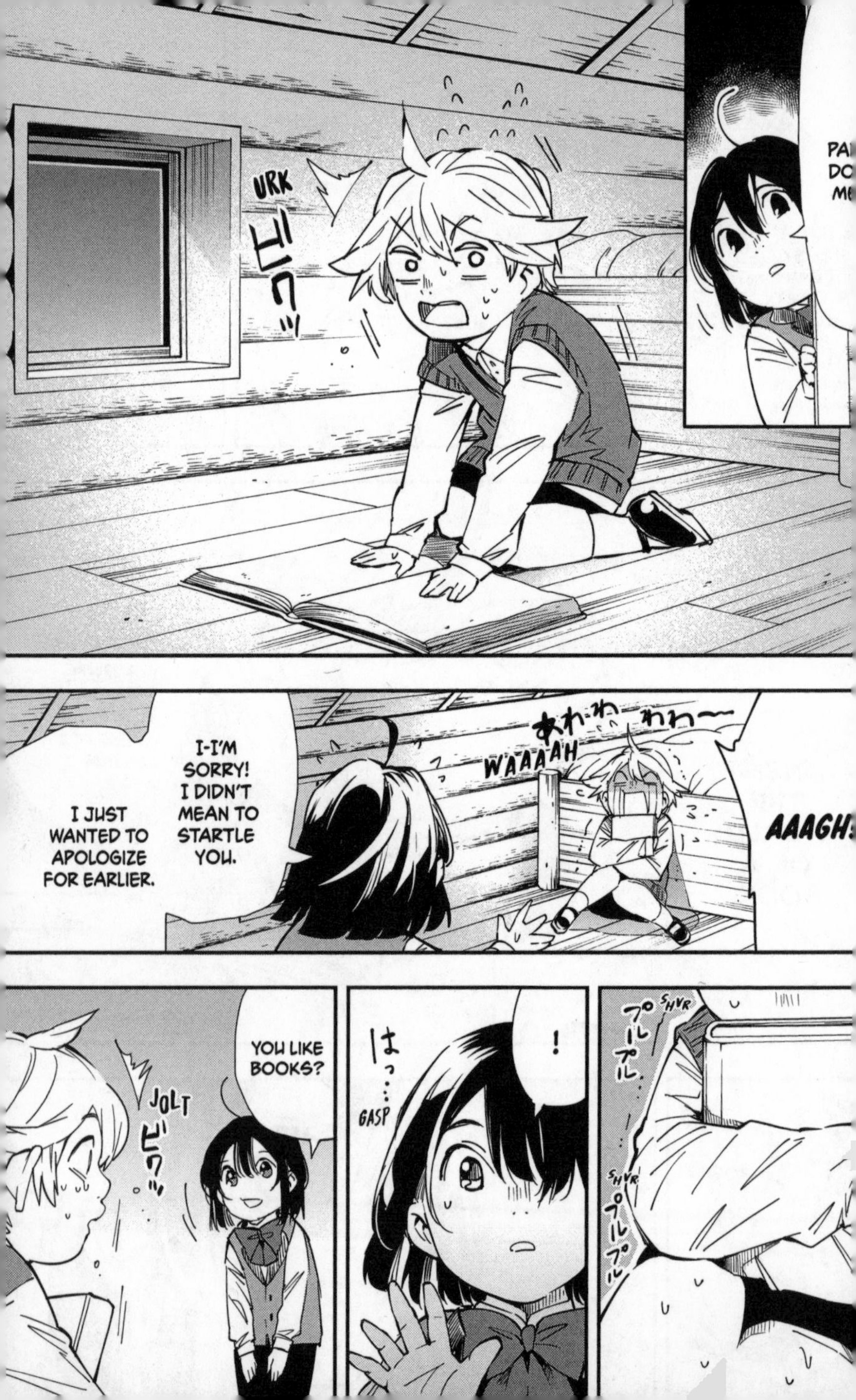
URK
ビクッ
AAAGH!
あわわ わわ〜
WAAAAH
I-I'M SORRY! I DIDN'T MEAN TO STARTLE YOU.
I JUST WANTED TO APOLOGIZE FOR EARLIER.
SHVR
プルプル
SHVR
プルプル
!
はっ…
GASP
YOU LIKE BOOKS?
JOLT
ビクッ

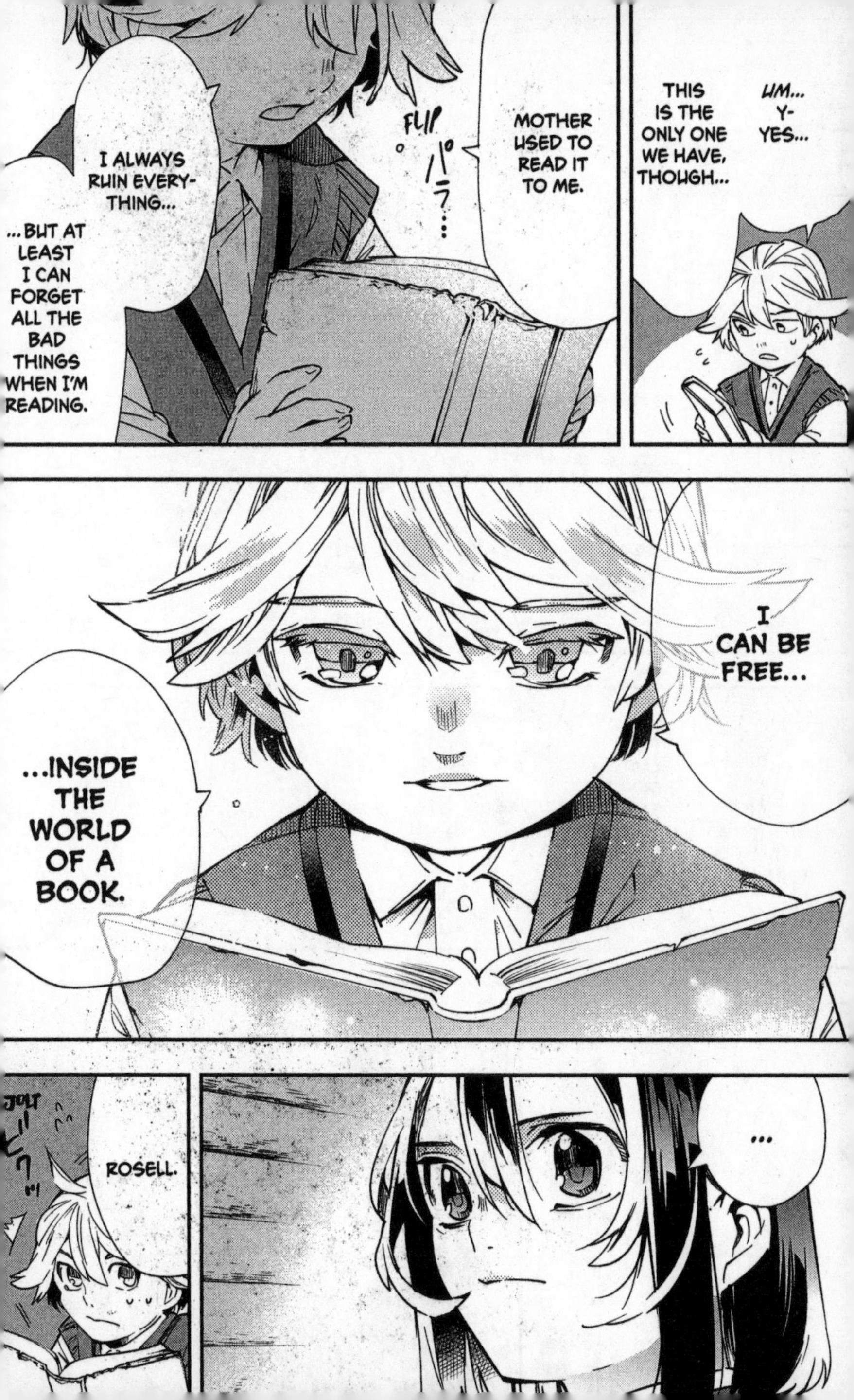

UM... Y-YES...
THIS IS THE ONLY ONE WE HAVE, THOUGH...
MOTHER USED TO READ IT TO ME.
FLIP
パラ…
I ALWAYS RUIN EVERYTHING...
...BUT AT LEAST I CAN FORGET ALL THE BAD THINGS WHEN I'M READING.
I CAN BE FREE...
...INSIDE THE WORLD OF A BOOK.
...
ROSELL.
JOLT

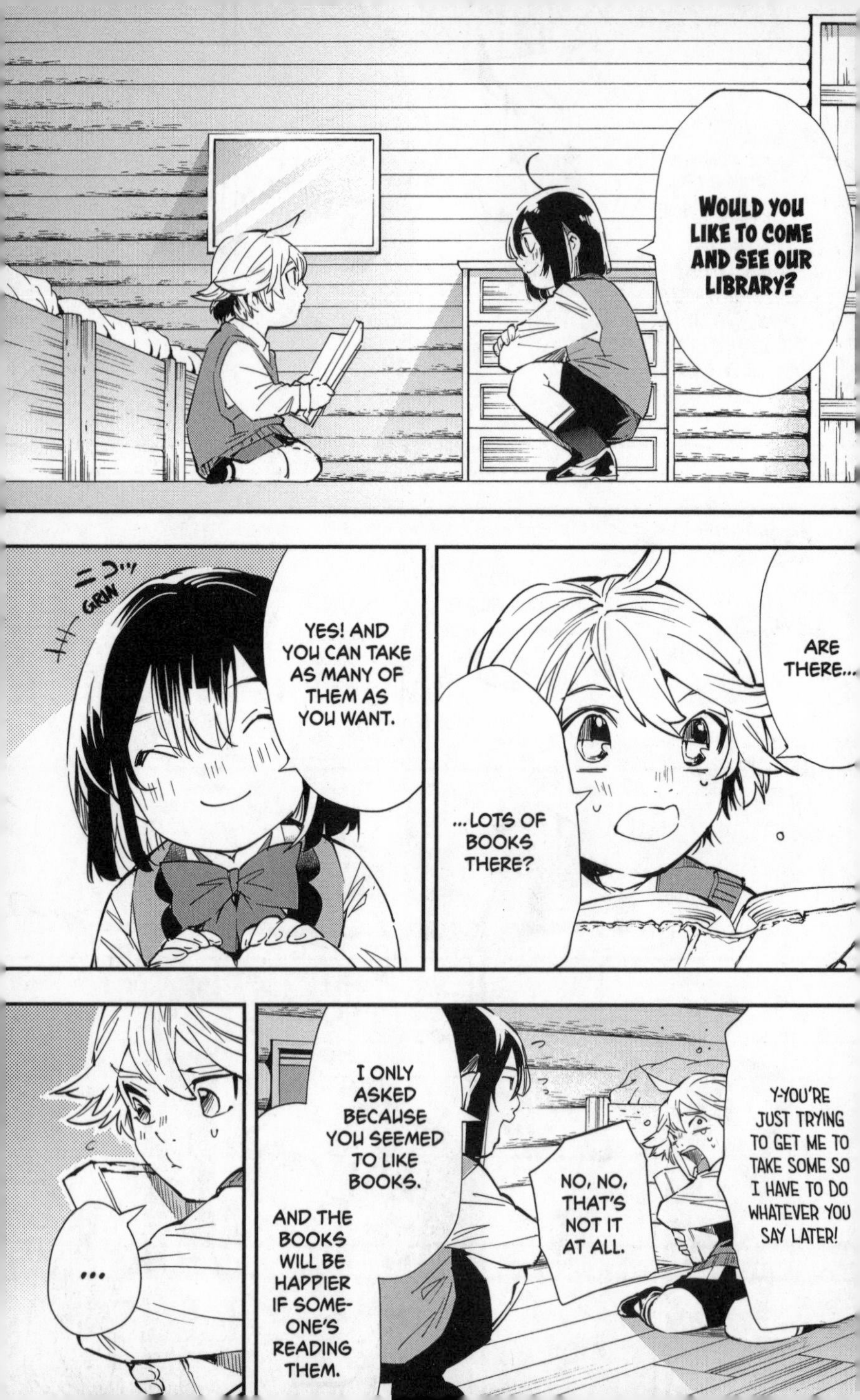

WOULD YOU LIKE TO COME AND SEE OUR LIBRARY?
ARE THERE...
...LOTS OF BOOKS THERE?
GRIN
YES! AND YOU CAN TAKE AS MANY OF THEM AS YOU WANT.
Y-YOU'RE JUST TRYING TO GET ME TO TAKE SOME SO I HAVE TO DO WHATEVER YOU SAY LATER!
NO, NO, THAT'S NOT IT AT ALL.
I ONLY ASKED BECAUSE YOU SEEMED TO LIKE BOOKS.
AND THE BOOKS WILL BE HAPPIER IF SOME-ONE'S READING THEM.
...

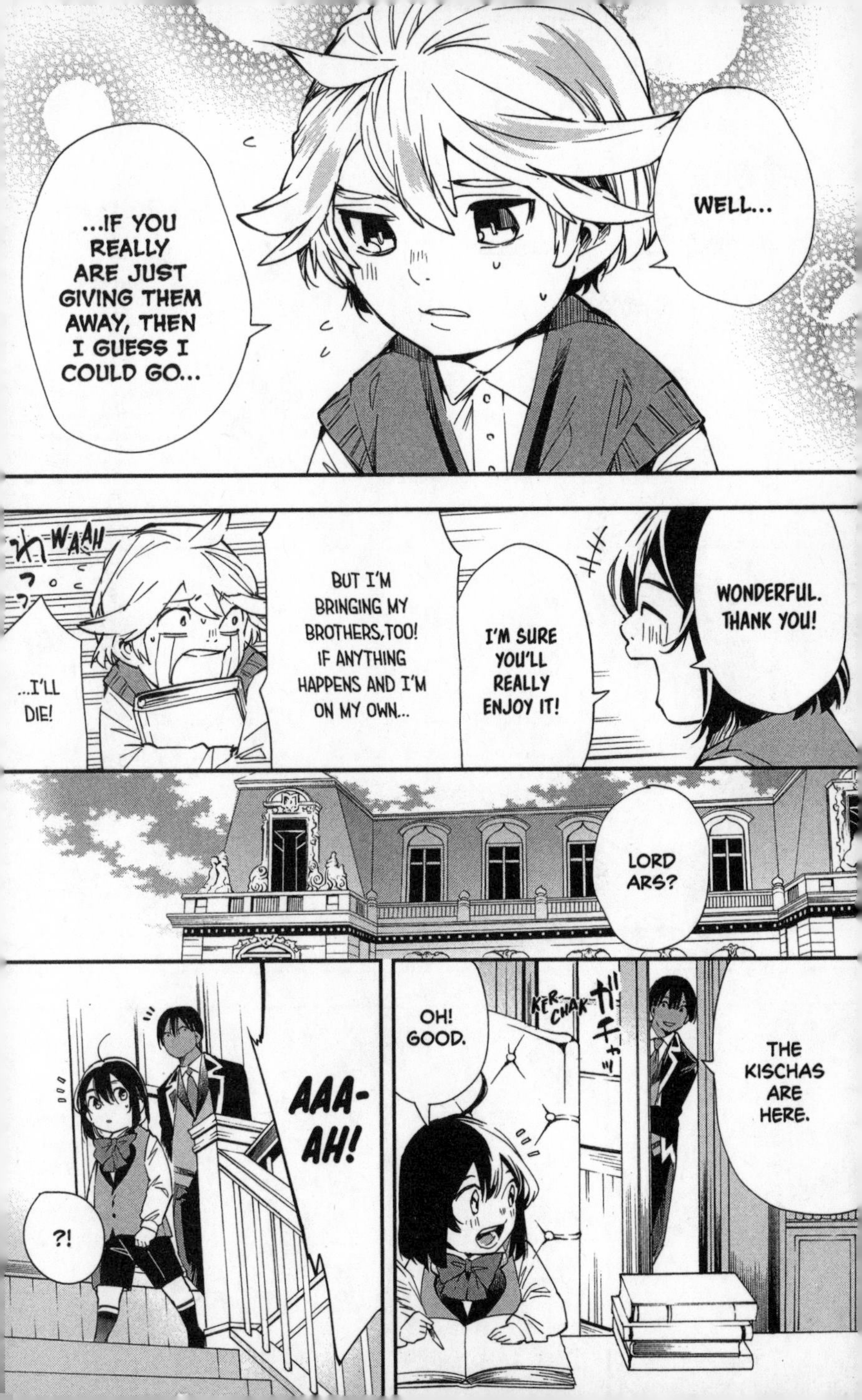
WELL...
...IF YOU REALLY ARE JUST GIVING THEM AWAY, THEN I GUESS I COULD GO...
WONDERFUL. THANK YOU!
I'M SURE YOU'LL REALLY ENJOY IT!
BUT I'M BRINGING MY BROTHERS, TOO! IF ANYTHING HAPPENS AND I'M ON MY OWN...
WAAH
...I'LL DIE!
LORD ARS?
THE KISCHAS ARE HERE.
KER-CHAK
OH! GOOD.
AAAA-AH!
?!

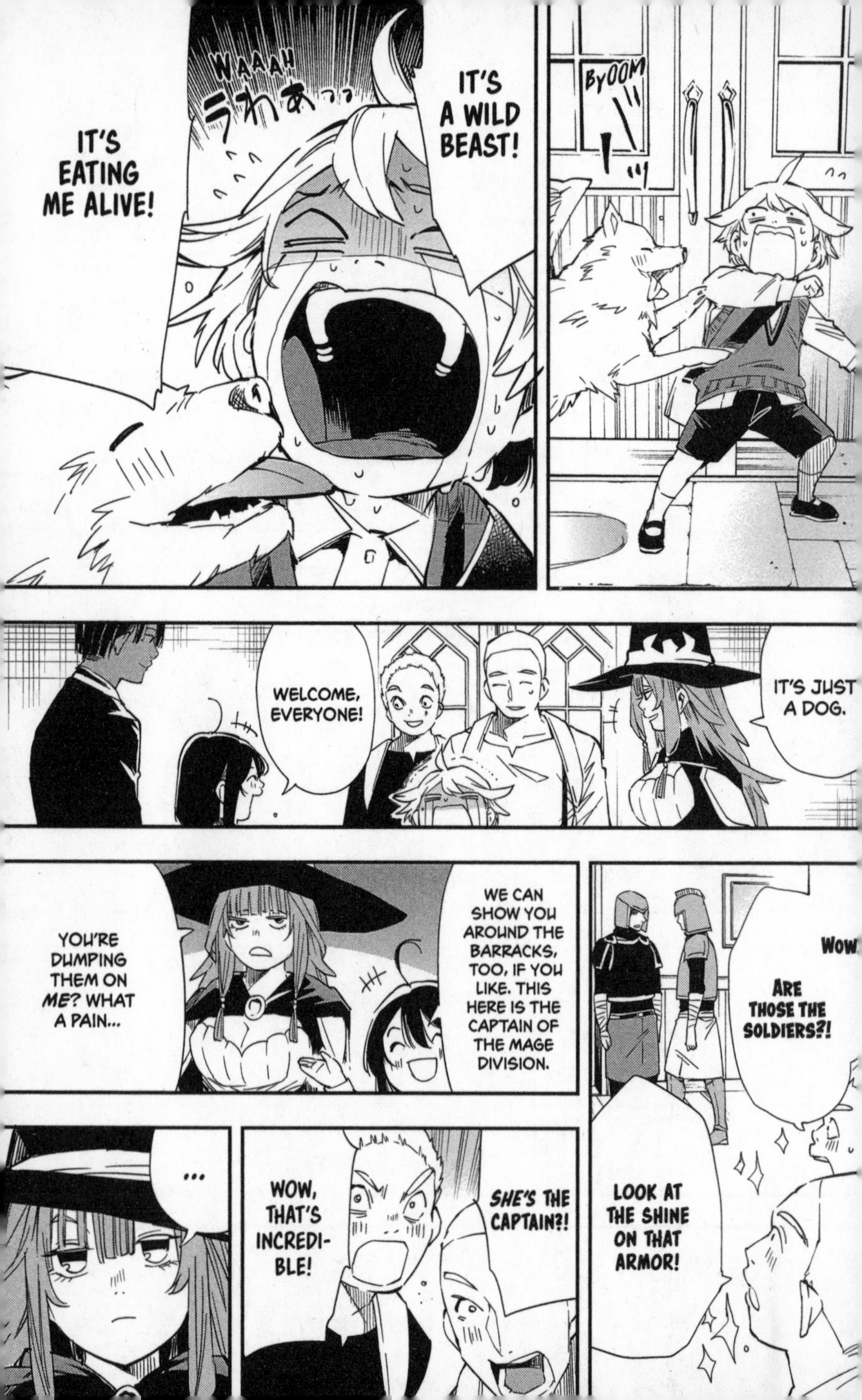
ByOOM
WAAAH
IT'S A WILD BEAST!
IT'S EATING ME ALIVE!
IT'S JUST A DOG.
WELCOME, EVERYONE!
WOW.
ARE THOSE THE SOLDIERS?!
LOOK AT THE SHINE ON THAT ARMOR!
WE CAN SHOW YOU AROUND THE BARRACKS, TOO, IF YOU LIKE. THIS HERE IS THE CAPTAIN OF THE MAGE DIVISION.
YOU'RE DUMPING THEM ON *ME*? WHAT A PAIN...
SHE'S THE CAPTAIN?!
WOW, THAT'S INCREDIBLE!
...

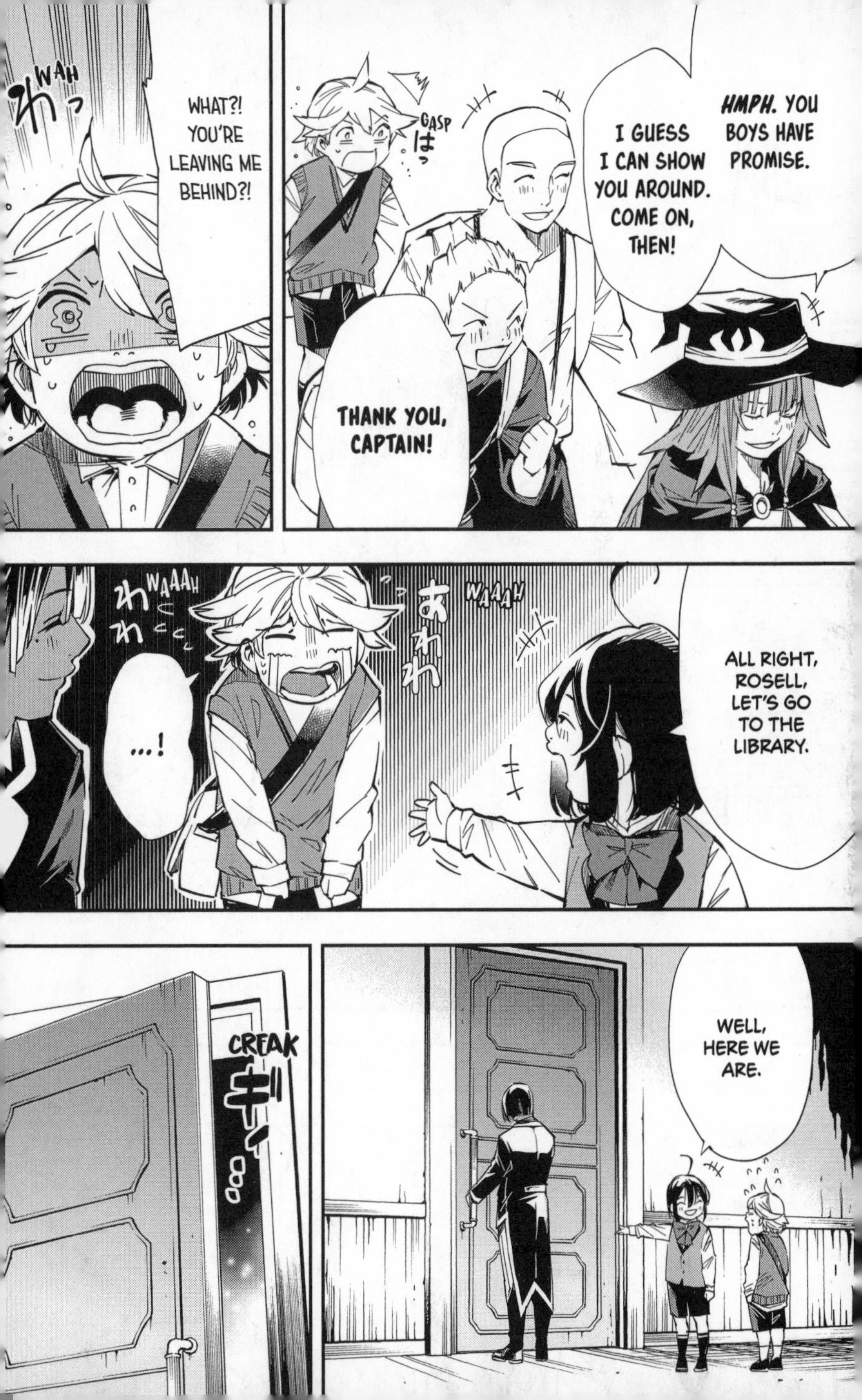
HMPH. YOU BOYS HAVE PROMISE.
I GUESS I CAN SHOW YOU AROUND. COME ON, THEN!
GASP
THANK YOU, CAPTAIN!
WAH
WHAT?! YOU'RE LEAVING ME BEHIND?!
ALL RIGHT, ROSELL, LET'S GO TO THE LIBRARY.
WAAAH
WAAAH
...!
WELL, HERE WE ARE.
CREAK

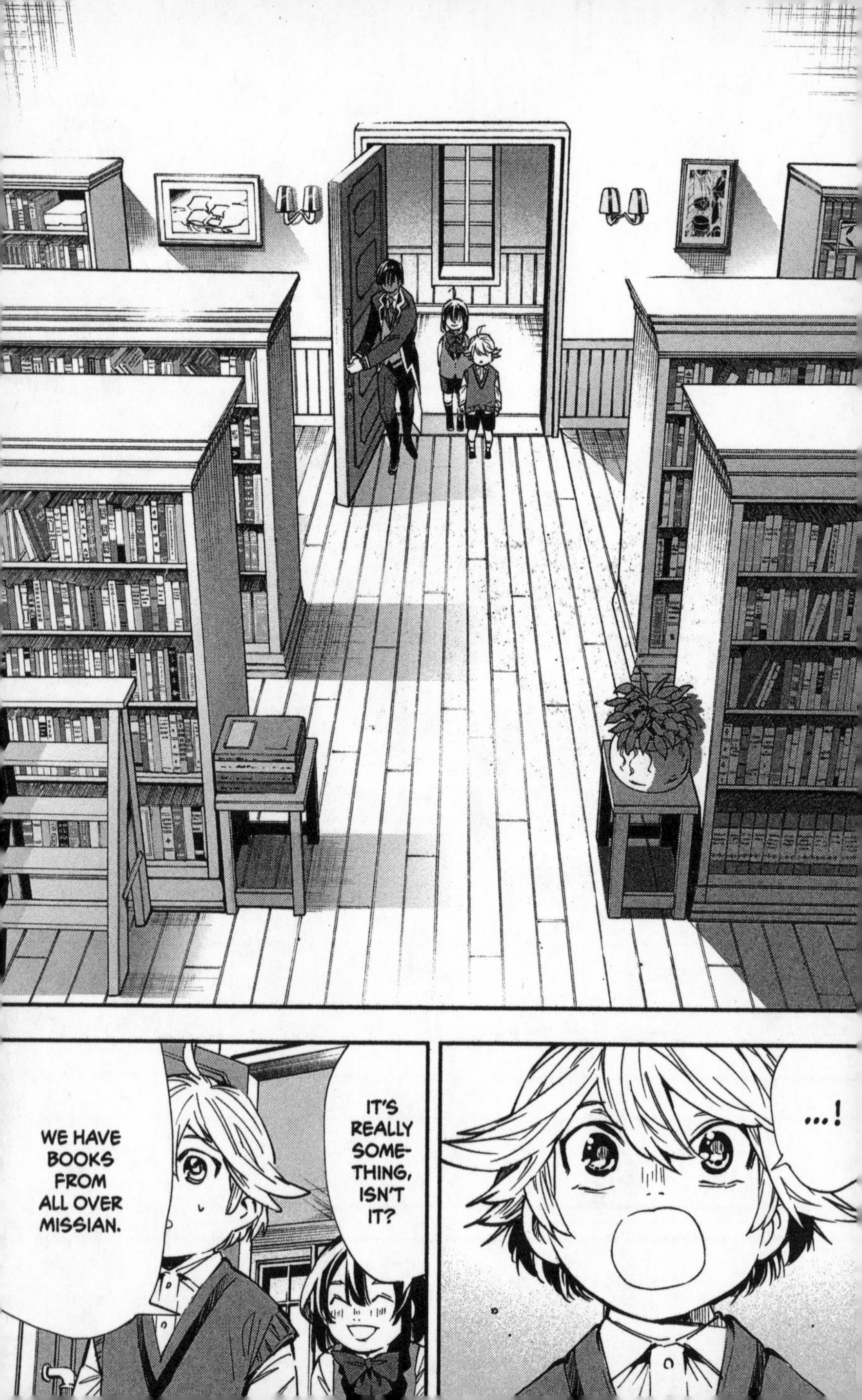
...!
IT'S REALLY SOMETHING, ISN'T IT?
WE HAVE BOOKS FROM ALL OVER MISSIAN.

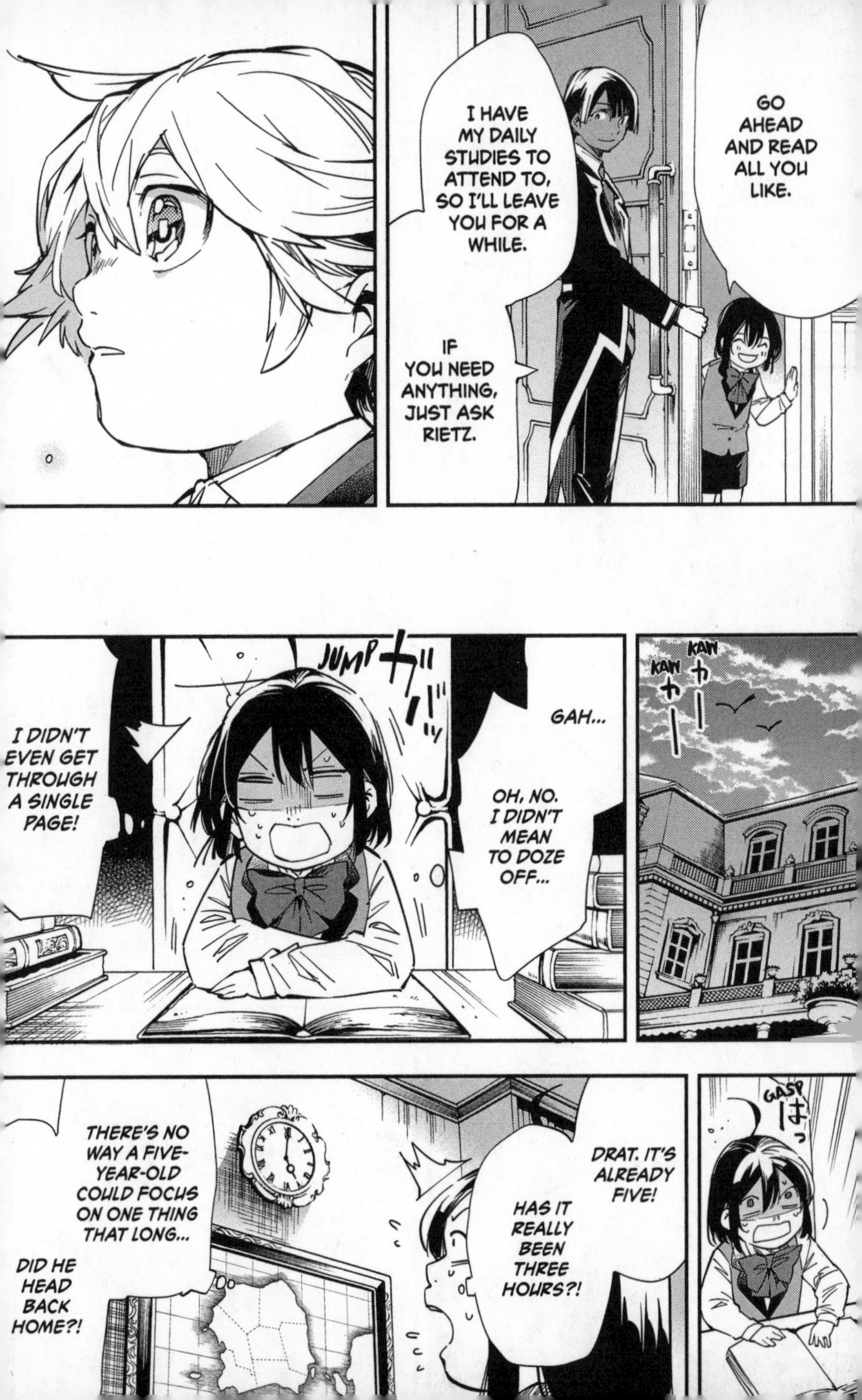
GO AHEAD AND READ ALL YOU LIKE.
I HAVE MY DAILY STUDIES TO ATTEND TO, SO I'LL LEAVE YOU FOR A WHILE.
IF YOU NEED ANYTHING, JUST ASK RIETZ.
KAW
KAW
JUMP
GAH...
OH, NO. I DIDN'T MEAN TO DOZE OFF...
I DIDN'T EVEN GET THROUGH A SINGLE PAGE!
GASP
DRAT. IT'S ALREADY FIVE!
HAS IT REALLY BEEN THREE HOURS?!
THERE'S NO WAY A FIVE-YEAR-OLD COULD FOCUS ON ONE THING THAT LONG...
DID HE HEAD BACK HOME?!

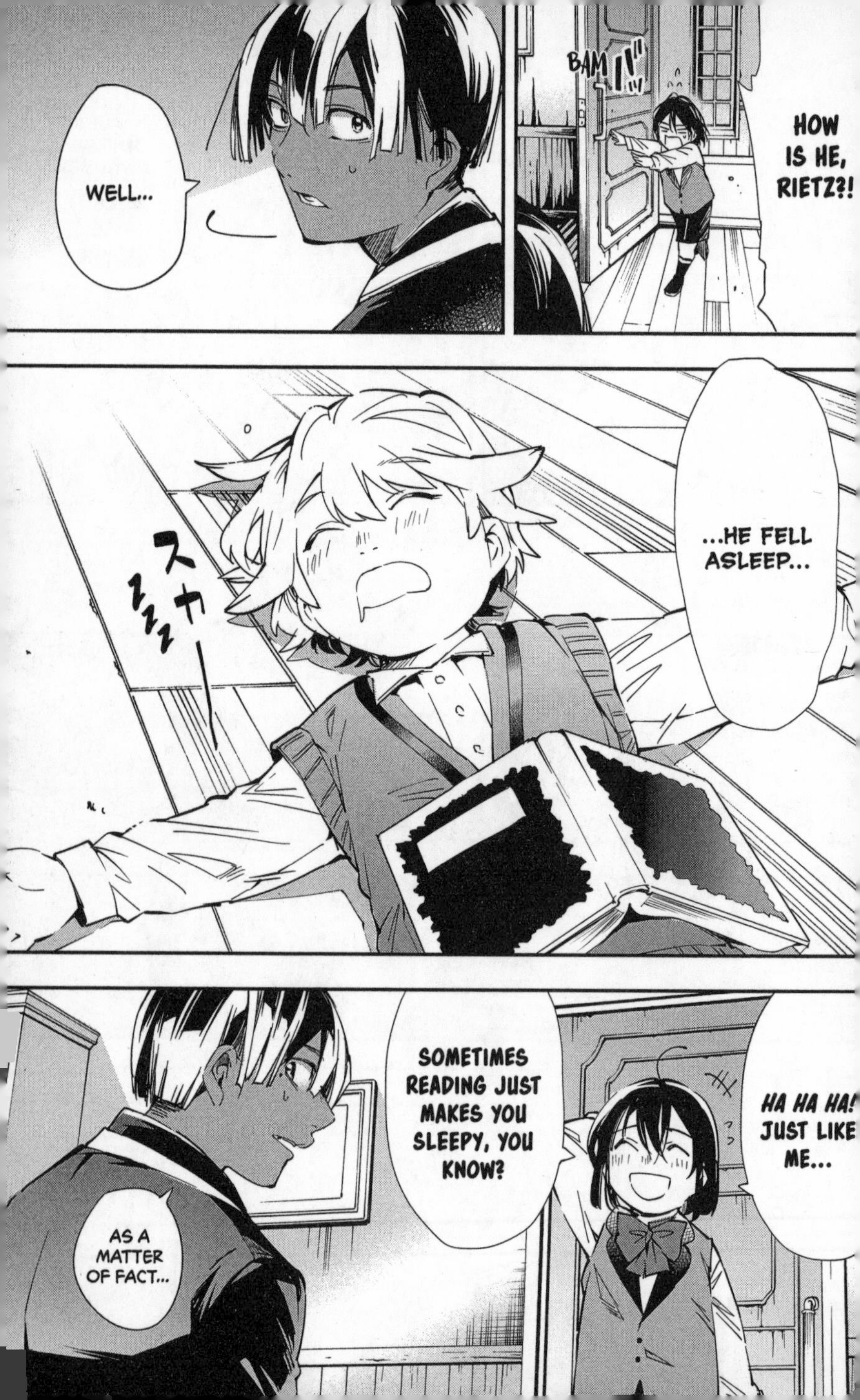
BAM
HOW IS HE, RIETZ?!
WELL...
...HE FELL ASLEEP...
スカー
ZZZZ
HA HA HA! JUST LIKE ME...
SOMETIMES READING JUST MAKES YOU SLEEPY, YOU KNOW?
AS A MATTER OF FACT...

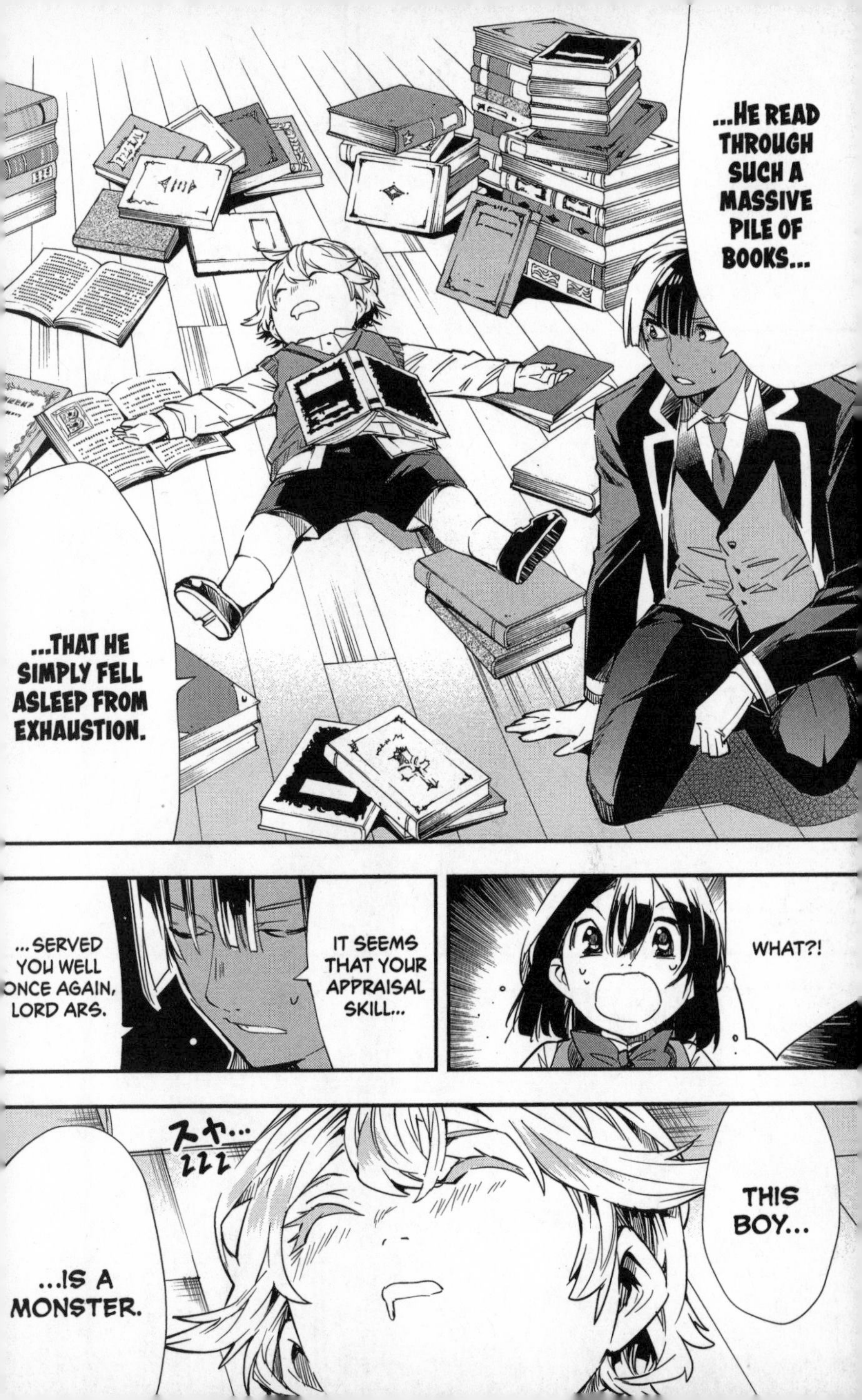
...HE READ THROUGH SUCH A MASSIVE PILE OF BOOKS...
...THAT HE SIMPLY FELL ASLEEP FROM EXHAUSTION.
WHAT?!
IT SEEMS THAT YOUR APPRAISAL SKILL...
...SERVED YOU WELL ONCE AGAIN, LORD ARS.
THIS BOY...
スヤ...
zzz
...IS A MONSTER.

As a Reincarnated
ARISTOCRAT,
I'll Use My Appraisal Skill to
Rise in the World

As a Reincarnated ARISTOCRAT, I'll Use My Appraisal Skill to Rise in the World

Chapter 14: Where Talent Lies

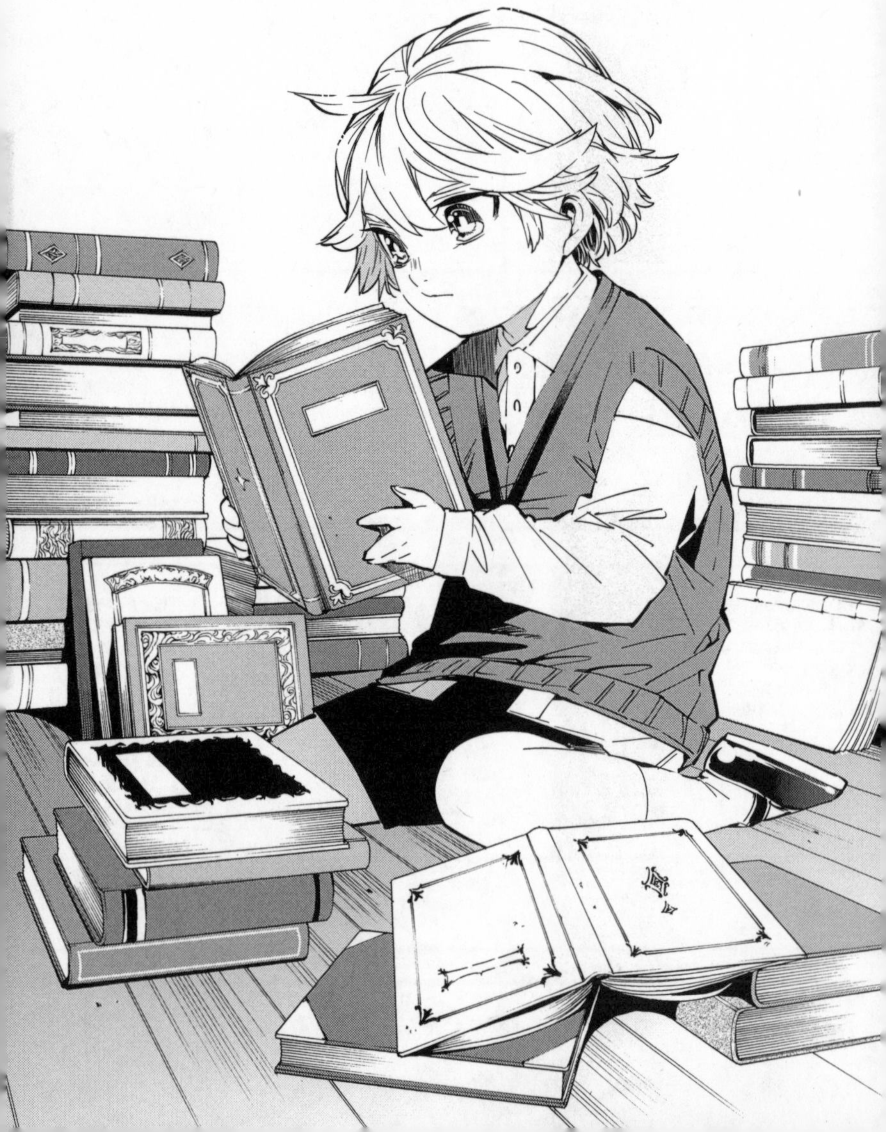

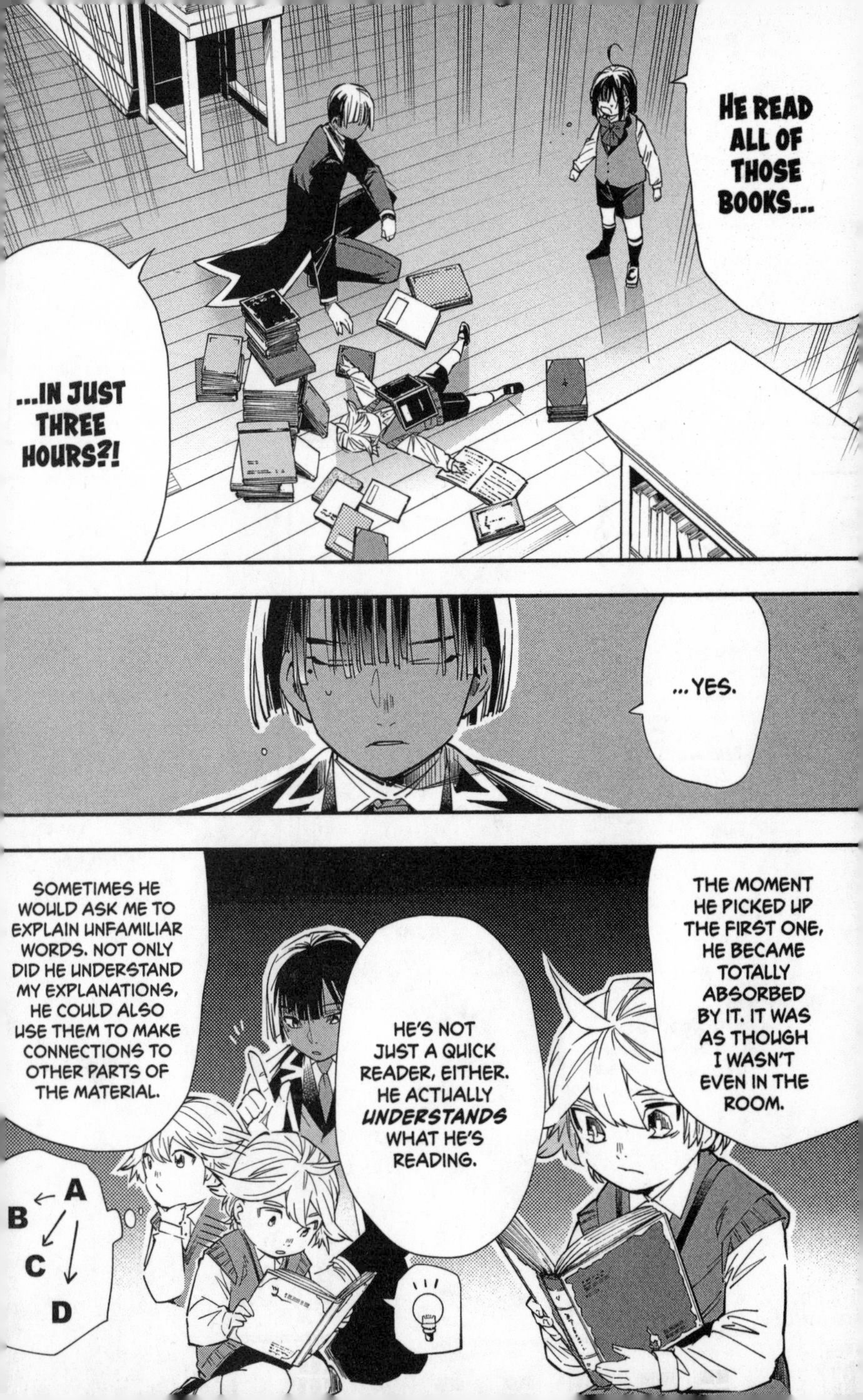
HE READ ALL OF THOSE BOOKS...
...IN JUST THREE HOURS?!
...YES.
THE MOMENT HE PICKED UP THE FIRST ONE, HE BECAME TOTALLY ABSORBED BY IT. IT WAS AS THOUGH I WASN'T EVEN IN THE ROOM.
HE'S NOT JUST A QUICK READER, EITHER. HE ACTUALLY *UNDERSTANDS* WHAT HE'S READING.
SOMETIMES HE WOULD ASK ME TO EXPLAIN UNFAMILIAR WORDS. NOT ONLY DID HE UNDERSTAND MY EXPLANATIONS, HE COULD ALSO USE THEM TO MAKE CONNECTIONS TO OTHER PARTS OF THE MATERIAL.
A
B
C
D

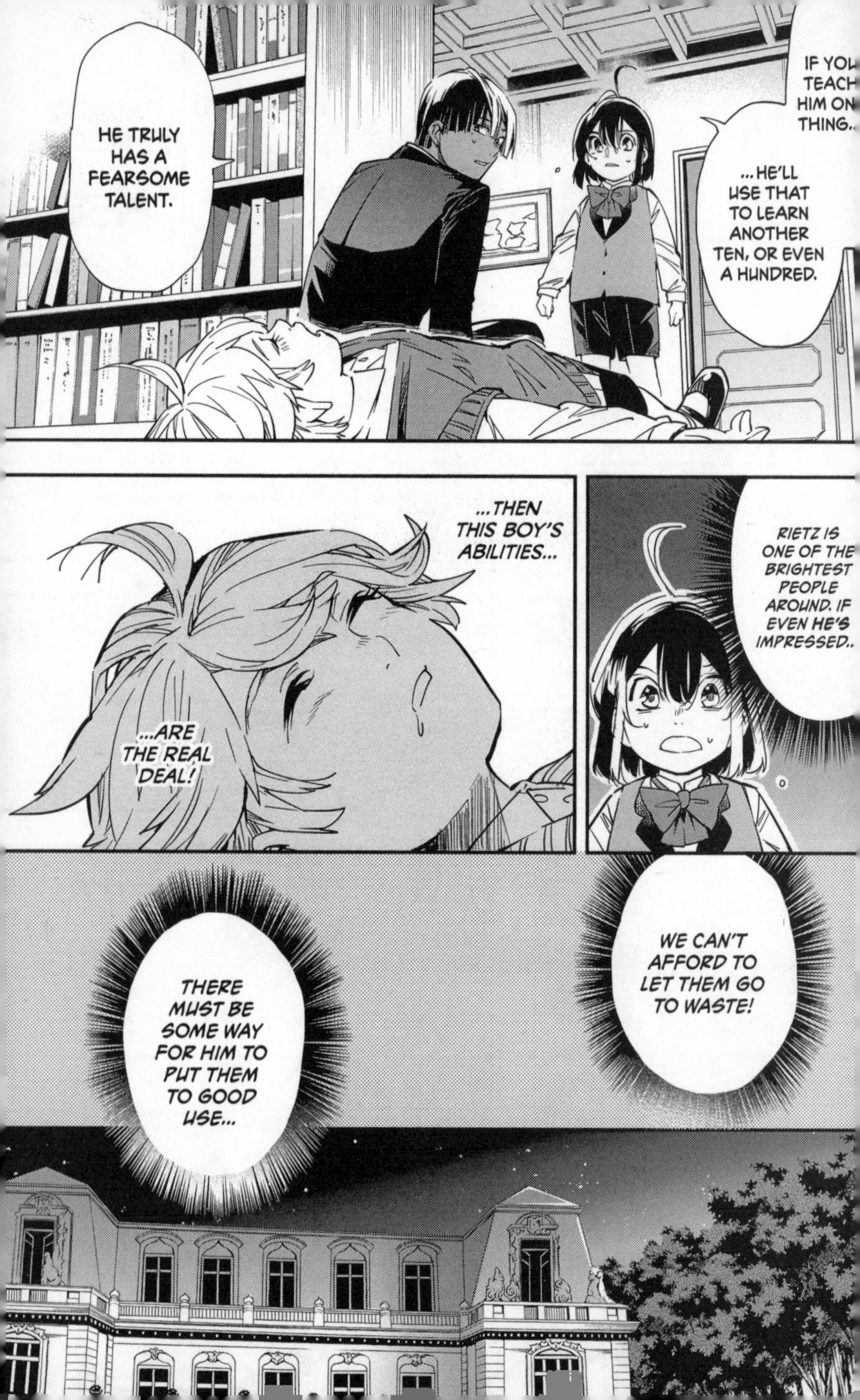
IF YOU TEACH HIM ONE THING...
...HE'LL USE THAT TO LEARN ANOTHER TEN, OR EVEN A HUNDRED.
HE TRULY HAS A FEARSOME TALENT.
RIETZ IS ONE OF THE BRIGHTEST PEOPLE AROUND. IF EVEN HE'S IMPRESSED...
...THEN THIS BOY'S ABILITIES...
...ARE THE REAL DEAL!
WE CAN'T AFFORD TO LET THEM GO TO WASTE!
THERE MUST BE SOME WAY FOR HIM TO PUT THEM TO GOOD USE...

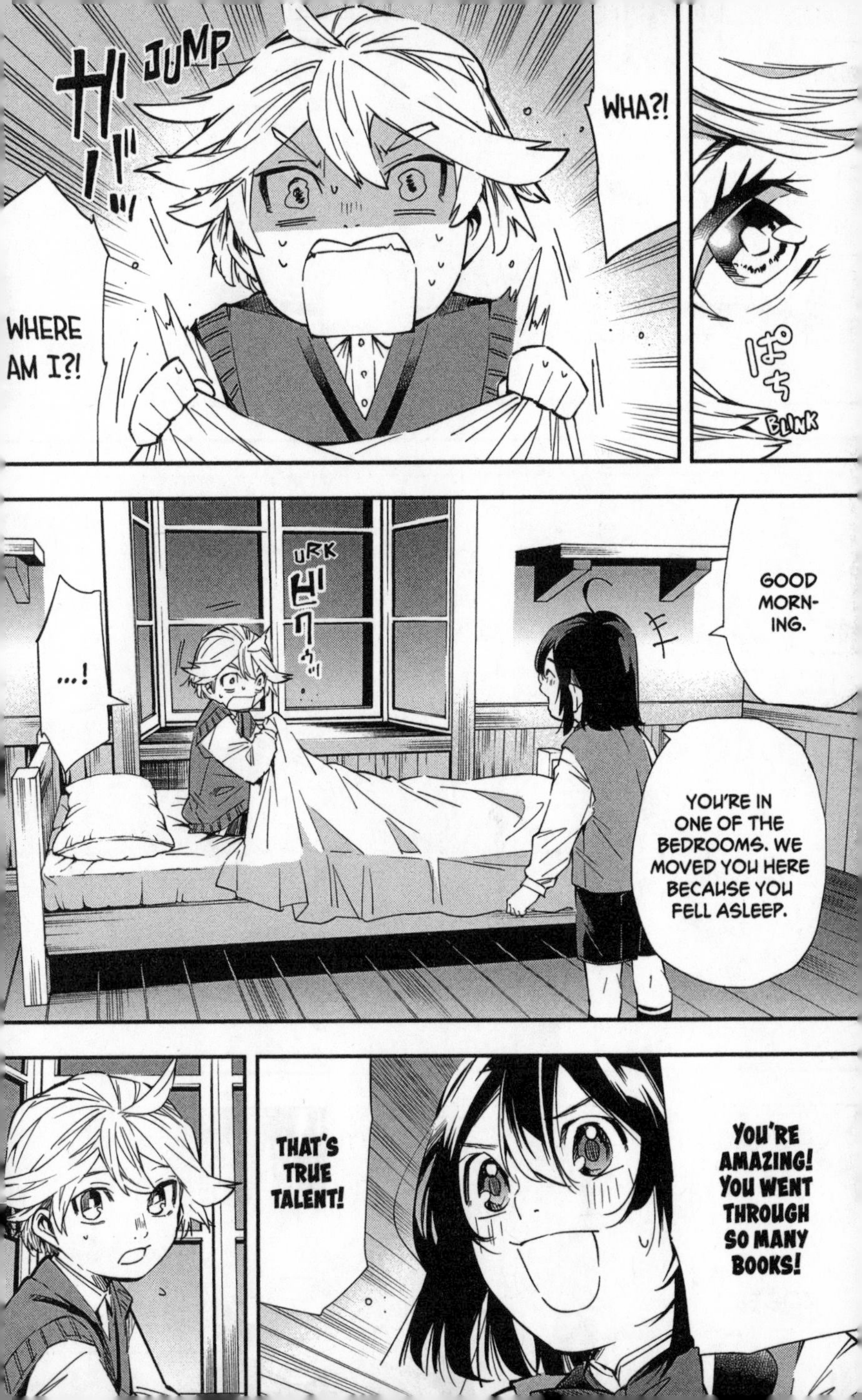
ぱち
BLINK
WHA?!
JUMP
WHERE AM I?!
GOOD MORNING.
URK
...!
YOU'RE IN ONE OF THE BEDROOMS. WE MOVED YOU HERE BECAUSE YOU FELL ASLEEP.
YOU'RE AMAZING! YOU WENT THROUGH SO MANY BOOKS!
THAT'S TRUE TALENT!

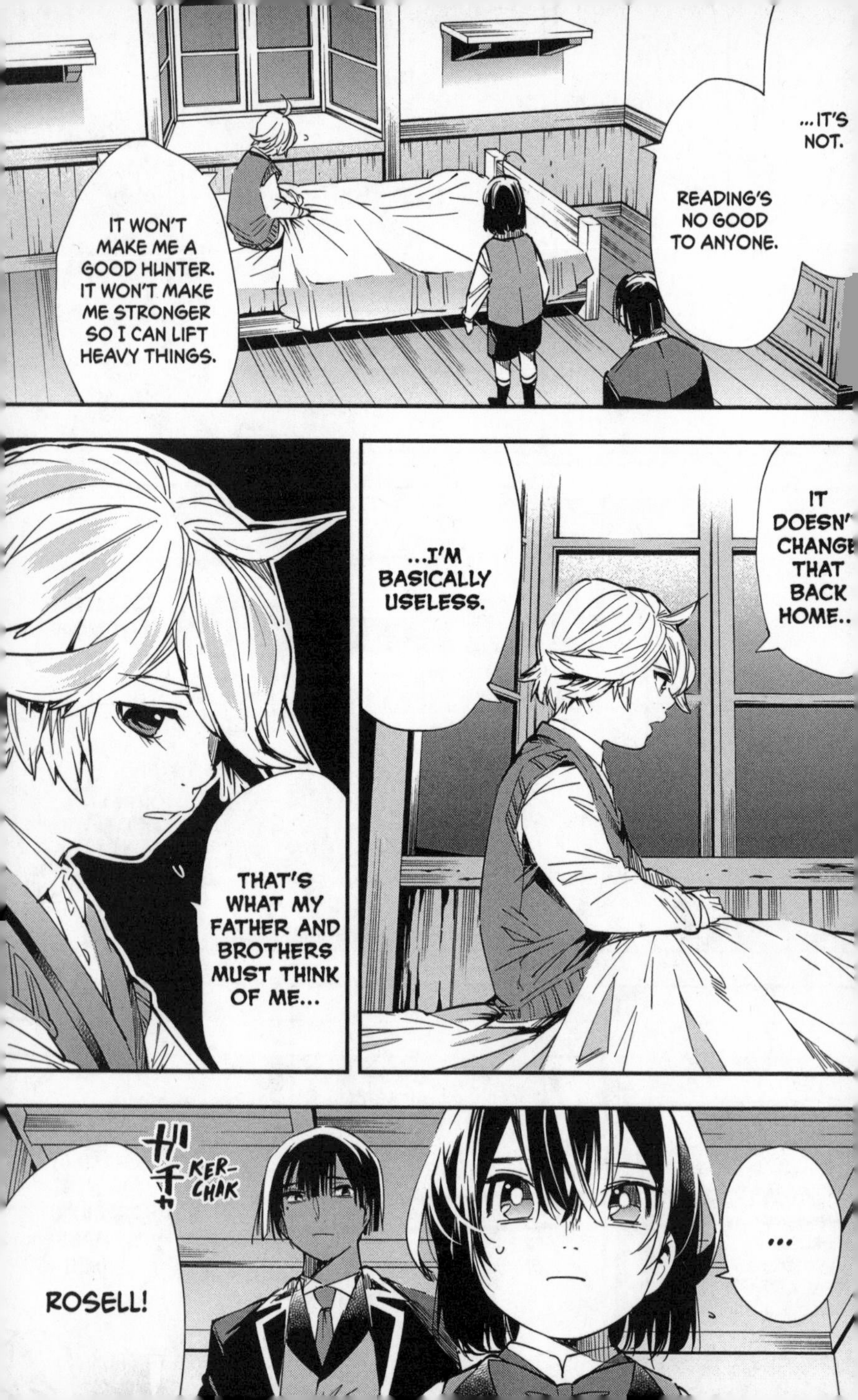
...IT'S NOT.
READING'S NO GOOD TO ANYONE.
IT WON'T MAKE ME A GOOD HUNTER. IT WON'T MAKE ME STRONGER SO I CAN LIFT HEAVY THINGS.
IT DOESN' CHANGE THAT BACK HOME..
...I'M BASICALLY USELESS.
THAT'S WHAT MY FATHER AND BROTHERS MUST THINK OF ME...
...
ガチャ
KER-CHAK
ROSELL!

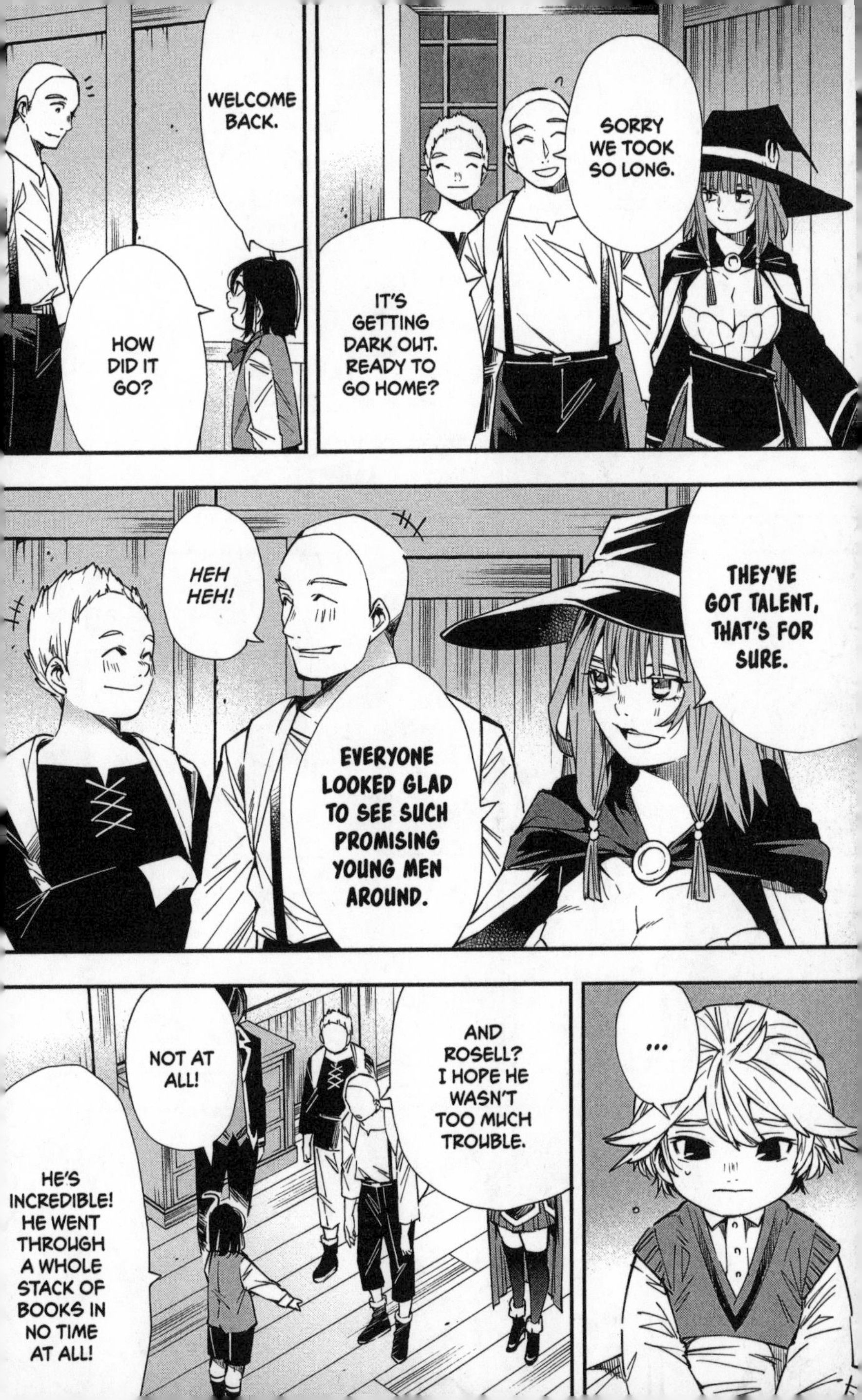
SORRY WE TOOK SO LONG.
IT'S GETTING DARK OUT. READY TO GO HOME?
WELCOME BACK.
HOW DID IT GO?
THEY'VE GOT TALENT, THAT'S FOR SURE.
EVERYONE LOOKED GLAD TO SEE SUCH PROMISING YOUNG MEN AROUND.
HEH HEH!
...
AND ROSELL? I HOPE HE WASN'T TOO MUCH TROUBLE.
NOT AT ALL!
HE'S INCREDIBLE! HE WENT THROUGH A WHOLE STACK OF BOOKS IN NO TIME AT ALL!

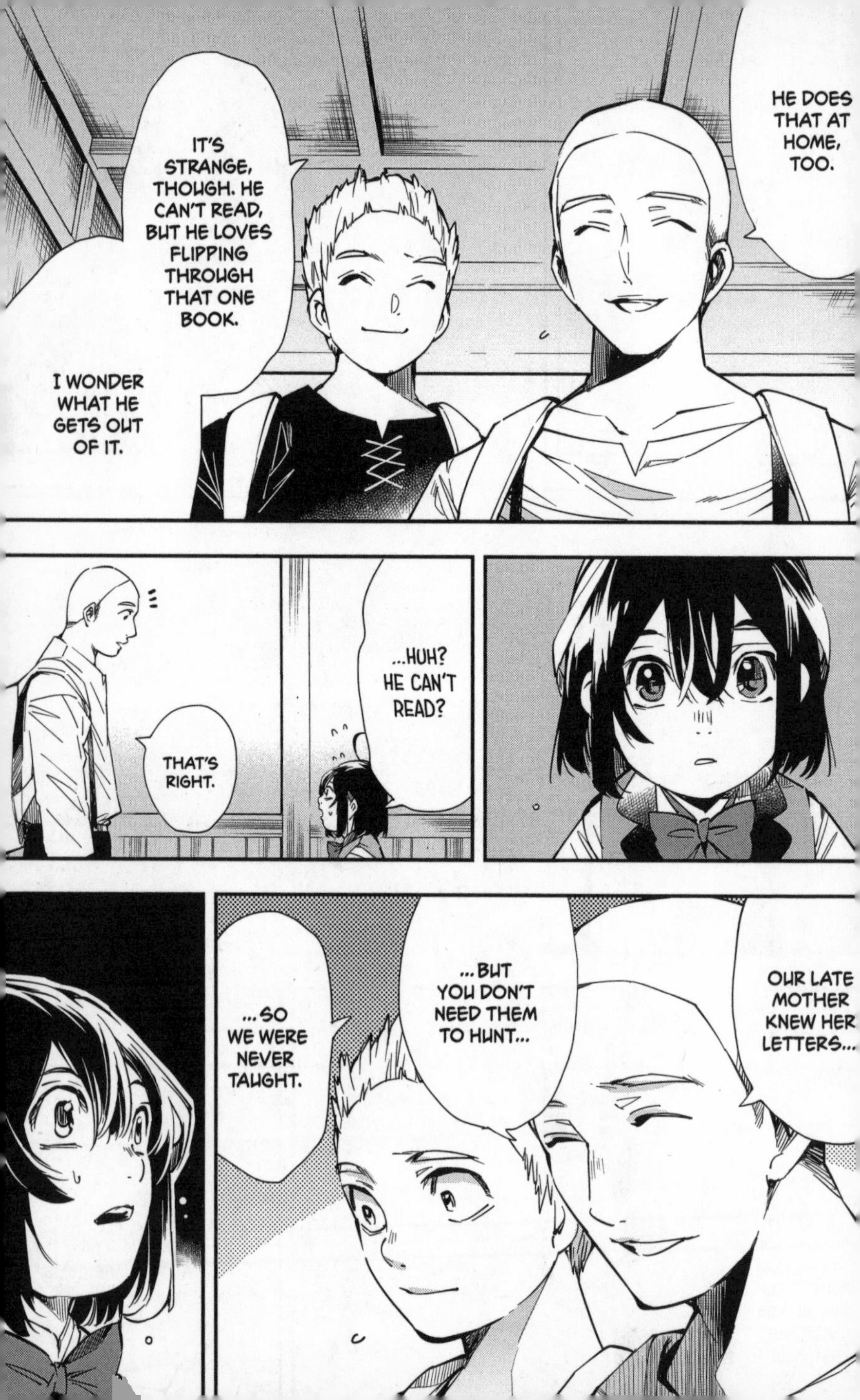
HE DOES THAT AT HOME, TOO.
IT'S STRANGE, THOUGH. HE CAN'T READ, BUT HE LOVES FLIPPING THROUGH THAT ONE BOOK.
I WONDER WHAT HE GETS OUT OF IT.
...HUH? HE CAN'T READ?
THAT'S RIGHT.
OUR LATE MOTHER KNEW HER LETTERS...
...BUT YOU DON'T NEED THEM TO HUNT...
...SO WE WERE NEVER TAUGHT.

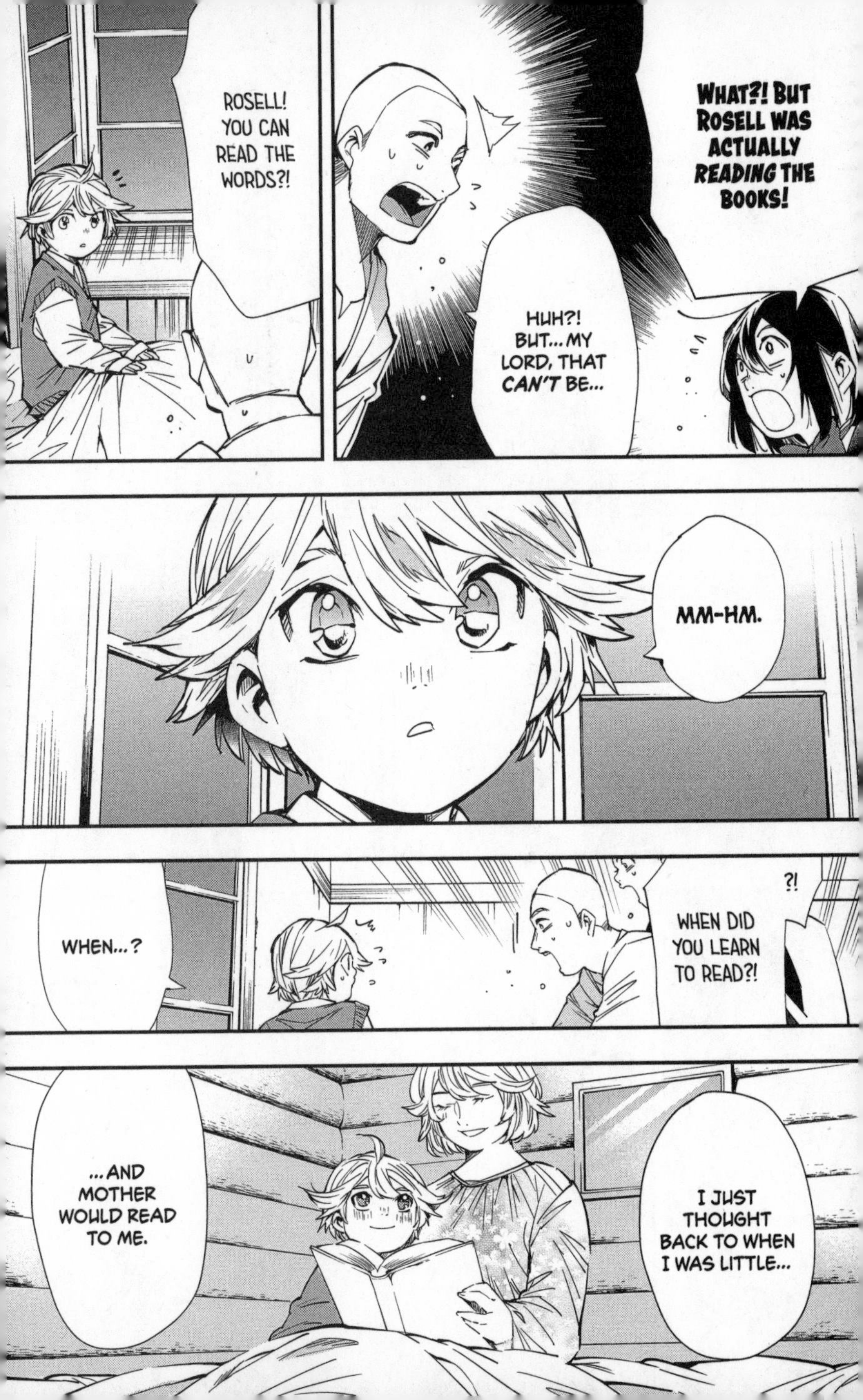
WHAT?! BUT ROSELL WAS ACTUALLY *READING* THE BOOKS!
HUH?! BUT... MY LORD, THAT *CAN'T* BE...
ROSELL! YOU CAN READ THE WORDS?!
MM-HM.
?!
WHEN DID YOU LEARN TO READ?!
WHEN...?
I JUST THOUGHT BACK TO WHEN I WAS LITTLE...
...AND MOTHER WOULD READ TO ME.

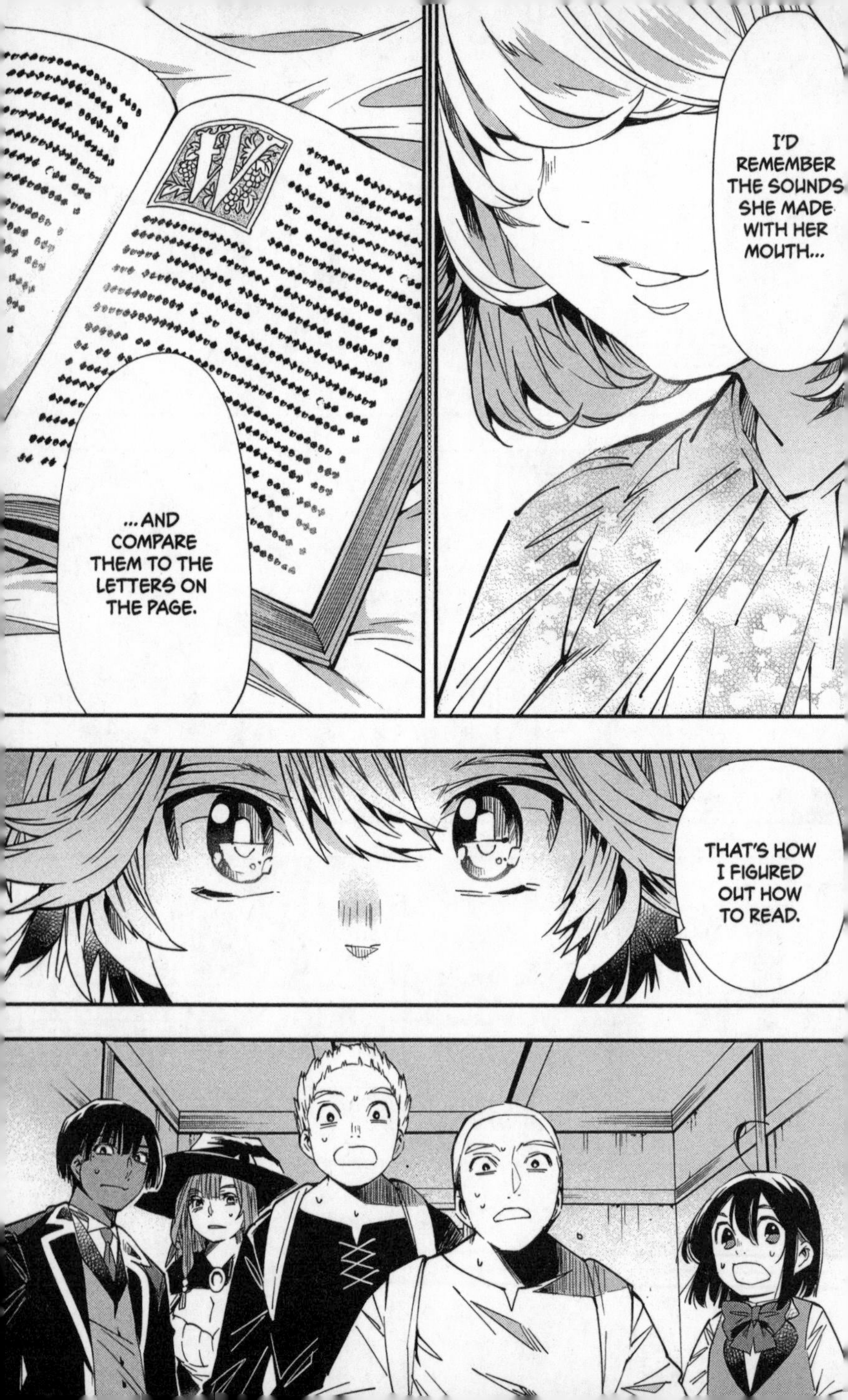
I'D REMEMBER THE SOUNDS SHE MADE WITH HER MOUTH...
...AND COMPARE THEM TO THE LETTERS ON THE PAGE.
THAT'S HOW I FIGURED OUT HOW TO READ.

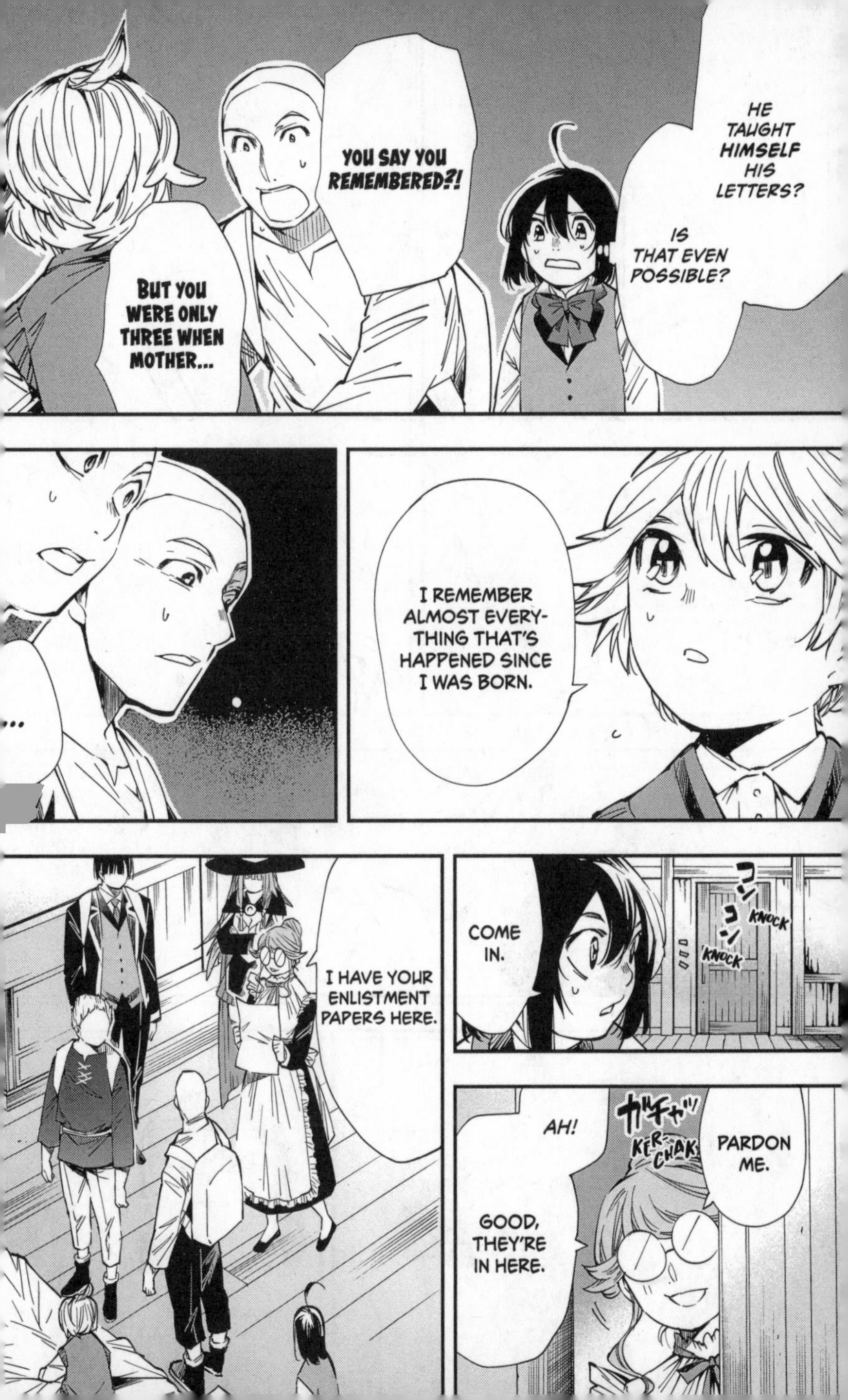
HE TAUGHT HIMSELF HIS LETTERS?
IS THAT EVEN POSSIBLE?
YOU SAY YOU REMEMBERED?!
BUT YOU WERE ONLY THREE WHEN MOTHER...
I REMEMBER ALMOST EVERY-THING THAT'S HAPPENED SINCE I WAS BORN.
...
KNOCK
KNOCK
COME IN.
PARDON ME.
KER-CHAK
AH!
GOOD, THEY'RE IN HERE.
I HAVE YOUR ENLISTMENT PAPERS HERE.

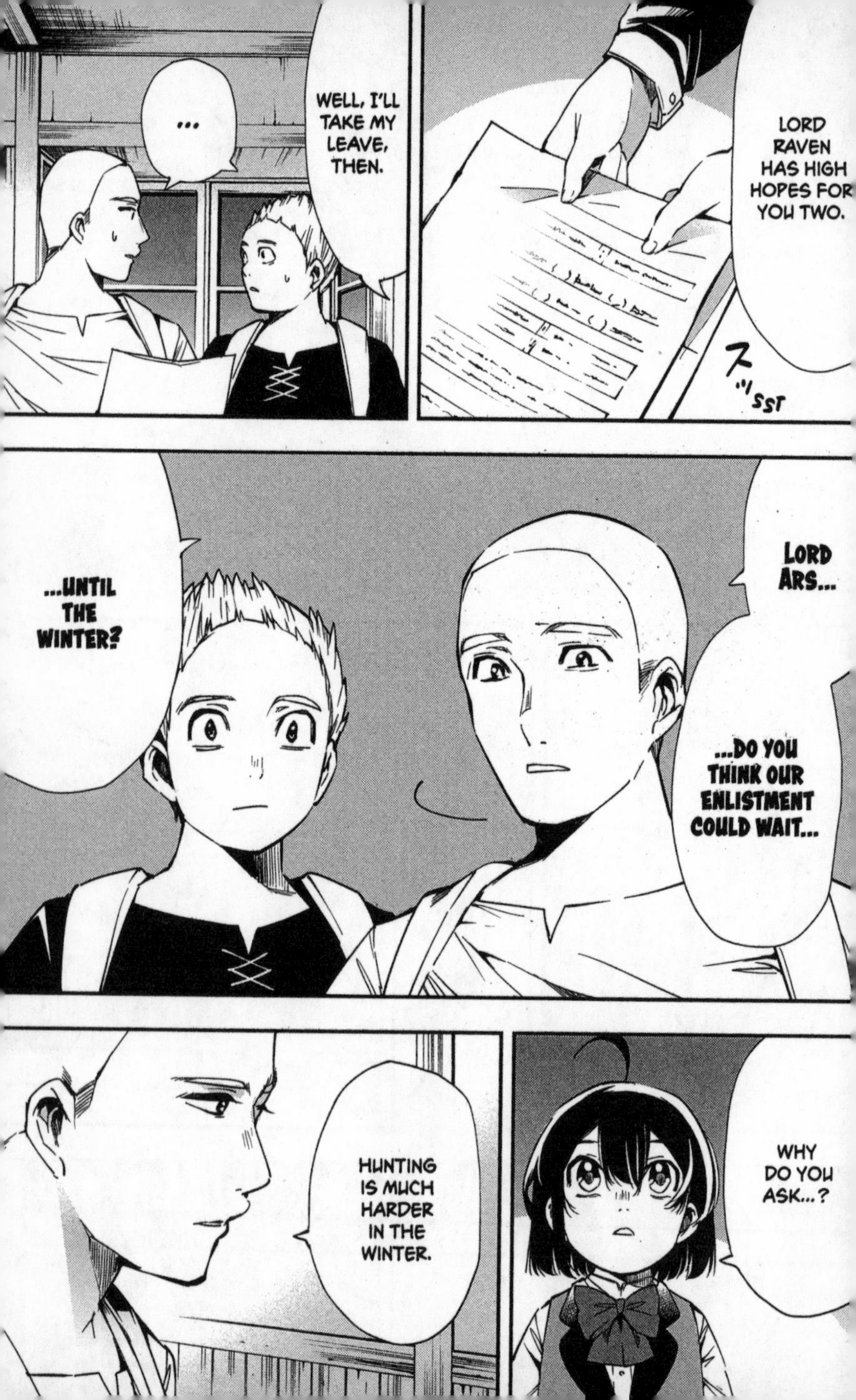
LORD RAVEN HAS HIGH HOPES FOR YOU TWO.
SST
WELL, I'LL TAKE MY LEAVE, THEN.
...
LORD ARS...
...DO YOU THINK OUR ENLISTMENT COULD WAIT...
...UNTIL THE WINTER?
WHY DO YOU ASK...?
HUNTING IS MUCH HARDER IN THE WINTER.

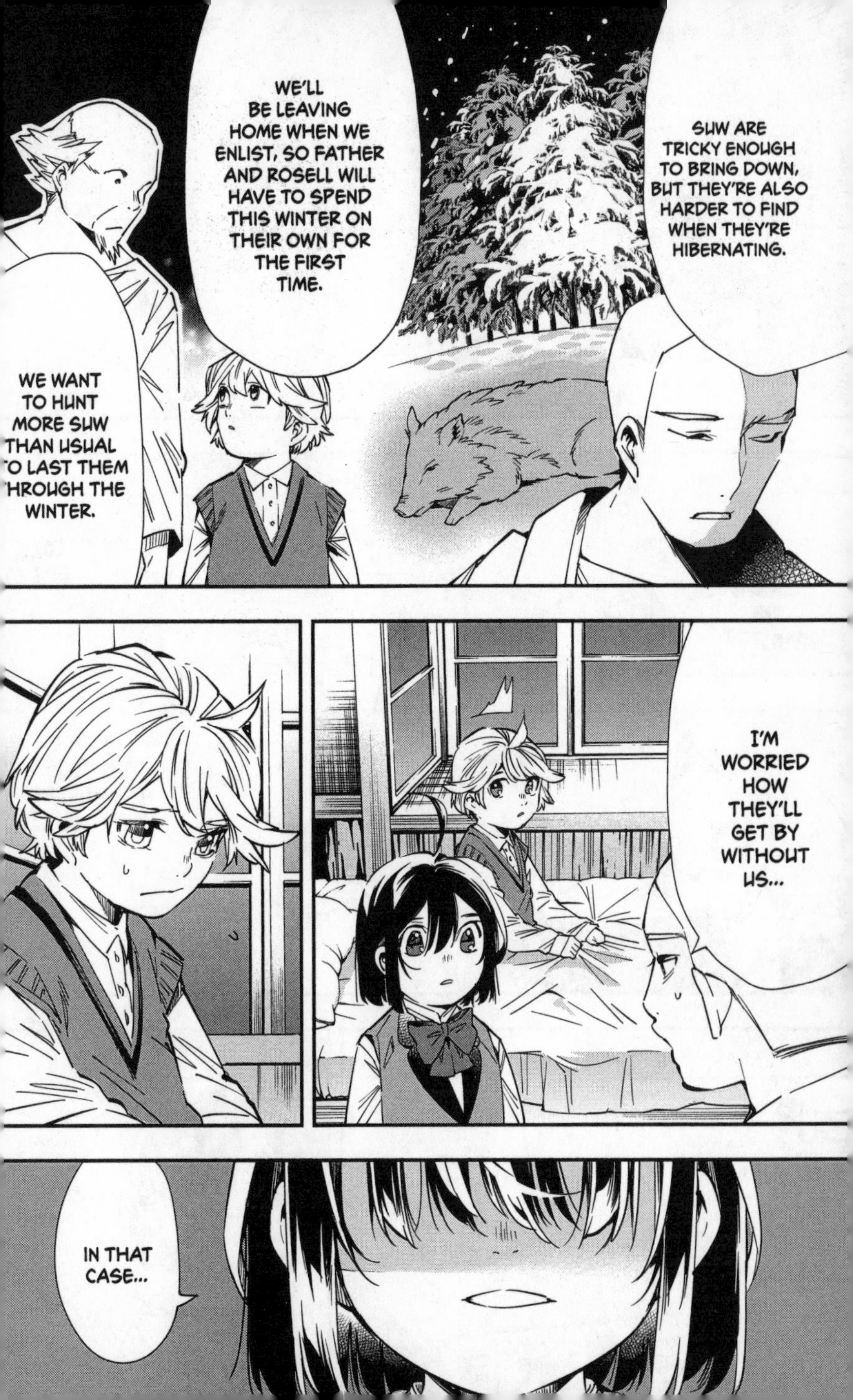
SUW ARE TRICKY ENOUGH TO BRING DOWN, BUT THEY'RE ALSO HARDER TO FIND WHEN THEY'RE HIBERNATING.
WE'LL BE LEAVING HOME WHEN WE ENLIST, SO FATHER AND ROSELL WILL HAVE TO SPEND THIS WINTER ON THEIR OWN FOR THE FIRST TIME.
WE WANT TO HUNT MORE SUW THAN USUAL O LAST THEM HROUGH THE WINTER.
I'M WORRIED HOW THEY'LL GET BY WITHOUT US...
IN THAT CASE...

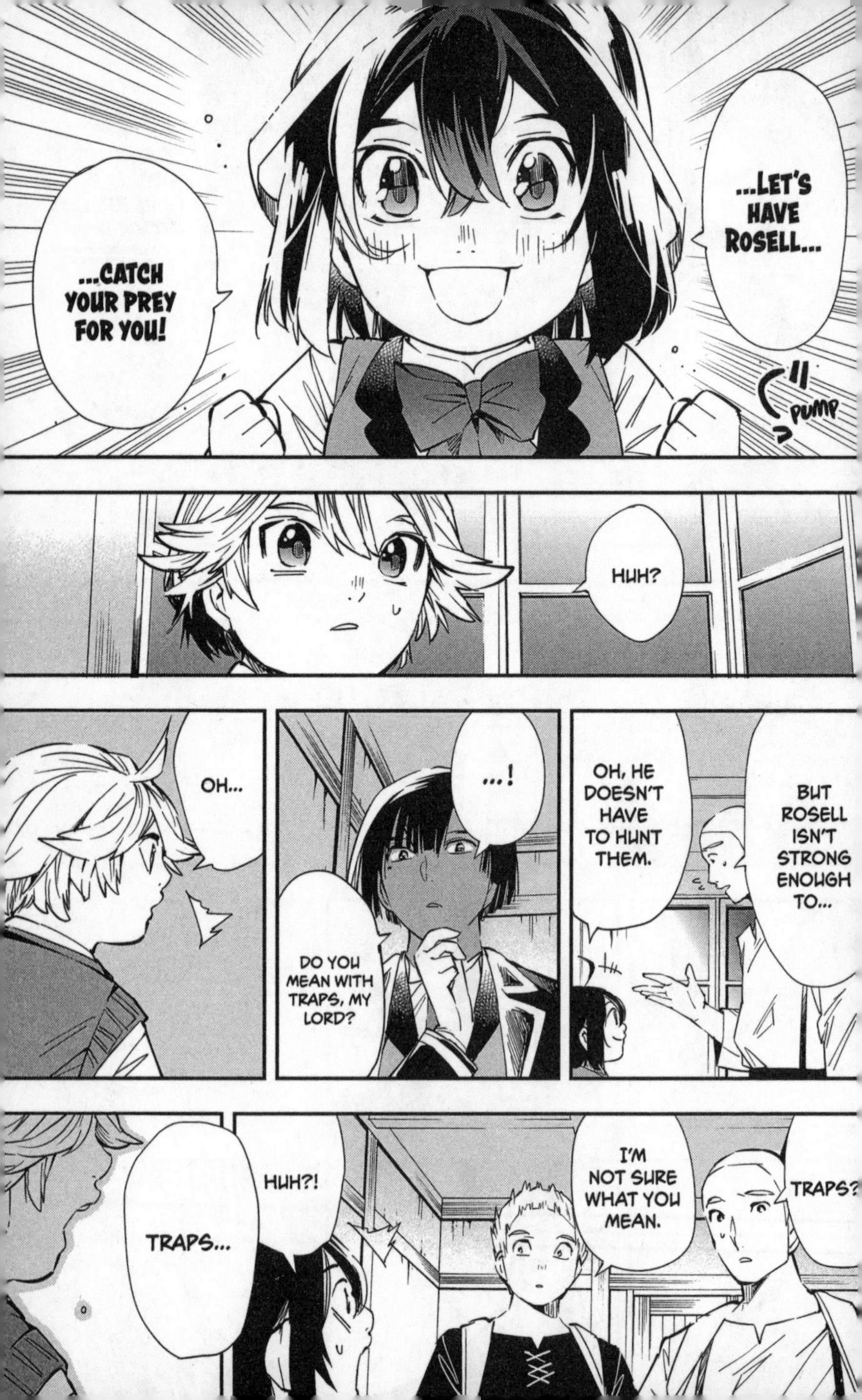
...LET'S HAVE ROSELL...
...CATCH YOUR PREY FOR YOU!
PUMP
HUH?
BUT ROSELL ISN'T STRONG ENOUGH TO...
OH, HE DOESN'T HAVE TO HUNT THEM.
...!
DO YOU MEAN WITH TRAPS, MY LORD?
OH...
TRAPS?
I'M NOT SURE WHAT YOU MEAN.
HUH?!
TRAPS...

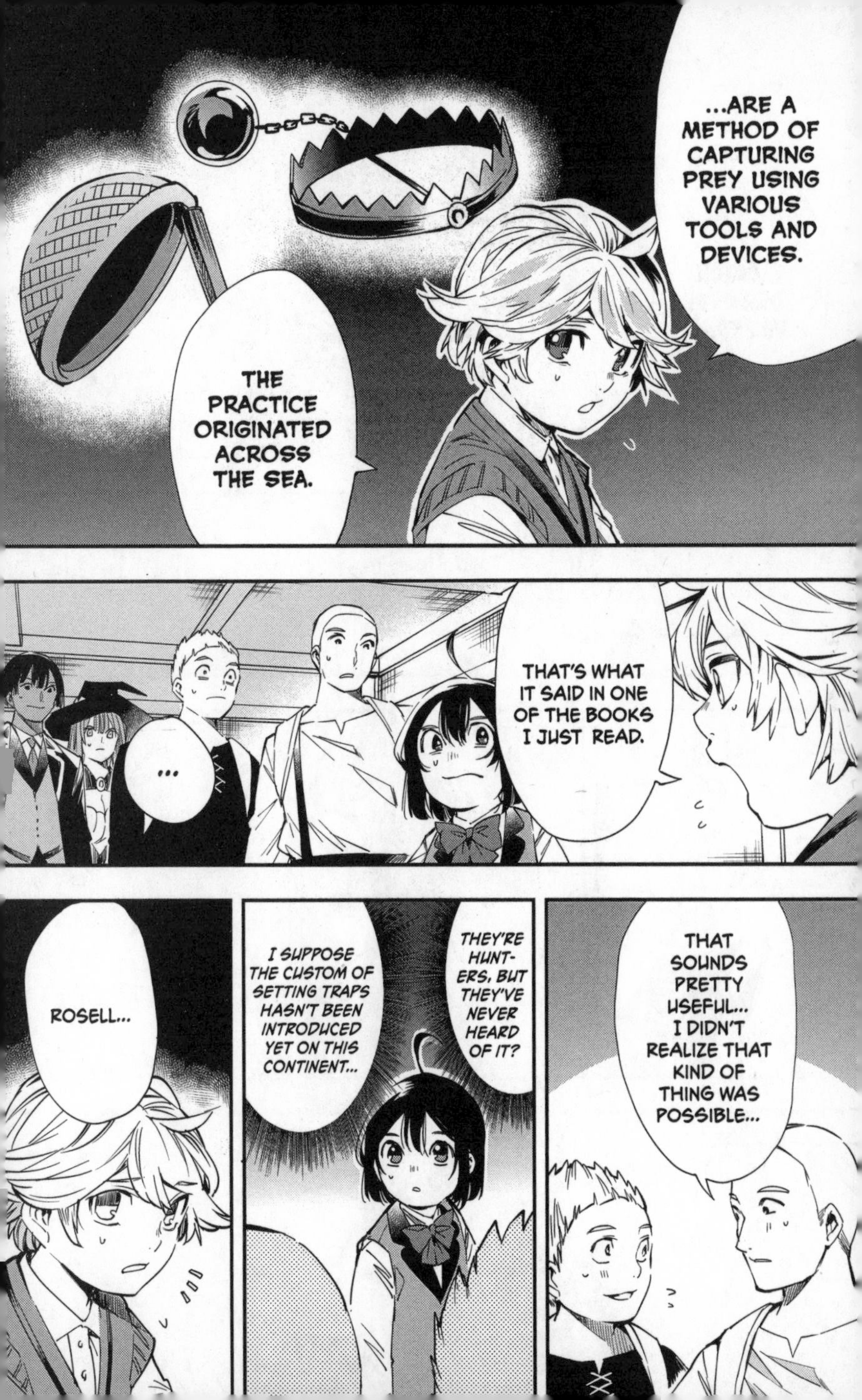
...ARE A METHOD OF CAPTURING PREY USING VARIOUS TOOLS AND DEVICES.
THE PRACTICE ORIGINATED ACROSS THE SEA.
THAT'S WHAT IT SAID IN ONE OF THE BOOKS I JUST READ.
...
THAT SOUNDS PRETTY USEFUL... I DIDN'T REALIZE THAT KIND OF THING WAS POSSIBLE...
THEY'RE HUNTERS, BUT THEY'VE NEVER HEARD OF IT?
I SUPPOSE THE CUSTOM OF SETTING TRAPS HASN'T BEEN INTRODUCED YET ON THIS CONTINENT...
ROSELL...

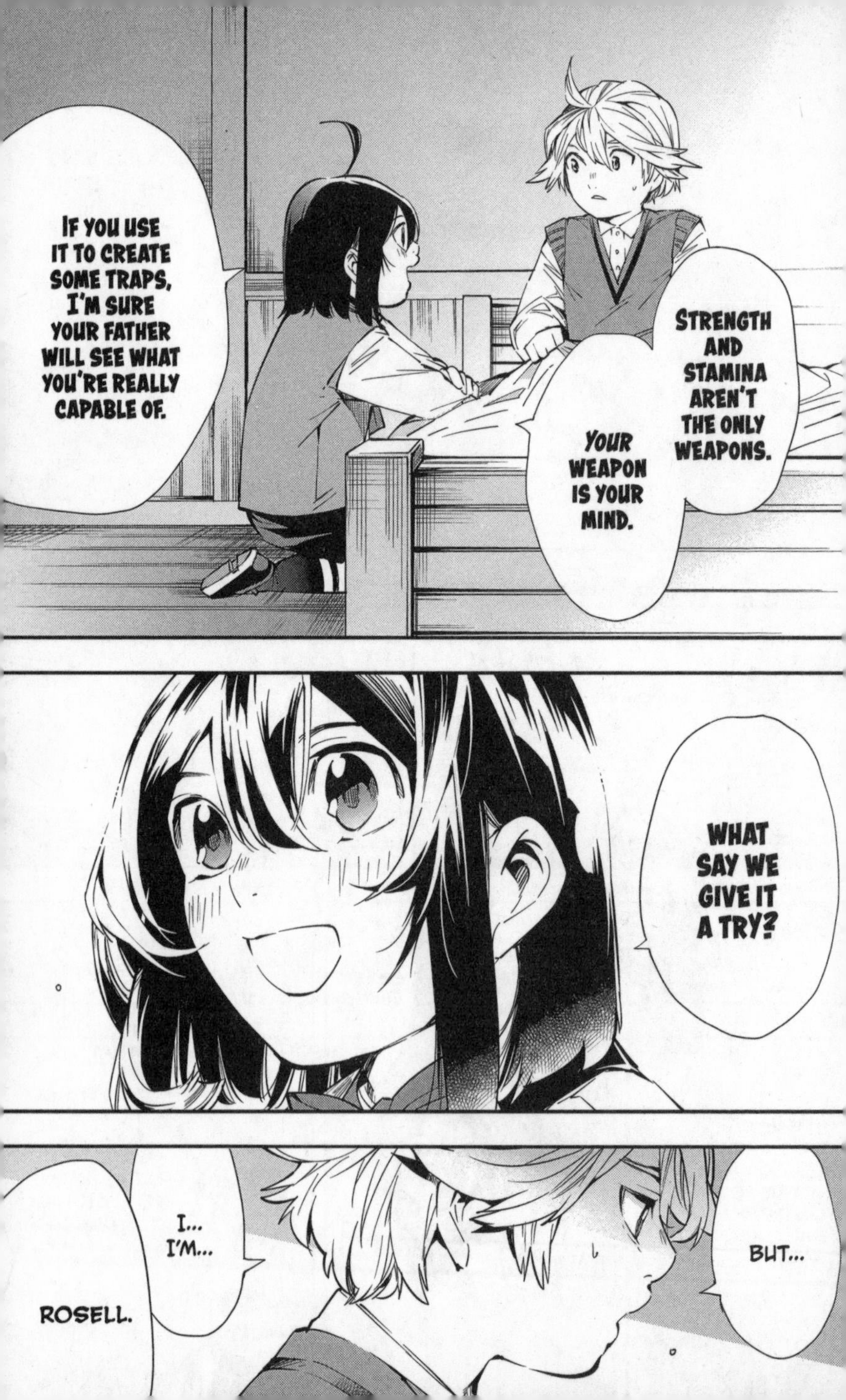
STRENGTH AND STAMINA AREN'T THE ONLY WEAPONS.
YOUR WEAPON IS YOUR MIND.
IF YOU USE IT TO CREATE SOME TRAPS, I'M SURE YOUR FATHER WILL SEE WHAT YOU'RE REALLY CAPABLE OF.
WHAT SAY WE GIVE IT A TRY?
BUT...
I... I'M...
ROSELL.

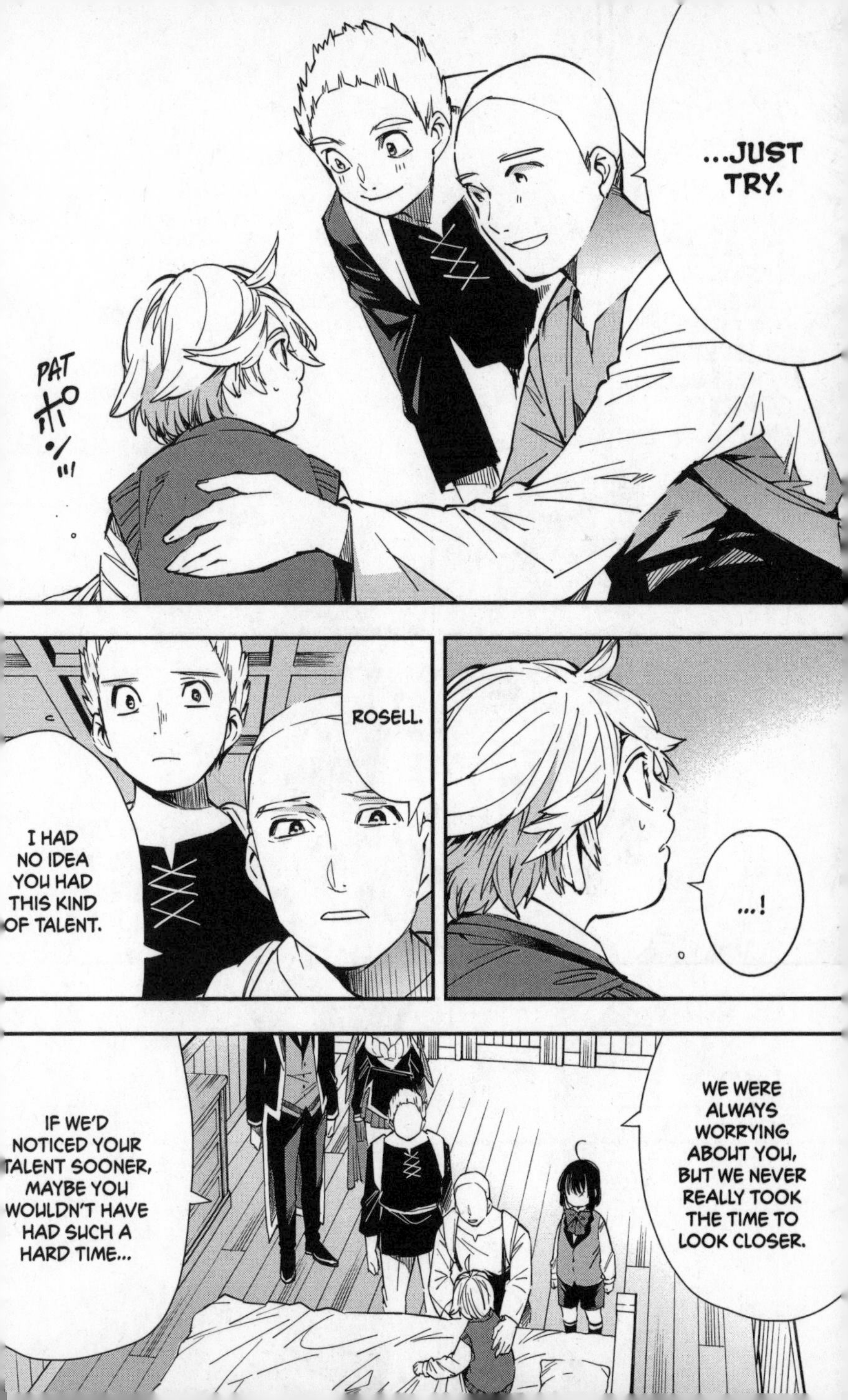

...JUST TRY.
PAT
...!
ROSELL.
I HAD NO IDEA YOU HAD THIS KIND OF TALENT.
WE WERE ALWAYS WORRYING ABOUT YOU, BUT WE NEVER REALLY TOOK THE TIME TO LOOK CLOSER.
IF WE'D NOTICED YOUR TALENT SOONER, MAYBE YOU WOULDN'T HAVE HAD SUCH A HARD TIME...

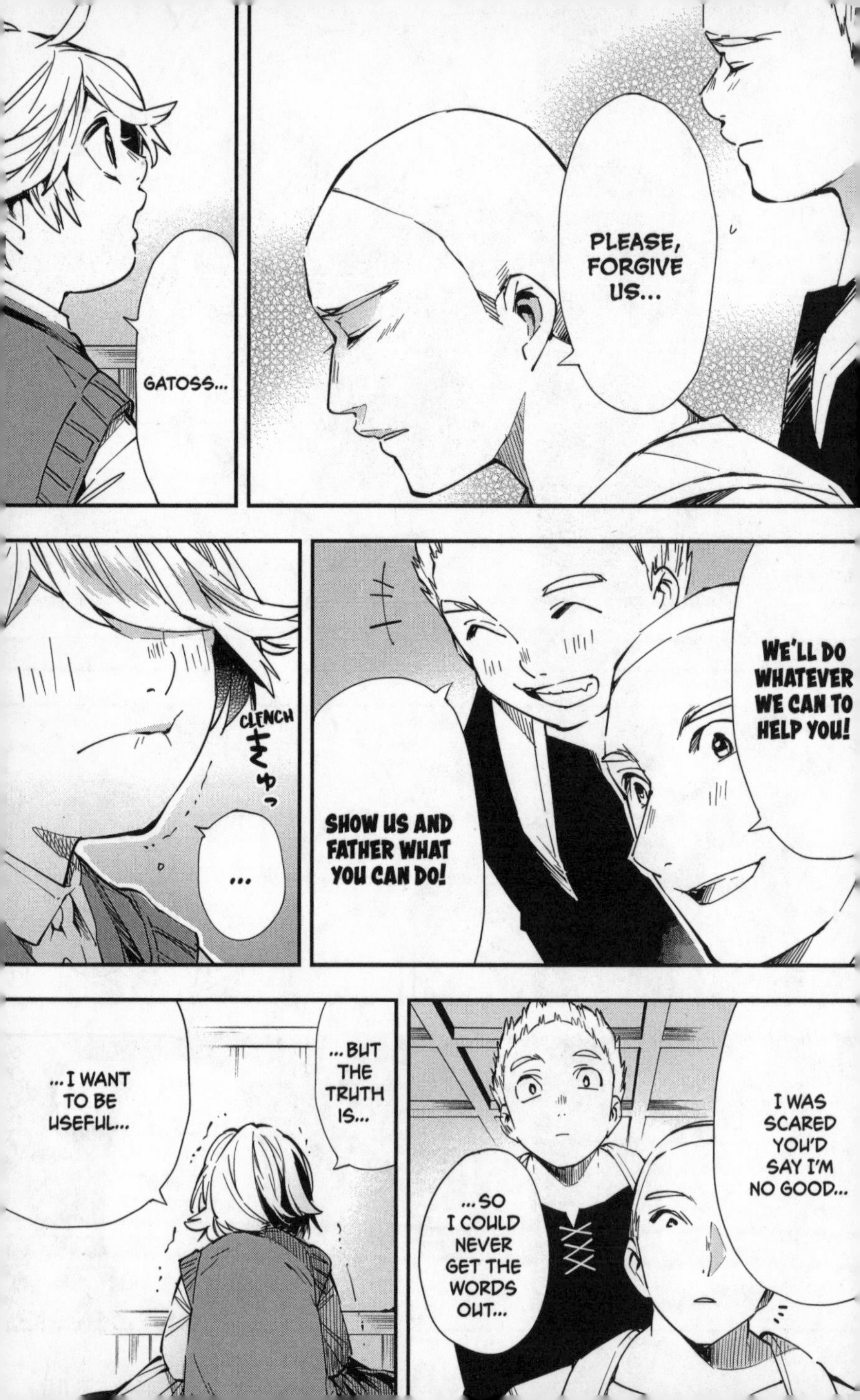
PLEASE, FORGIVE US...
GATOSS...
WE'LL DO WHATEVER WE CAN TO HELP YOU!
SHOW US AND FATHER WHAT YOU CAN DO!
CLENCH
きゅっ
...
I WAS SCARED YOU'D SAY I'M NO GOOD...
...SO I COULD NEVER GET THE WORDS OUT...
...BUT THE TRUTH IS...
...I WANT TO BE USEFUL...

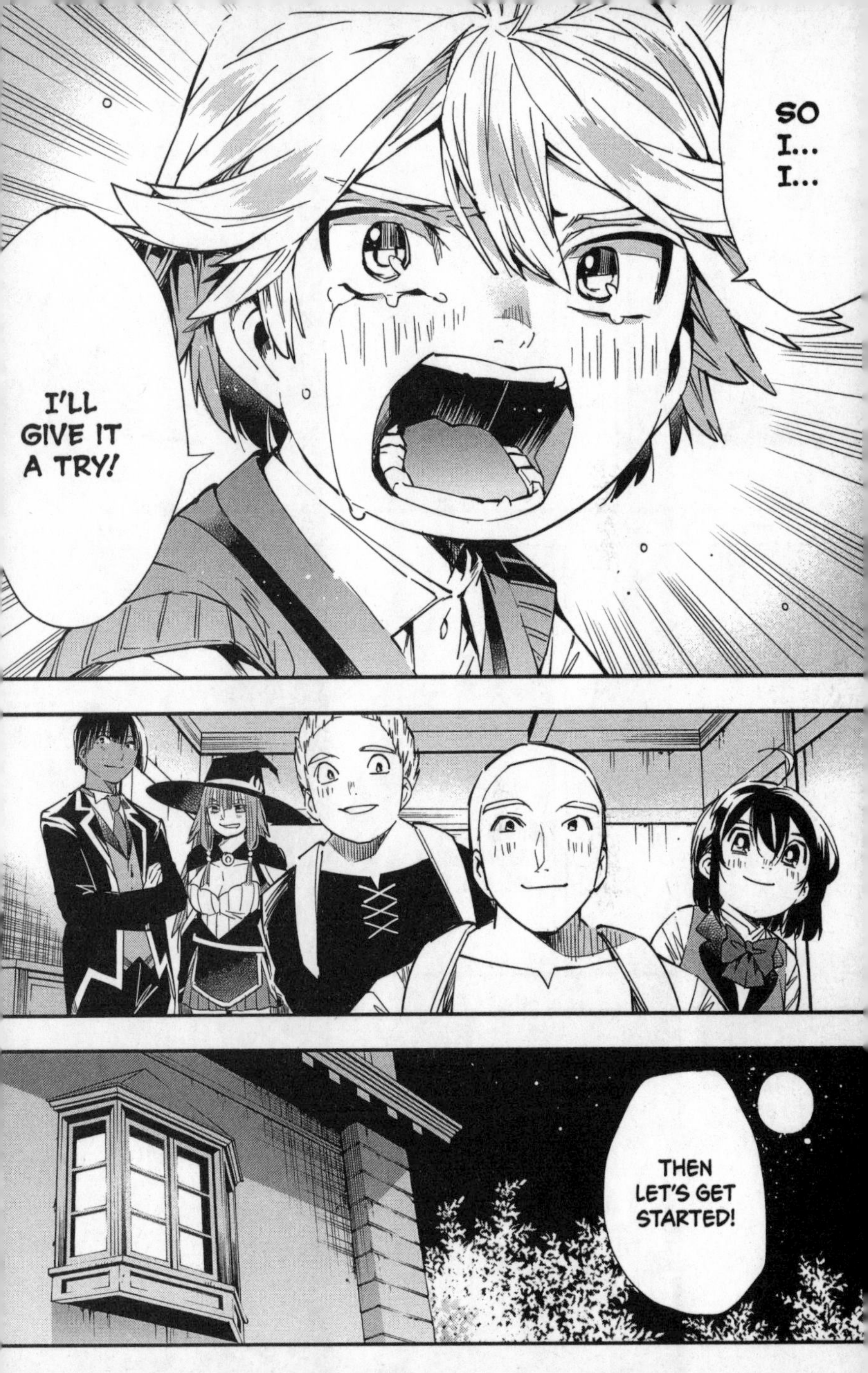
SO I... I...
I'LL GIVE IT A TRY!
THEN LET'S GET STARTED!

As a Reincarnated
ARISTOCRAT,
I'll Use My **Appraisal Skill** to
Rise in the World

As a Reincarnated
ARISTOCRAT,
I'll Use My Appraisal Skill to
Rise in the World

Chapter 15: A Stroke of Genius

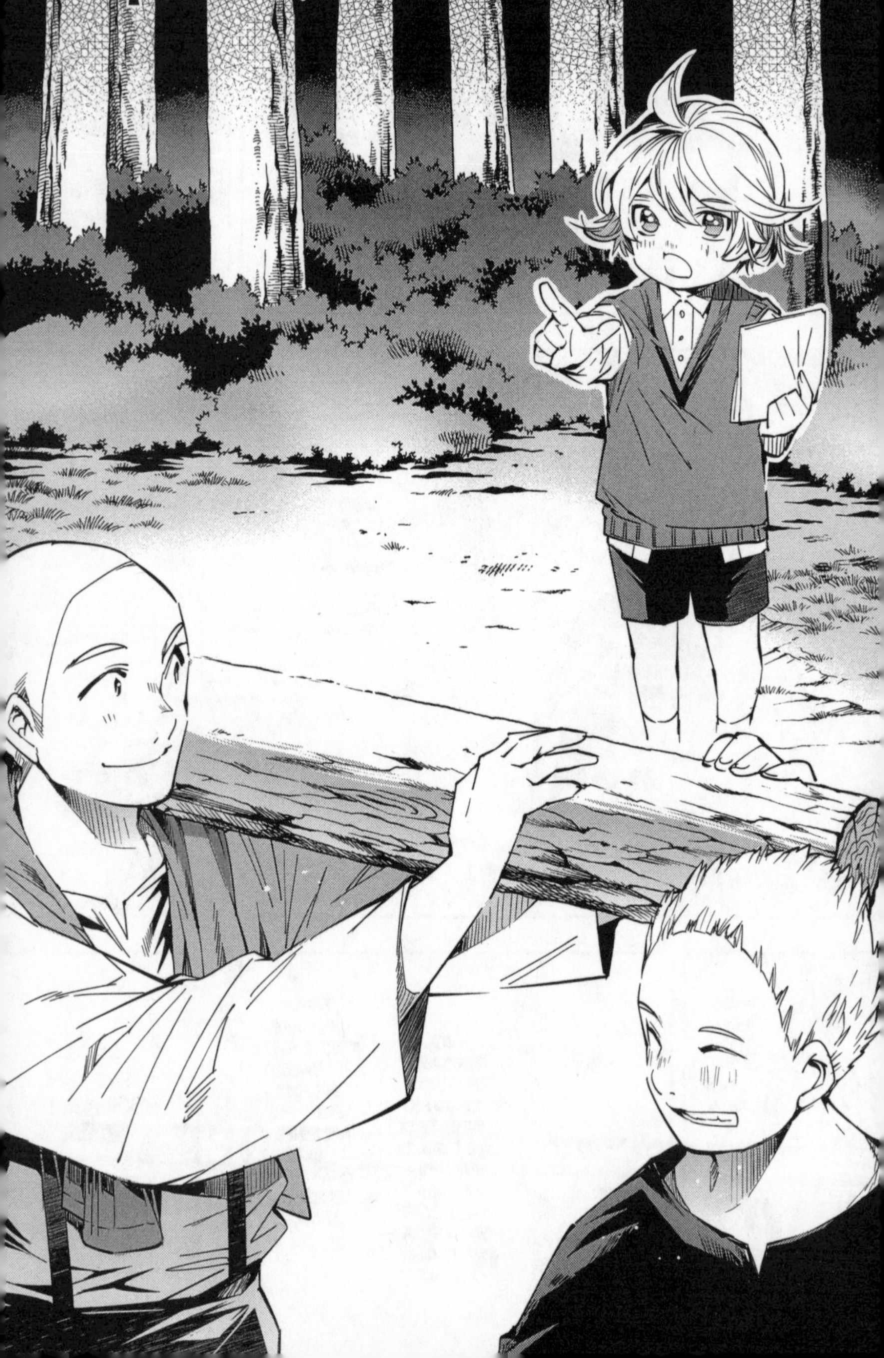

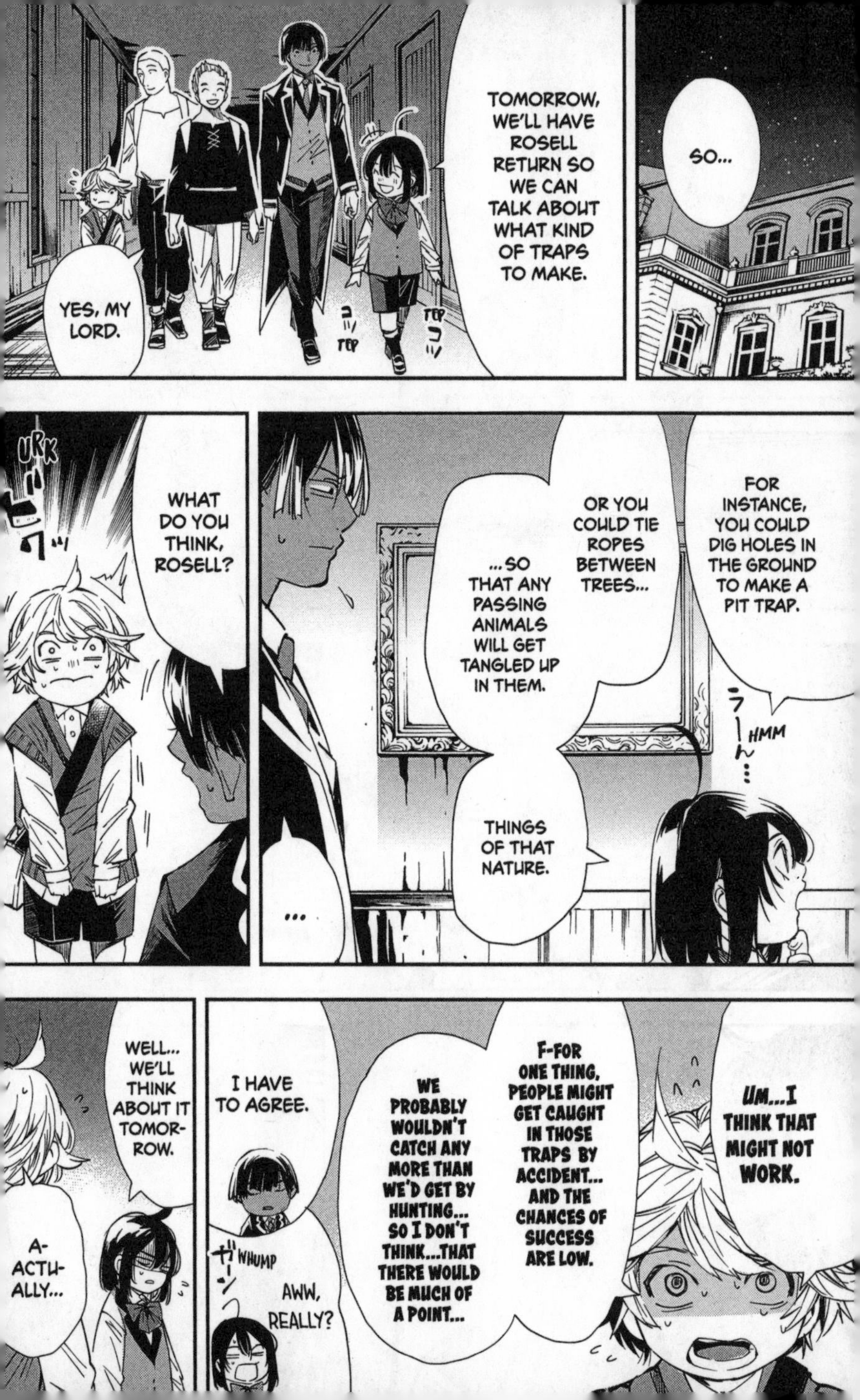
SO...
TOMORROW, WE'LL HAVE ROSELL RETURN SO WE CAN TALK ABOUT WHAT KIND OF TRAPS TO MAKE.
TEP
TEP
YES, MY LORD.
FOR INSTANCE, YOU COULD DIG HOLES IN THE GROUND TO MAKE A PIT TRAP.
HMM
OR YOU COULD TIE ROPES BETWEEN TREES...
...SO THAT ANY PASSING ANIMALS WILL GET TANGLED UP IN THEM.
THINGS OF THAT NATURE.
...
URK
WHAT DO YOU THINK, ROSELL?
UM...I THINK THAT MIGHT NOT WORK.
F-FOR ONE THING, PEOPLE MIGHT GET CAUGHT IN THOSE TRAPS BY ACCIDENT... AND THE CHANCES OF SUCCESS ARE LOW.
WE PROBABLY WOULDN'T CATCH ANY MORE THAN WE'D GET BY HUNTING... SO I DON'T THINK...THAT THERE WOULD BE MUCH OF A POINT...
I HAVE TO AGREE.
WHUMP
AWW, REALLY?
WELL... WE'LL THINK ABOUT IT TOMOR-ROW.
A-ACTU-ALLY...

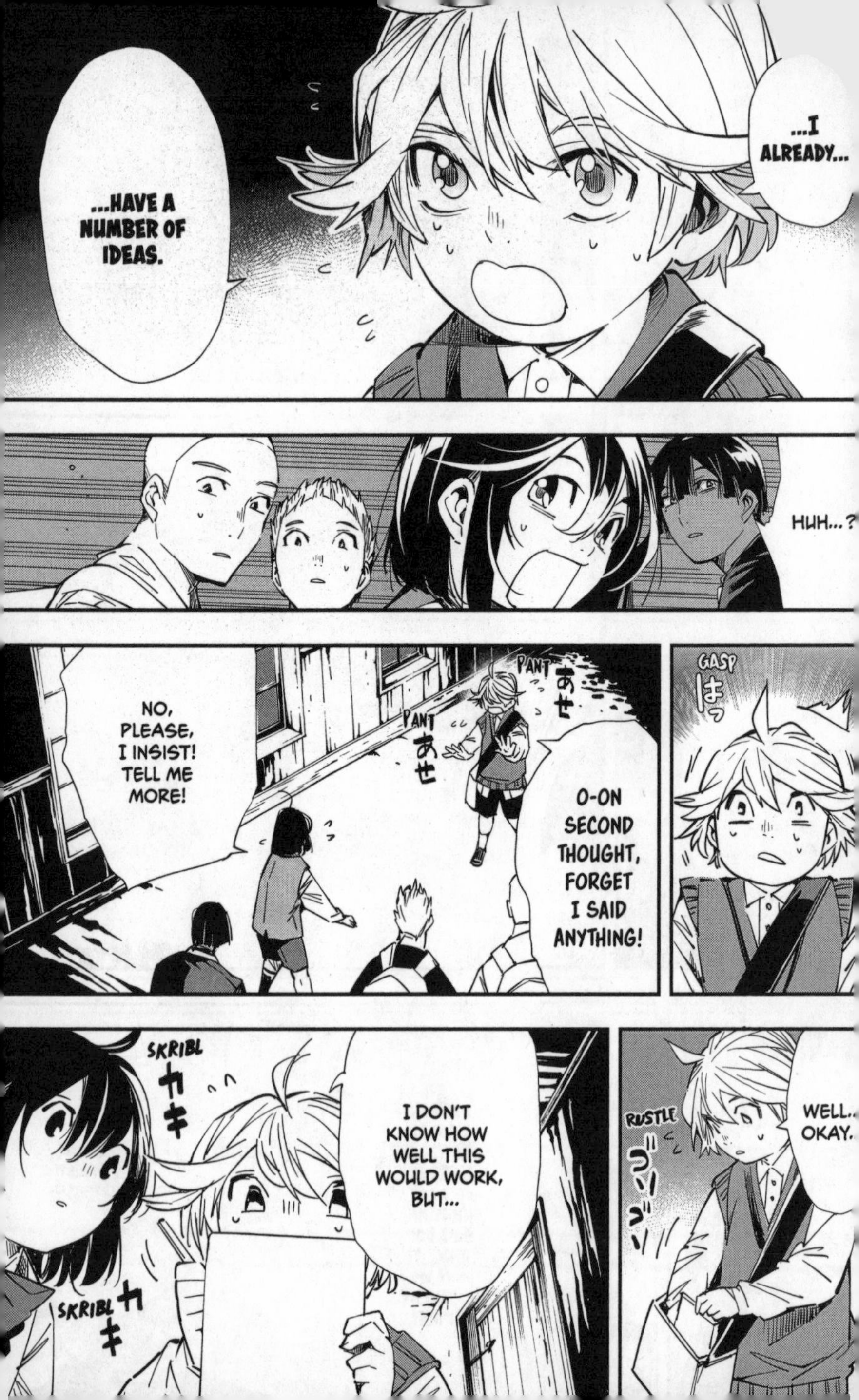

...I ALREADY...
...HAVE A NUMBER OF IDEAS.
HUH...?
GASP
はっ
O-ON SECOND THOUGHT, FORGET I SAID ANYTHING!
PANT
あせ
PANT
あせ
NO, PLEASE, I INSIST! TELL ME MORE!
WELL... OKAY.
RUSTLE
ゴソゴソ
I DON'T KNOW HOW WELL THIS WOULD WORK, BUT...
SKRIBL
カキ
SKRIBL
カキ

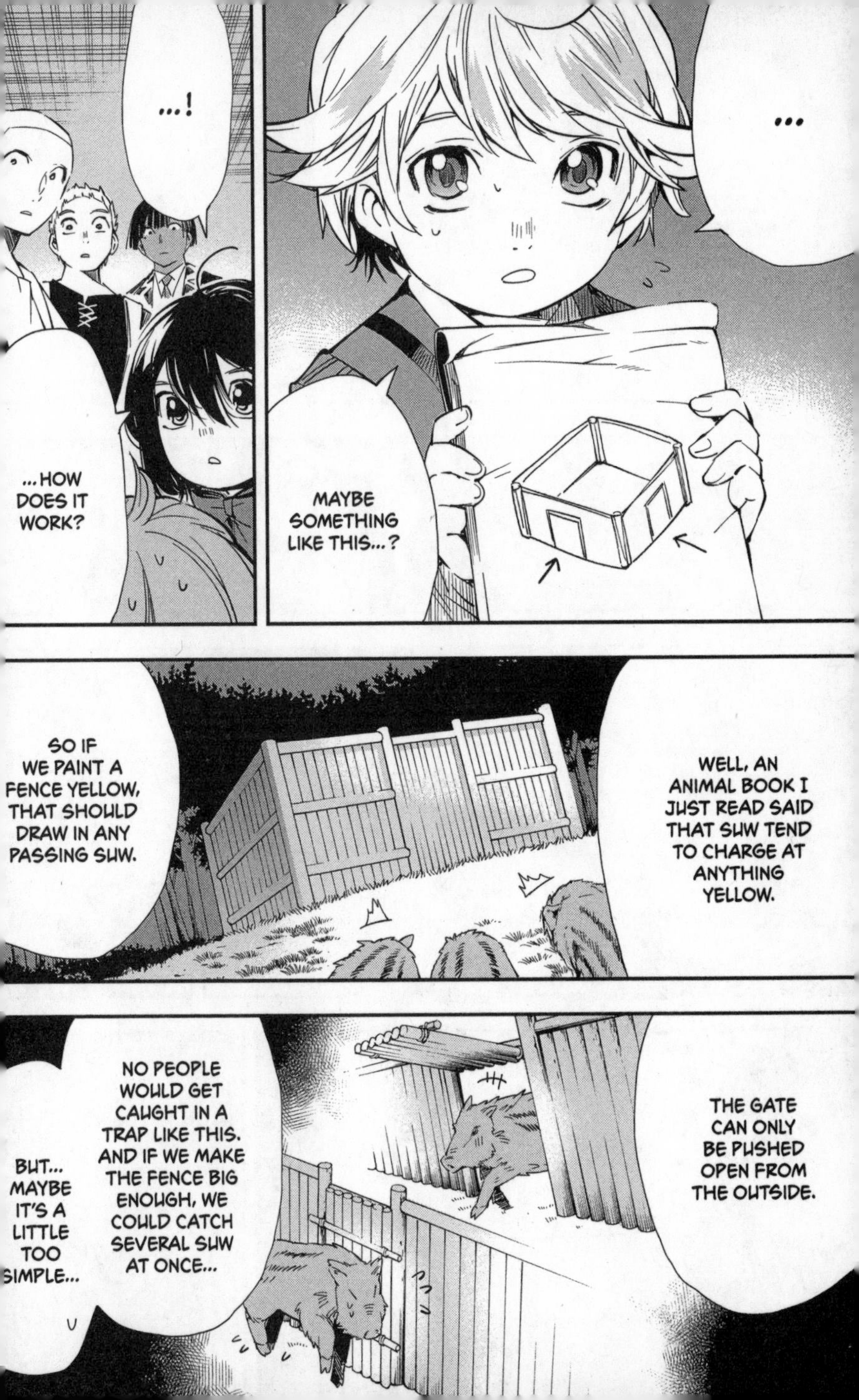
...
MAYBE SOMETHING LIKE THIS...?
...!
...HOW DOES IT WORK?
WELL, AN ANIMAL BOOK I JUST READ SAID THAT SUW TEND TO CHARGE AT ANYTHING YELLOW.
SO IF WE PAINT A FENCE YELLOW, THAT SHOULD DRAW IN ANY PASSING SUW.
THE GATE CAN ONLY BE PUSHED OPEN FROM THE OUTSIDE.
NO PEOPLE WOULD GET CAUGHT IN A TRAP LIKE THIS. AND IF WE MAKE THE FENCE BIG ENOUGH, WE COULD CATCH SEVERAL SUW AT ONCE...
BUT... MAYBE IT'S A LITTLE TOO SIMPLE...

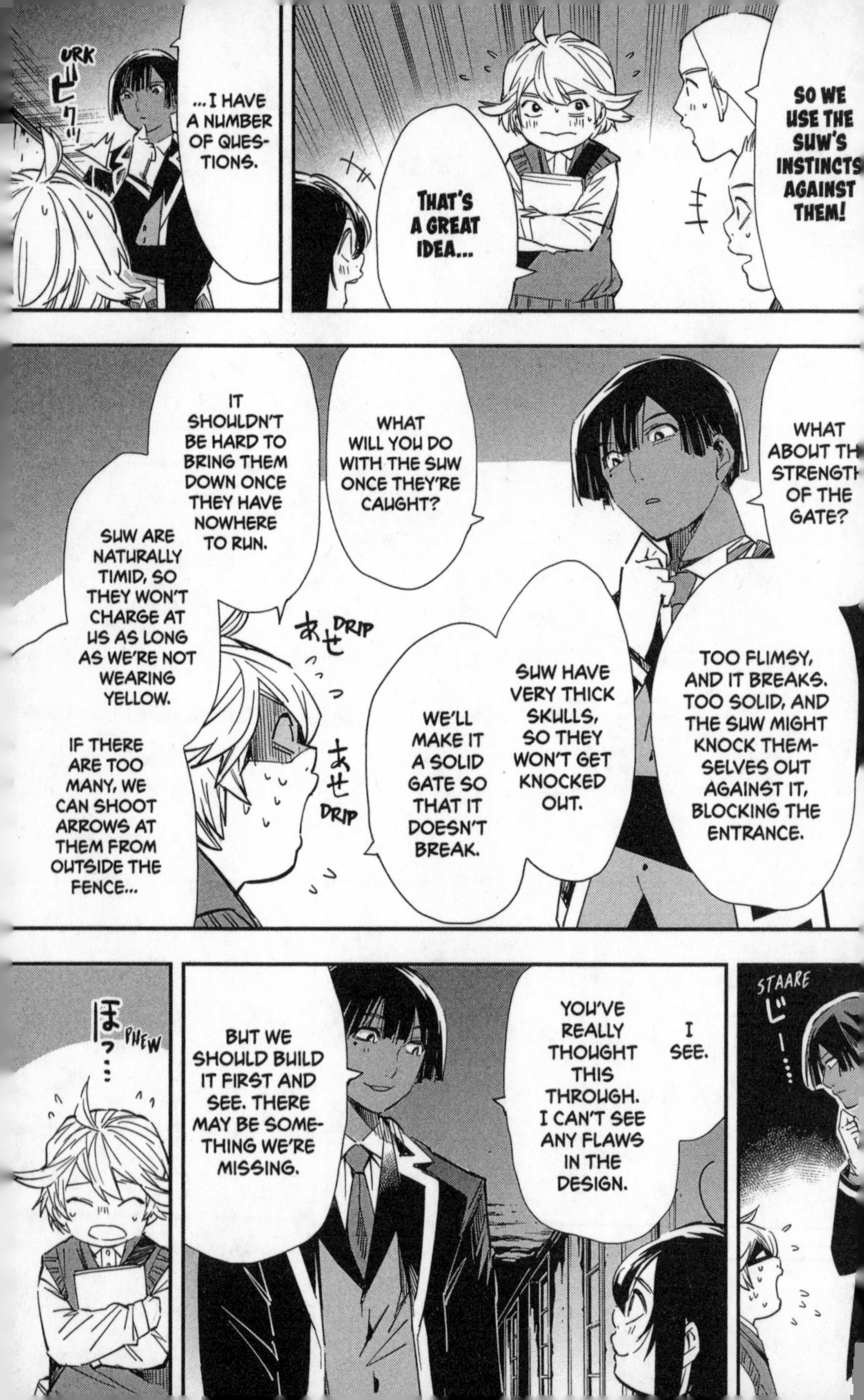
SO WE USE THE SUW'S INSTINCTS AGAINST THEM!
THAT'S A GREAT IDEA...
URK ビクッ
...I HAVE A NUMBER OF QUES-TIONS.
WHAT ABOUT TH STRENGTH OF THE GATE?
WE'LL MAKE IT A SOLID GATE SO THAT IT DOESN'T BREAK.
TOO FLIMSY, AND IT BREAKS. TOO SOLID, AND THE SUW MIGHT KNOCK THEM-SELVES OUT AGAINST IT, BLOCKING THE ENTRANCE.
SUW HAVE VERY THICK SKULLS, SO THEY WON'T GET KNOCKED OUT.
あせ DRIP
あせ DRIP
WHAT WILL YOU DO WITH THE SUW ONCE THEY'RE CAUGHT?
IT SHOULDN'T BE HARD TO BRING THEM DOWN ONCE THEY HAVE NOWHERE TO RUN.
SUW ARE NATURALLY TIMID, SO THEY WON'T CHARGE AT US AS LONG AS WE'RE NOT WEARING YELLOW.
IF THERE ARE TOO MANY, WE CAN SHOOT ARROWS AT THEM FROM OUTSIDE THE FENCE...
STAARE ジー…
I SEE.
YOU'VE REALLY THOUGHT THIS THROUGH. I CAN'T SEE ANY FLAWS IN THE DESIGN.
BUT WE SHOULD BUILD IT FIRST AND SEE. THERE MAY BE SOME-THING WE'RE MISSING.
ほっ… PHEW

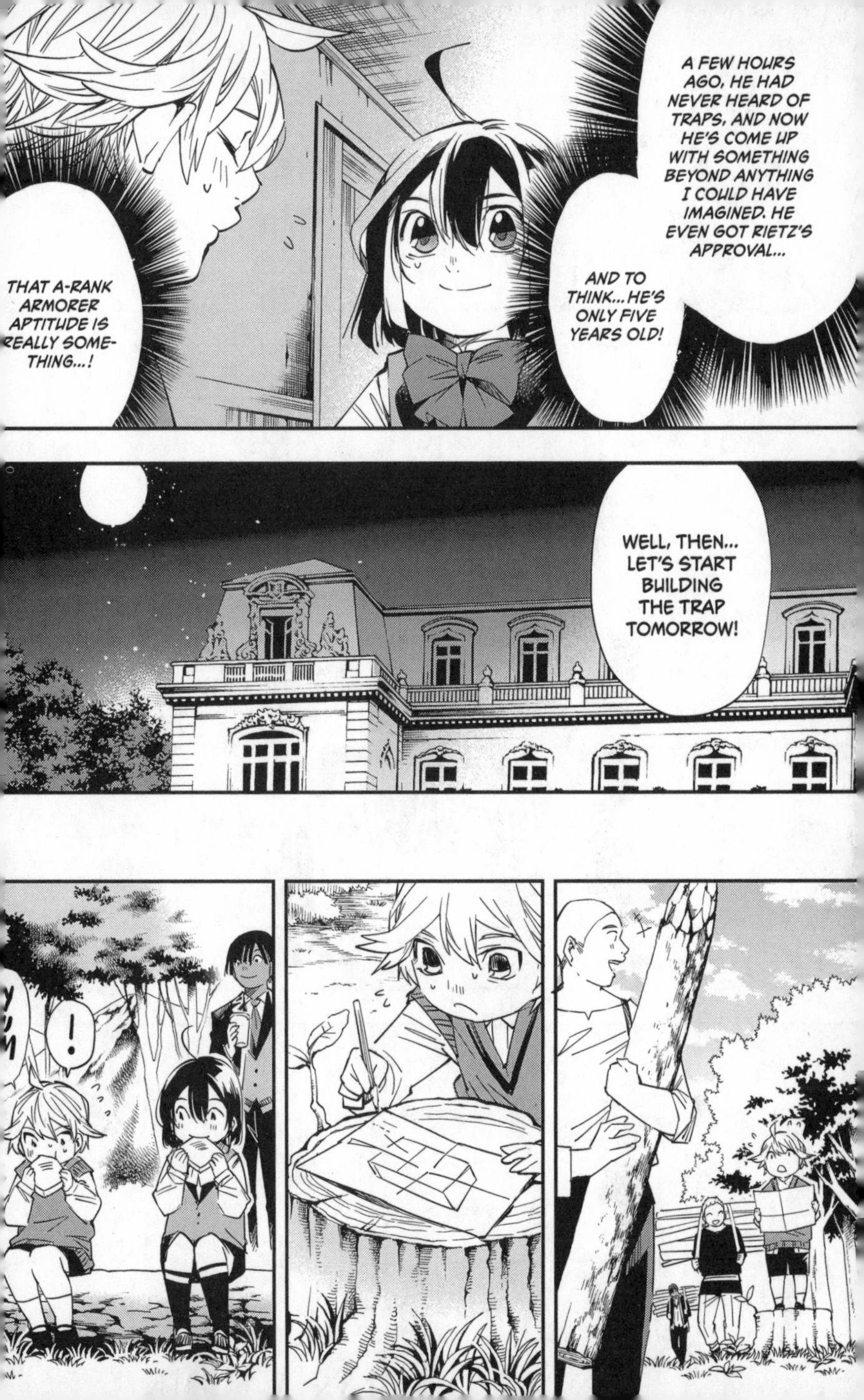

A FEW HOURS AGO, HE HAD NEVER HEARD OF TRAPS, AND NOW HE'S COME UP WITH SOMETHING BEYOND ANYTHING I COULD HAVE IMAGINED. HE EVEN GOT RIETZ'S APPROVAL...
AND TO THINK... HE'S ONLY FIVE YEARS OLD!
THAT A-RANK ARMORER APTITUDE IS REALLY SOME-THING...!
WELL, THEN... LET'S START BUILDING THE TRAP TOMORROW!
!
YUM

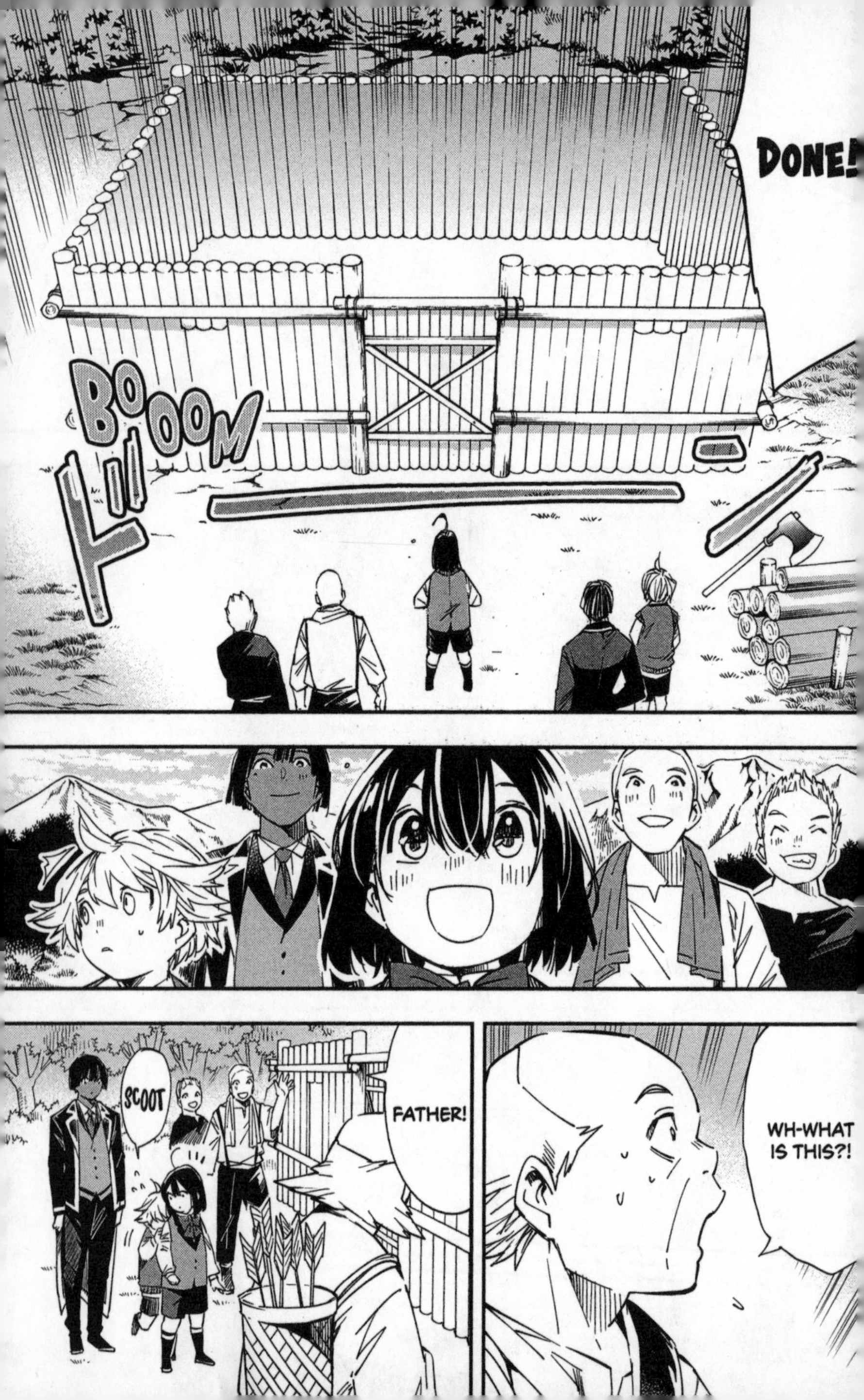
DONE!
BOOOM
WH-WHAT IS THIS?!
FATHER!
SCOOT

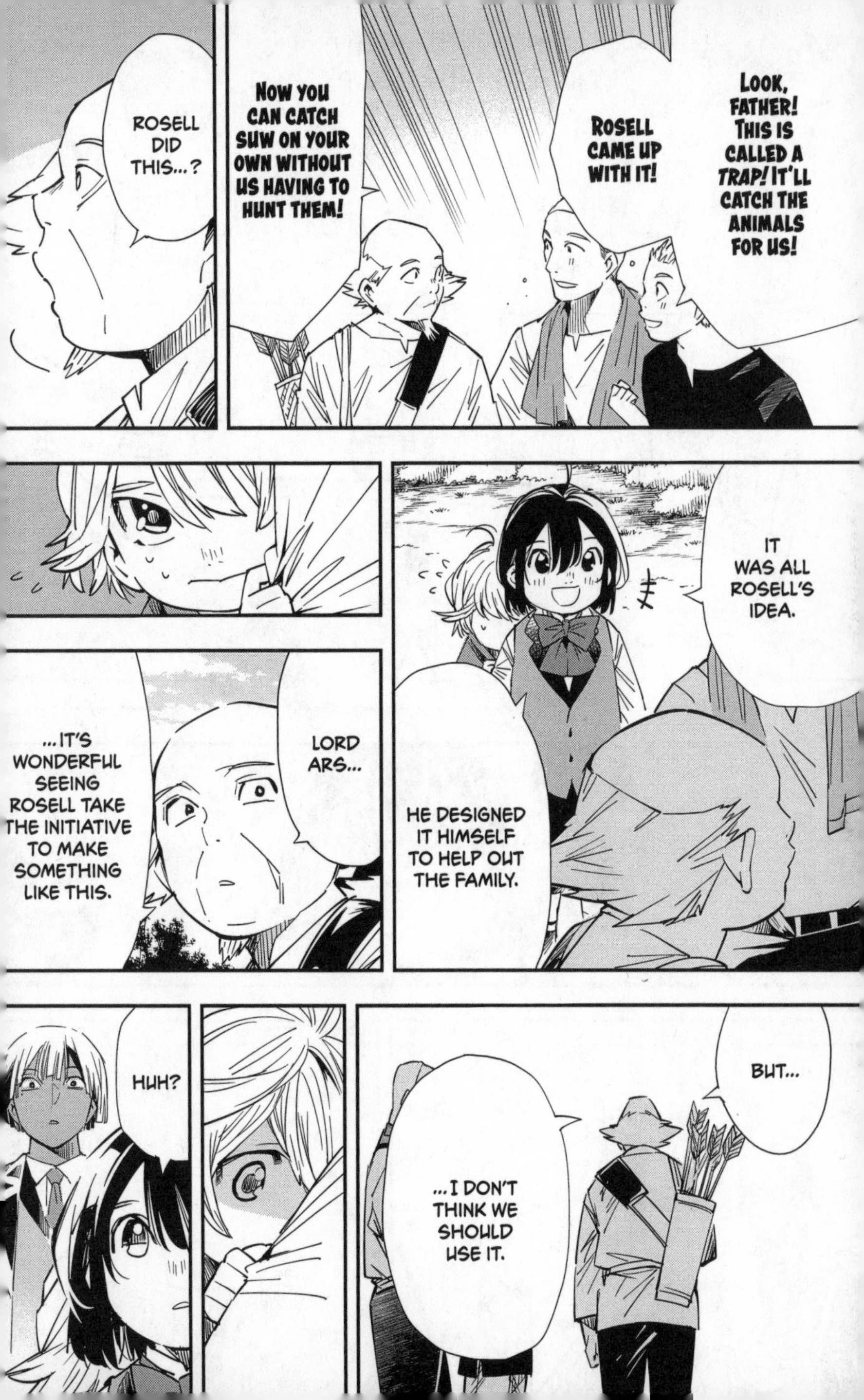
LOOK, FATHER! THIS IS CALLED A *TRAP!* IT'LL CATCH THE ANIMALS FOR US!
ROSELL CAME UP WITH IT!
NOW YOU CAN CATCH SUW ON YOUR OWN WITHOUT US HAVING TO HUNT THEM!
ROSELL DID THIS...?
IT WAS ALL ROSELL'S IDEA.
HE DESIGNED IT HIMSELF TO HELP OUT THE FAMILY.
LORD ARS...
...IT'S WONDERFUL SEEING ROSELL TAKE THE INITIATIVE TO MAKE SOMETHING LIKE THIS.
BUT...
...I DON'T THINK WE SHOULD USE IT.
HUH?

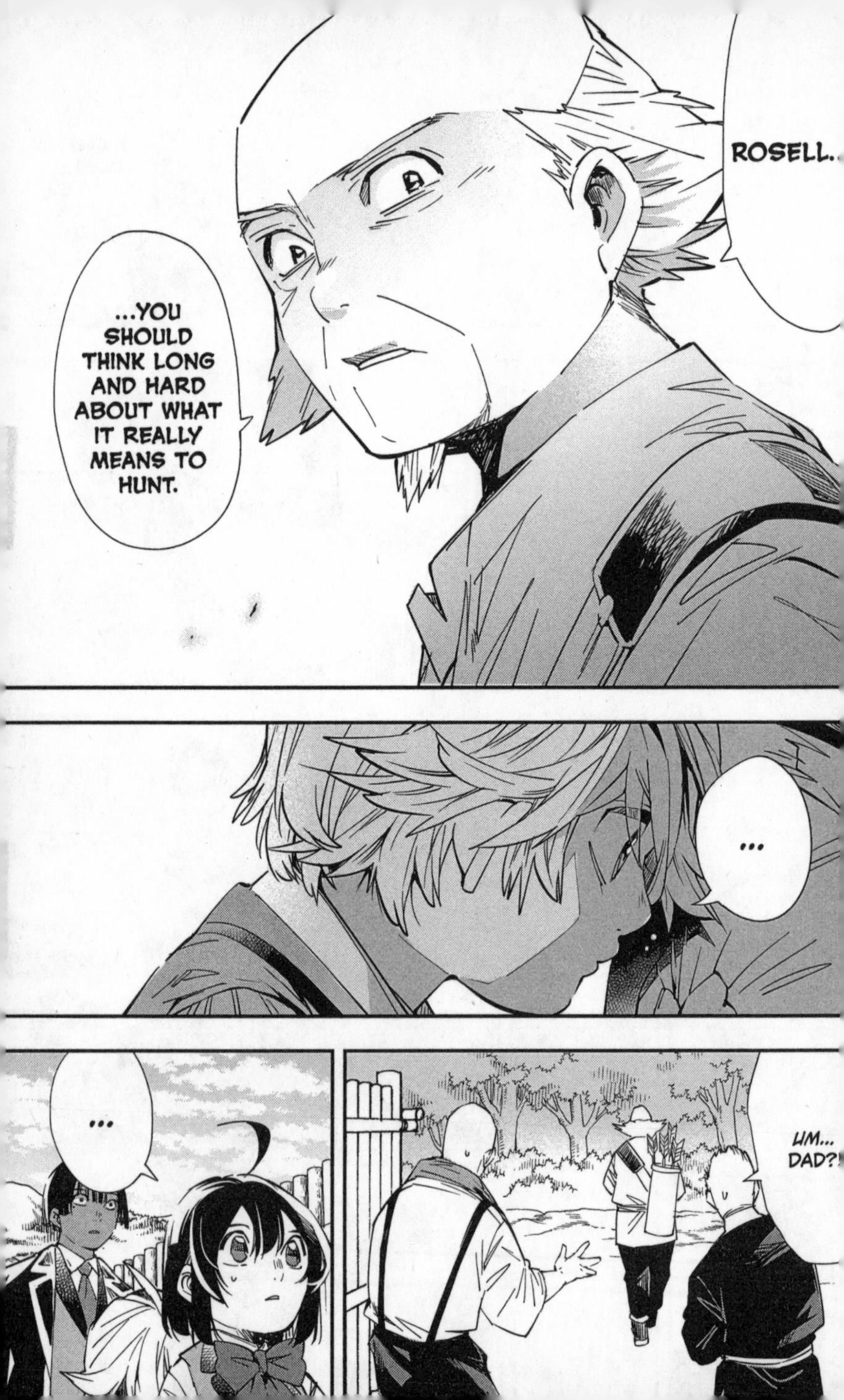
ROSELL...
...YOU SHOULD THINK LONG AND HARD ABOUT WHAT IT REALLY MEANS TO HUNT.
...
UM... DAD?!
...

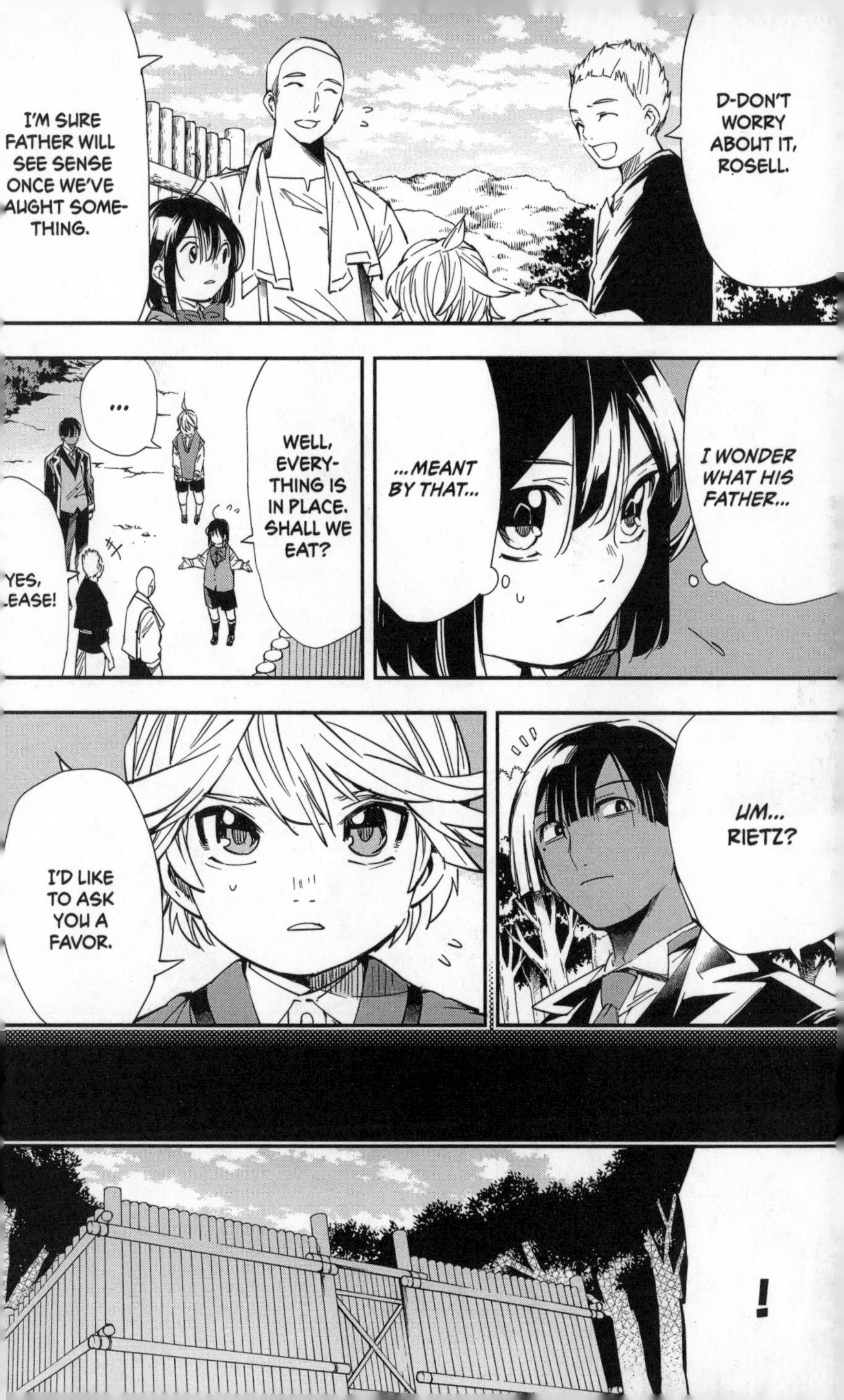
D-DON'T WORRY ABOUT IT, ROSELL.
I'M SURE FATHER WILL SEE SENSE ONCE WE'VE AUGHT SOME-THING.
I WONDER WHAT HIS FATHER...
...MEANT BY THAT...
WELL, EVERY-THING IS IN PLACE. SHALL WE EAT?
...
YES, LEASE!
UM... RIETZ?
I'D LIKE TO ASK YOU A FAVOR.
!

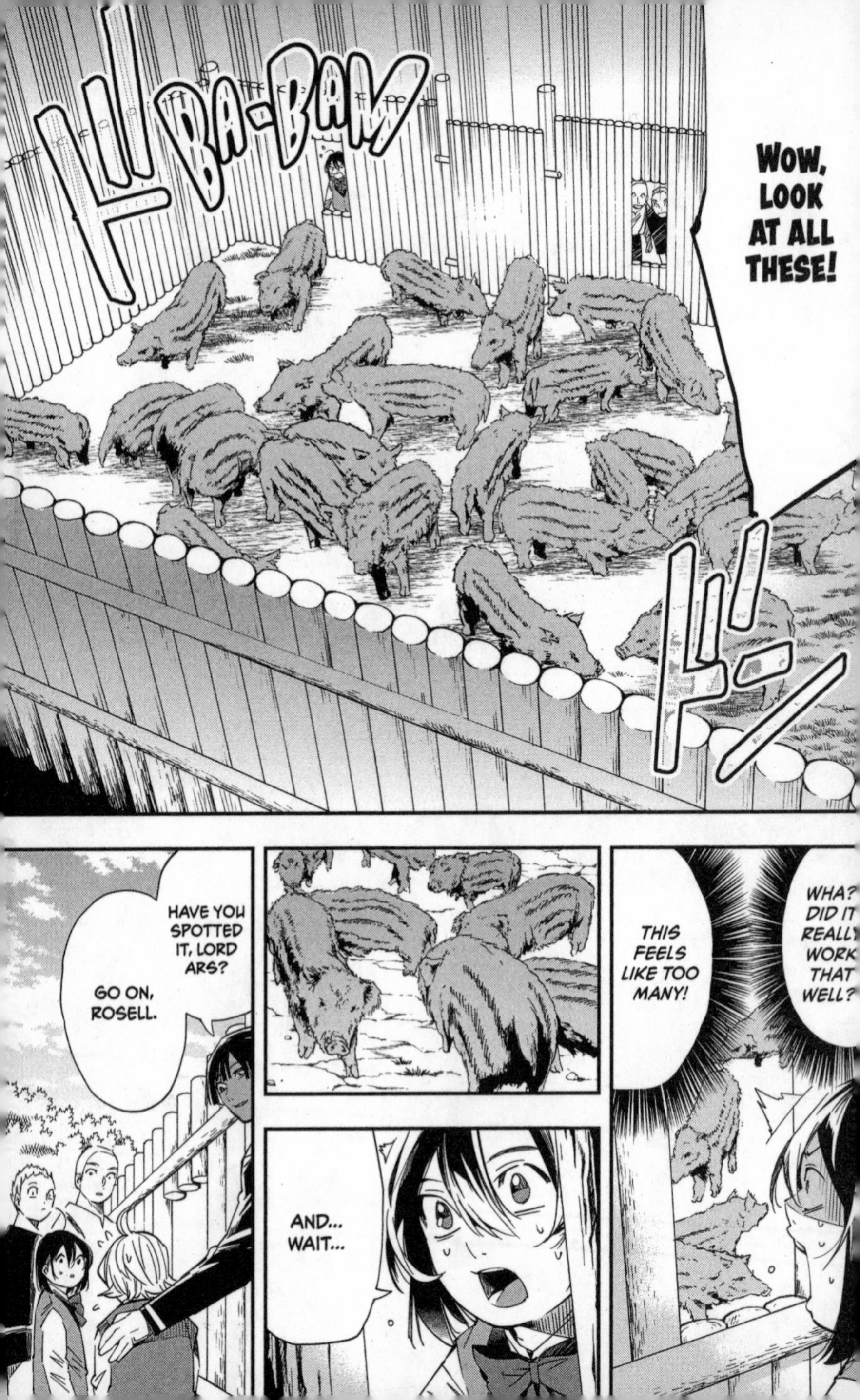
BA-BAM
WOW, LOOK AT ALL THESE!
WHA? DID IT REALLY WORK THAT WELL?
THIS FEELS LIKE TOO MANY!
AND... WAIT...
HAVE YOU SPOTTED IT, LORD ARS?
GO ON, ROSELL.

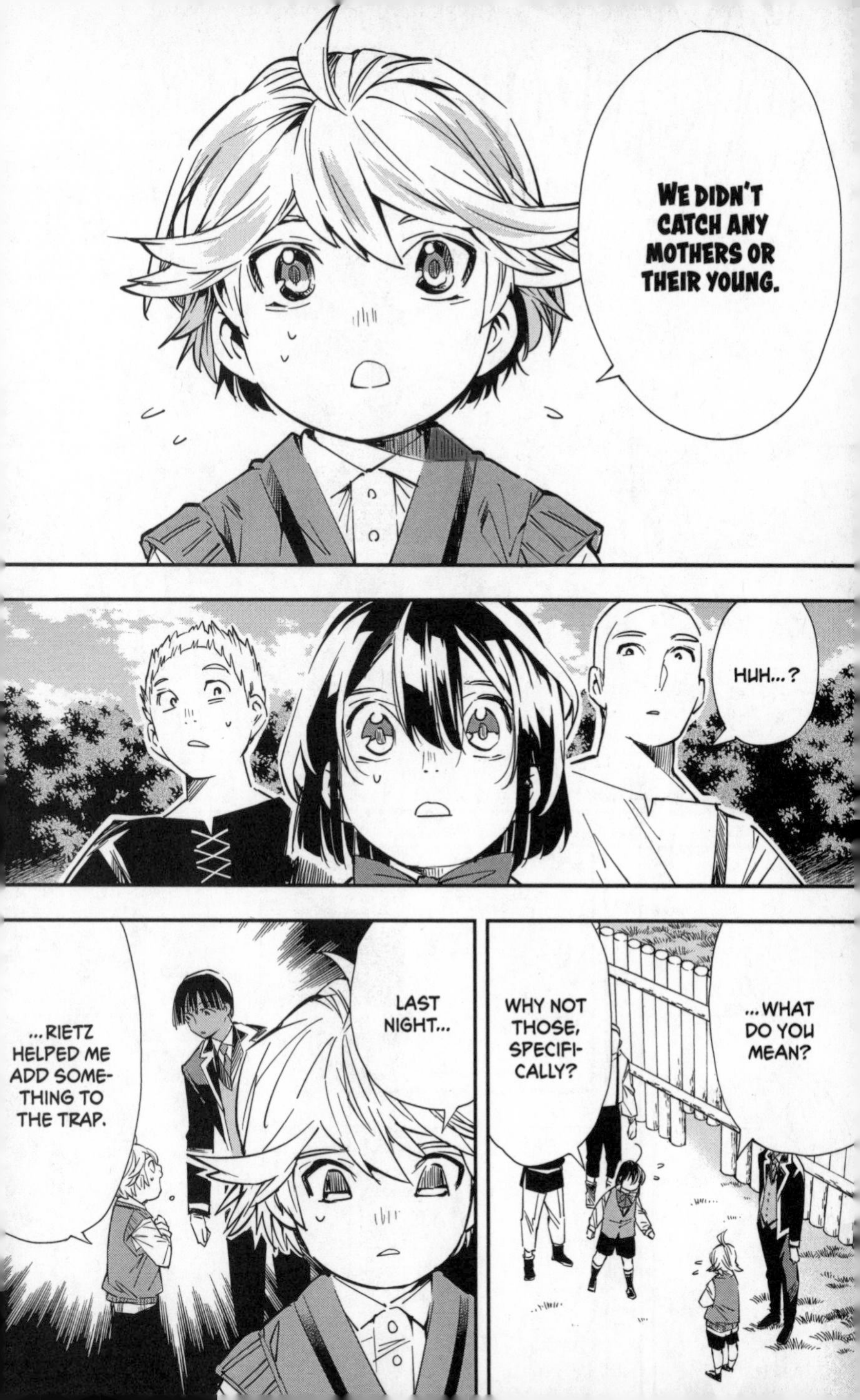
WE DIDN'T CATCH ANY MOTHERS OR THEIR YOUNG.
HUH...?
...WHAT DO YOU MEAN?
WHY NOT THOSE, SPECIFI-CALLY?
LAST NIGHT...
...RIETZ HELPED ME ADD SOME-THING TO THE TRAP.

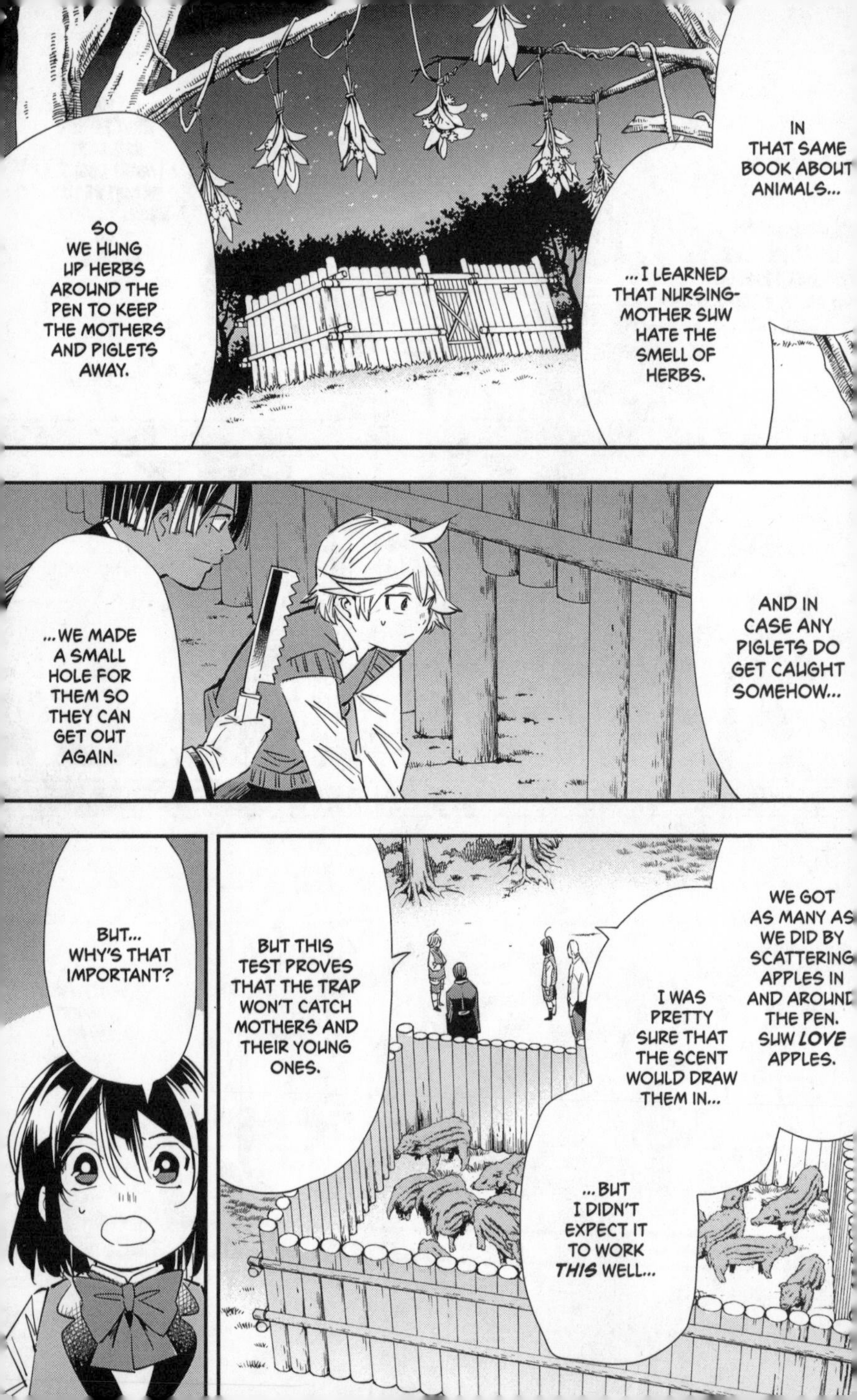
IN THAT SAME BOOK ABOUT ANIMALS...
...I LEARNED THAT NURSING-MOTHER SUW HATE THE SMELL OF HERBS.
SO WE HUNG UP HERBS AROUND THE PEN TO KEEP THE MOTHERS AND PIGLETS AWAY.
AND IN CASE ANY PIGLETS DO GET CAUGHT SOMEHOW...
...WE MADE A SMALL HOLE FOR THEM SO THEY CAN GET OUT AGAIN.
WE GOT AS MANY AS WE DID BY SCATTERING APPLES IN AND AROUND THE PEN. SUW *LOVE* APPLES.
I WAS PRETTY SURE THAT THE SCENT WOULD DRAW THEM IN...
...BUT I DIDN'T EXPECT IT TO WORK *THIS* WELL...
BUT THIS TEST PROVES THAT THE TRAP WON'T CATCH MOTHERS AND THEIR YOUNG ONES.
BUT... WHY'S THAT IMPORTANT?

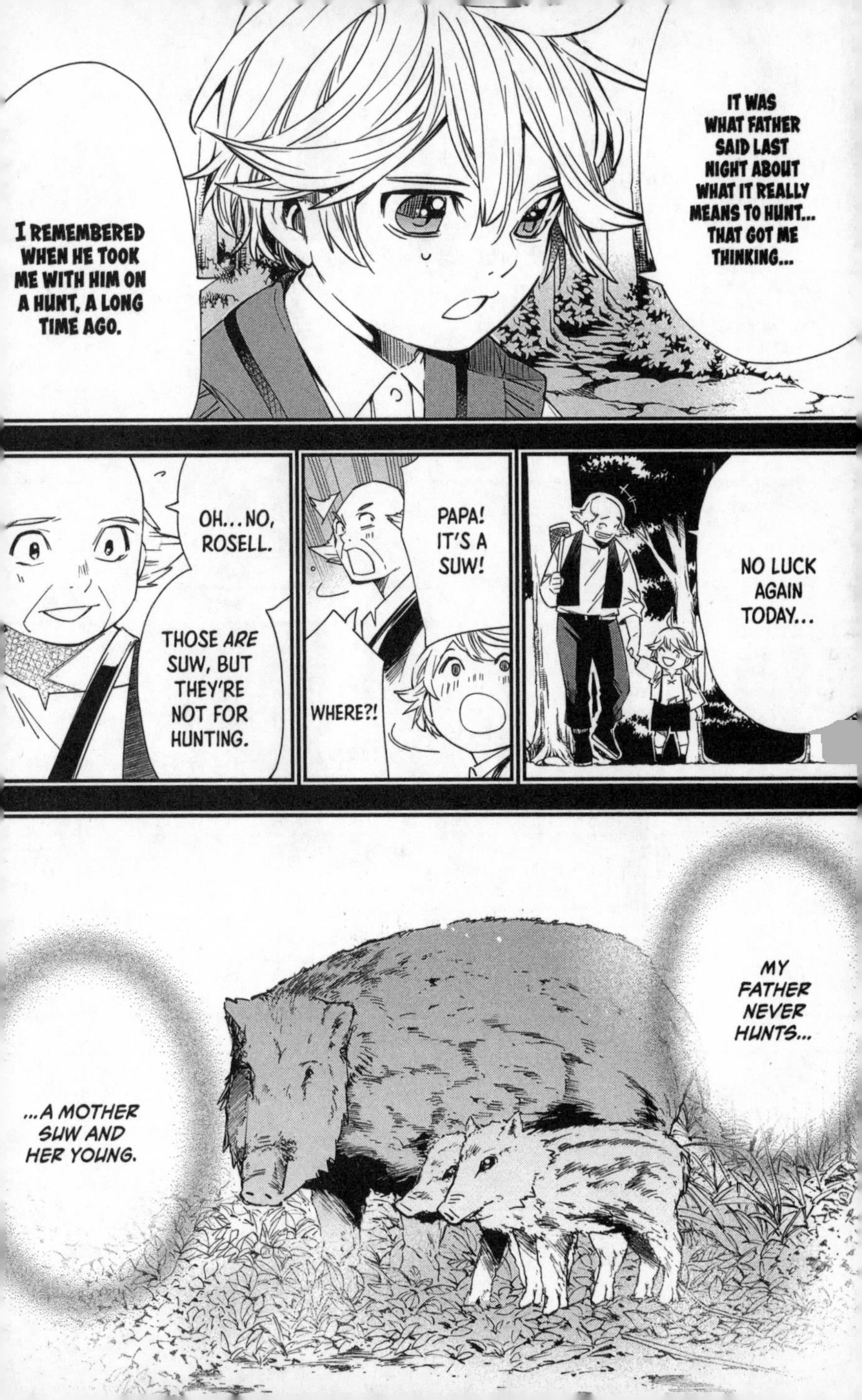
IT WAS WHAT FATHER SAID LAST NIGHT ABOUT WHAT IT REALLY MEANS TO HUNT... THAT GOT ME THINKING...
I REMEMBERED WHEN HE TOOK ME WITH HIM ON A HUNT, A LONG TIME AGO.
NO LUCK AGAIN TODAY...
PAPA! IT'S A SUW!
WHERE?!
OH...NO, ROSELL.
THOSE ARE SUW, BUT THEY'RE NOT FOR HUNTING.
MY FATHER NEVER HUNTS...
...A MOTHER SUW AND HER YOUNG.

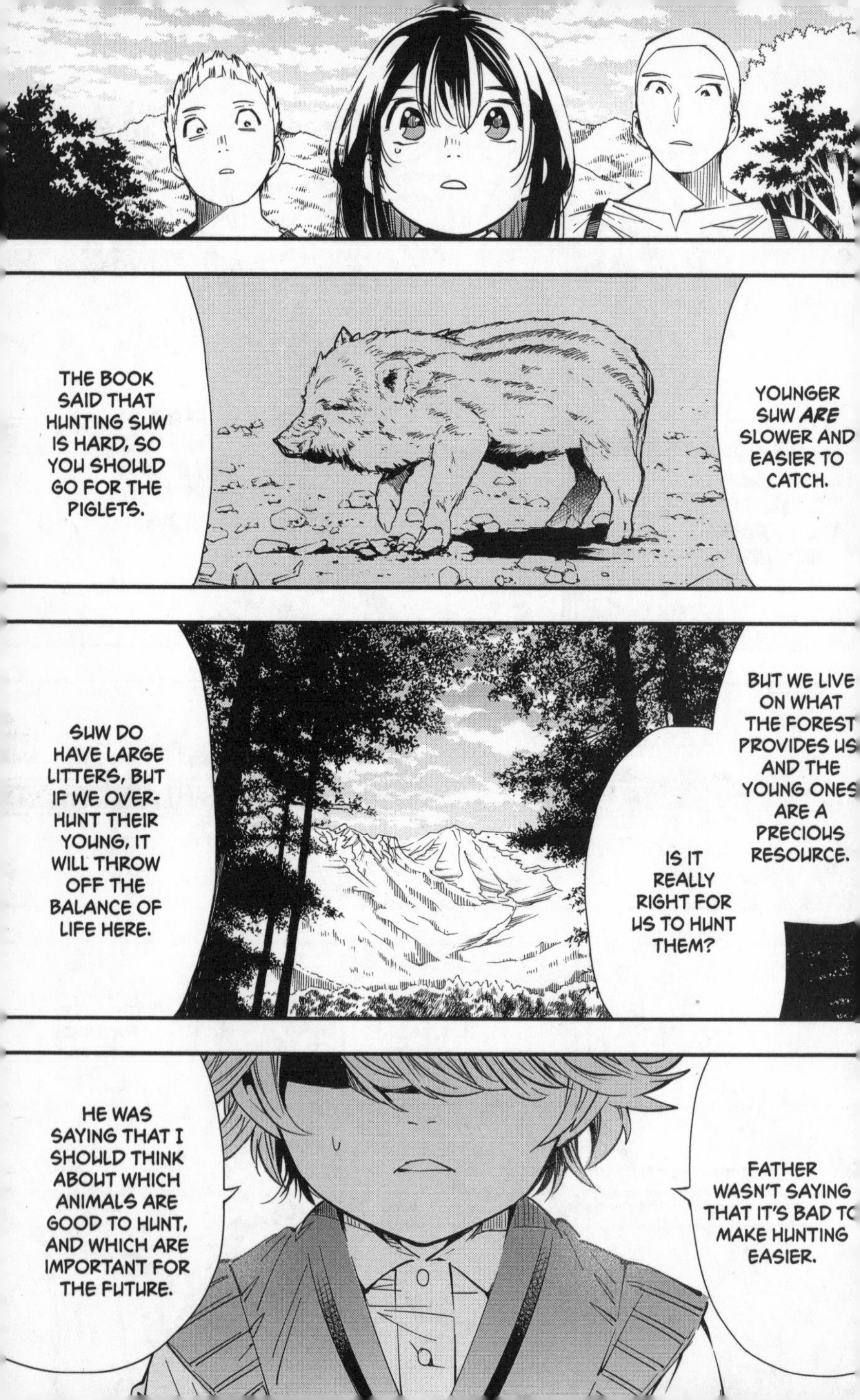

YOUNGER SUW ***ARE*** SLOWER AND EASIER TO CATCH.
THE BOOK SAID THAT HUNTING SUW IS HARD, SO YOU SHOULD GO FOR THE PIGLETS.
BUT WE LIVE ON WHAT THE FOREST PROVIDES US AND THE YOUNG ONES ARE A PRECIOUS RESOURCE.
IS IT REALLY RIGHT FOR US TO HUNT THEM?
SUW DO HAVE LARGE LITTERS, BUT IF WE OVER-HUNT THEIR YOUNG, IT WILL THROW OFF THE BALANCE OF LIFE HERE.
FATHER WASN'T SAYING THAT IT'S BAD TO MAKE HUNTING EASIER.
HE WAS SAYING THAT I SHOULD THINK ABOUT WHICH ANIMALS ARE GOOD TO HUNT, AND WHICH ARE IMPORTANT FOR THE FUTURE.

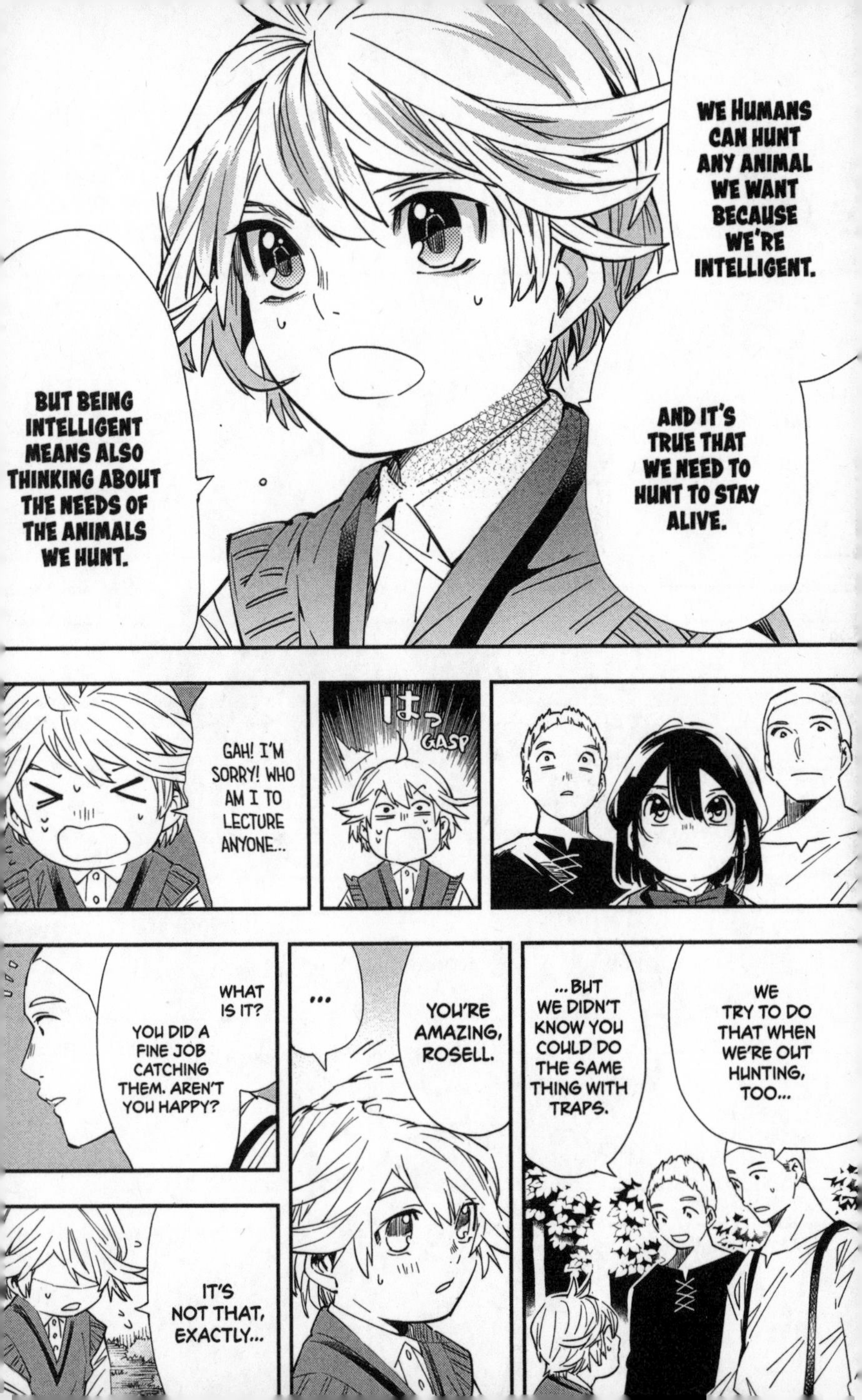
WE HUMANS CAN HUNT ANY ANIMAL WE WANT BECAUSE WE'RE INTELLIGENT.
AND IT'S TRUE THAT WE NEED TO HUNT TO STAY ALIVE.
BUT BEING INTELLIGENT MEANS ALSO THINKING ABOUT THE NEEDS OF THE ANIMALS WE HUNT.
はっ
GASP
GAH! I'M SORRY! WHO AM I TO LECTURE ANYONE...
WE TRY TO DO THAT WHEN WE'RE OUT HUNTING, TOO...
...BUT WE DIDN'T KNOW YOU COULD DO THE SAME THING WITH TRAPS.
YOU'RE AMAZING, ROSELL.
...
WHAT IS IT?
YOU DID A FINE JOB CATCHING THEM. AREN'T YOU HAPPY?
IT'S NOT THAT, EXACTLY...

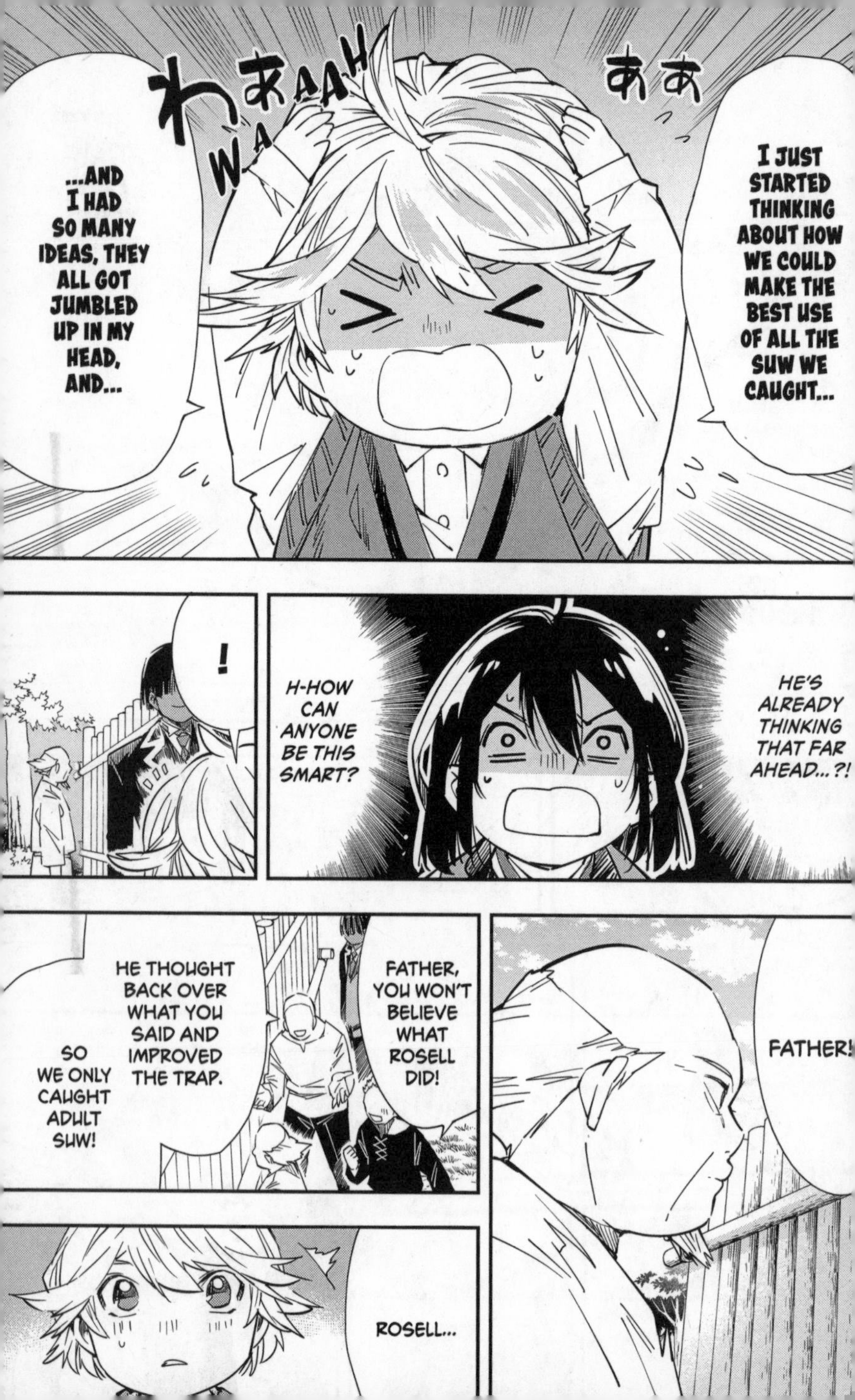
I JUST STARTED THINKING ABOUT HOW WE COULD MAKE THE BEST USE OF ALL THE SUW WE CAUGHT...
ああ
わあ
WAAAH
...AND I HAD SO MANY IDEAS, THEY ALL GOT JUMBLED UP IN MY HEAD, AND...
HE'S ALREADY THINKING THAT FAR AHEAD...?!
H-HOW CAN ANYONE BE THIS SMART?
!
FATHER!
FATHER, YOU WON'T BELIEVE WHAT ROSELL DID!
HE THOUGHT BACK OVER WHAT YOU SAID AND IMPROVED THE TRAP.
SO WE ONLY CAUGHT ADULT SUW!
ROSELL...

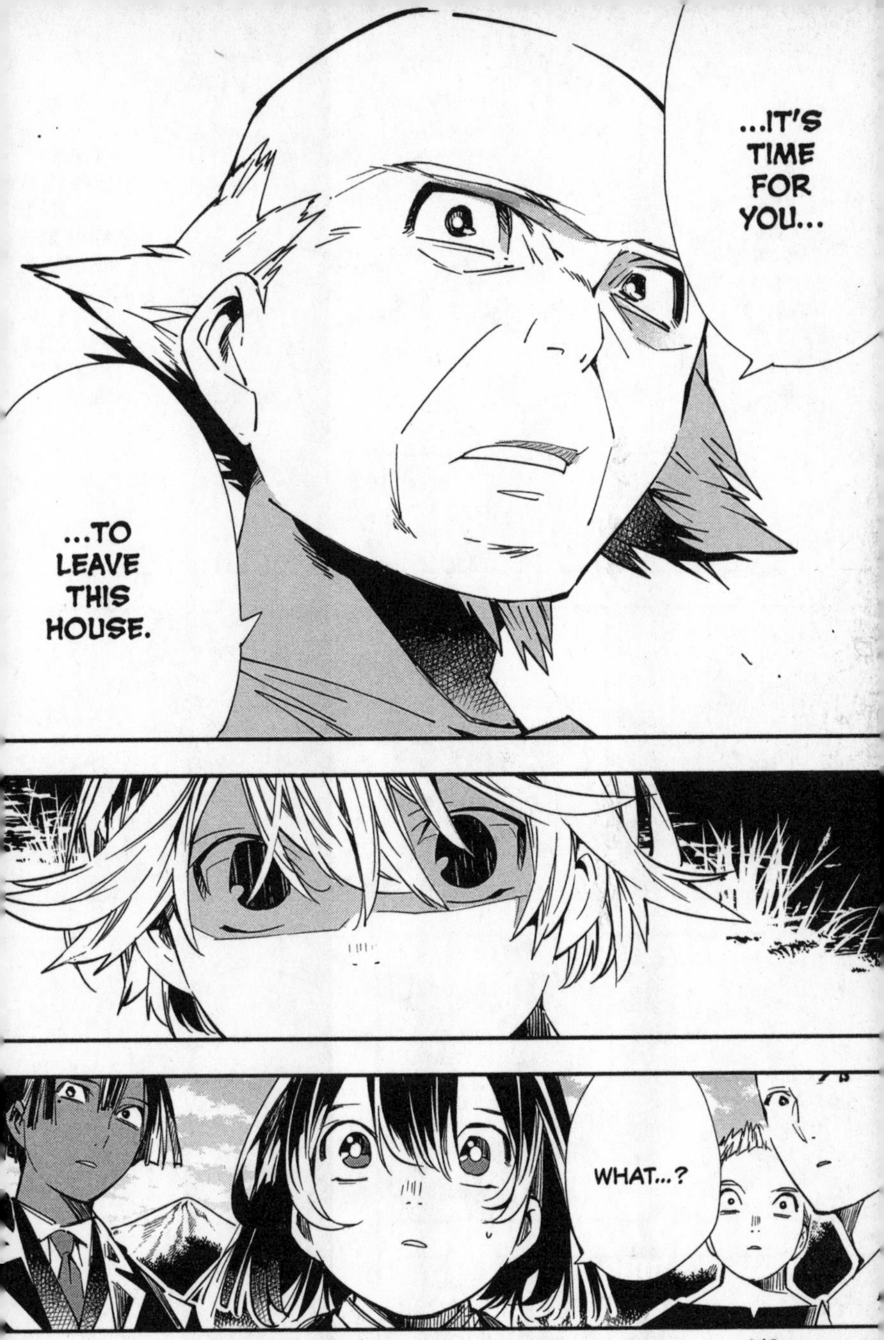
...IT'S TIME FOR YOU...
...TO LEAVE THIS HOUSE.
WHAT...?

As a Reincarnated
ARISTOCRAT,
I'll Use My Appraisal Skill to
Rise in the World

As a Reincarnated **ARISTOCRAT,** I'll Use My Appraisal Skill to **Rise in the World**

Chapter 16: The Shape of Family

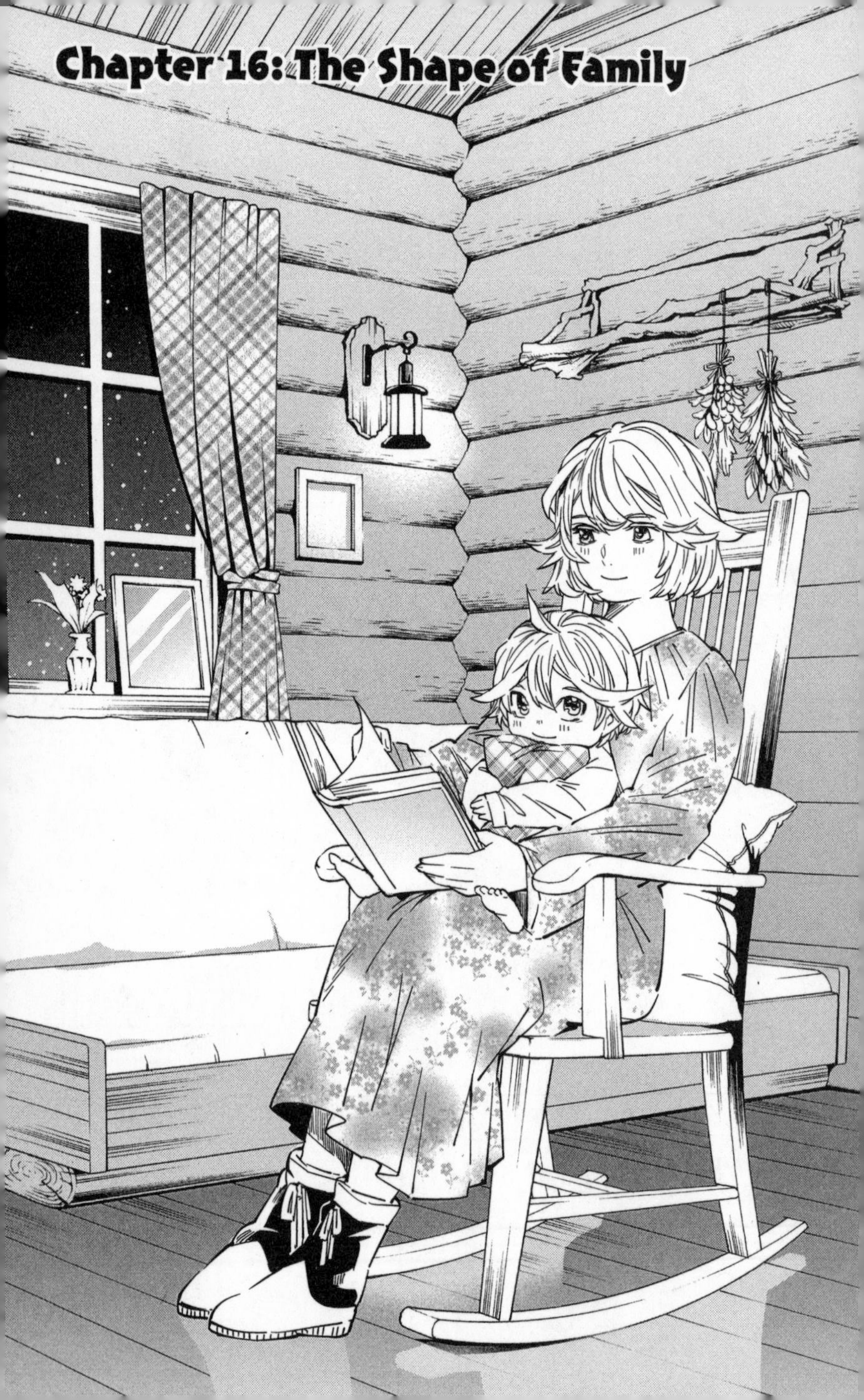

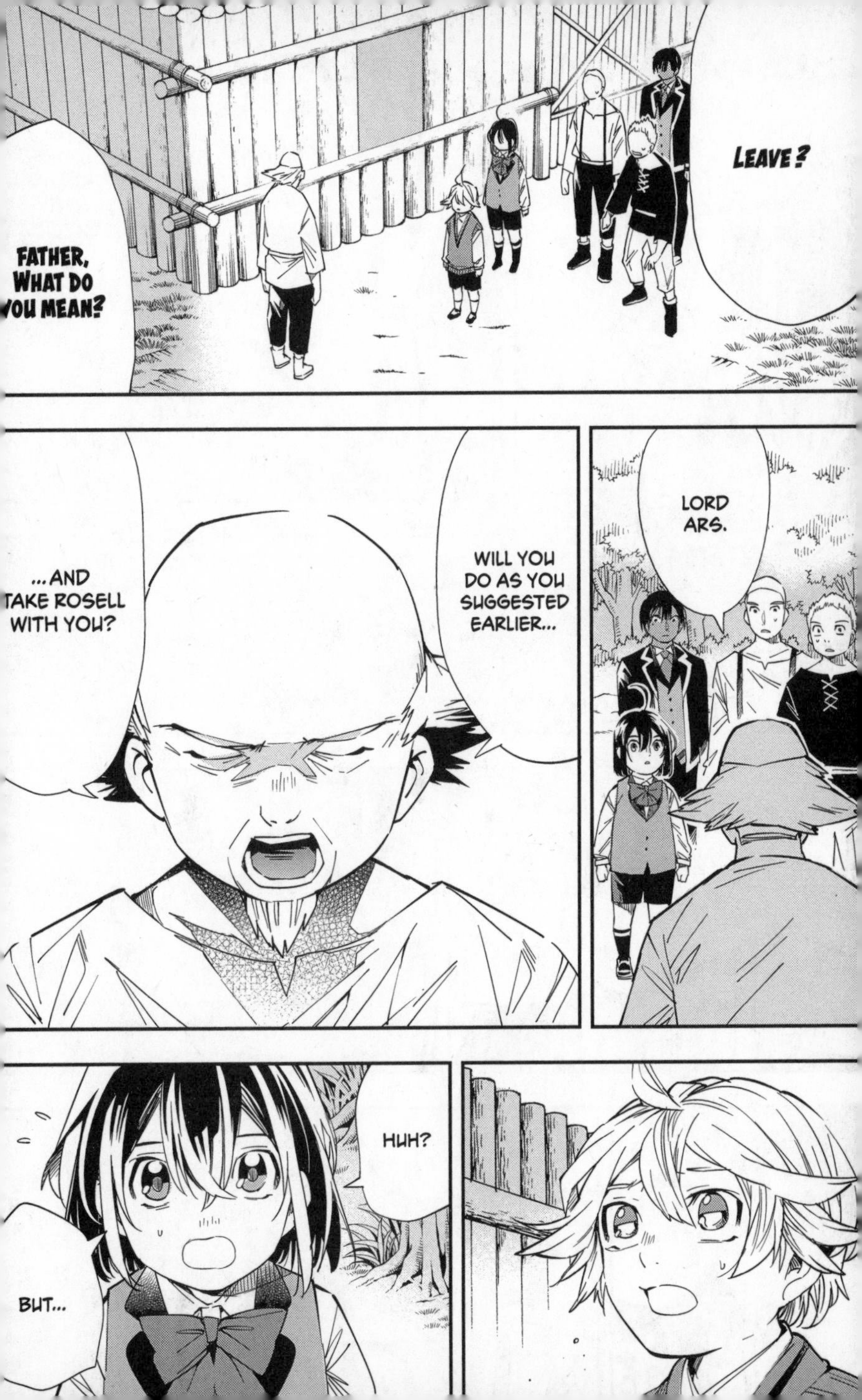
LEAVE?
FATHER, WHAT DO YOU MEAN?
LORD ARS.
WILL YOU DO AS YOU SUGGESTED EARLIER...
...AND TAKE ROSELL WITH YOU?
HUH?
BUT...

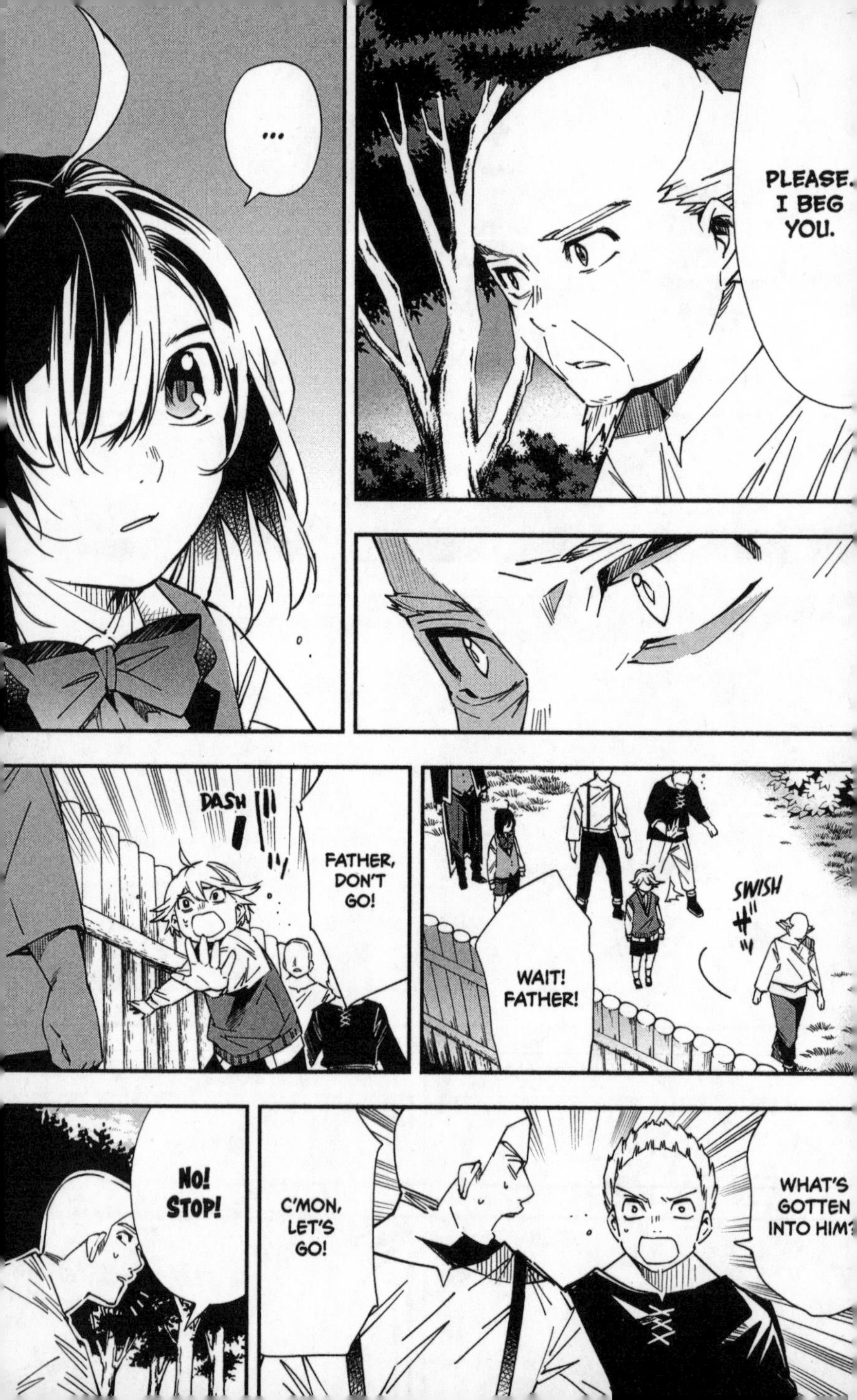
PLEASE. I BEG YOU.
...
SWISH
WAIT! FATHER!
FATHER, DON'T GO!
DASH
WHAT'S GOTTEN INTO HIM?
C'MON, LET'S GO!
NO! STOP!

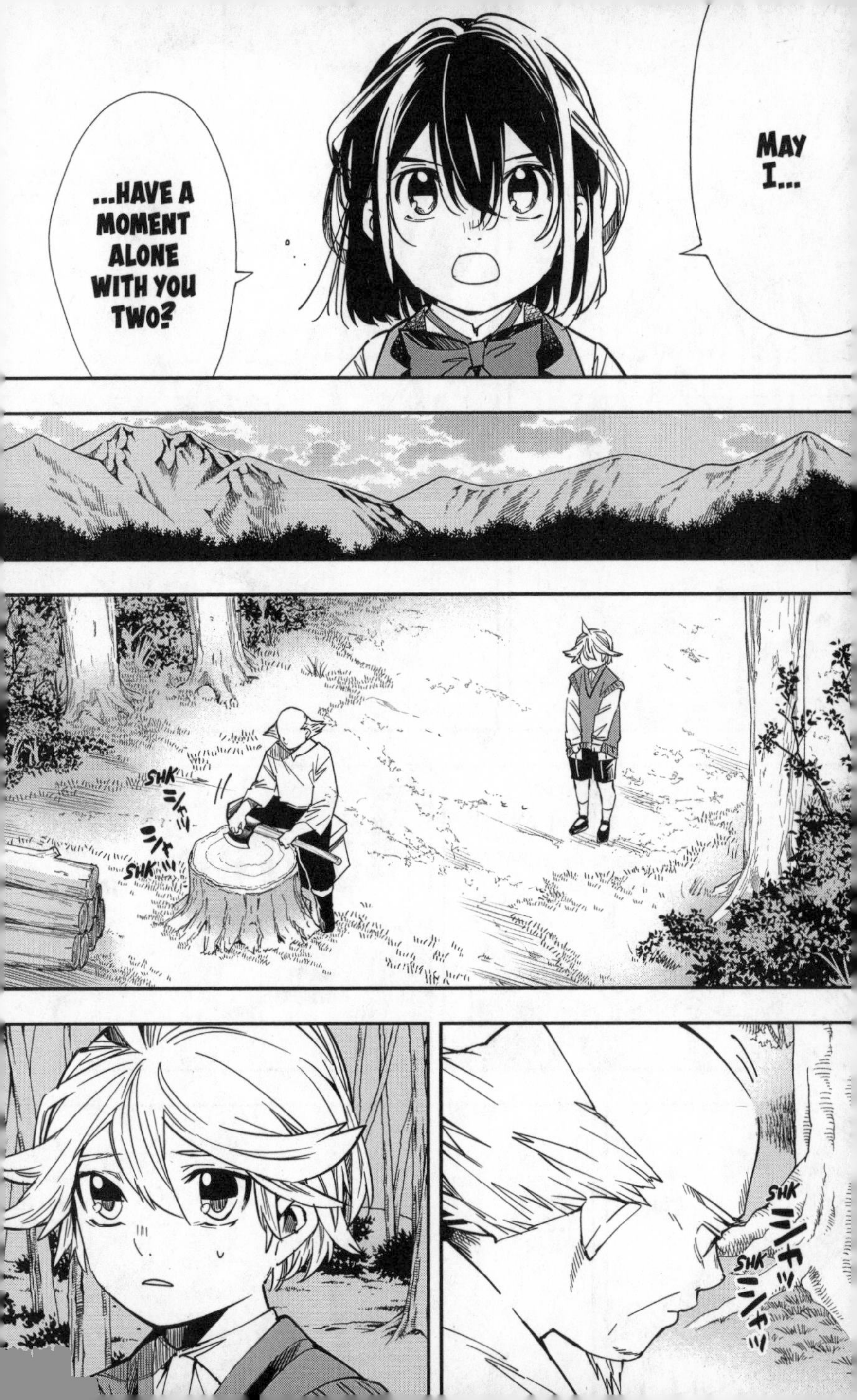
MAY I...
...HAVE A MOMENT ALONE WITH YOU TWO?
SHK
SHK
SHK
SHK

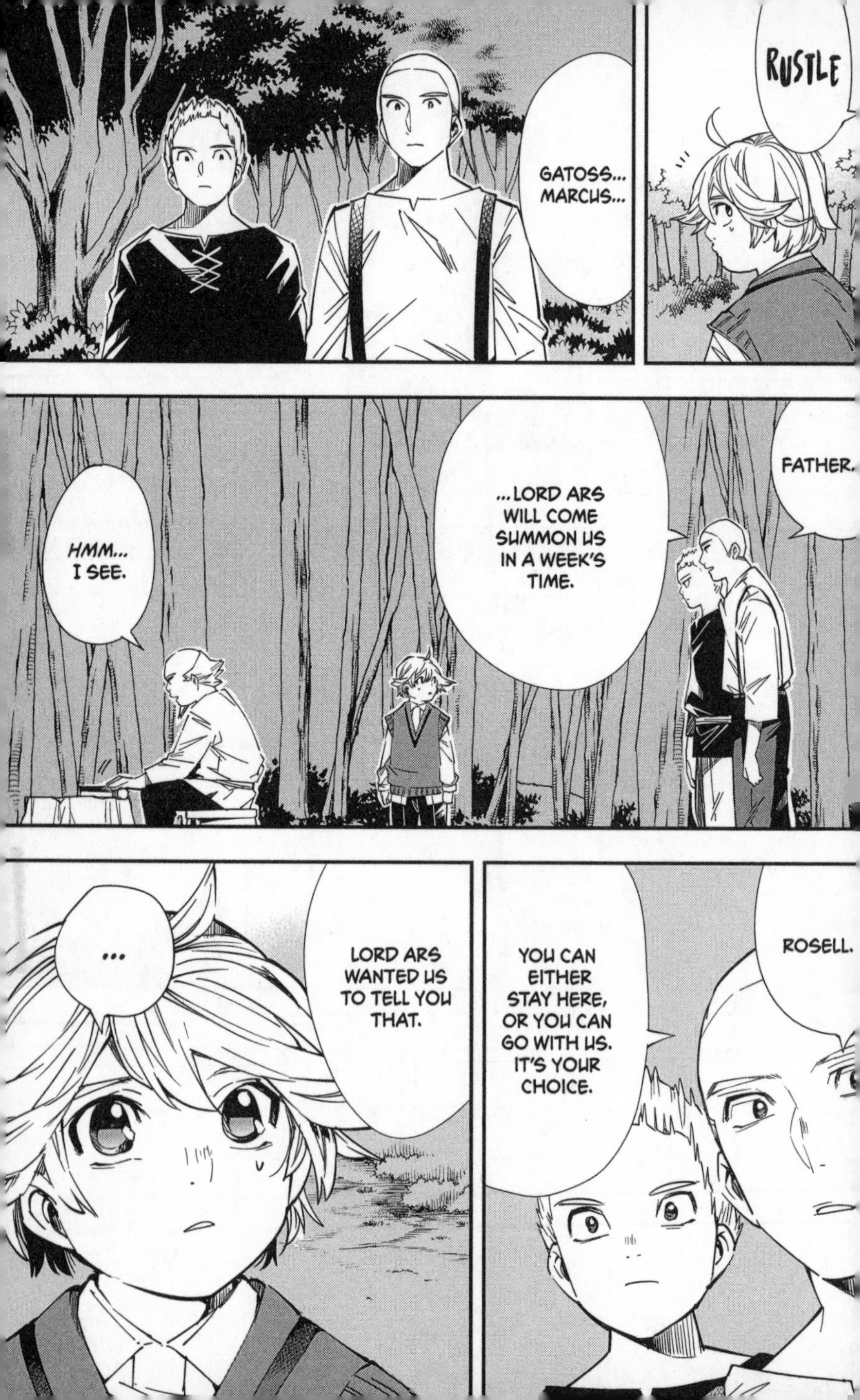
RUSTLE
GATOSS... MARCUS...
FATHER.
...LORD ARS WILL COME SUMMON US IN A WEEK'S TIME.
HMM... I SEE.
ROSELL.
YOU CAN EITHER STAY HERE, OR YOU CAN GO WITH US. IT'S YOUR CHOICE.
LORD ARS WANTED US TO TELL YOU THAT.
...

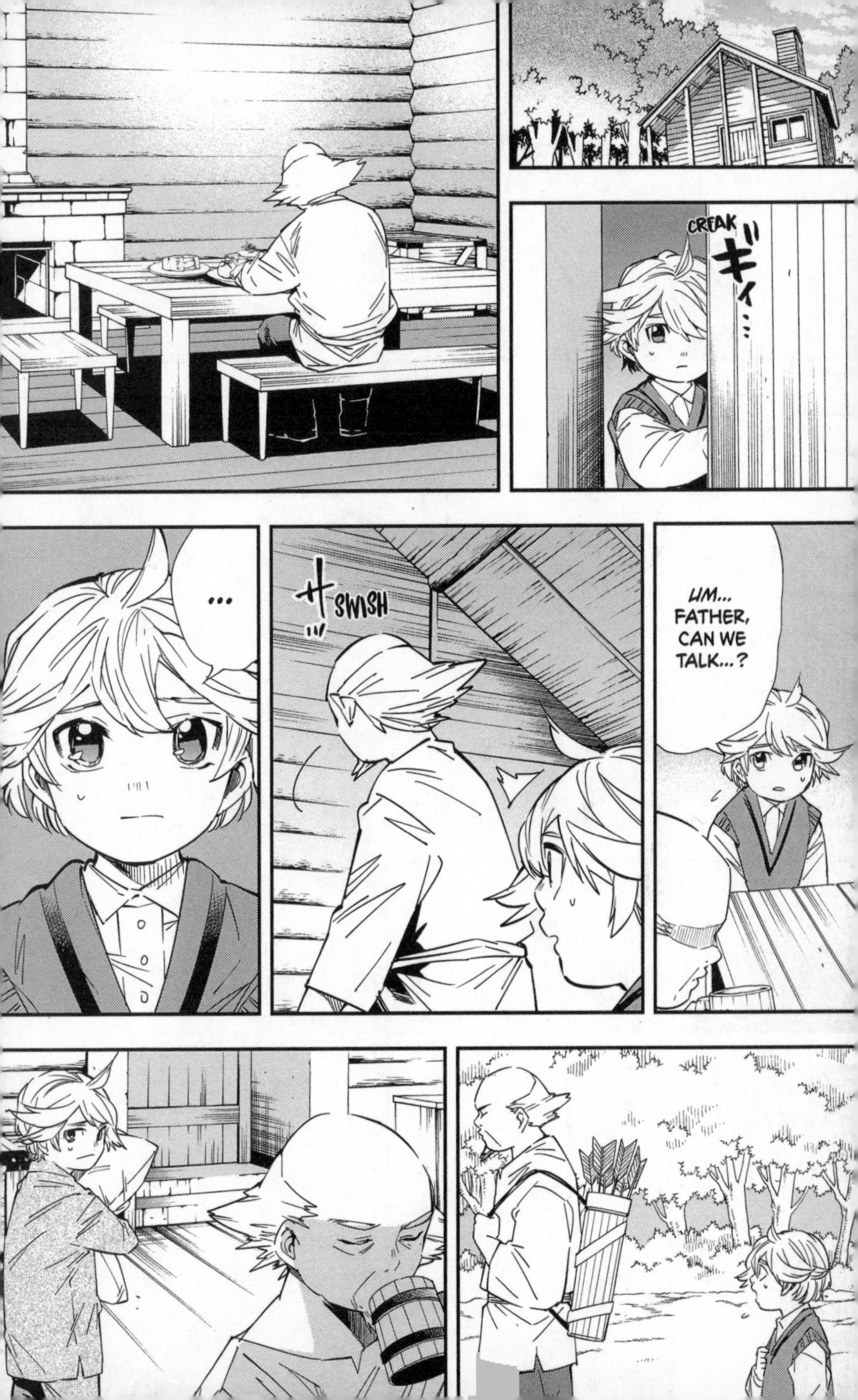
CREAK
ギィ…
UM... FATHER, CAN WE TALK...?
SWISH
...

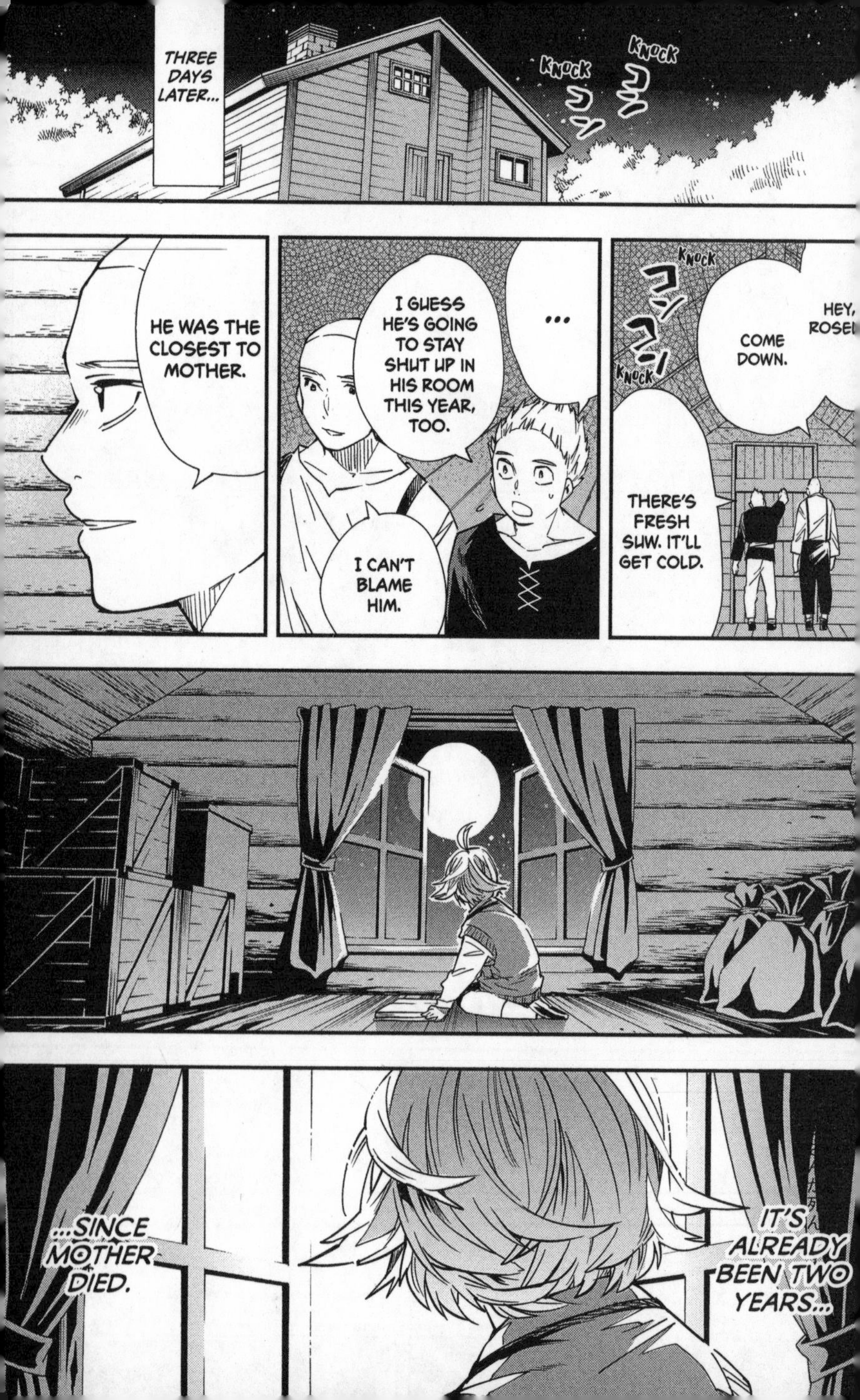
KNOCK
KNOCK
THREE DAYS LATER...
KNOCK
HEY, ROSE!
COME DOWN.
KNOCK
THERE'S FRESH SUW. IT'LL GET COLD.
...
I GUESS HE'S GOING TO STAY SHUT UP IN HIS ROOM THIS YEAR, TOO.
I CAN'T BLAME HIM.
HE WAS THE CLOSEST TO MOTHER.
IT'S ALREADY BEEN TWO YEARS...
...SINCE MOTHER DIED.

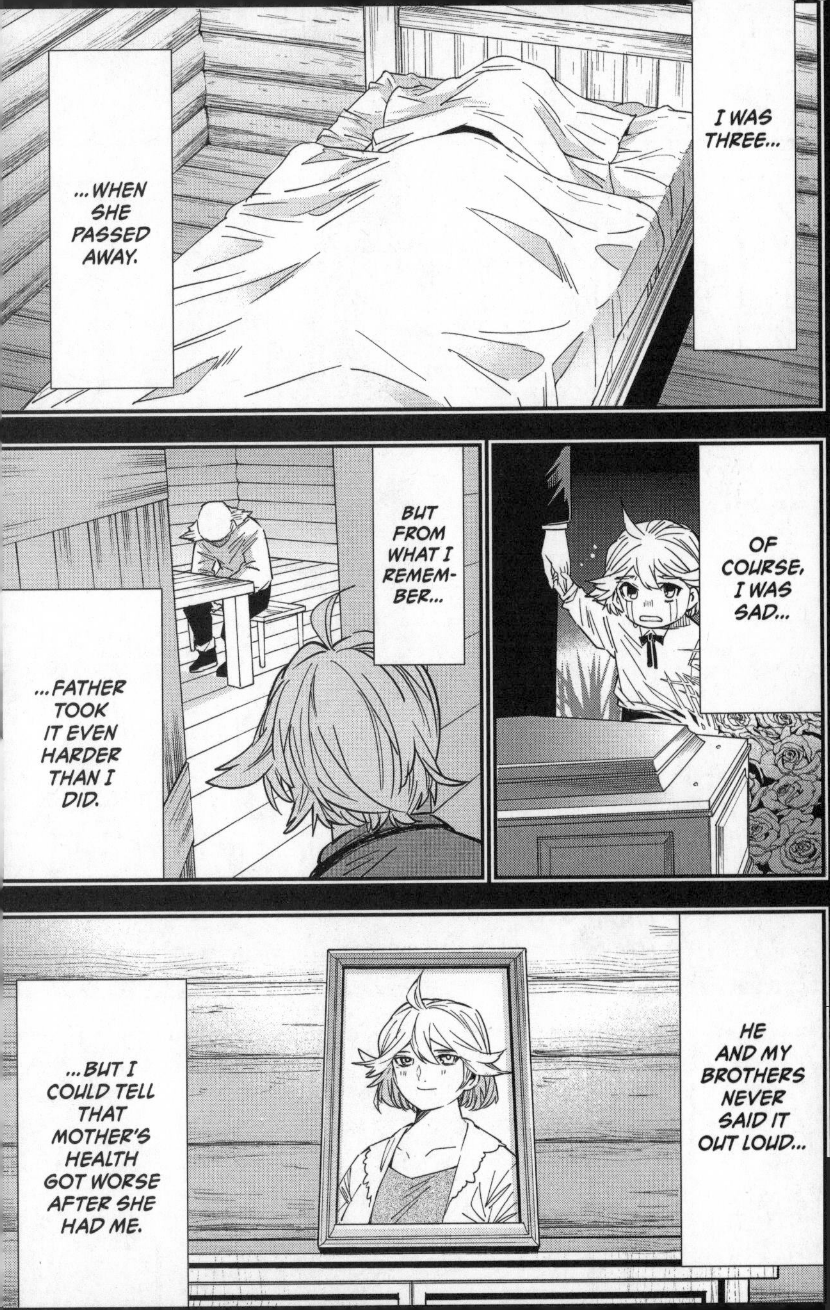
I WAS THREE...
...WHEN SHE PASSED AWAY.
OF COURSE, I WAS SAD...
BUT FROM WHAT I REMEMBER...
...FATHER TOOK IT EVEN HARDER THAN I DID.
HE AND MY BROTHERS NEVER SAID IT OUT LOUD...
...BUT I COULD TELL THAT MOTHER'S HEALTH GOT WORSE AFTER SHE HAD ME.

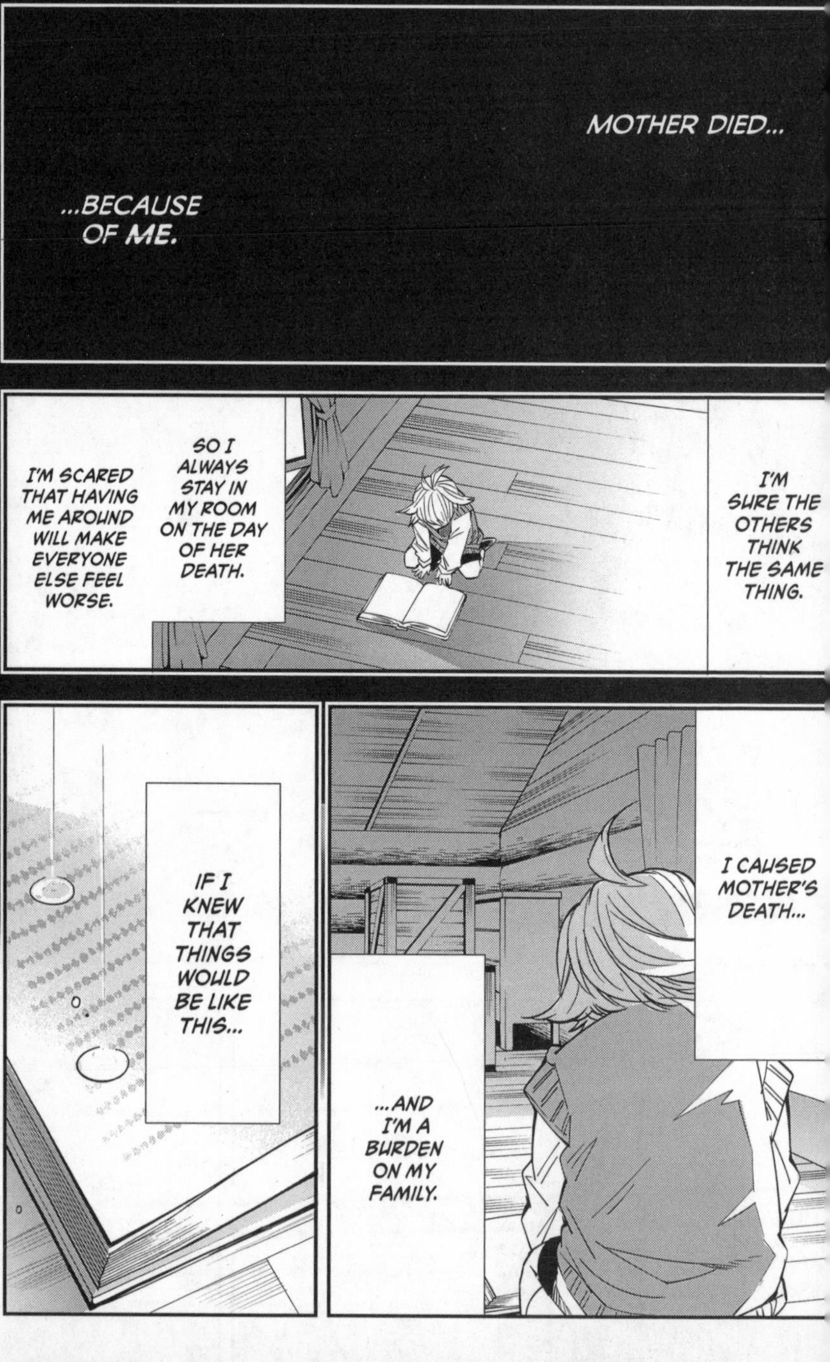
MOTHER DIED...
...BECAUSE OF ME.
I'M SURE THE OTHERS THINK THE SAME THING.
SO I ALWAYS STAY IN MY ROOM ON THE DAY OF HER DEATH.
I'M SCARED THAT HAVING ME AROUND WILL MAKE EVERYONE ELSE FEEL WORSE.
I CAUSED MOTHER'S DEATH...
...AND I'M A BURDEN ON MY FAMILY.
IF I KNEW THAT THINGS WOULD BE LIKE THIS...

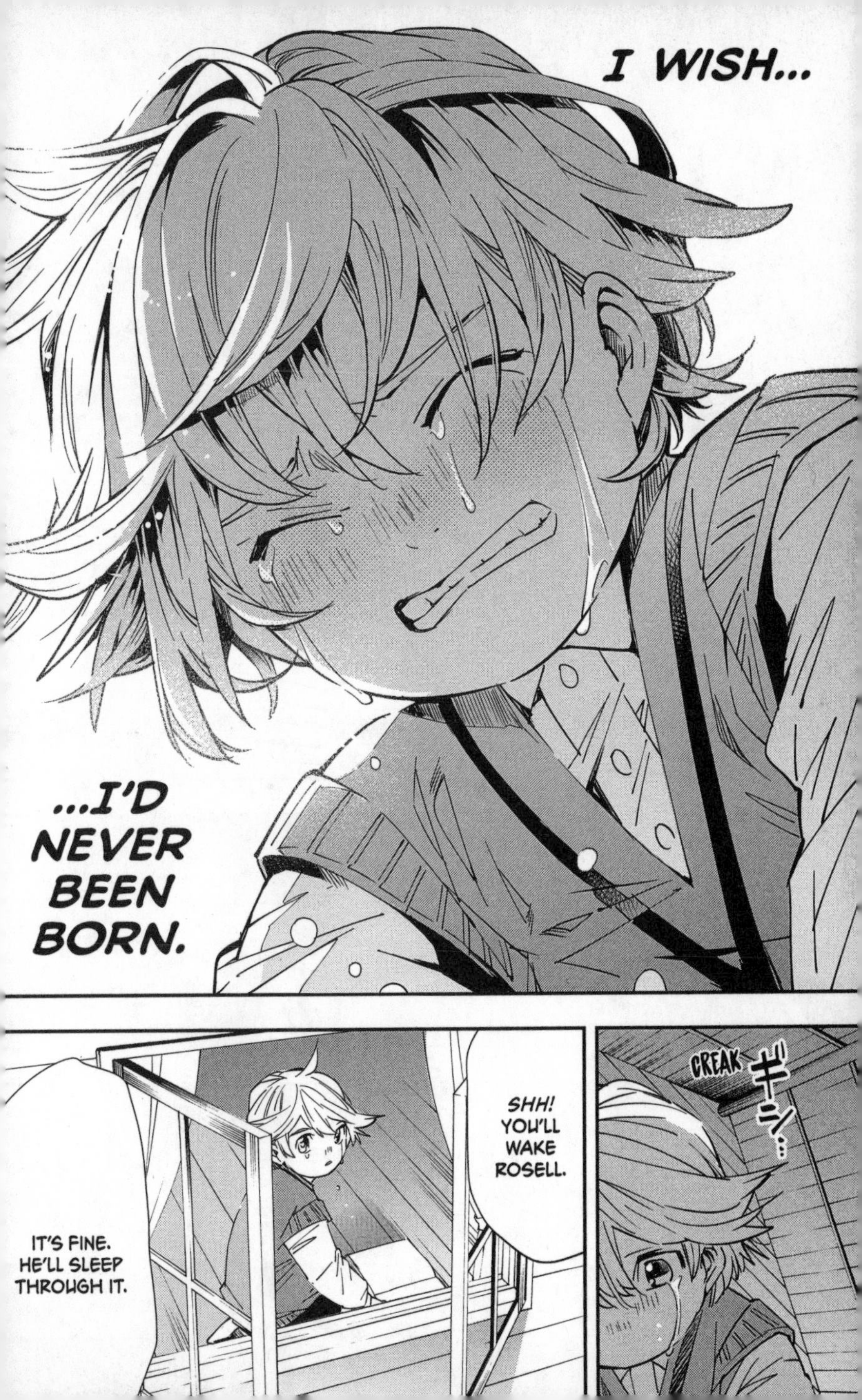
I WISH...
...I'D NEVER BEEN BORN.
CREAK
SHH! YOU'LL WAKE ROSELL.
IT'S FINE. HE'LL SLEEP THROUGH IT.

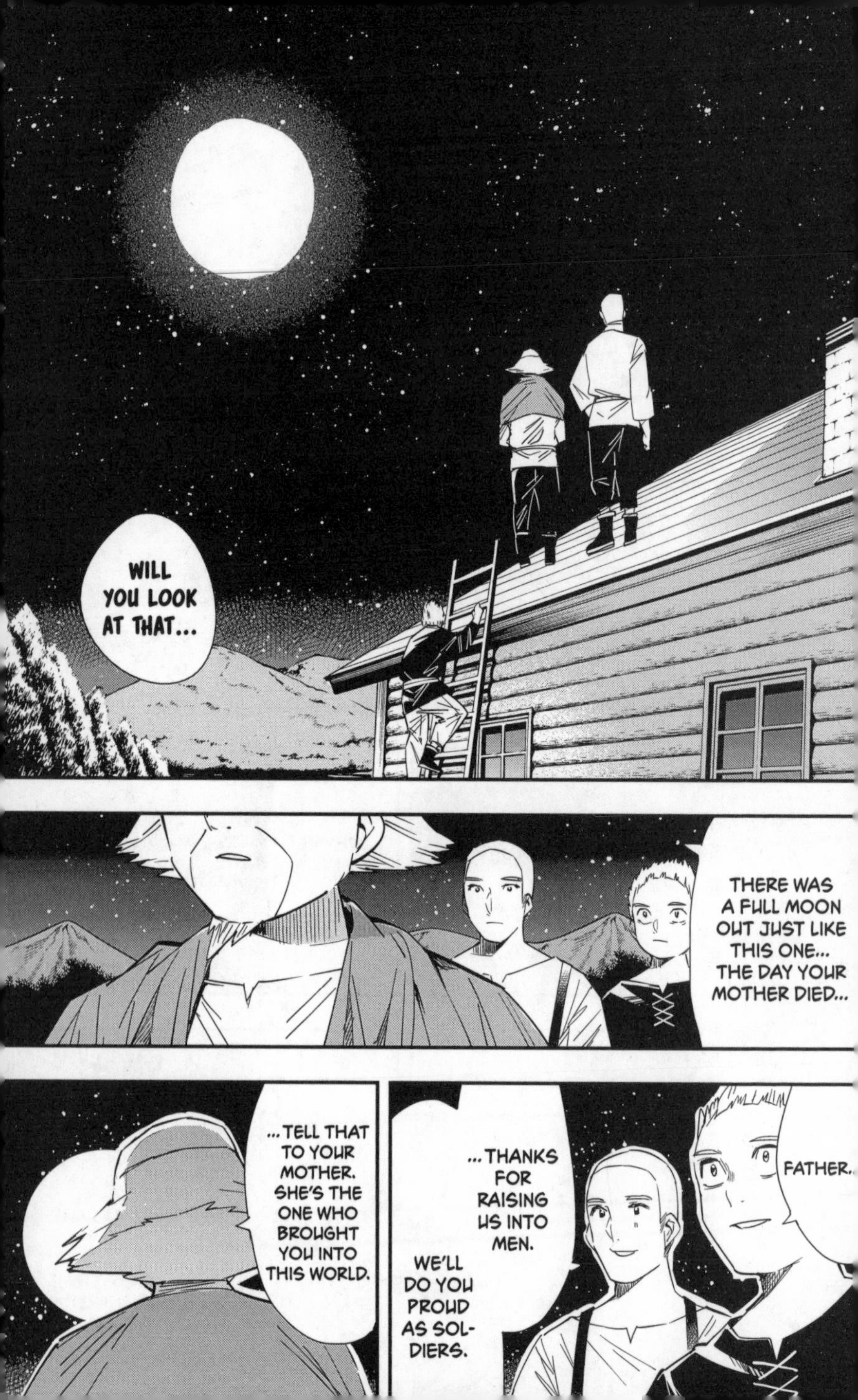
WILL YOU LOOK AT THAT...
THERE WAS A FULL MOON OUT JUST LIKE THIS ONE... THE DAY YOUR MOTHER DIED...
FATHER.
...THANKS FOR RAISING US INTO MEN.
WE'LL DO YOU PROUD AS SOL-DIERS.
...TELL THAT TO YOUR MOTHER. SHE'S THE ONE WHO BROUGHT YOU INTO THIS WORLD.

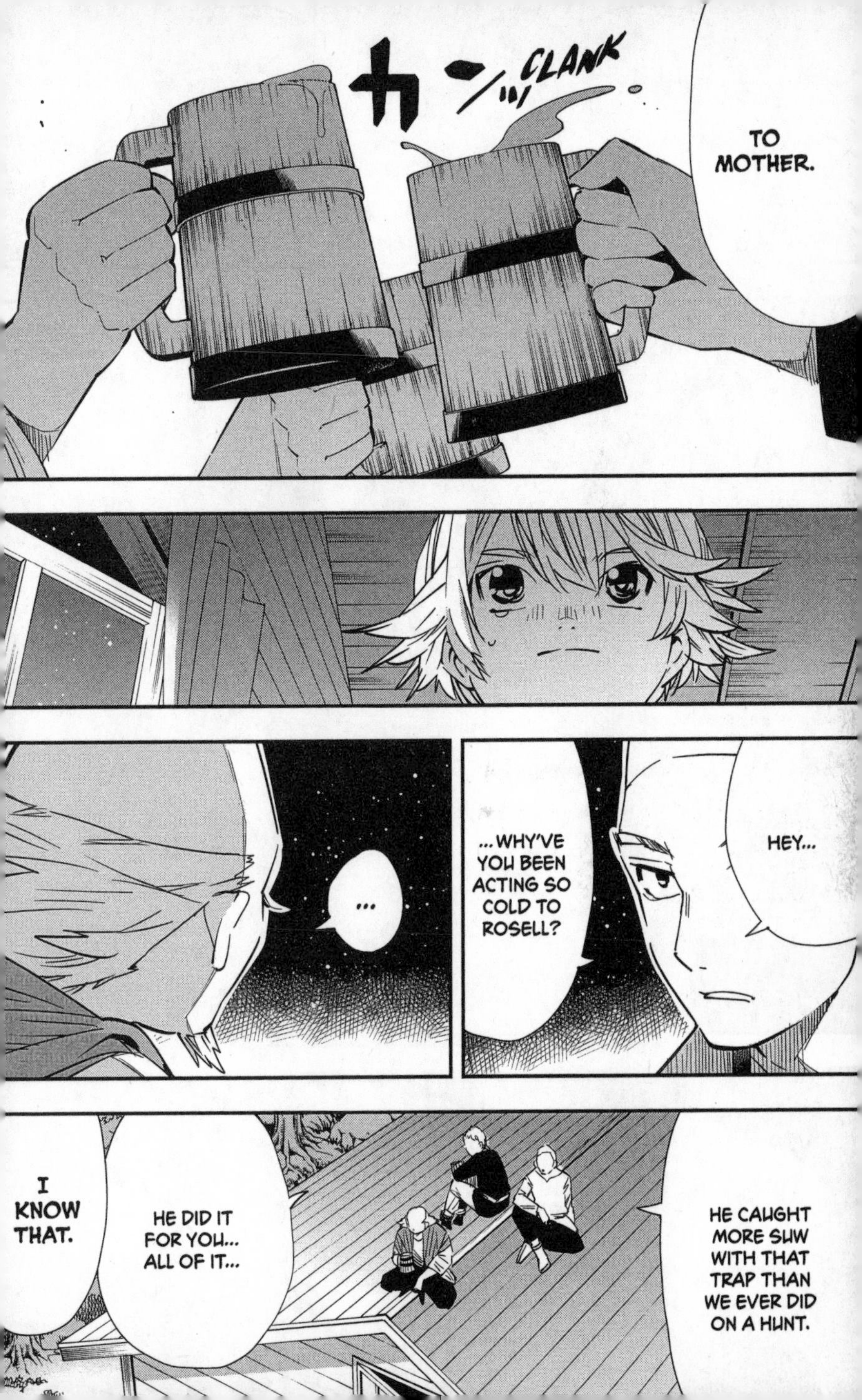
TO MOTHER.
カン
CLANK
HEY...
...WHY'VE YOU BEEN ACTING SO COLD TO ROSELL?
...
HE CAUGHT MORE SUW WITH THAT TRAP THAN WE EVER DID ON A HUNT.
HE DID IT FOR YOU... ALL OF IT...
I KNOW THAT.

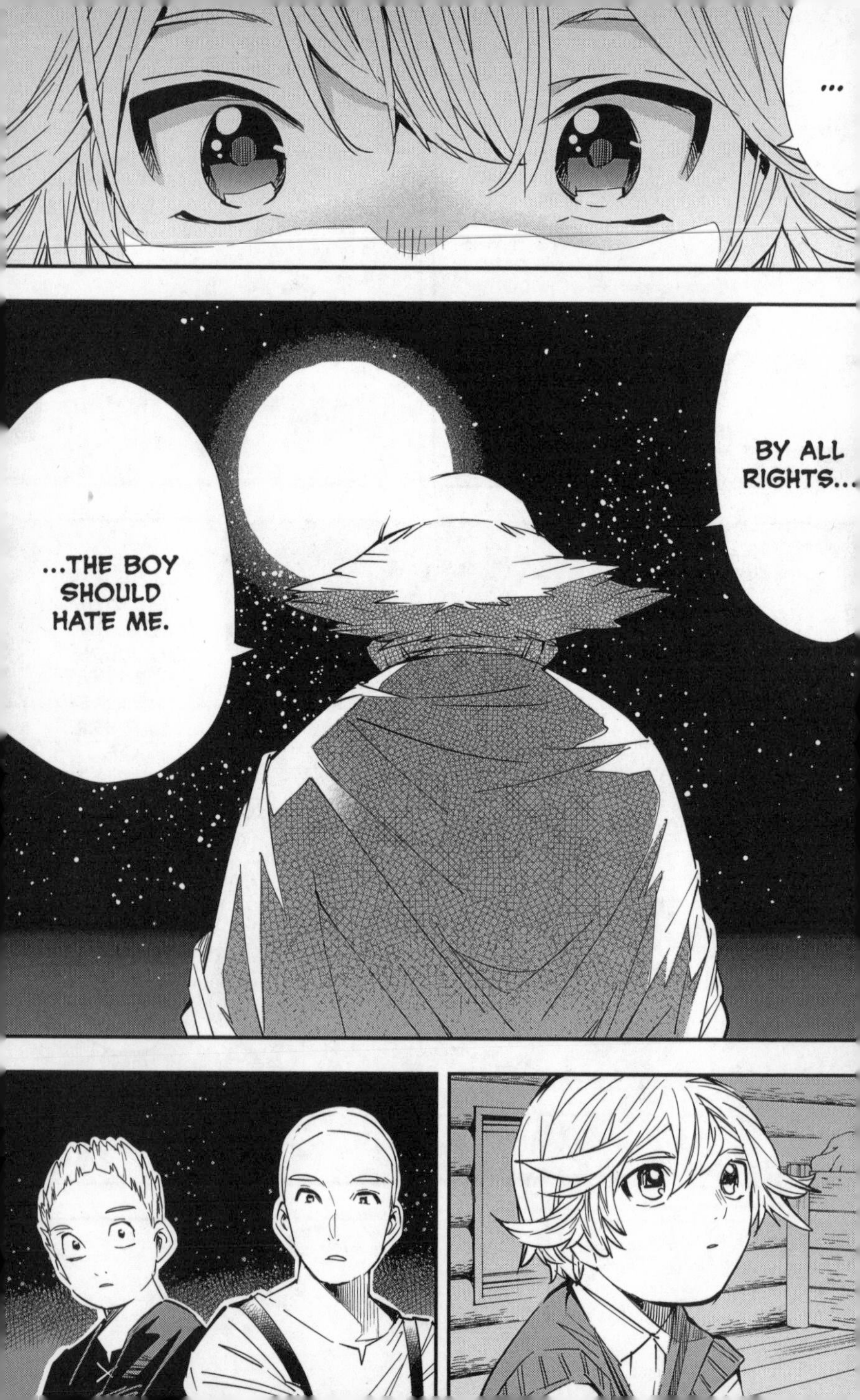
...
BY ALL RIGHTS...
...THE BOY SHOULD HATE ME.

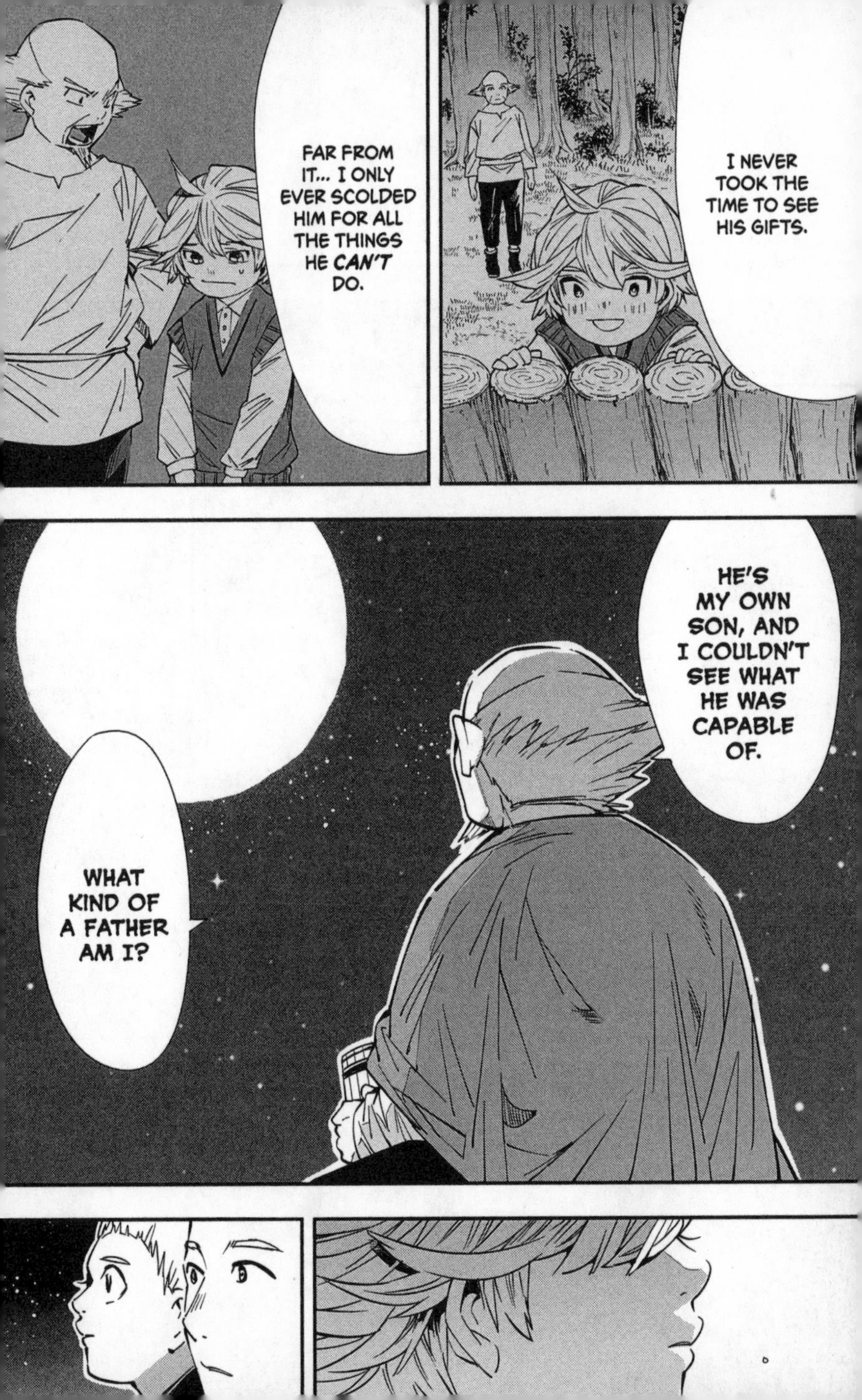
I NEVER TOOK THE TIME TO SEE HIS GIFTS.
FAR FROM IT... I ONLY EVER SCOLDED HIM FOR ALL THE THINGS HE *CAN'T* DO.
HE'S MY OWN SON, AND I COULDN'T SEE WHAT HE WAS CAPABLE OF.
WHAT KIND OF A FATHER AM I?

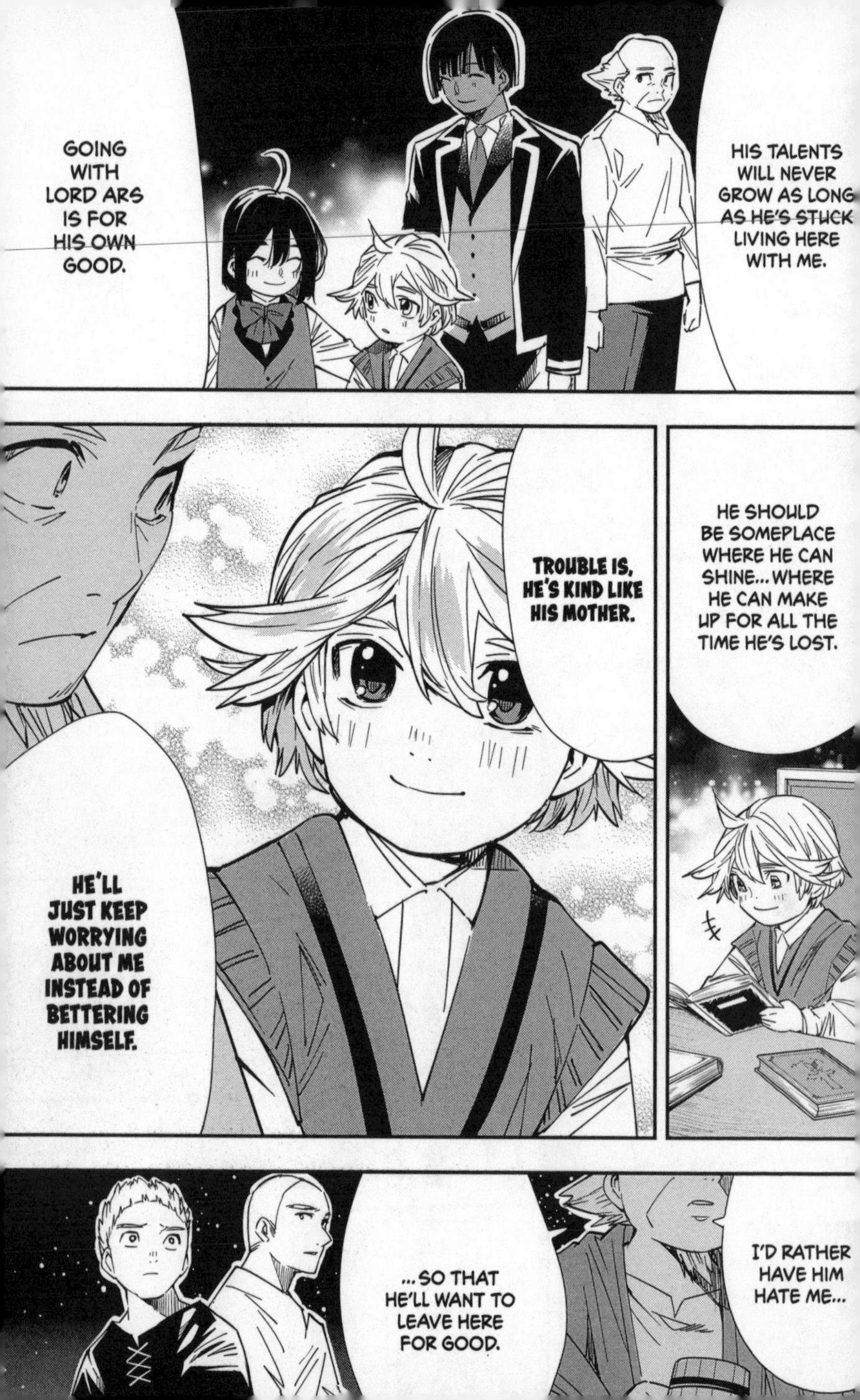
HIS TALENTS WILL NEVER GROW AS LONG AS HE'S STUCK LIVING HERE WITH ME.
GOING WITH LORD ARS IS FOR HIS OWN GOOD.
HE SHOULD BE SOMEPLACE WHERE HE CAN SHINE... WHERE HE CAN MAKE UP FOR ALL THE TIME HE'S LOST.
TROUBLE IS, HE'S KIND LIKE HIS MOTHER.
HE'LL JUST KEEP WORRYING ABOUT ME INSTEAD OF BETTERING HIMSELF.
I'D RATHER HAVE HIM HATE ME...
...SO THAT HE'LL WANT TO LEAVE HERE FOR GOOD.

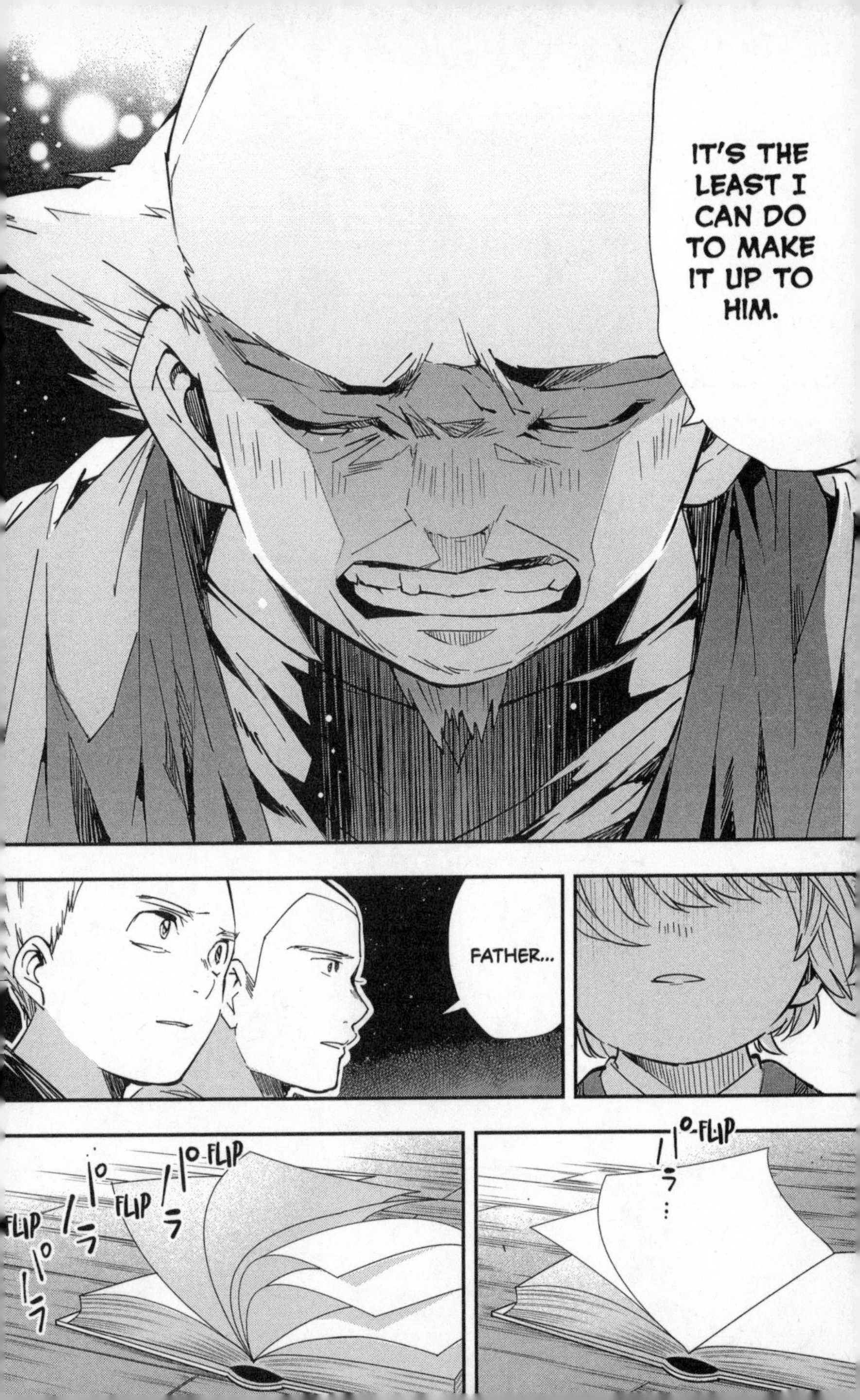
IT'S THE LEAST I CAN DO TO MAKE IT UP TO HIM.
FATHER...
パラ… FLIP
パラ FLIP
パラ FLIP
パラ FLIP
パラ FLIP

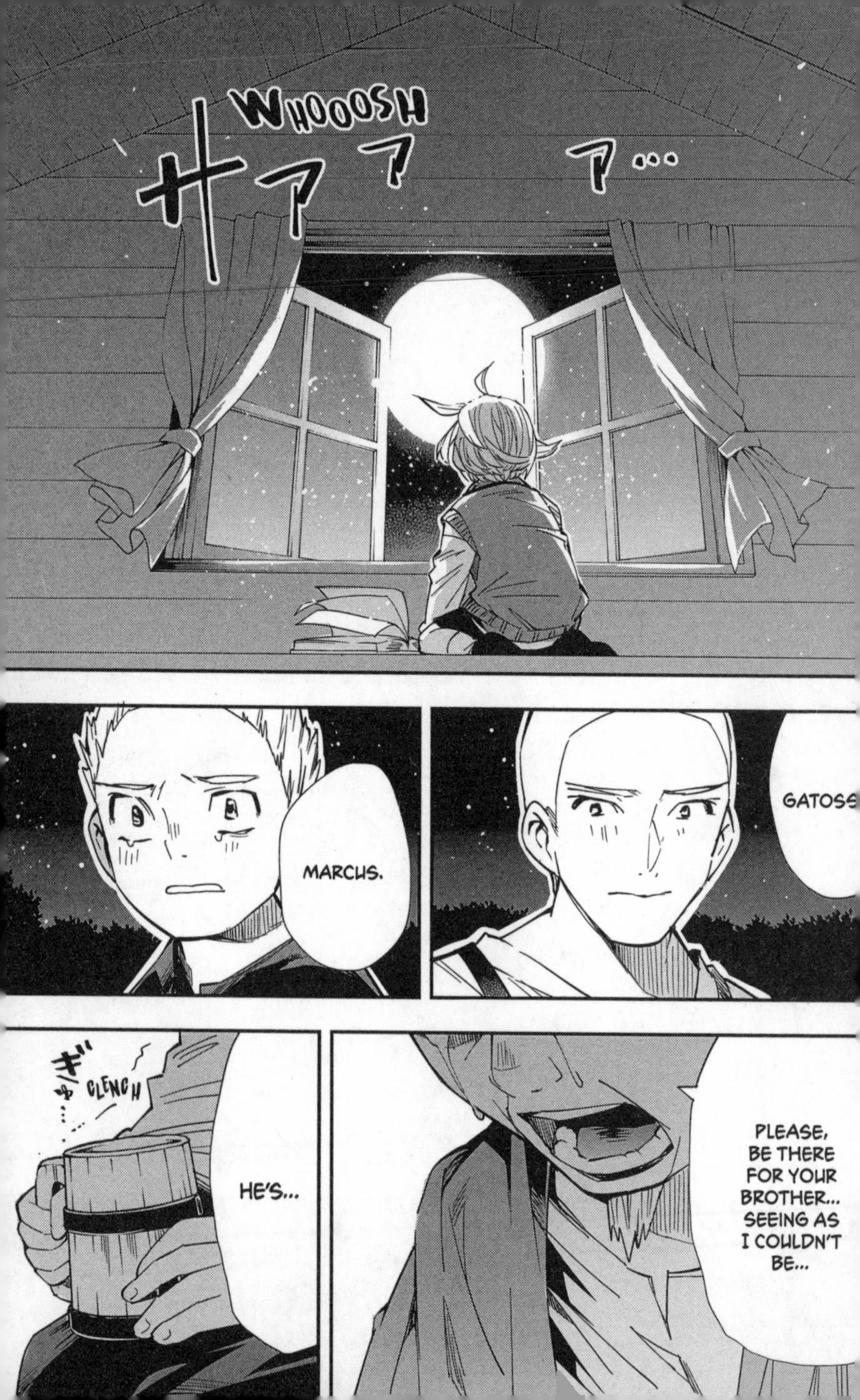

WHOOOSH
サァァ ァ…
GATOSS
MARCUS.
PLEASE, BE THERE FOR YOUR BROTHER... SEEING AS I COULDN'T BE...
CLENCH
HE'S...

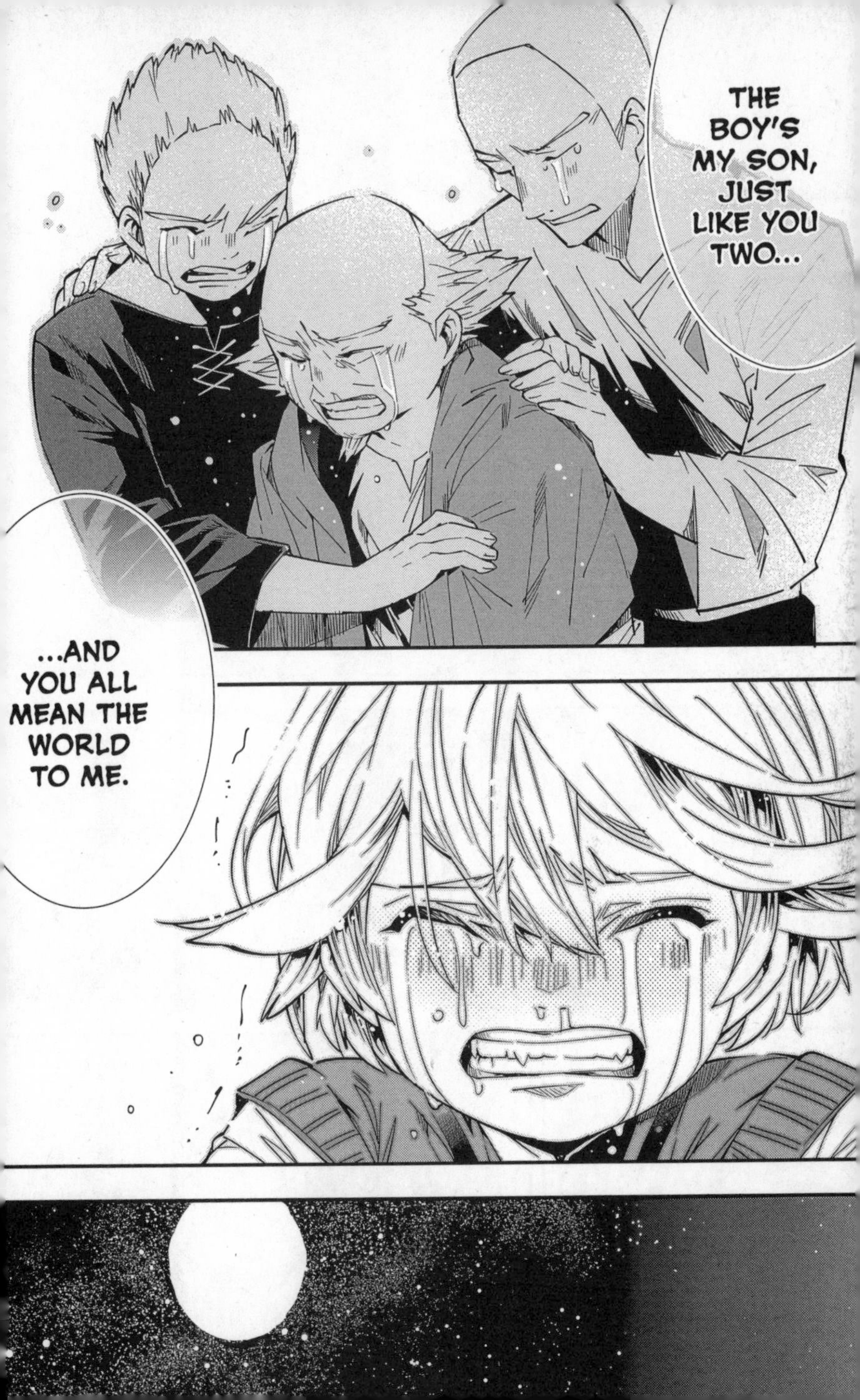
THE BOY'S MY SON, JUST LIKE YOU TWO...
...AND YOU ALL MEAN THE WORLD TO ME.

As a Reincarnated
ARISTOCRAT,
I'll Use My Appraisal Skill to
Rise in the World

As a Reincarnated ARISTOCRAT, I'll Use My Appraisal Skill to Rise in the World

Chapter 17: Farewell

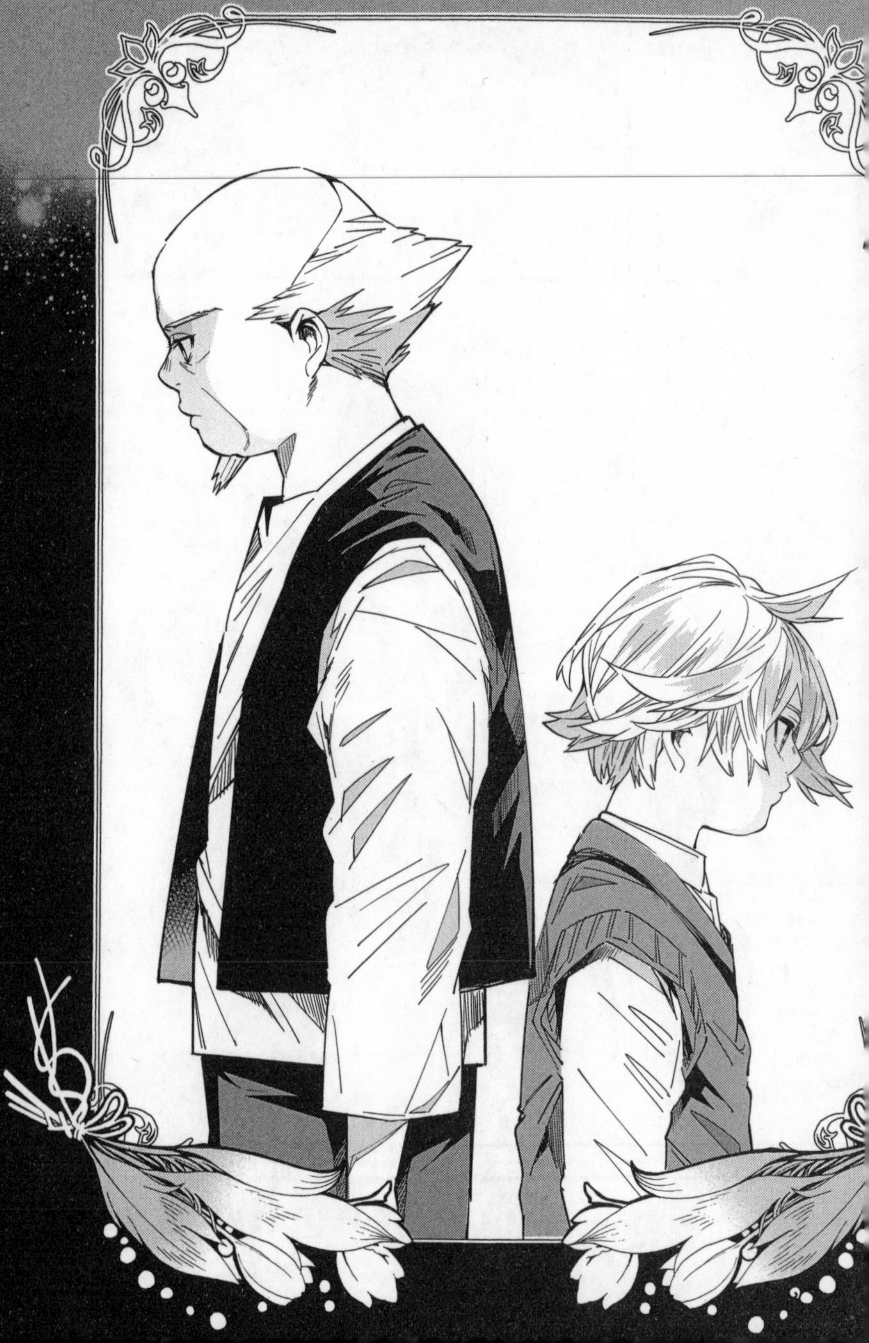

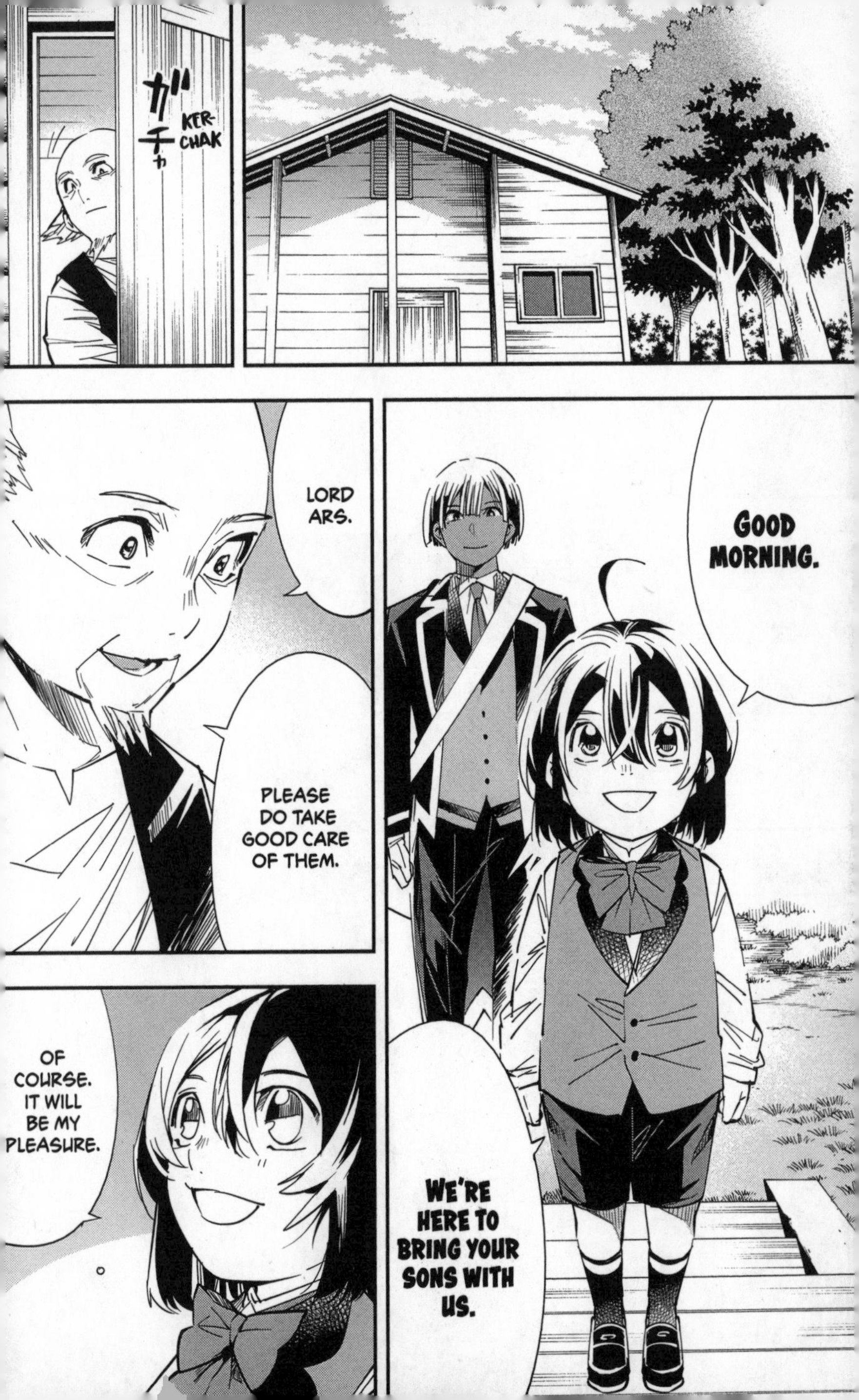
ガチャ
KER-CHAK
GOOD MORNING.
WE'RE HERE TO BRING YOUR SONS WITH US.
LORD ARS.
PLEASE DO TAKE GOOD CARE OF THEM.
OF COURSE. IT WILL BE MY PLEASURE.

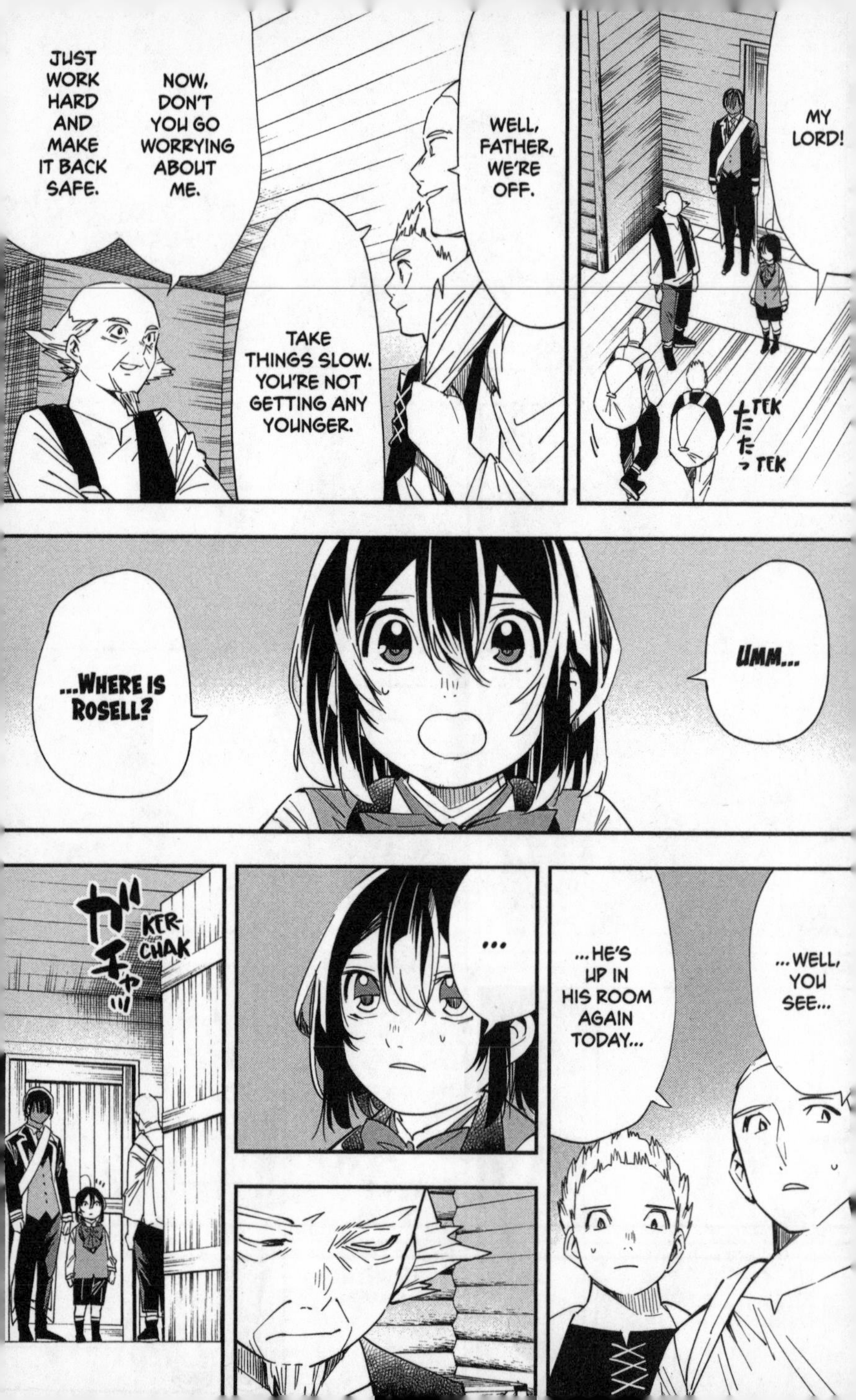
MY LORD!
TEK TEK
WELL, FATHER, WE'RE OFF.
TAKE THINGS SLOW. YOU'RE NOT GETTING ANY YOUNGER.
NOW, DON'T YOU GO WORRYING ABOUT ME.
JUST WORK HARD AND MAKE IT BACK SAFE.
UMM...
...WHERE IS ROSELL?
...WELL, YOU SEE...
...HE'S UP IN HIS ROOM AGAIN TODAY...
...
KER-CHAK

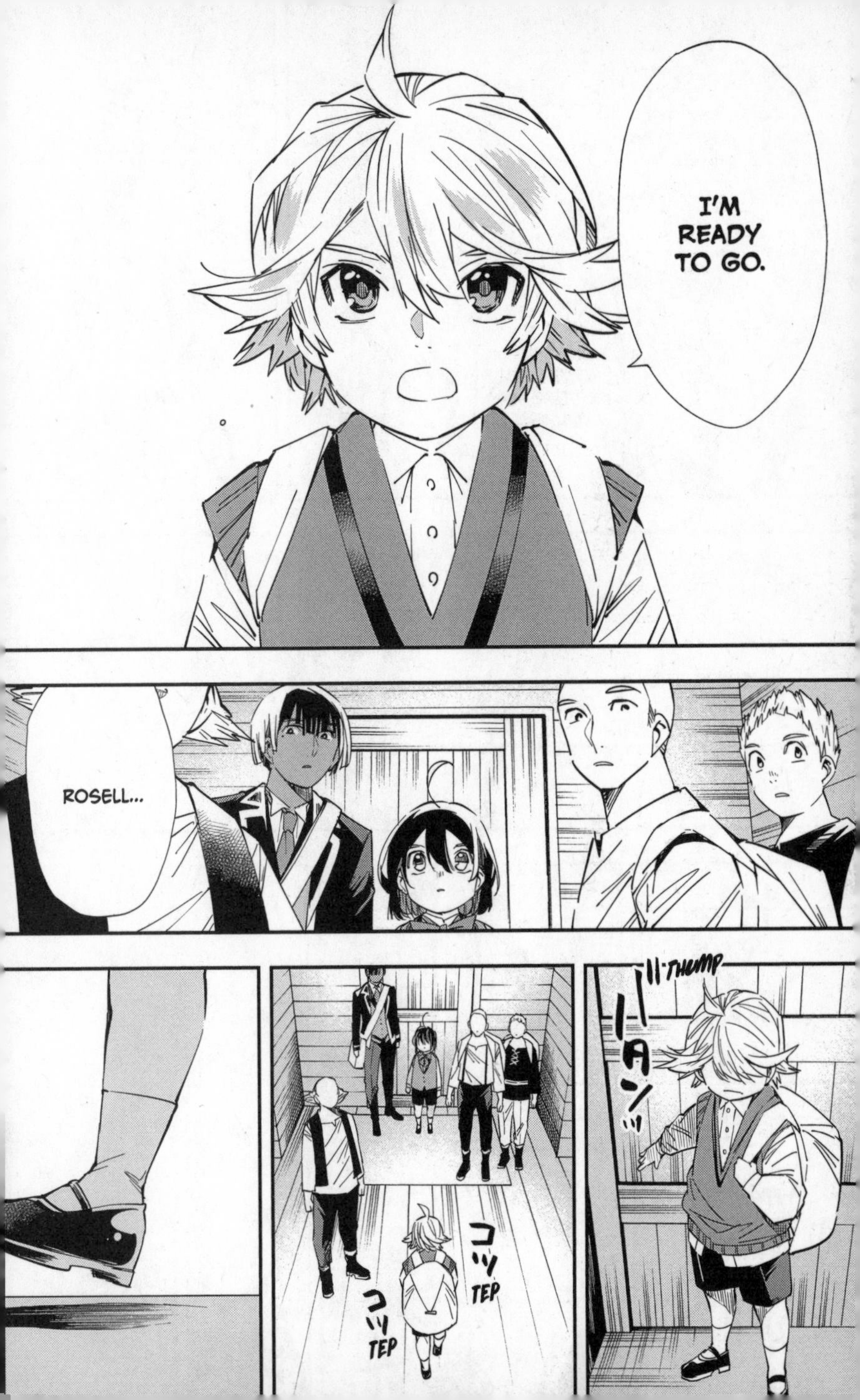
I'M READY TO GO.
ROSELL...
THUMP
ダンッ
コツ
TEP
コツ
TEP

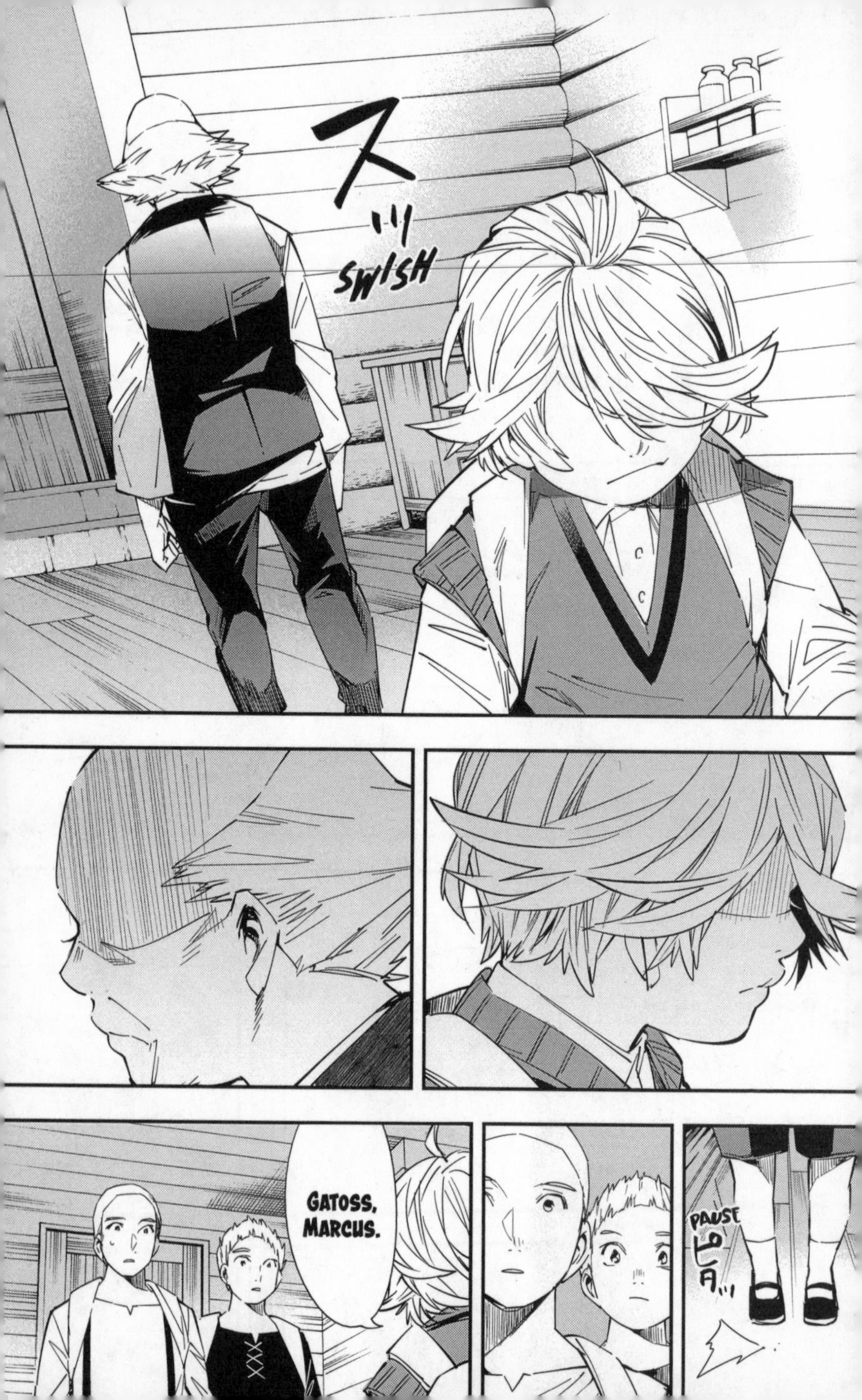
スッ
SWISH
PAUSE
ピタ
GATOSS, MARCUS.

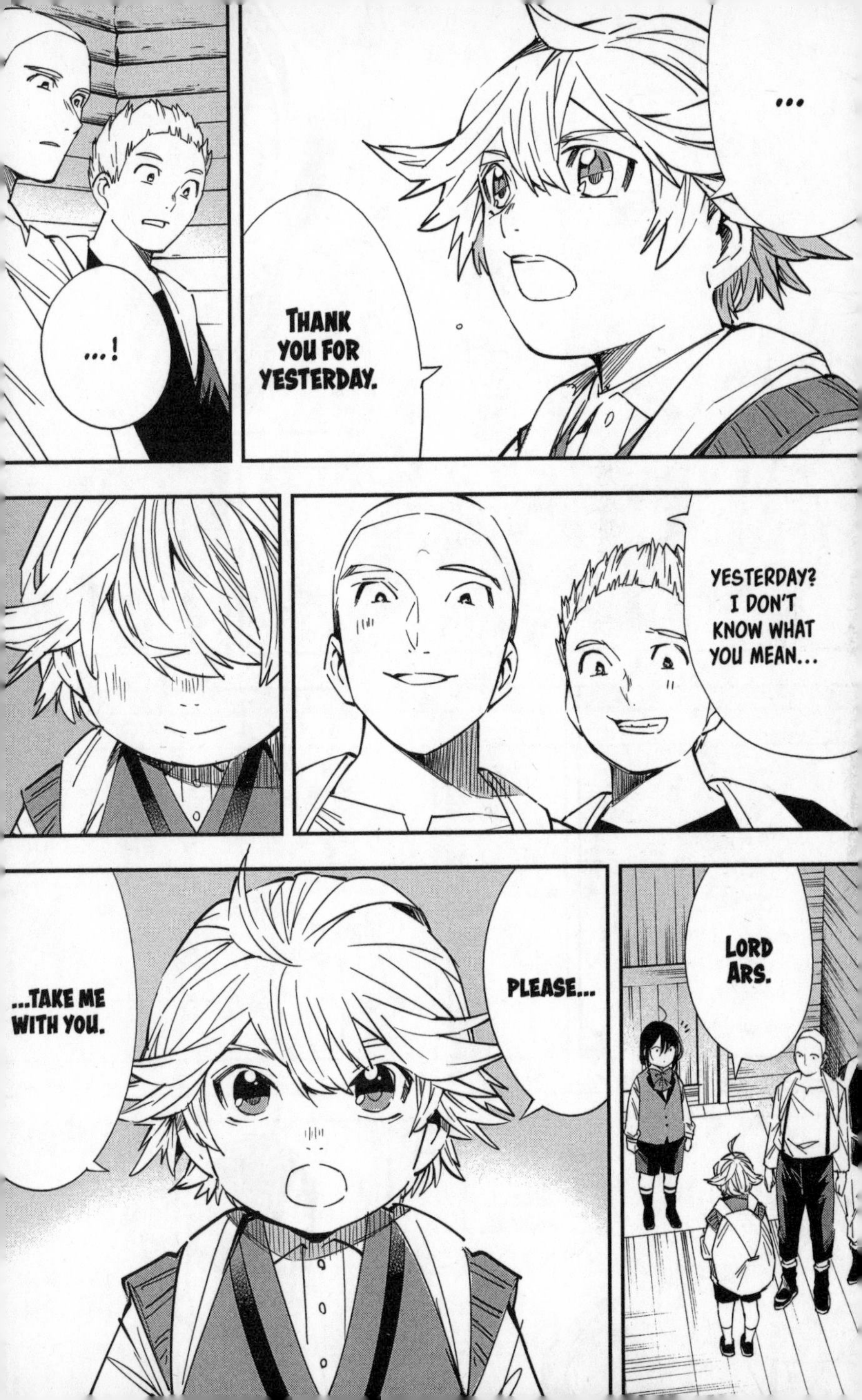
...
THANK YOU FOR YESTERDAY.
...!
YESTERDAY? I DON'T KNOW WHAT YOU MEAN...
LORD ARS.
PLEASE...
...TAKE ME WITH YOU.

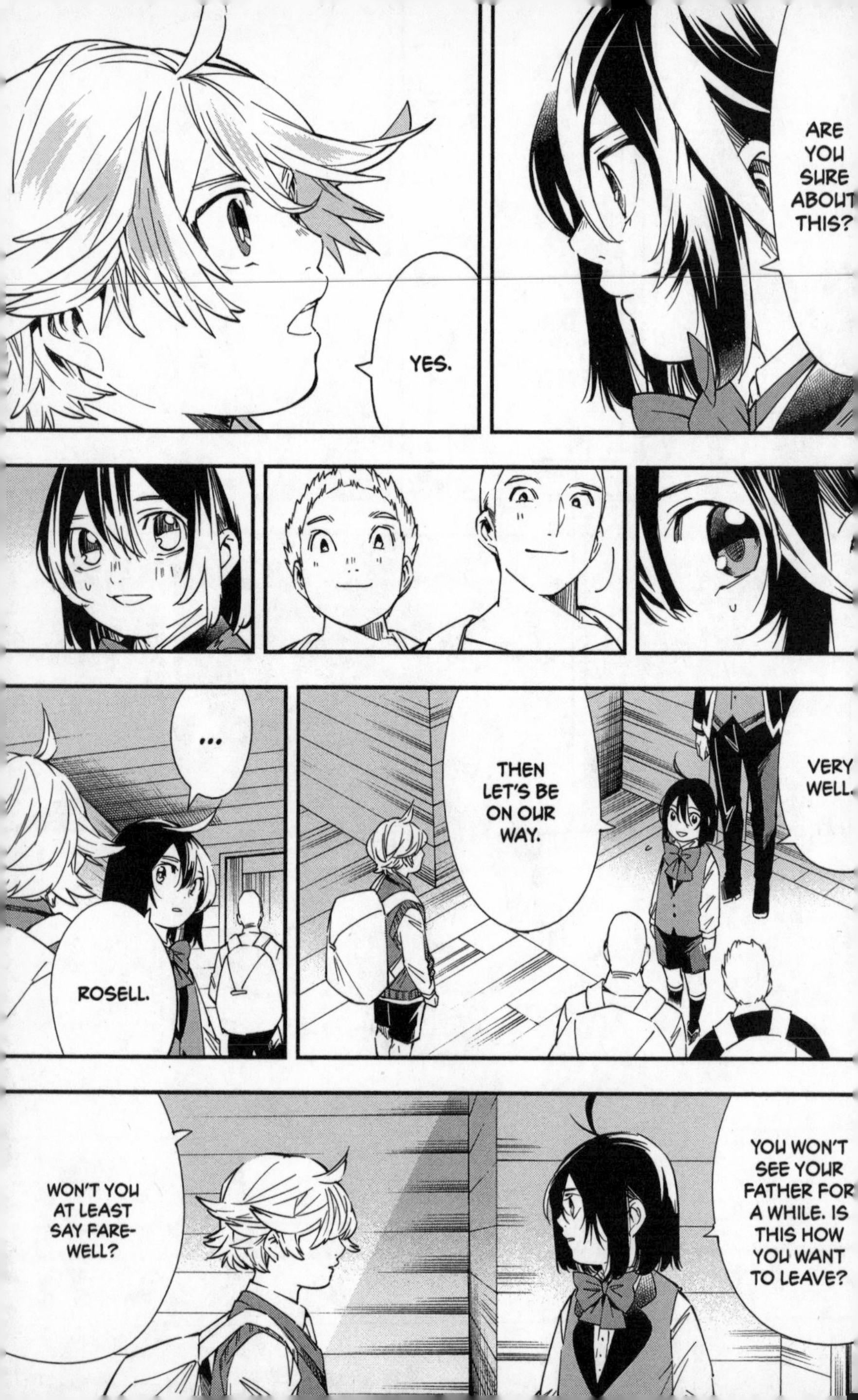
ARE YOU SURE ABOUT THIS?
YES.
VERY WELL.
THEN LET'S BE ON OUR WAY.
...
ROSELL.
YOU WON'T SEE YOUR FATHER FOR A WHILE. IS THIS HOW YOU WANT TO LEAVE?
WON'T YOU AT LEAST SAY FARE-WELL?

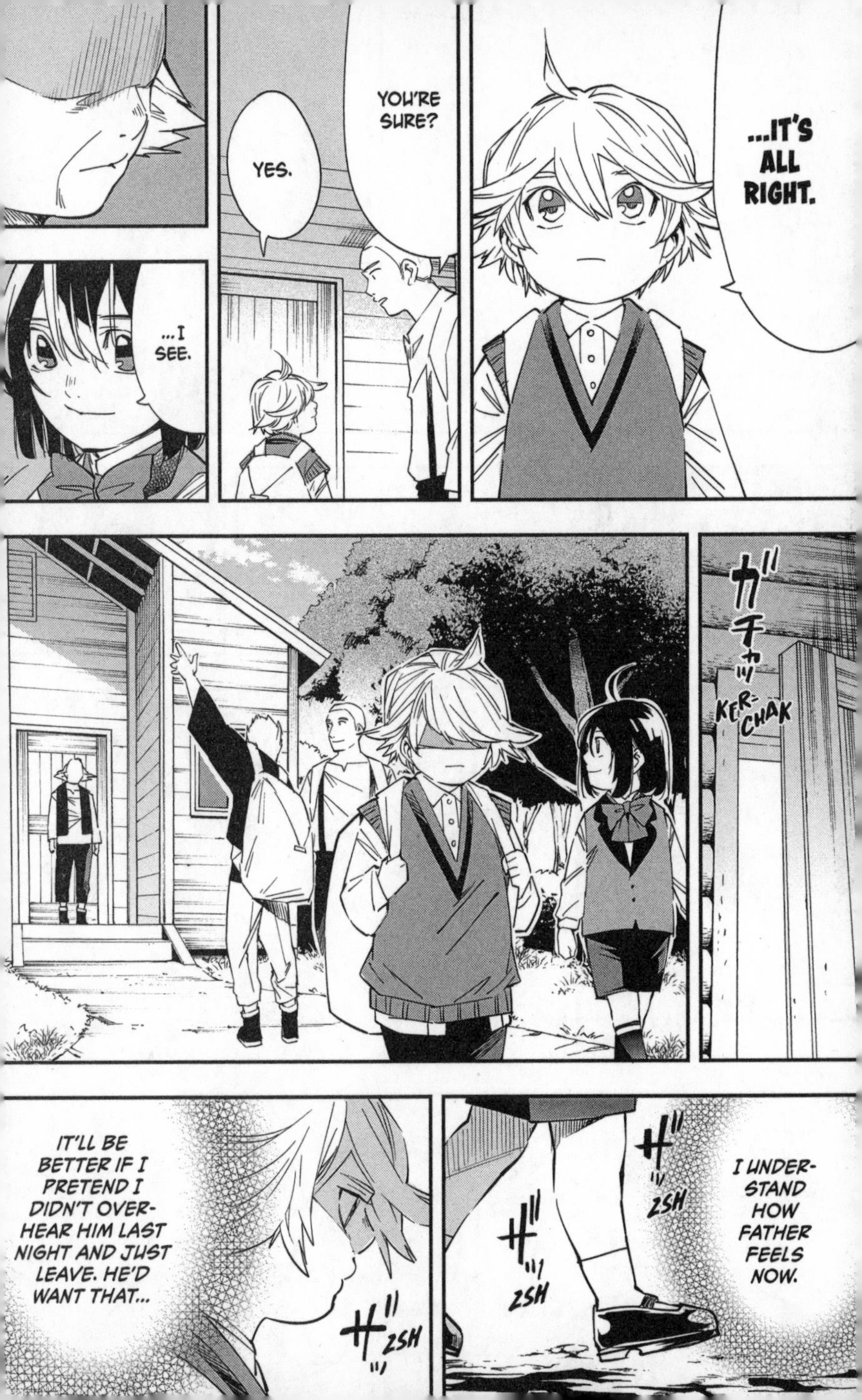
...IT'S ALL RIGHT.
YOU'RE SURE?
YES.
...I SEE.
ガチャッ
KER-CHAK
ザッ
ZSH
ザッ
ZSH
I UNDER-STAND HOW FATHER FEELS NOW.
IT'LL BE BETTER IF I PRETEND I DIDN'T OVER-HEAR HIM LAST NIGHT AND JUST LEAVE. HE'D WANT THAT...
ザッ
ZSH

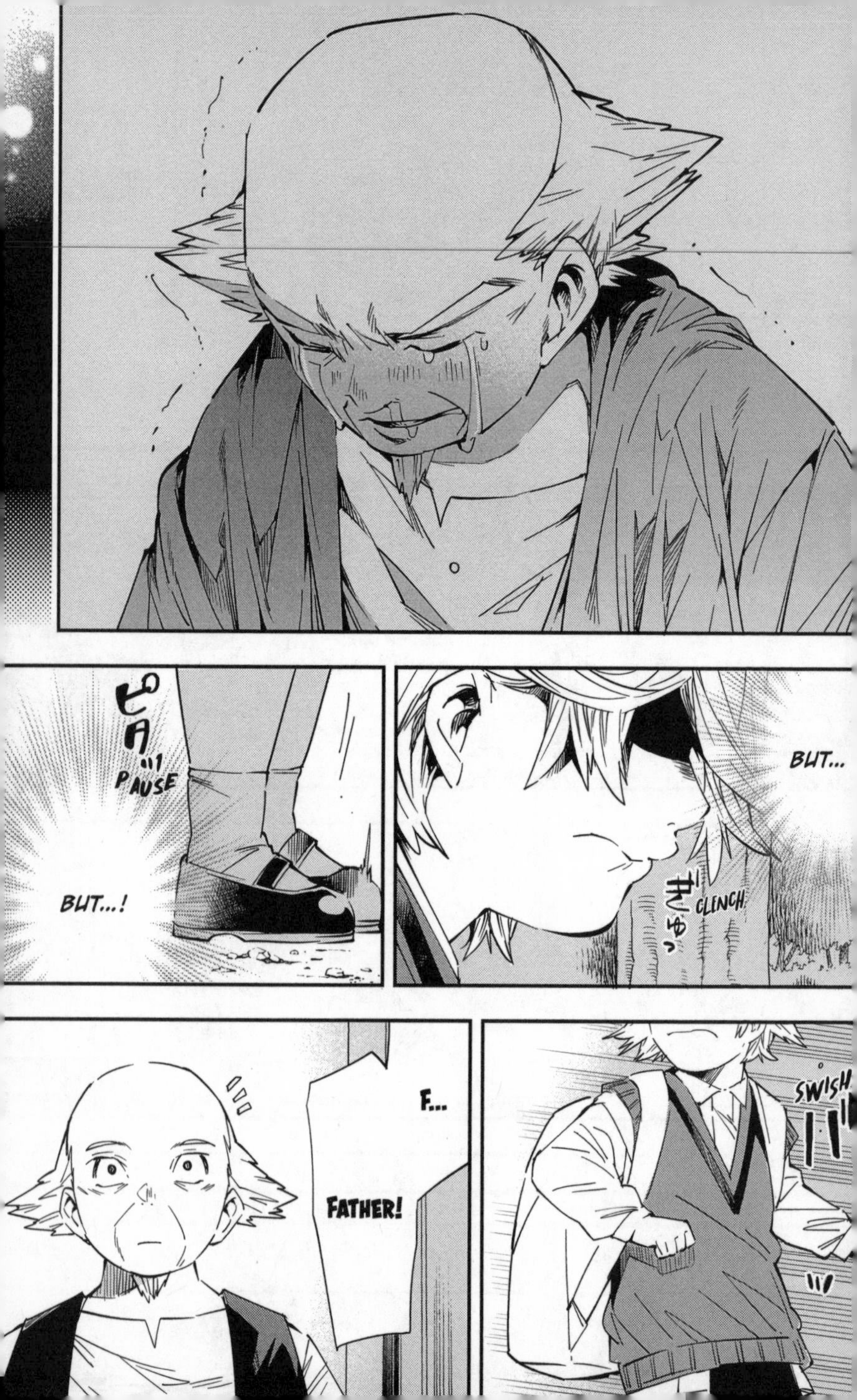
BUT...
ぎゅっ CLENCH
ピタッ PAUSE
BUT...!
SWISH
F...
FATHER!

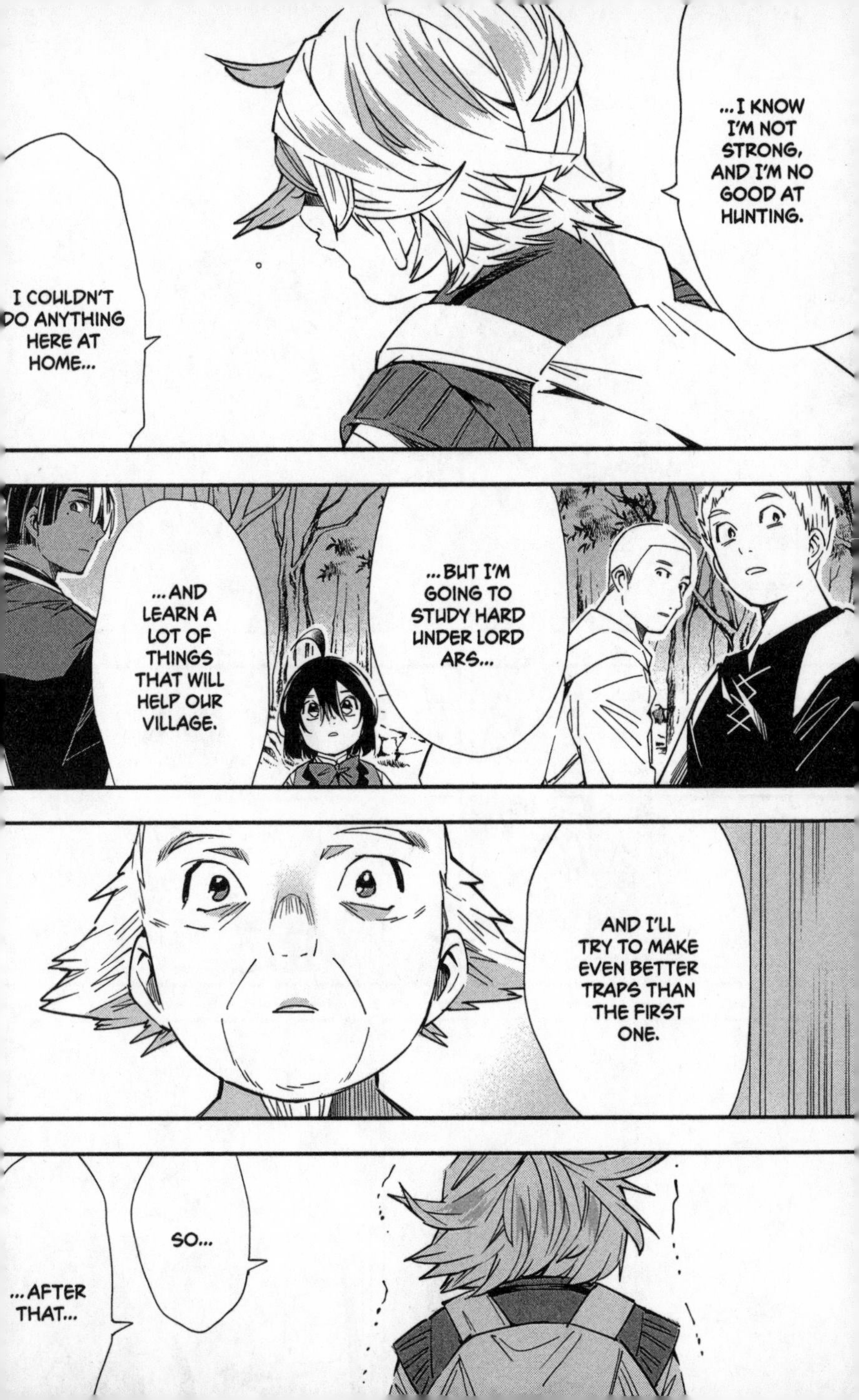
...I KNOW I'M NOT STRONG, AND I'M NO GOOD AT HUNTING.
I COULDN'T DO ANYTHING HERE AT HOME...
...BUT I'M GOING TO STUDY HARD UNDER LORD ARS...
...AND LEARN A LOT OF THINGS THAT WILL HELP OUR VILLAGE.
AND I'LL TRY TO MAKE EVEN BETTER TRAPS THAN THE FIRST ONE.
SO...
...AFTER THAT...

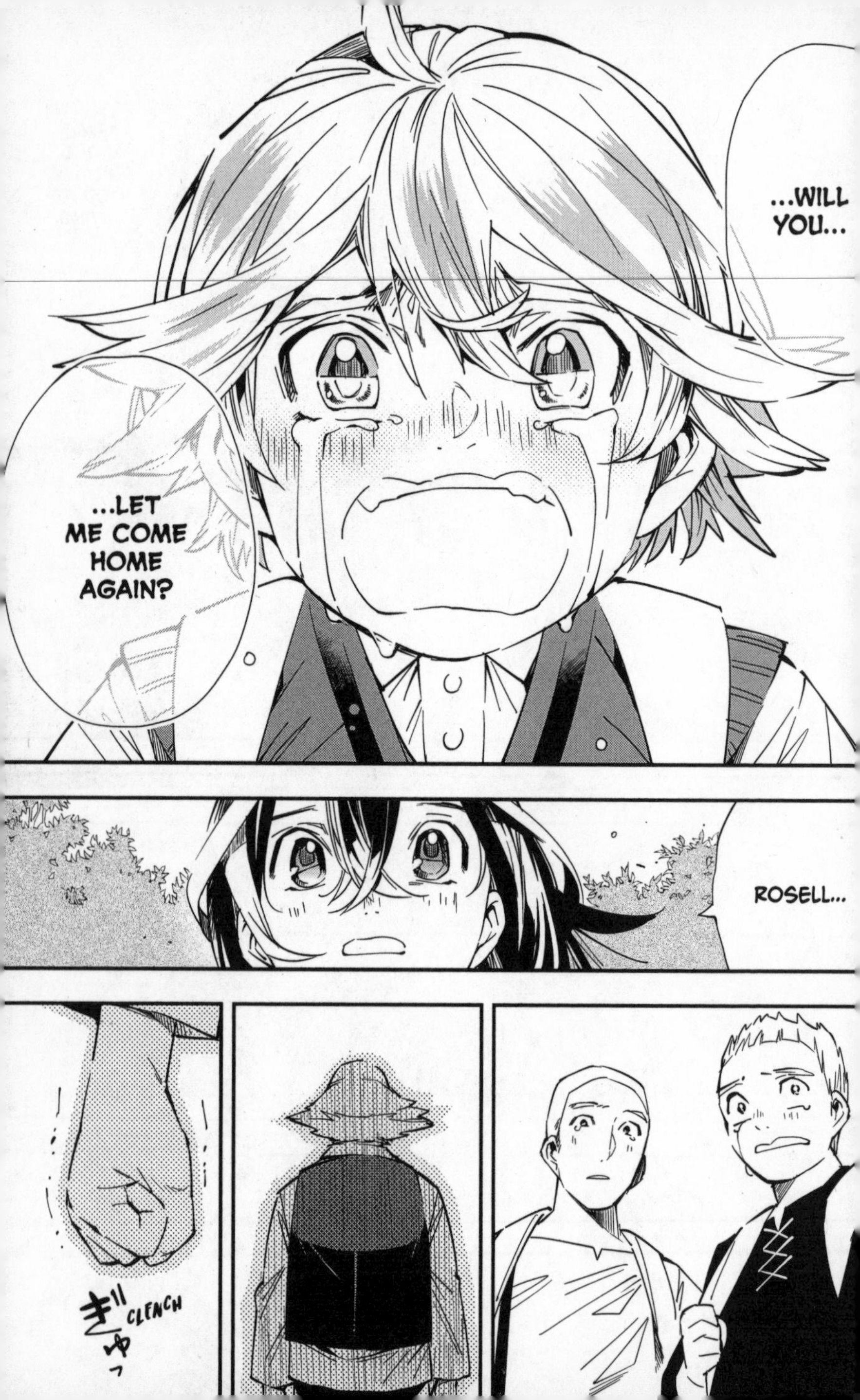
...WILL YOU...
...LET ME COME HOME AGAIN?
ROSELL...
CLENCH

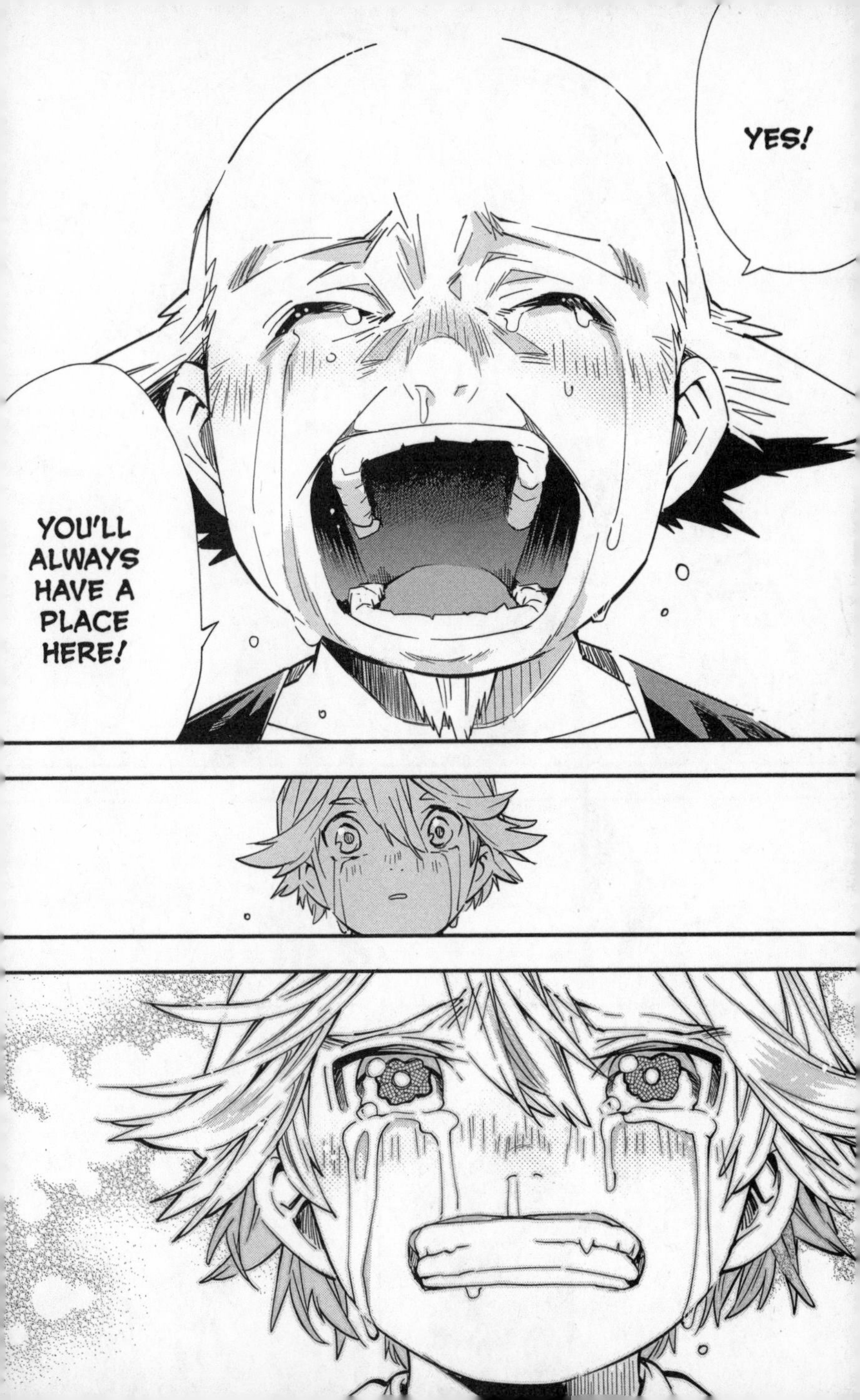
YES!
YOU'LL ALWAYS HAVE A PLACE HERE!

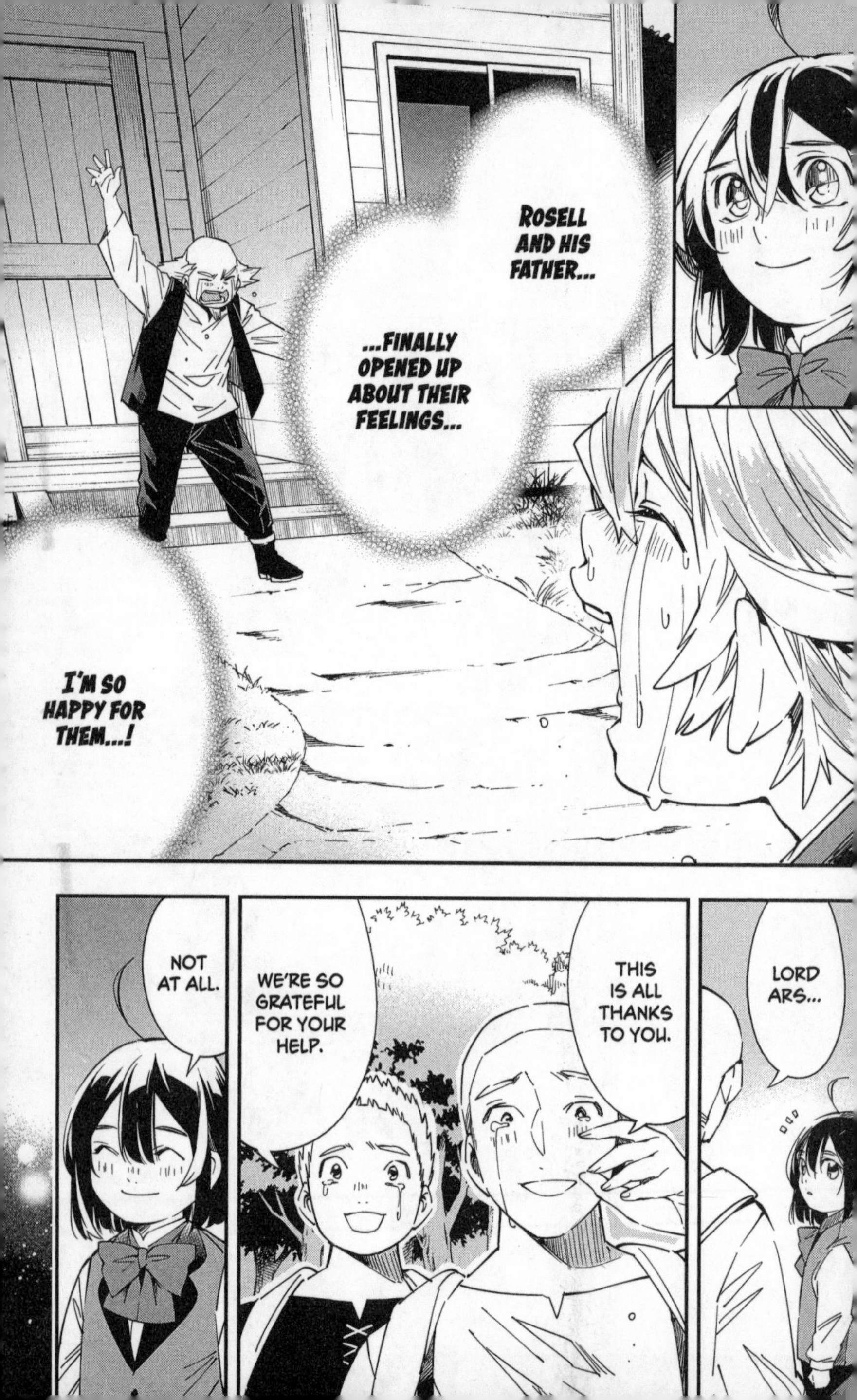
ROSELL AND HIS FATHER...
...FINALLY OPENED UP ABOUT THEIR FEELINGS...
I'M SO HAPPY FOR THEM...!
LORD ARS...
THIS IS ALL THANKS TO YOU.
WE'RE SO GRATEFUL FOR YOUR HELP.
NOT AT ALL.

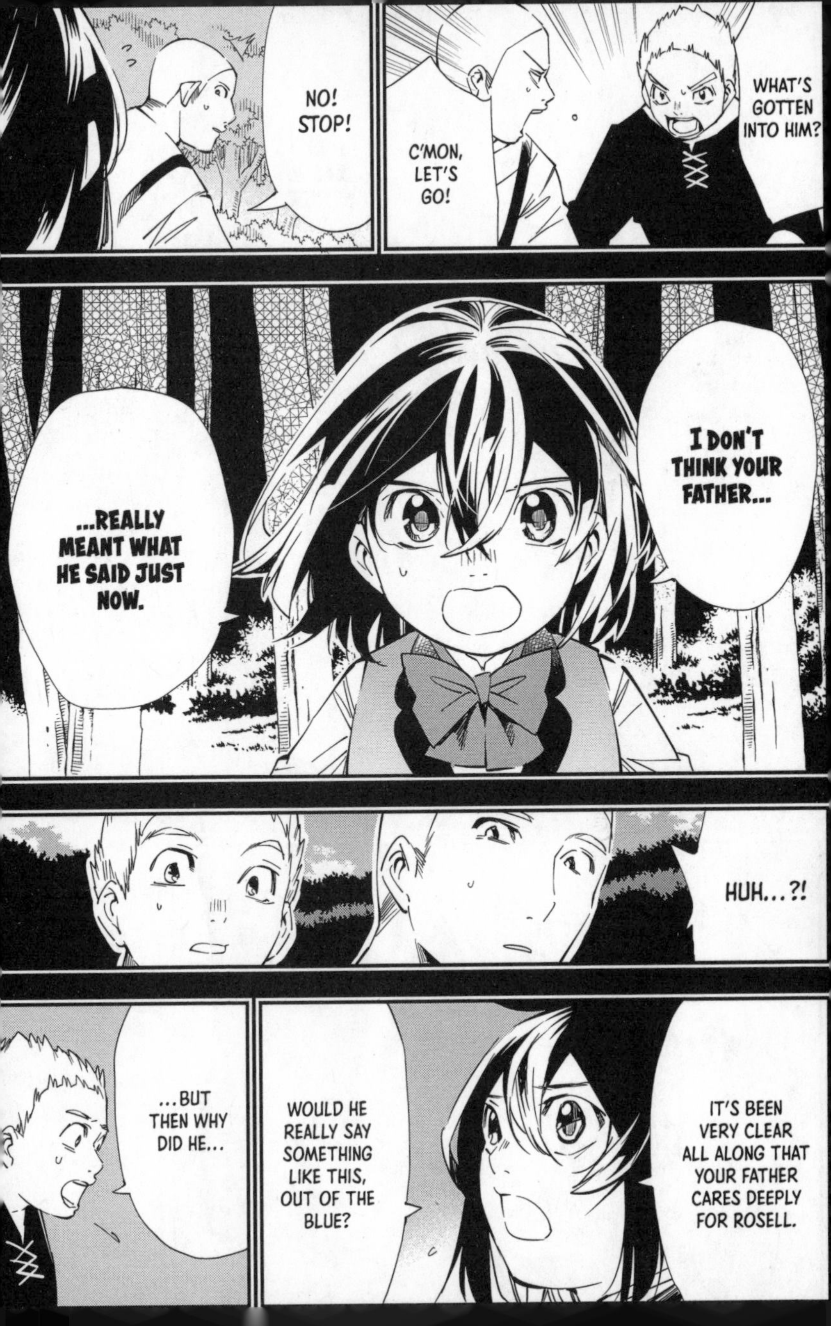
WHAT'S GOTTEN INTO HIM?
C'MON, LET'S GO!
NO! STOP!
I DON'T THINK YOUR FATHER...
...REALLY MEANT WHAT HE SAID JUST NOW.
HUH...?!
IT'S BEEN VERY CLEAR ALL ALONG THAT YOUR FATHER CARES DEEPLY FOR ROSELL.
WOULD HE REALLY SAY SOMETHING LIKE THIS, OUT OF THE BLUE?
...BUT THEN WHY DID HE...

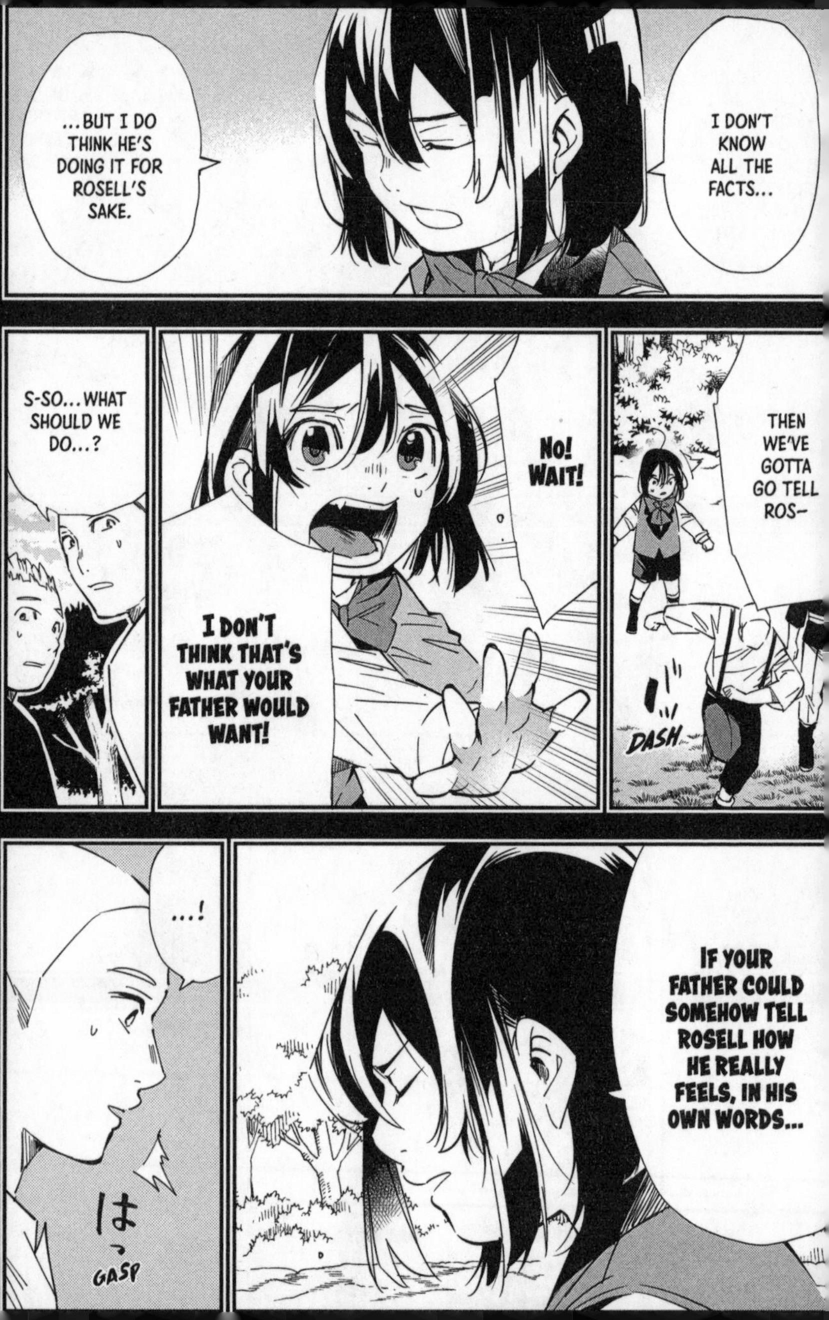
I DON'T KNOW ALL THE FACTS...
...BUT I DO THINK HE'S DOING IT FOR ROSELL'S SAKE.
THEN WE'VE GOTTA GO TELL ROS–
DASH
NO! WAIT!
I DON'T THINK THAT'S WHAT YOUR FATHER WOULD WANT!
S-SO...WHAT SHOULD WE DO...?
IF YOUR FATHER COULD SOMEHOW TELL ROSELL HOW HE REALLY FEELS, IN HIS OWN WORDS...
...!
はっ
GASP

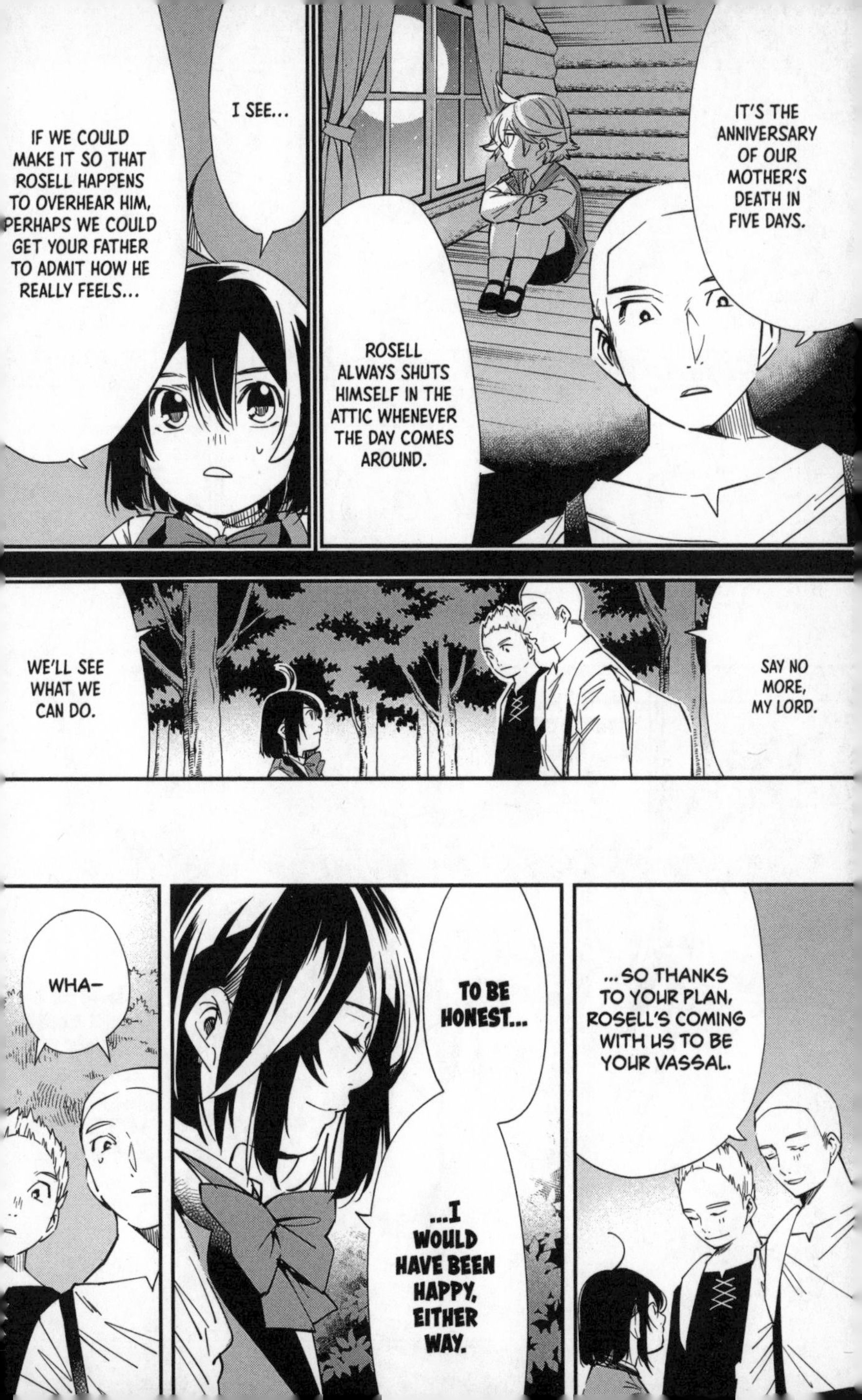
IT'S THE ANNIVERSARY OF OUR MOTHER'S DEATH IN FIVE DAYS.
ROSELL ALWAYS SHUTS HIMSELF IN THE ATTIC WHENEVER THE DAY COMES AROUND.
I SEE...
IF WE COULD MAKE IT SO THAT ROSELL HAPPENS TO OVERHEAR HIM, PERHAPS WE COULD GET YOUR FATHER TO ADMIT HOW HE REALLY FEELS...
SAY NO MORE, MY LORD.
WE'LL SEE WHAT WE CAN DO.
...SO THANKS TO YOUR PLAN, ROSELL'S COMING WITH US TO BE YOUR VASSAL.
TO BE HONEST...
...I WOULD HAVE BEEN HAPPY, EITHER WAY.
WHA-

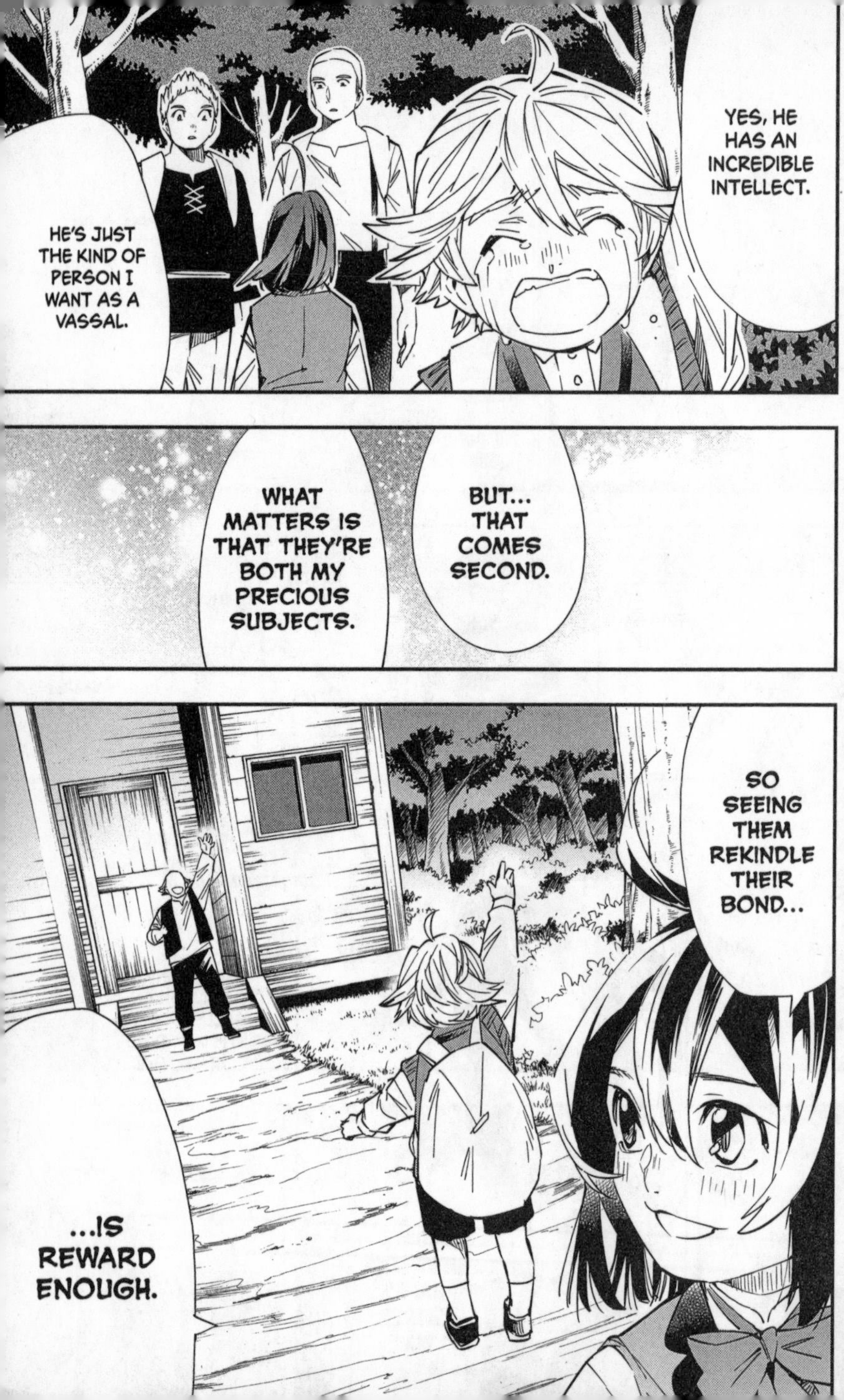
YES, HE HAS AN INCREDIBLE INTELLECT.
HE'S JUST THE KIND OF PERSON I WANT AS A VASSAL.
BUT... THAT COMES SECOND.
WHAT MATTERS IS THAT THEY'RE BOTH MY PRECIOUS SUBJECTS.
SO SEEING THEM REKINDLE THEIR BOND...
...IS REWARD ENOUGH.

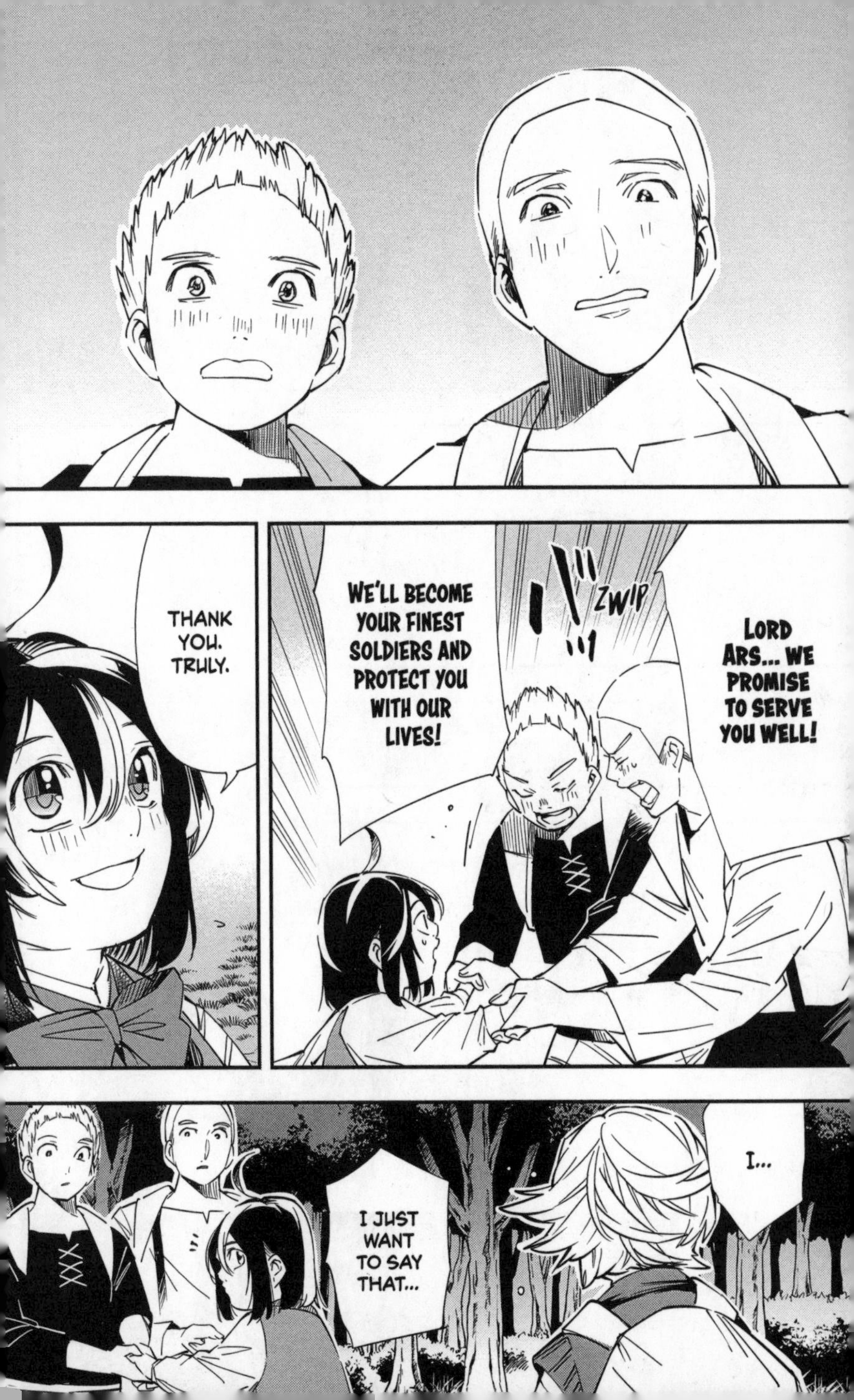
LORD ARS... WE PROMISE TO SERVE YOU WELL!
ZWIP
WE'LL BECOME YOUR FINEST SOLDIERS AND PROTECT YOU WITH OUR LIVES!
THANK YOU. TRULY.
I...
I JUST WANT TO SAY THAT...

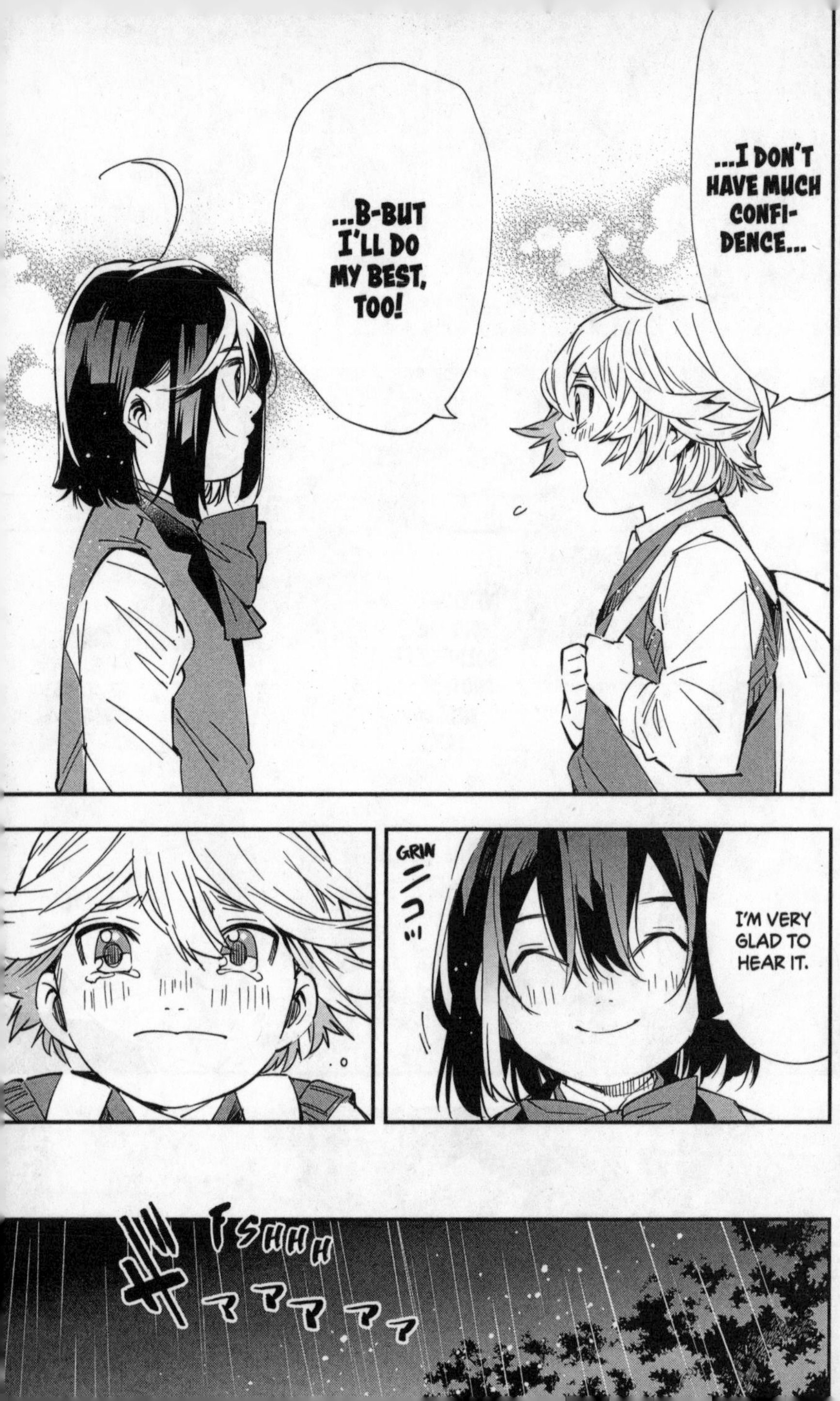
...I DON'T HAVE MUCH CONFI-DENCE...
...B-BUT I'LL DO MY BEST, TOO!
GRIN
ニコッ
I'M VERY GLAD TO HEAR IT.
FSHHH
ザァァァァ

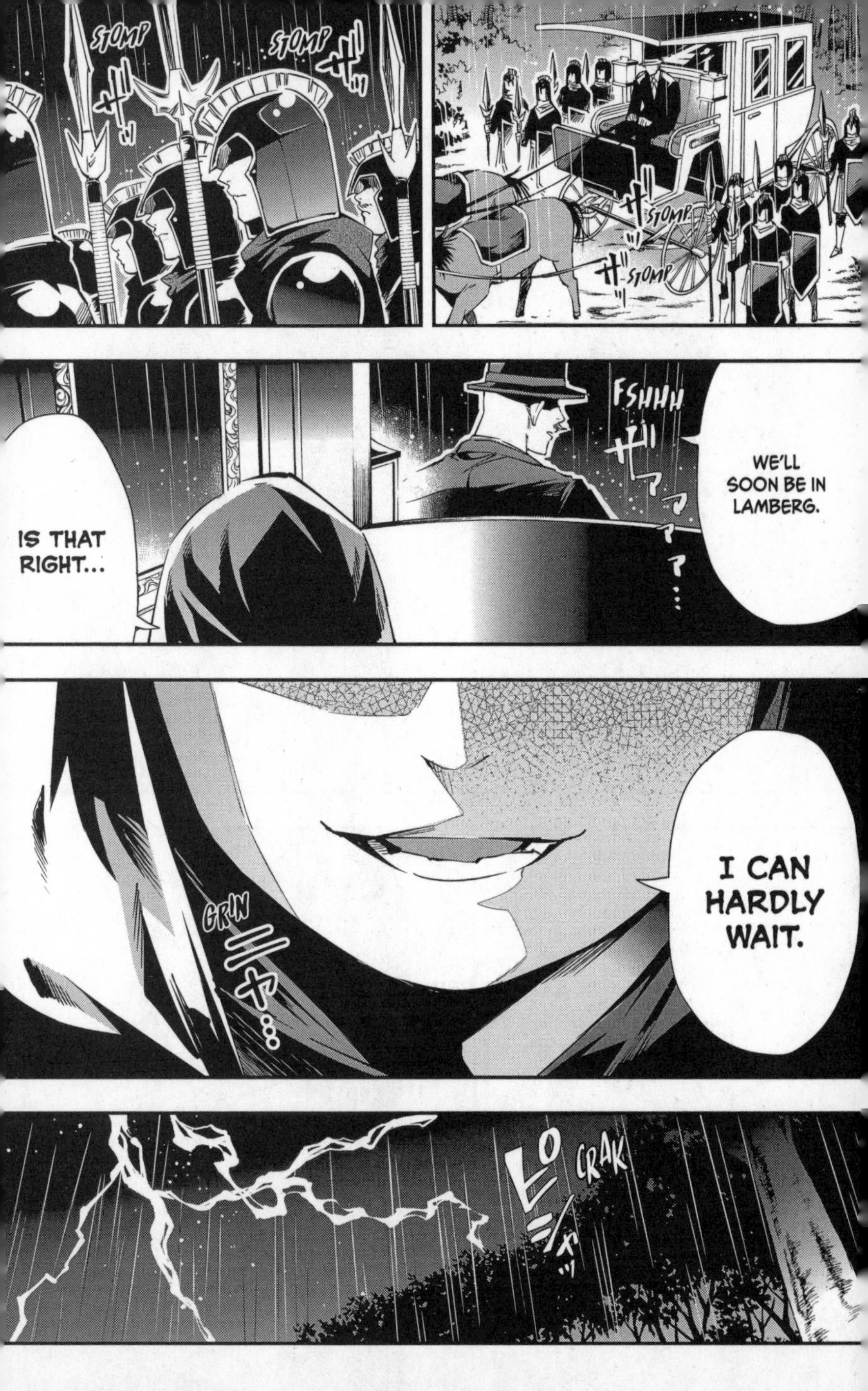
STOMP
STOMP
STOMP
STOMP
WE'LL SOON BE IN LAMBERG.
FSHHH
IS THAT RIGHT...
I CAN HARDLY WAIT.
GRIN
CRAK

Bonus Story

by Miraijin A

Having resolved the incident in Canarre, Ars returned to Louvent Manor with Charlotte in tow. He then informed his father, Raven Louvent, of his intention to make Charlotte a vassal, at which Lord Raven refused flat out to elevate a girl to such a position. However, he promptly reconsidered after seeing the true nature of Charlotte's skill as a mage. And so, practically overnight, Charlotte became a vassal of House Louvent.

"Well, that's a relief," said Ars with a sigh. "I'm so glad Father realized how valuable you really are." He had spent the entire journey home fretting about what he would do if Lord Raven refused to accept Charlotte.

Casting a measured eye over the manor, Charlotte said, "This place is enormous. Must be nice, being born a noble." For her part, she didn't seem particularly concerned about the whole affair.

Ars beamed. "You're one of our vassals now, Charlotte. That means this is your home, too. I hope you'll like it."

"I get to live here...? It still doesn't feel real," Charlotte added in a murmur, as though thinking back on her life up to that point.

Rietz cut across these thoughts, saying, "My lord, if Charlotte is to be a vassal, then there are things that need doing. I'd say the first is to have some proper clothes made for her."

"Clothes?" asked Charlotte. "But you already bought me clothes." This was true enough; Ars had purchased a new outfit for her in Canarre before emptying his purse on the slave trader. As a result, Charlotte was wearing finer clothes now than when she had first met him.

"Those are your everyday clothes," Rietz explained. "You'll need special mage gear to wear into battle."

"Huh," said Charlotte disinterestedly. "To be honest, I couldn't care less what I wear."

"Well, you should! And you might at least pretend to have some manners, seeing as you'll be representing this house."

"Manners?"

"Yes, manners. I still cringe every time I remember how you addressed Lord Raven earlier. I understand that being a commoner means you know nothing of etiquette, but you'd do best to learn. Anyone would expect as much from one of Lord Ars's vassals."

"Bo—ring. I'm getting hungry. Can we eat?"

"What do you mean, 'boring'?!"

Ars stepped in quickly before the squabble could escalate. "A-actually, I'm hungry, too. This discussion can wait, so let's have lunch!"

"See?" said Charlotte. "Ars agrees. Let's eat."

Rietz sighed. "Very well. We'll continue this later, Charlotte."

Thankfully, this put an end to the argument, and the three settled down for lunch. Charlotte's eyes went wide as she saw the feast laid out on the dining table.

"Wow, that looks tasty. Can I start?" she drooled. She looked like she was barely keeping a hold of herself.

"Yes, go ahead and eat as much as you like," said Ars. The words had hardly left his mouth when Charlotte began doing just that.

Ars had been hoping that Charlotte would warm to life at the manor, so he felt relieved to see her enthusiasm for the meal. However, Charlotte was a commoner with no knowledge of etiquette, and it showed; her table manners were atrocious.

"The girl really *could* use a lesson in manners," Rietz muttered.

Having polished off her plate, Charlotte gave a groan of satisfaction, saying, "Now *that* was a meal. Time for a nap."

As Charlotte made as though to rise from her seat, Rietz said, "Now's no time for sleeping. Like I said earlier, you'll need to learn some manners. What if you get asked to accompany Lord Ars to a social dinner? You'll bring shame on the entire house. Let's get started right away!"

"Whaaat?" Charlotte moaned. "No, thanks. What a chore. Besides, manners are beyond me."

"I wasn't born knowing manners, either," said Rietz. "It took practice. You can learn, too, provided you put in the effort."

"Ugh. This is why I can't stand aristocrats."

Ars was suddenly filled with dread at the sight of Charlotte's disgusted expression. What if she decided she'd had enough of being a vassal and simply up and left?

"Um, Rietz... I don't think we need to be *quite* that strict with her..."

"There you are," Charlotte gloated. "Even Ars is on my side."

"My lord! You really mustn't spoil her!" said Rietz, sounding exasperated. "It may not seem like an issue now, but we don't know how Lord Raven will react in the future. He acknowledged her today, but if she forgets herself around him, he might decide to dismiss her."

"That *would* be a problem..." Ars agreed.

Being of common birth himself, Lord Raven wasn't particularly rigid when it came to manners. Even so, that didn't mean that he was beyond taking offense. Best to avoid that altogether.

Charlotte let out a heavy sigh. "Well, this is no fun... But the food here is great, and you did help me out before. I don't want to get thrown out, either. I guess I can work at it."

"Really?!" said Rietz in surprise.

"But not today. I need to sleep this off," Charlotte yawned. She started back to her private quarters, Rietz following behind her with a string of imprecations.

The End

[Story] Miraijin A

Hello, I'm Miraijin A, the author of this work.
Volume 2 differs in places from the original light novels,
but it had some touching emotional moments, so I'm very
happy with it. This is just such a wonderful adaptation,
and I'm extremely grateful to Natsumi Inoue-sensei
for illustrating it. I think Volume 3 will be extremely
entertaining, so if you've read the first two volumes,
I definitely encourage you to pick up the third.
Thank you so much for buying Volume 2!

[Character Design] jimmy

Congratulations on volume two of the manga!

jimmy

②

Ars kinda looks like Rosell's big brother when they're next to each other...

TRANSLATION NOTE

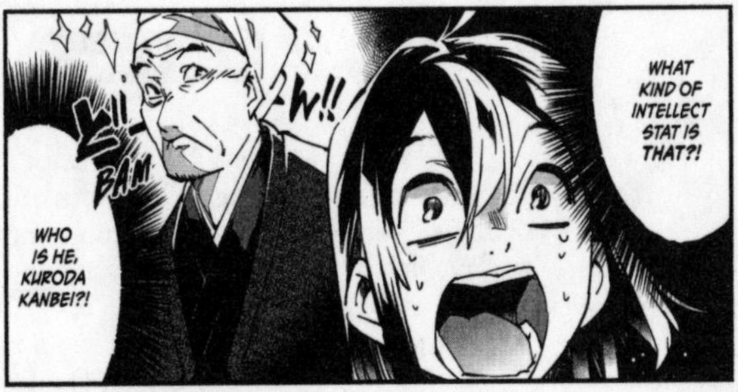
WHAT KIND OF INTELLECT STAT IS THAT?!
-W!!
BAM
WHO IS HE, KURODA KANBEI?!

pg. 80
Kuroda Kanbei

Kuroda Yoshitaka (1546-1604), also known as Kuroda Kanbei, was a Japanese *daimyo* who served as strategist and advisor to Oda Nobunaga and Toyotomi Hideyoshi. He became widely celebrated as a master tactician.

Charlotte Lace · Age 14

Stats

	CURRENT	MAX
Command	73	92
Prowess	101	116
Intellect	34	45
Diplomacy	31	40
Ambition	1	

Aptitude

Fighter	D	Cavalier	D	Archer	D
Mage	S	Engineer	D	Armorer	D
Mariner	D	Pilot	D	Tactician	D

A Kodansha Trade Paperback Original

As a Reincarnated Aristocrat, I'll Use My Appraisal Skill to Rise in the World 2 copyright © 2021 Miraijin A/Natsumi Inoue/jimmy
English translation copyright © 2022 Miraijin A/Natsumi Inoue/jimmy

Published in the United States by
Kodansha USA Publishing, LLC, New York.

Publication rights for this English edition arranged through
Kodansha Ltd., Tokyo.

First published in Japan in 2021 by Kodansha Ltd., Tokyo
as *Tensei kizoku, kantei sukiru de nariagaru*, volume 2.

ISBN 978-1-64651-513-4

Printed in the United States of America.

9 8 7 6 5 4 3 2 1

Translation: Stephen Paul
Lettering: Nicole Roderick
Editing: Andres Oliver
Kodansha USA Publishing edition cover design by Pekka Luhtala

Publisher: Kiichiro Sugawara

Director of Publishing Services: Ben Applegate
Director of Publishing Operations: Dave Barrett
Associate Director of Publishing Operations: Stephen Pakula
Publishing Services Managing Editors: Alanna Ruse, Madison Salters, with Grace Chen

KODANSHA.US